# Openness for Prosperity

# Openness for Prosperity

Essays in World Economics

Herbert Giersch

The MIT Press
Cambridge, Massachusetts
London, England

This book was set in Palatino by Asco Trade Typesetting Ltd., Hong Kong, and was printed and bound in the United States of America.

Library of Congress Cataloging-in-Publication Data

Giersch, Herbert.
    Openness for prosperity / Herbert Giersch.
        p.   cm.
    Includes bibliographical references and index.
    ISBN 0-262-07148-7
    1. Economic policy. 2. Monetary policy. 3. Commercial policy. 4. Inflation (Finance)
5. Foreign exchange rates. I. Title.
HD87.G54   1993
338.9—dc20                                                          92-35940
                                                                        CIP

# Contents

## II Monetary Policy, Inflation, and Exchange Rates

# 1  Introduction

Friends and colleagues encouraged me, and MIT Press agreed, to publish as a book a collection of articles for which I have responsibility as an author or coauthor, in addition to a complementary work that appeared elsewhere in 1991 (Giersch 1991). They deserve my gratitude, as does Joachim Fels, who spent much time selecting and assembling the material. Two articles are a translation from German, the language of my usual audience and readership. Nobody except myself, however, bears any responsibility for what is presented in this book.

I gave my consent to the project after I received encouragement from previous readers who had happened to find several essays in scattered and even obscure publications. I was told that some pieces contained arguments and insights that were worth preserving and might even have some bearing on ongoing debates in the economic profession.

All articles are policy oriented. The main motivation to write and publish them was not to accelerate my academic career; rather I thought that if there was any merit in being an economist, in addition to earning one's living in an honest way, it would have to come from one's contribution to the economic policy debate.

What, in the end, is economics good for if economists ignore its potential as a means of understanding and ultimately improving the social order so that it enables people to enjoy a better life? Elsewhere I spelled out how the Great Depression in Germany affected my family during my formative years and led me to adopt such a point of view (Giersch 1986).

Contributions aiming at policy relevance cannot be entirely value free. A professional economist may try to camouflage the normative bias as much as possible by using masses of data and a highly sophisticated methodology, but when it comes to policy implications, one cannot but admit that they largely follow from our preferences and prejudices. Knowledgeable readers will soon discover them, just as the public is usually not unaware of the value system behind an articulate professional economist's pronouncements. I do not hesitate to confess my bias: I am for trustworthy, informal cooperation within small groups (that is, among people who know each other well); I am for unrestricted competition with more distant rivals in anonymous markets all over the world—in other words, for free trade; I favor limits to government through either constitutional constraints or competition among governments; and I have a high esteem for openness toward the future in the sense that individuals and firms should be free to experiment and discover, to invent and innovate. The term *openness* in the title of this book is meant to spell this out. It includes both forms of openness: in regard to the outside world and to the future.

Prosperity is what we expect from such openness. This is why *prosperity* figures in the title. *Economic development* or *growth* would have been alternative terms; however, I prefer *prosperity*, not only because it reminds me of Gottfried Haberler's macroeconomic masterwork *Prosperity and Depression* (1937) but also because it has less holistic connotations than anything related to gross national product. *Prosperity* also covers a wider field, including leisure and cultural life, aesthetic and environmental values, and creative and scientific activities, which tend to become more and more important in advanced countries. *Prosperity*, in contrast to *growth*, smacks less of aggregation and unwarranted quantification, more of individual opportunity and subjective satisfaction.

*Evolution* would have been my second choice. In fact, more and more of my thinking during the past two decades has tended to move closer to the biological analogy. But *evolution* sounds slightly more deterministic than *prosperity*, at least to those who view evolution more as a process of selection and necessity than of creation and opportunity. *Progress* would have fitted my prejudices almost perfectly, as I confess to being an optimist despite all environmental concerns, but the term would have nurtured expectations going much beyond the contents of this book.

The chapters have been arranged in two parts; the first focuses on economic growth and structural change, the second on issues of inflation and exchange rates. In both parts, the sequence is chronological according to the dates of publication or writing. The chronology has been preserved for the benefit of readers who are curious to see how the topics and the emphasis have changed over time. After all, political economy is a historical discipline.

Many of the chapters in the first part have a Schumpeterian cast. In fact, I found that Schumpeter's way of thinking became more and more appropriate when we moved into the fourth quarter of this century, leaving behind the decades of reconstruction in Europe after World War II and the period of fast growth that compensated my generation for the miserable economic performance of the interwar period. Schumpeter had to come onto the scene, together with the entrepreneur as his hero, when it seemed that growth would no longer be pushed by tailwinds but had to be pulled —like a front-wheel-driven car—by forces eager to gain ground in the fields of new technology. It may be worth recalling in this connection that this was also the time when Hayek's interpretation of competition as a procedure of discovery found increasing resonance in the public policy debate, at least in Germany.

"Aspects of Growth, Structural Change, and Employment: A Schumpeterian Perspective" (chapter 2) was originally presented at an international conference in Kiel in 1979 but written largely in 1978 during a stay at Yale University. It originated from an attempt to formulate a policy paradigm that was in line with the gist of the discussion we had in Germany on what was called supply-oriented policies: more growth, yes, but growth that would be sustainable and noninflationary in the medium run. It would have to be growth propelled more by investment and saving rather than more government consumption and, specifically, by private investment geared to the creation of jobs, and new productive capacity, preferably by firms and sectors leading in the process of structural change. Impressionistic as the Schumpeterian approach may have appeared to the neoclassical growth theorist who discussed the original paper at a conference, it was not without some influence on the public policy discussion in Europe.

Chapter 3, "Problems of Adjustment to Imports from Less Developed Countries," resumes the discussion of structural change in the context of an advanced open economy that is under increasing import competition from low-wage countries that are in a process of catching up. The country of reference is again West Germany. The message is that if the authorities adopted a forward-looking Schumpeterian policy of promoting flexibility —rather than a policy of protection derived from the Stolper-Samuelson theorem—the country would grow faster and would simultaneously assist its partners in the less developed world. The empirical research cited clearly supports the view that it is possible to implement such a forward-looking answer to the then-fashionable demands for a so-called New International Economic Order.

"The Role of Entrepreneurship in the 1980s" (chapter 4) starts from the classical solution to the policy assignment problem: If the central bank has as its sole task preventing inflation and Keynesian unemployment and if responsibility for preventing classical unemployment rests with labor market institutions, including the unemployment insurance system, then it is the group of genuine economic entrepreneurs—and the scope left to them in society—that will determine the speed of productivity advance and the scope for real wage increases at given levels of employment. After enumerating the qualities of entrepreneurship essential for searching and taking timely decisions, the argument is presented that the supply of entrepreneurship is not genetically limited but can well be extended under favorable conditions within firms (decentralization) and in society, if we limit the growth of bureaucracy and are prepared to enlarge the scope for free action, self-reliance, and individual responsibility.

Chapter 5 was written as a comment on the address that Paul Samuelson gave to the opening plenary session of the Sixth World Congress of the International Economic Association held in Mexico City in 1980 under the title "The World Economy at Century's End." It has been included not so much because of the detailed points it raises as a criticism of Samuelson's position and vision, though this may interest quite a few readers, who will then wish to consult the paper to which it refers; rather, the main purpose was to present my own views on the subject. They focus on classical rather than Keynesian unemployment, on the clash between protectionist pressure groups in advanced countries and the requirements of a prosperous world economy, on the tendency of governments in mixed economies to expand in size, and on the hope that intellectuals will behave symmetrically, criticizing not only the market in support of socialism as Schumpeter thought but throwing their weight also against government and bureaucracy when they become excessive. The piece ends with a list of points related to the role of the European Community in the world economy.

Chapter 6, "Toward an Explanation of the Productivity Slowdown: An Acceleration-Deceleration Hypothesis," coauthored by Frank Wolter, was an invited paper for the 1982 annual meeting of the Royal Economic Society in London. It tries to explain the preceding productivity slowdown as a complex phenomenon defying a monocausal explanation. This slowdown is perceived to exhibit the characteristics of a long vicious circle following a similarly long virtuous circle. What seems to be at stake is the coordination system, which can work smoothly if the trend growth of output is fairly constant but is overtaxed once bottlenecks and serious adjustment requirements cause partial delays (like accidents), a loss of coherence, or even chaos (similar to traffic congestion). Some participants in the discussion felt reminded of a Kondratieff cycle.

If Kondratieff was behind the scene in London, the German economist Johann Heinrich von Thünen was quite on center stage when the contents of chapter 7, "Labor, Wages, and Productivity," was presented in German to an interdisciplinary audience on the occasion of Mannheim University's seventy-fifth anniversary in late 1982. Although the words in the title are borrowed from Thünen and although the approach is close to his model, the subject is actually unemployment in a classical perspective. This subject figured prominently in the public policy discussion in Germany. The main message is that fighting classical unemployment by monetary expansion rather than wage moderation may help in the Keynesian short run but will lead to more persistent forms of unemployment—capital shortage unemployment and technological unemployment—in the medium run. In the circumstances prevailing at the time, a combination of monetary expansion and wage moderation was suggested as the appropriate policy implication. Wage moderation at the collective bargaining table, where minimum wages are fixed, would also permit firms to pay incentive wages for workers promising entrepreneurial behavior.

Schumpeter comes into the limelight in the following chapter, a lecture given to the American Economic Association at its annual meeting in 1983 to commemorate Schumpeter's birth one hundred years before. The title, "The Age of Schumpeter," indicates the bold prediction that the fourth quarter of this century, following the age of demand management, which Hicks called the Age of Keynes, would be characterized by an increasing importance of entrepreneurship, innovation, and knowledge production. A look at the world economy from a Thünen-Schumpeter perspective directs attention to growth centers, which benefit from external economies of agglomeration and a social atmosphere conducive to knowledge production. The chapter expresses the hope that world economic growth would accelerate, perhaps already in the late 1980s.

The two chapters that follow were prepared in 1987 and 1988 when I addressed the Mont Pèlerin Society as its president. Under the heading "Openness and Incentives" (chapter 9), a European perspective is presented. It focuses on the drawbacks of the corporatist system and its sclerotic tendencies and calls for privatization, deregulation, and liberalization as means to improving Europe's competitiveness. Competitiveness in this context is not related to the export performance; rather, it means attractiveness for internationally mobile resources, such as investment capital and human capital. The goal of competitiveness in this sense calls for a restraint of populism in taxation policy and welfare spending. As a reward for limited government it offers the prospect of faster growth as a result of the attraction of future-oriented resources.

The 1988 address "Individual Freedom for Worldwide Prosperity" (chapter 10), makes the point that progress in lowering communication costs, despite the Orwellian danger and thanks to our awareness, will work in favor of a decentralization of decision making everywhere. In retrospect, it appears as if the scent of dramatic changes in Central and Eastern Europe was already in the air. But mention is also made of interventionist tendencies arising from environmental concerns as politicians and bureaucrats prefer direct controls, of the fear that competition among governments and among central banks will be subdued by policy cartels established under the name of cooperation, and of selective industrial policies to protect new as well as old industries at consumers' or taxpayers' expense. The costs are high; there is evidence to suppose that a world without so much government interference would experience more growth on a permanent basis and allow people to enjoy more economic prosperity.

The following chapter, on Europe 1992, was presented to a conference in Montreal in early 1989 when the completion of the European Community (EC) internal market was still high up on the agenda of the public policy debate. The message is that increased competition of all sorts—among locations and institutions just as among firms—would meet with improved conditions for medium-run growth so that Western Europe could look forward to achieving real growth rates of 4 to 5 percent by the mid-1990s. More intense competition would lift the trend rate of growth and productivity advance, a factor to be added to the once-for-all gains from the lowering of transaction costs after 1992. Such prosperity should permit governments to compensate farmers for the loss of income they would suffer under a free trade solution to the agricultural problem; if this compensation were capitalized in the form of government bonds, farmers would obtain the means for making investment in alternative land uses. Other policy remarks and suggestions refer to monetary unification, tax harmonization, and the highly debatable demand for a social dimension of the single market.

Chapter 12 addresses economists interested in Central and Eastern Europe who are eager to learn from West Germany's experience after 1945. One conclusion, which shocked participants when the paper was discussed at an Organization of Economic Cooperation and Development–World Bank conference, was that catching up with the West may require the efforts of a whole generation—twenty-five years. Another implication is that full currency convertibility need not be delayed for ten years, as in the case of West Germany; the costs would be too high for countries that desperately need capital imports in all forms and could obtain them as participants in a well-developed world capital market as it exists now, in contrast to the immediate postwar period.

The last chapter of part I, "The Progressive Order" (chapter 13), is the slightly amended version of a paper for a recent (1992) conference on the future of the world economy. The original assignment sounded much more ambitious and specific than the reflections I was able to present under the broad title I chose. The progressive order is to be understood as a collection of institutions and people aiming at an increase of knowledge (in the creative order), at the application of this knowledge (in the innovative order), and at improving economic welfare (in the productive order). The reflections center around the hypothesis that the growth of knowledge is promoted by an increasing division of labor among minds, thanks to declining communication costs, and that this will raise the potential for overall productivity growth in the future. The actual outcome is supposed to depend on numerous conditions, including impediments to progress, that merit intense discussion and further study, possibly in the context of what is being called the "new growth theory."

Part II begins with a paper submitted to the 1969 Bürgenstock Conference on greater exchange rate flexibility, which was organized by Fred Bergsten, Georg Halm, Fritz Machlup, and Robert Roosa. The paper was intended to convince other participants in the debate that a move to flexible exchange rates would not increase entrepreneurial risk and, hence, not impair growth and prosperity. The argument, which I still support in a modified form, assumes that central banks do not pursue an interventionist exchange rate policy (managed floating) but concentrate on a predictable monetary policy. No additional risk would then be introduced from the policy side, and exporting and importing firms would gain when, in a domestic recession, monetary policy would be free to expand and the exchange rate would depreciate, giving relief to firms producing exportables and import substitutes. The advantage for firms of greater price flexibility and smaller changes in output would, of course, be the greater, the smaller the country and the more open it is. As this was, and still is, in contrast to conventional wisdom, readers will wish to find out what it is that makes all the difference and led to disappointments in practice. Is it the risk arising from temptation to manage the floating? Is it the risk that central banks make an unproductive use of their increased discretion in conducting monetary policy? Or what else creates volatility and distorts the signals in flexprice markets? On the other hand and in a historical perspective, the volatility observed did not harm the world economy so much as one would have expected in an ex ante evaluation.

Chapter 15, "On the Desirable Degree of Flexibility of Exchange Rate," was written in 1972 before the period of general floating. It leads to the discussion of fifteen cases in which exchange rate changes could form part of a policy package together with demand management (monetary policy) and wage behavior (incomes policy). The targets are balance of payments equilibrium, insulation against external inflation and cyclical disturbances from abroad, a smoothing of cycles in domestic absorption, and an improvement (or worsening) of the country's attractiveness to internationally mobile resources. In most cases, a free float appears sufficient for accommodating a policy of preventing or correcting an internal or external disequilibrium, with prevention requiring fewer exchange rate changes than correction. Only if a domestic boom or recession is to be corrected or if the country is to attract more (or less) foreign resources for more (less) growth of potential output will the exchange rate have to be manipulated in line with an appropriate wage policy. The case of decelerating growth is not as absurd as it might look if one contrasts the drawbacks of overindustrialization with the resource needs of peripheral countries eager to catch up. The point is also relevant for wage policy in different areas of an exchange rate union with irreversibly fixed rates.

Chapter 16 was written in 1972 to throw light on a number of neglected aspects of inflation in the international economy. These very diverse aspects have one common point: the average level of resource utilization compatible with price level stability is unsatisfactory, as there is insufficient sellers' competition. In periods of boom, when prices and wages lag behind demand, resource utilization is as high as desirable, but it is not sustainable without accelerating inflation. In periods of recession, monopolistic cost and price pressures are held at bay but at an unsatisfactory level of resource utilization. The trade-off can be improved by injecting additional doses of effective competition: more price competition from imports, more wage competition from immigrant workers, more openness also in domestic markets. In international monetary matters, the argument goes against the formation of exchange rate unions since flexible rates quickly operate on the prices of imports and of exportables when—in a small open economy —the monetary brakes are put on to curb an inflationary boom. If competition is good for prosperity, price cartels—even in monetary matters— have their drawbacks, at least in the medium run.

Chapter 17, on indexation, translated from a paper written in 1973, assumes that there was little or no money illusion left and that past inflation rates would be incorporated in collective bargaining contracts reaching into the future. Under such conditions, efforts at reducing inflation, if successful, would boost real wages much beyond the scope of productivity advance and lead to a severe stabilization crisis, with a fall in employment and output. Escalator clauses, exactly tuned to the inflation rate, would prevent this; they would fix the real wage increase by making the nominal increase flexible. A point to be added as a postscript is that wage indexation can make matters worse when it is not instantaneous but provides for a delayed adjustment that alleviates wage pressures when contracts are concluded but makes them stronger after the switch to a policy of disinflation. The offering of purchasing power bonds was suggested mainly as a hedge against inflation to compete with the wasteful alternative of building houses, thus producing a housing crisis in the following period of disinflation. The proposals were rejected by the German authorities for being inflationary, which implies that the belief in the existence and the potential merits of money illusion still prevailed.

"IMF Surveillance over Exchange Rates" (chapter 18) was presented at a conference on the New International Monetary System held at International Monetary Fund headquarters in Washington, D.C., in November 1976 as a memorial to the late J. Marcus Fleming. It was the time when the IMF was looking for a new role after the breakdown of the Bretton Woods system. The paper, which was discussed by Walter Salant, is based on several assumptions: expectations have become fairly rational after inflation destroyed money illusion; major central banks have announced money supply targets; the level of output and employment is determined by those who fix prices and wages; and currencies are convertible on all accounts. Leaving out competition for internationally mobile resources (international investment) by tax policy, I believed that exchange rates would be quite predictable in the absence of portfolio shifts. The latter would be tantamount to a shrinking or enlarging of currency areas—shifts in the structure of demand. These shifts had to be accommodated. What was left for the IMF was to survey that it occurred properly and that central banks would not deliberately intervene in foreign exchange markets. Therefore I proposed the rule, no intervention without notification.

Chapter 19, on central bank independence, was written with Harmen Lehment and presented to the 1980 meeting of the Mont Pèlerin Society. It first explains why the best solution of the policy assignment problem consists of giving the central bank the sole responsibility for price level stability, while leaving the balance of payment objective to a flexible exchange rate and the employment objective to those setting prices and wages. A brief survey of German central bank history since 1875 is given to show that formal independence is not enough and that even after 1948 the bank's hands were tied (for example, by the government's responsibility for the exchange rates). In conflicts with the Bundesbank, the West German government always adopted a more expansionary stance. Policy-oriented readers whose focus is on Europe's future monetary order will also think about how money holders can be protected against monetary mismanagement and whether it is possible to find institutional substitutes for the historical experience of the two great inflations that certainly played a role in forming the cultural wall against which the Bundesbank could lean.

The final chapter originally had a less specific title ("Real Exchange Rates and Economic Development") when it was written in 1984 (in honor of Alan Peacock). At that time the real exchange rate between the dollar and the deutsche mark was about the same as in 1950, when few people thought that the dollar was overvalued. But the dollar was high compared to 1970, perhaps due "either to the cut in business taxes or to technological innovation or to the downward flexibility of real wages." Cyclical and structural modifications of the purchasing power parity doctrine are reviewed to see whether they could account for temporary or sustained changes of the real exchange rate. The conclusion drawn is that the United States at the time of the high dollar had raised the marginal efficiency of investment, thus attracting capital imports for a faster growth of output. The conclusion that the dollar would remain at rather high levels was not borne out by subsequent events. In retrospect, some of the assumptions that were mentioned and taken for granted did not turn out to be realistic: the monetary regime changed toward more expansion, the tax cuts that had raised the marginal efficiency of investment were reversed, and EC Europe made efforts to catch up by reducing classical unemployment (by wage moderation) and raising its competitiveness (by tax cuts). If the real exchange rate reflects a country's competitive position relative to others, it is as unpredictable as the outcome of a competitive race.

This introduction can be concluded with a fairly general statement leading back to the title of the book: if open competition is good for prosperity, we have no reason to deplore that it makes economics less of a science than we would like to have it. After all, it is better merely to understand prosperity and have it than to serve under a determining visible hand.

## References

Giersch, Herbert. 1986. "Economics as a Public Good." *Banca Nazionale del Lavoro Quarterly Review* 158:251–273. Reprinted in Giersch (1991, 3–22).

Giersch, Herbert. 1991. *The World Economy in Perspective: Essays on International Trade and European Integration.* Aldershot: Edward Elgar.

Haberler, Gottfried. 1937. *Prosperity and Depression: A Theoretical Analysis of Cyclical Movements* Geneva: League of Nations.

# I

## Growth, Structural Change, and Employment

# 2

Aspects of Growth,
Structural Change,
and Employment:
A Schumpeterian
Perspective

## The Conceptual Framework

This chapter aims to throw some light on problems of growth and employment that appear to have been somewhat neglected in the recent development of mainstream economics. As the subtitle suggests we shall make use
of a framework of thought that might be called "Schumpeterian," in honor
of Joseph Schumpeter, who taught in Vienna and Bonn as well as at Yale
and Harvard, and who deserves—as some people here in Kiel think—
more credit than he usually receives in the shadow of Keynes.

This system of thought emphasizes

• a medium run time horizon, as distinct from the Keynesian short run and
the classical, neoclassical, or Marxian long run;

• the cyclical nature of capitalist development, rather than the notions of
short run or long run equilibrium, as a basic postulate;

• the catallactic features of activity in the private sector and hence the
information and coordination problems arising in decentralized systems—
in contrast to a view which Hicks calls "plutologist" or "social accounting
Keynesianism" (Hicks 1976);

• active or dynamic competition of all sorts (Schumpeter's creative destruction) among entrepreneurs, whom Schumpeter (1912) defined as everyone
who "carries out new combinations";

• autonomy, spontaneity, curiosity, experimenting, and risk taking as essentials of human action under competitive conditions in business as well
as in research—in contrast to the notion of perfect competition and its
implicit "situational determinism" (Latsis 1976);

Reprinted with permission from *Weltwirtschaftliches Archiv* 115 (1979): 629–652. Copyright
1979 by Institut für Weltwirtschaft, Kiel.

• entrepreneurial supply activities (supply pull) rather than demand mechanics such as demand induced accelerator investments or multiplier processes (demand push) as driving forces in economic development.

This approach certainly is supply oriented, in contrast to the demand bias of short-run macroeconomics. Effective demand is taken to be a consequence (multiplier effect) of private supply activities, that is, of autonomous investments. A shortfall of demand can be explained in this framework as a consequence of unfavorable conditions for autonomous investments, including

• a shortage of technological breakthroughs,
• a shortage of factors complementary to investments,
• institutional constraints,
• a shortage of entrepreneurs, and
• a distortion of relative prices depressing profits and profit expectations.

The last point allows one to take account of short-run impediments to growth and lapses from full employment conditioned by

• excessive real rates of interest (shortage of money relative to goods at given prices) implying that hoarding is too attractive relative to investment in physical assets (Keynesian underemployment of all factors of production);

• excessive real wages that create classical unemployment of labor even if the real rate of interest is not excessive;

• a breakdown of consumers' and investors' confidence (a confidence or liquidity trap) and hence of the conditions for the functioning of the price mechanism as a device for coordinating decentralized decisions (Leijonhufvud 1968).

These distortions may arise

• from deceleration of the money supply unanticipated on capital markets,

• from minimum wage legislation, from changes in the degree of monopoly on the supply side of the labor market, or from decelerations of the money supply unanticipated on labor markets, or

• from secondary deflation or a cumulation of structural changes due, for example, to supply shocks or sharp variations in real exchange rates and other relative prices, which lead to a temporary breakdown of confidence, that is, of the methods of projection used in households and firms.

Conversely, cyclical upswings and growth spurts are characterized by changes in relative prices favorable to profits and profit expectations, due, for example, to

• unanticipated accelerations of monetary growth resulting in a decline of real rates of interest (interest lag),

• price inflation not anticipated in previous wage contracts (wage lag), or

• uncertainty-reducing additional information supplied as a public good, such as preannounced credible policy targets, development programs, and other substitutes for futures markets.[1]

The Schumpeterian framework focuses on time, that is, on the forces determining the speed and the cyclical pattern of spontaneous development; it leaves, however, a gap with respect to space and therefore the questions of where development takes place and why development differs from country to country and—within countries—from region to region. This gap, it is suggested, can most easily be closed by combining the Schumpeterian framework with a spatial model derived from Thünen (1826) who, incidentally, anticipated the marginalist revolution. Let me first describe the essentials of a Thünen-Schumpeter model before using it as a tool for understanding some features of postwar economic growth and their relevance for present world economic problems.

Imagine a homogenous plane, with transportation costs proportional to distance and weight. A central point (Thünen City) is bound to emerge because of

• scale economies in the supply of public goods, such as security and contract enforcement, which also determine—together with transportation costs—the border of the political system,

• scale economies in the supply of private goods, and

• economies of conglomeration (external economies).[2]

Locational equilibrium (in a stationary setting) requires an allocation of mobile labor and capital in such a way that all transportation costs are shifted onto the owners of land and other immobile resources. Hence the rent of land monotonically declines from the center to the periphery, while the reward of mobile factors is the same all over the plane. Relatively transport-intensive products are attracted by the center inasmuch as it pays to incur higher land costs and to substitute labor and capital for land. The system can be conceived as a cone, if the density of population or the GDP per unit of land is measured in the third dimension. When labor is not perfectly mobile, even wages and per capita incomes decline from the center to the periphery.

With a homogenous plane and given knowledge, we have only one set of private goods. Trade theorists call them Heckscher-Ohlin goods, but the honor should really go to Thünen. If we introduce differences in climate and natural resource endowment, we also have trade in Ricardo goods. They are named after Ricardo for his pedagogic decision to have England export humidity-intensive cloth against sun-intensive wine from Portugal. But had he anticipated Alfred Weber's theory of industrial location, he would have referred to raw material deposits as a source of rent and to coal from Newcastle as a resource-based good. If a resource rent enables a government to efficiently supply peace and contract enforcement, or private firms to get a head start in industrialization, it may be decisive for center formation. For explaining long-run growth we need a third type of good, which has the property of being new in the sense that the production function is still a secret, or that the preference for it has not yet been revealed. These goods, often referred to as product cycle goods, can be called Schumpeter goods. Being the result of innovation, they will be produced where human capital is abundant and where the social atmosphere and the institutional arrangements are attractive to firms and persons who are prepared to devote resources to R&D and to risky ventures in expectation of transitory monopoly gains. An innovative sector added to a Thünen cone transforms the cone into a volcano. Center-periphery trade now also includes the lava of knowledge (transfer of technology) incorporated in Schumpeter goods. When knowledge flows down from the top, it raises total factor productivity wherever it is applied, but once it is applied in competitive places it destroys the original gains from innovation in the center (assuming that the center is in fact the generator of new knowledge or that the center moves to places where innovative firms and persons have found a convenient location). Thus in order to maintain these gains, the center must continuously generate new knowledge and Schumpeter goods. With transportation costs and some immobility of labor, these gains are partly shifted to local labor that is or becomes complementary to Schumpeter entrepreneurs and firms. Under these conditions even wages for manual workers will decline from the center to the periphery.

The world economy could once be thought of as one great Thünen-Schumpeter system, in the eighteenth and nineteenth centuries with London as the center of the Pax Britannica, and in this century with New York as the center of the Pax Americana. Now it seems that the Western world has at least three centers. Apart from the United States, there is a distinct

Asian and a distinct European center. The cone shape of income dispersion in Europe is most pronounced, if the subnational regions located in the northwest-southeast direction from the estuary of the Rhine are presumed to have a per capita income dependent upon the distance from Düsseldorf. This is shown for the European Economic Community (EEC) in figure 2.1, which is based on 1974 data. Additional evidence supports the presumption that the center tends to shift southward. The picture is less impressive in the northeast-southwest direction, unless we take the capitals of the Scandinavian countries and Paris as part of the cone's top and ignore the areas in between. More specifically, most national economies have an income cone of their own, often with the national capital as a center. In the United States several subnational income cones can be observed, with New York City, Chicago, and San Francisco as centers.

How was it possible for two new world economic centers to develop outside the United States in Europe and Asia in the postwar period? Will the countries close to the top of the European cone be able to maintain an income position comparable to the United States? Will it even be possible for these countries to overtake the United States in terms of gross hourly earnings or is such overtaking a temporary process bound to fail in the medium run? What are the problems of trilateral policy coordination in the triple top system of the West? These are the questions that arise from the Thünen-Schumpeter framework sketched above.

**The Catching-Up Process**

A cone of its own may well develop in any place outside the center if conditions emerge or are created that raise the marginal efficiency of capital which under static conditions would be the same everywhere. This can be illustrated by the lower part of figure 2.2, where the increase in the marginal efficiency of capital is shown by the shaded area (hollow). Such an increase can come about

• through wartime destruction of parts of the old capital stock that depresses the income per unit of immobile factors as shown by the shaded area in the upper part of figure 2.2 but makes room for new and superior vintages (Schumpeter's creative destruction decomposed into (I) a sudden exogenous destruction first and (2) a faster than normal creation afterward),

• through a forced influx (refugees) of manual labor and entrepreneurship amounting to an increase in the stock of human capital,

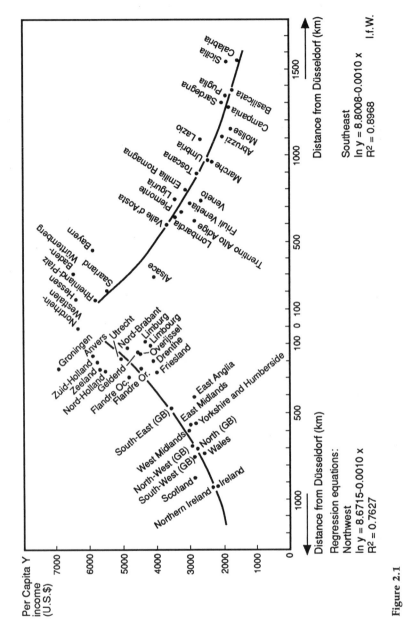

**Figure 2.1**
Center-periphery income differences in the European Community: cross-section from Düsseldorf to Northwest and Sourheast (GDP per capita, 1974)

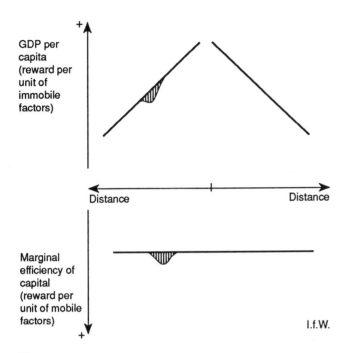

**Figure 2.2**
Model of a Thünen-Schumpeter income cone

• through public infrastructure investments, government efforts to raise the domestic supply of human capital, low wages with impediments to emigration, and institutional measures to make the area more attractive for autonomous investment and entrepreneurs.

This catalog includes the main features of a starting base for postwar recovery as they existed in West Germany. Assuming fixed coefficients in industry, the unemployment prevailing at the time could be called capital shortage unemployment (Giersch 1978). As to wages they were

• presumably equal to the low marginal product of labor in overcrowded agriculture,

• probably below the marginal product of labor employed in industry, implying "exploitation,"

• below those in neighboring countries and held in check by impediments to emigration.

With an exchange rate set to avoid balance of payments deficits and to allow import liberalization, unit labor costs in the international sector (the tradable goods sector) were so low in international comparison that capital was bound to flow in and to be accumulated out of domestic profits. Low wages and high profits, combined with an unexploited potential of human capital and skill, thus appears to have been essential for producing a laissez-faire catching-up process—sometimes called a virtuous circle. This mechanism was facilitated by information about an appropriate structure of production (reconstruction) and development path (imitation).

Neighboring countries benefit from such a virtuous circle as far as

- their firms produce complementary goods (demand effect);

- their consumers are supplied with more attractive goods, which in addition may contribute to improving work incentives (incentive effect);

- their firms mobilize their innovative forces to transform the challenge of competition into a stimulus to better achievement.

The last two points are basic to a supply-oriented "locomotive theory," in contrast to the popular "locomotive theory" based on demand multiplier effects.

If virtuous circle growth is to become more than a short-lived acceleration to regain a previous position on the world income scale it must obviously either benefit from strong domestic positive feedback mechanisms or from a foreign "locomotive."

The foreign locomotive for postwar Europe certainly was the United States as a source of demand and as a pacemaker for domestic supplier activities. Foreign demand is of little help unless domestic suppliers are keen on exploiting it. They can do so by making their product mix complementary to present foreign demand (static linking) and by concentrating their competitive activities on those segments of demand that promise a high income elasticity (dynamic linking). Foreign demand for exports of domestic firms will, of course, rise when foreign firms give up in the competitive race. To be forced to give up on certain established products is beneficial for growth in the pacemaker country, if this contributes to shifting resources to the development of Schumpeter goods: more volcano activity under the pressure of competition from a lower part of the Thünen-Schumpeter system.

Among the competitors who give up may be exporters from neighboring countries who fail to develop the supply activities required for effective linking to a pacemaker. Instead of being or becoming Schumpeter entrepreneurs, they are passive and decide to wait for the foreign trade multiplier to work. Perhaps they fail for the simple reason of relying too much on demand delivered by the government. In such a case the Schumpeter country crowded with active suppliers will surpass its more complacent neighbors: a new cone begins to emerge on the gradient after the hollow (figure 2.2) has been filled up.

Positive feedback mechanisms in the catching-up economy can arise

• from the psychological mechanisms underlying the dictum that nothing succeeds like success;

• from learning by doing, for example, in the export business, a practice which can be systematically developed when the way upwards to the top level in the management hierarchy usually passes over the hurdle of an export department;

• from the creation of a growth-minded tradition of thought and behavior, which supports an initial decision in favor of open markets (the historic Erhard decision) and institutions conducive to active suppliers' competition, and which deemphasizes the equality element in the "big trade-off" between equity and growth (rather than efficiency).[3]

Will a catching-up country run an export surplus? Demand-biased social accounting interpretations suggest that it obviously will, because this is the way the foreign trade multiplier functions. In German social accounting language the export surplus is called "Außenbeitrag," meaning "the foreign contribution." Supply-oriented economists (and laymen) wonder what the foreign countries "contribute" to. The social accounting answer is, of course, "to total demand." But this interpretation meets with doubts in a medium-run perspective when supply activities and supply bottlenecks have to be taken into account. Can a country really catch up while it loses resources that would have had a potential social productivity of domestic investment much above the interest earned abroad? The answer becomes obvious when we consider that a catching-up country is likely to be strong in unfolding suppliers' activities both at home and in export markets. Exports are being fought for and markets are conquered by investing in sales organizations abroad, while imports just come in, sometimes at an accelerated speed when domestic supply bottlenecks arise (Giersch 1953). An export surplus and domestic growth thus have a common source: vigorous suppliers' activities. We may call this the case of a "Sturm und Drang" economy.

Other cases of a persistent export surplus[4] that can be related to suppliers' activities include

- the *mature* economy, which has ceased to offer enough attractive opportunities to entrepreneurs and investors, and has thus become a supplier of capital to poorer countries further down on the Thünen gradient,

- the *aging* economy, which no longer offers the social atmosphere congenial to active persons, letting them emigrate—together with their capital assets—to "virgin" lands, and

- the *decaying* economy, where capital and labor feel expelled from the area or region, which then suffers from what regional economists sometimes call "passive rehabilitation."

In none of these cases would it be justified to accuse the country of pursuing a beggar-thy-neighbor policy.[5]

It is tempting at this stage to integrate the export surplus cases with deficit cases into a "life cycle hypothesis" of trade balances.[6]

- A *poor* but *young* economy may be able to raise, or to attract from abroad, entrepreneurs who become dynamic importers of capital goods. If they fail to bring with them or to attract foreign capital in the first instance, their impact as autonomous importers of capital goods is to raise the price of foreign exchange, thus making domestic resources more attractive to foreign investors and suppliers of capital (wealth effect). In other words: autonomous importer-investors can raise the marginal efficiency of capital as seen from outside in a similar way as the factors that contributed to West Germany's postwar recovery, as described above.

The cases to come next would be

- the surplus economy in its *catching-up* process;

- the capital-exporting *mature* economy;

- the *aging* surplus economy, losing human capital as well;

- the *rentier* economy, which runs a current account deficit in order to consume the capital previously invested abroad; and

- eventually the *decaying* economy.

This life cycle hypothesis gives rise to the following conjectures about trade policies. It appears most likely

- for the poor and young economy to turn toward free trade and convertibility once it has discovered that youthfulness can be transformed into strength and—in a virtuous circle—into attractiveness with regard to foreign capital,

• for the catching-up economy to pursue a free trade policy under the influence of aggressive exporters who must be presumed to be in favor of open markets everywhere, and

• for the rentier economy to be protectionist and to be favorable to applying (perversely) the infant industry argument to senile industries and activities.[7]

While the rentier economy is likely to be very concerned about (static) optimum tariffs and the best (static) commodity terms of trade, the youthful catching-up economy has a longer time horizon. People are prepared to sacrifice—or plow back—part of their potential gains from trade for the sake of improving the external income terms of trade and, in the end, their external double factorial terms of trade. For this, they will hear, from foreign competitors, complaints about "dumping," "disorderly marketing," and "market disruption." The target of raising the double factorial terms of trade (i.e., of catching-up through trade) can be achieved

• by giving priority to export products which promise to benefit from a high income elasticity of world demand (dynamic linking),

• by exploiting economies of learning through specialization in international trade,

• by absorbing whatever technology can be imported and applied to raise efficiency (process innovations) and to capture transitory monopoly gains (product innovations).

More briefly, while the rentier economy adopts a zero sum mentality, the youthful catching-up economy exploits its conversion potential and the profits held out for future-oriented activities.

It appears that the advanced parts of Europe, after having caught up with the United States in many respects, find themselves in a critical stage of transition characterized by declining supply elasticities. This highly tentative judgment is based on very limited and casual observations, mostly, if not exclusively, relating to Germany. Several points come to mind immediately:

• an increasing concern about the costs of economic growth, fueled by the 1972 Club of Rome report, combined with a reluctance to consider that the costs could well be internalized, and the fashion among intellectuals of preaching a new austerity;

• the widespread nuclear power anxiety;

• a microprocessor allergy (technological unemployment);

• a noticeable resistance to structural change, and a related concern about rents and windfall profits;

• a shift in collective bargaining from pay increases to safeguard provisions, income maintenance clauses, longer vacations, and shorter work weeks, which is more pronounced than in the past;

• a decline in the share of fixed investments (in West German GNP from 26 percent in the mid-sixties to less than 21 percent after 1974 (current prices));

• a marked increase of net direct investment abroad.

While the first points seem to apply to most advanced countries or regions all over the world, supporting the hypothesis that the mid-seventies may mark the end of a thirty-year period of accelerated growth in the West,[8] the points further down the list appear to be characteristic for countries having succeeded in catching up. Without having a pacemaker to follow, these countries find themselves in great uncertainty on the way from (a rather) imitative to (a more) innovative growth pattern.

**Problems of Transatlantic Equilibrium**

The transition was inaugurated in 1969 with the deutsche mark revaluation. The series of appreciations of German currency vis-à-vis the U.S. dollar proved to be more than a monetary phenomenon; it was real, that is, in excess of differences in price level changes. As the upward revaluation of the deutsche mark measured on a cost basis was even greater (SVR, 1978–79, 141), catapulting hourly wage costs above the U.S. average,[9] profitability deteriorated. Similar developments occurred in the Benelux countries, and even stronger ones in Switzerland. Part of this is presumably due to short-term phenomena, including

• the substitution of deutsche marks and Swiss francs for "oversupplied" U.S. dollars as international money, and

• a cyclical lead of the U.S. economy in the post-1975 upswing.

However, what is relevant here are not the monetary and cyclical aspects but the structural element: the real appreciation of the deutsche mark was a necessary condition for accommodating structural change on both sides of the Atlantic.[10]

For one thing, postwar recovery in Japan and Germany started on an exchange rate track appropriate for overcoming what was called the dollar shortage. It thus became profitable to build up capacities in the tradables sector for earning dollars. Not surprisingly, the U.S. economy, supplying the dollars, tended to become import biased with a relatively weak international sector. After the structural development had gone on for two decades, only a sharp real appreciation of the deutsche mark (and the yen) could be expected to break the underlying structural trend by allowing the price of traded goods to fall relative to domestic goods and push resources out of that sector.

For another thing, and surely not unrelated, underlying sectoral productivity developments in the United States and Germany differ (Heitger and Weiss 1979). In Germany, the productivity advance in tradables relative to nontradables has been faster than in the United States. Hence, equilibrium prices of tradables in Germany should have fallen relative to prices of domestic goods. As long as the deutsche mark remained undervalued in real terms, there was a disparity between actual prices and static equilibrium prices of German tradables; this gave broad scope for quantity expansion. Only a real appreciation of the deutsche mark in terms of wages or domestic goods prices could break the quantity expansion and bring about an upward pressure on the prices (in U.S. dollars) of German tradables.

When the real appreciation took place, West Germany came under more severe pressure to give up some of the more imitative and labor-intensive activities in the international sector. These activities are no longer sufficiently competitive. The future of the tradables sector lies in human capital intensive activities. The nontradables sector can best contribute to such activities by providing human capital and by supplying new knowledge as a condition for innovation.

Transatlantic equilibrium thus seems (or seemed?) to require that West Germany expand her domestic sector in order to reduce her export bias while the United States would have to build up her import substitution and her export industries (strategy A). But should the diagnosis for the world economy be that the Third World and the newly industrialized countries (NICs) suffer from a capital shortage but are able to develop their absorptive capacities, all of the rich countries ought to run a surplus on current account to be underpinned by capital exports. In this case, West Germany (and Japan) might just have the right balance between the domestic and international sectors, and it would be only the United States that would have to undergo a substantial structural change in the next couple of years (strategy B). To clarify this point might be worth closer study and another summit meeting, with capital exports to Third World countries included on the agenda. The point is to regard export surpluses as the form of resource transfer which is needed to stimulate supply activities in Third World countries. It would also be appropriate to discuss institutional arrangements for overcoming the political risks impeding the flow of private capital.

At least until recently (1978) the situation in West Germany and in countries of a similar position was characterized by a lack of investors' confidence, notably in the international sector of the economy (covering in West Germany 47 percent of employment (1975), more than in any other OECD country). This reflects the adjustment process that has been going on since the beginning of the decade:

• Between 1970 and 1971 and again after 1973 the international sector of the West German economy has grown less than would have been normal (Heitger and Weiss 1979, Chart I).

• How the adjustment was enforced can be inferred from a comparison of the percentage of after-tax profits over total sales in the United States and Germany since the mid-sixties. While the U.S. percentage in 1973−76 (5.1) was again almost as high as it had been in 1965−68 (5.3), after a drop in 1969−72 (4.3), the percentage for Germany shows an uninterrupted decline over the three periods by one-third (1.9 for 1973−76 as compared to 2.9 for 1965−68). It has also been calculated (Strigel 1978, 23) that in the United States the before-tax percentage in 1976 was again as high as at the beginning of the sixties (II), in contrast to Germany where it had declined (from 7 to 5).

• In 1978 profit rates in German manufacturing, which practically covers the international sector, further declined below the 1977 level, but they appear to have risen in the domestic sector, notably in new construction (SVR 1978−79, 49).

• While in the United States gross fixed investment in manufacturing at constant prices showed an average growth rate of 5.2 percent over the period 1961−77, the corresponding rate for Germany was only 2.2 percent, exclusively due to the worse performance since 1971.

• This is in line with the observation that firms with headquarters in West Germany have an increasing propensity to invest abroad and to concentrate on the United States, thus reversing the transatlantic flow of investment that prevailed in the sixties (see SVR 1978−79, Graph 29).

• Surveys conducted among international businessmen reveal an increasing preference for investment in the United States. The reasons given include: better profits, less labor unrest, increasingly more favorable labor costs, less governmental intervention, greater investment security, and improved security of materials supply (U.S. Department of Commerce 1976, G-4). In addition, German businessmen refer to the absence of codetermination in the United States.

But is it not legitimate to argue that without those factors favorable to foreign investments in the United States, the dollar would be even weaker and German unit labor costs in the international sector correspondingly higher? In a similar vein it has been suggested that wage restraint in Germany would not raise the marginal efficiency of investment within the country but merely lead to a further decline of the dollar–deutsche mark exchange rate. It can be shown, however, that wage restraint in relation to the productivity increase, or any other development favorable to investment in Germany, will not be fully wiped out by exchange rate adjustments even as far as the international sector is concerned (Lehment 1979). Wage restraint can be expected to be yet a stronger factor for growth in the domestic sector, and it is the domestic sector that must grow faster, if Germany is to further correct the export bias in her production structure under strategy A. To put it differently: if the internal terms of trade of the domestic sector were not allowed to improve (relative to the international sector), strategy A could only work via a slowdown in growth of the whole German economy, that is, via a flow of German investment to the United States at the expense not only of the international but also of the domestic sector in Germany. Under strategy B, the United States would concentrate on strengthening the import substitution and the export sector, thus supporting the dollar to an extent which would help the German international sector to grow in proportion with the domestic sector.

**Policies toward Growth and Employment**

The key to stimulating growth in West Germany and her European partner countries is investment. One form is public investment, an avenue pursued by demand-oriented economists. They expect more public spending to produce more growth of real GNP, more employment, and possibly an even faster increase in labor productivity (DIW 1979). This view is supported by simulations with an econometric model for the Federal Republic of Germany (Krelle 1976). The crucial questions raised by this demand-oriented approach concern the supply side, notably the supply elasticities of domestic resources, particularly labor and the capital stock. The demand-oriented approach obviously assumes conditions which are similar to those in the sixties,

• when the currency was notoriously undervalued;

• when the economy was allowed to grow under conditions of an almost unlimited supply of labor (guest workers);

• when unit labor costs were so low relative to unit labor costs in most other countries that firms could fill existing jobs and create new ones without concern about competitiveness;

• when low unit labor costs attracted direct investment and superior technology from abroad;

• when the excess demand for labor induced firms to pursue search activities and active labor market policies, thus reducing search unemployment and frictional unemployment among the domestic labor force to an insignificant percentage;

• when serious indications for the existence or emergence of a grey (untaxed) part of the economy did not yet exist; and

• when the pressure of competition from low-wage countries did not yet manifest itself in a need for structural adjustment.

Since the second half of the seventies at the latest, West Germany (and some of her neighbors) no longer enjoys the advantages of a catching-up economy. In these circumstances there is reason to fear that a program of inflating demand without a concern for the capacity and productivity effects of investment will have much lower output effects and much higher price effects than the proponents of more government spending expect. Even without such a program, inflation is already accelerating at the present stage (May 1979) after the labor market shows signs of tension and after the decline of the dollar has been reversed. A program of demand expansion is not needed as a public good supporting the market mechanism, because the problem is uncertainty about medium-run competitiveness in a situation of structural change. The weak spots in the economy are industries and firms, including some large corporations, which are suffering from the storm of innovative competition originating in technologically more advanced parts of the world, including Japan, and from import competition in standardized goods originating in low-wage countries. In these circumstances, economic policy has two polar options to stimulate growth and promote unemployment:

• lowering unit labor costs relative to other countries by restraining real wage increases (Option I), and

• accelerating growth of total factor productivity by rejuvenating the economy and augmenting the supply of highly productive jobs (Option II).

Option I is similar to the way chosen by the United States after 1971 and by England in the thirties as a remedy against what Keynes called "The Economic Consequences of Mr. Churchill." In both countries the situation was characterized by an overvaluation of the currency and hence of domestic unit labor costs, with low profit margins and profit expectations as a consequence. The U.S. situation in the late sixties can be compared to that of Germany and related countries in Europe in the seventies: slow growth of the international sector in both cases was accompanied by an outflow of investment.

The basic question of Option I is whether an explicit policy of real wage restraint alone, that is, without elements of Option II, would be desirable or even feasible in West Germany. If the policy is limited to manipulating the price level, the answer is most likely "no" for the following reasons:

• While in the United States accelerating inflation between 1972 and 1974 lowered the rise in real wages (hourly earnings related to the CPI) from 2.8 percent in 1971 to an annual average close to zero (and below zero if 1975 is included), such inflation in Germany would have much less chance, if any, of depressing real wage increases below the rise in distributable productivity (output per man-hour corrected for changes in the terms of trade) for more than a year, given the inflation sensitivity of the population and the annual nationwide wage rounds. Prospects for a long wage lag in Germany have deteriorated in comparison to the 1960s when the great post-1967 expansion, supported by longer wage contracts, ended in a series of wildcat strikes in the fall of 1969.

• While the dollar devaluation can be considered to have had a positive employment effect in the United States (0.2 percentage points less unemployment in 1974 according to DRI (Data Resources, Inc.) simulations (Eckstein 1978, 141), a deutsche mark devaluation in the case of Germany must be expected to have a greater effect on inflation and an even lesser effect on employment, given the larger relative size of the international sector in a smaller economy.

• Lowering real wages via disguised inflation (from moral suasion to price controls) does not promise success, given that large parts of the population still vividly remember the pre-1948 repressed inflation. They would quickly lose confidence in price indexes upon discovering the quality deterioration of goods supplied under disguised inflation.

For the recent past, West Germany has found it more appropriate to favor policies along the lines of Option II, although the subject has been under constant debate since the 1975 recession. The ideal framework for Option II can be described as follows:

1. There is an implicit consensus about a solution to the policy assignment problem which attributes

• responsibility for maintaining price level stability without deflation (preventing Keynesian unemployment) to monetary policy;

• responsibility for removing Keynesian underemployment to a concerted action of monetary policy, fiscal policy, and wage policy;

• responsibility for preventing and removing classical unemployment to (fairly centralized) organized labor supported by expert information about an appropriate incomes policy;

• responsibility for lowering search and frictional unemployment to active labor market policies;

• responsibility for adequate growth of potential output and total factor productivity to the business community and to those branches of government which determine the institutional framework (*Ordnungspolitik*) and which influence the structure of incentives (*Rentabilitäts- und Strukturpolitik*).

2. There is a high degree of predictability (preannouncement) of government and central bank policy.

3. Additional efforts are undertaken to reduce investors' uncertainty by supplying information on trends of structural change from independent research institutions competing with each other.

Practice is, of course, much less than ideal. This holds for the implicit "consensus," for the correct diagnosis of specific government and market failures, for the reliability of government announcements, and for the quality of structural research and its information content.

The basic issue in Germany (and elsewhere) since 1974 is the nature of the unemployment problem. Adherents of Option II policies consider

• the uninterrupted decline of employment in German manufacturing since 1970 (by almost 12 percent until 1977) as a clear indication of longer-term structural changes, which have been predicted (Fels et al. 1971);

• the rise in the underlying unemployment rate since 1974 partly as a form of classical unemployment, conditioned by a rise of real hourly wage costs in excess of the distributable increase of labor productivity during the phase of decelerating inflation;

• the hard-core unemployment prevailing at the present stage of the up-swing (1979) as a reflection of a job gap,[11] which is due to

• wage-induced job obsolescence (capital destruction),

• strong import competition from less developed countries (LDCs),[12]

• an insufficient volume of job creation because of poor investment performance and induced labor-saving innovations, notably in the international sector, and

• an increase of the intended participation rate of women.

The job gap scenario for the future naturally depends upon the expected rate of growth of domestic investment outside the government sector and the expected capital intensity of the jobs incorporated in the new capital stock. For 1985, job gap estimates currently range between 2.25 and 4.5 percent of the labor force. In the absence of additional capital formation for closing the gap, the economy, according to the underlying scenario hypothesis,

• would fail to provide enough viable jobs for "reasonable" full employment at a level of real wages compatible with "reasonable" expectations, and

• might suffer from a vicious circle of stagflation implying,

    • disappointed wage and employment expectations,

    • wage-push inflation,

    • wildcat strikes or organized actions against imports from low-wage countries, against labor-saving innovations, and against a labor market without equitable forms of job rationing, and

    • general hostility toward the market system.

On the other hand, a new investment surge could stabilize or improve the German economy's competitive position close to the top of the European income cone. The country would then also feel vigorous enough to champion freeing imports from LDCs.

In contrast to the demand-oriented proposals a job creation program in line with Option II would be supply oriented. It would aim at

• the supply of jobs for new products (rather than the demand for traditional products),

• jobs in the private and potentially international sector (rather than in the domestic public sector),

• strengthening the engine of growth in the private enterprise system (rather than in the government bureaucracy).

The German government, including state governments, has taken a number of steps in this direction, including

• tax measures to widen the scope for accelerated depreciation (a device amounting to an interest free investment loan plus government participation in the risk of failure),

• a shift from direct to indirect taxation,

• more government support to R&D in manufacturing,

• government loans to support the creation of new firms,

• government-supported consulting for small business,

• investment loans, subsidies, and public infrastructure investment in the framework of regional policy.

However, as any major step in this direction tends to meet with strong political resistance on income distribution grounds, there will be no spectacular developments in the near future.

A disguised form of support for real growth in West Germany may arise from the European Monetary System (EMS), if the following conditions happen to be met:

• German labor unions accept a major responsibility for price level stability —as they did in the sixties—and will unintentionally contribute to an undervaluation of the deutsche mark relative to other EMS currencies;

• exchange rate adjustments within the EMS are delayed so that unit labor costs in Germany are artificially reduced for most of the time, making locations in Germany again more attractive (as in the sixties) to German and foreign investors;

• an EMS-controlled deutsche mark becomes less attractive relative to the dollar so that German unit labor costs are not artificially high in relation to unit labor costs in the United States.

Thus, Europe may use German unions as a disciplinary force in its monetary system and reward them with a supply of complementary investments
and more viable jobs for full employment at higher real wages in the
medium run. The counterpart would, of course, be less investment and
more unemployment in the more peripheral regions of Europe's Thünen-
Schumpeter cone and—once the mechanism has been understood—complaints about German beggar-thy-neighbor policies.

## Notes

I am grateful for helpful criticisms and suggestions to Gerhard Fels, Harmen Lehment, Bodo Risch, Klaus-Werner Schatz, Carsten Thoroe, and Frank Weiss. Shortcomings are mine.

1. Confidence in accustomed methods of projection can, of course, also be
strengthened by quantity signals arising from exogenous increases in government
demand. This is the rationale of public expenditure programs in deep recessions.
  As an example, one may think of suggestions submitted by the German Expert
Council in the 1967 recession and subsequently discussed by government authorities and business and labor organizations in the forum established explicitly for the
purpose of coordinating expectations and actions (Konzertierte Aktion) whenever
market coordination is thought to need public leadership. The Expert Council had
suggested such coordination efforts already in 1965 for attaining the target of
price level stabilization without stagnation (Sachverständigenrat (SVR) 1965–66).
The idea had been rejected by Chancellor Erhard because of its gradualist elements,
although it had been explained to him that gradualism was indispensable because
of the existence of old contracts anticipating higher rates of inflation. When the
1966–67 recession occurred—a "wanted" recession as the minister of economic
affairs admitted—the Expert Council (SVR 1967–68) thought that the market
required support and that a concerted anticipation of high employment equilibrium
would greatly contribute to attaining it. Although the official coordination effort
failed, the economy expanded fast, however strongly pushed by foreign demand
on the basis of an undervalued exchange rate (Giersch 1976). The theoretical basis
for public action to coordinate expectations seems to be implicit in Hayek (1948,
42 sqq.): "the concept of equilibrium (merely) means that the foresight of the
different members of the society ... must be correct in the sense that every
person's plan is based on the expectation of just those actions of other people
which those other people intend to perform and that all these plans are based on
the same set of external facts, so that under certain conditions nobody will have
any reason to change his plans.... But if the different plans were from the beginning incompatible, it is inevitable ... that somebody's plans will be upset ... and
that ... the whole complex of actions ... will not show those characteristics which
apply if all the actions ... can be understood as part of a single individual plan."
Moreover, "the problem ... is how the spontaneous interaction of a number of
people, each possessing only bits of knowledge, brings about a state of affairs ...

which could be brought about by deliberate direction only by somebody who possessed the combined knowledge of all those individuals."

2. For more details see Giersch (1949–50, 1959).

3. Put somewhat differently: Rapid growth, once it has gone on for some time, is likely to be extrapolated so that also the poorest expect a substantial rise in their incomes within the foreseeable future. This stretches the time element implicit in Rawlsian type (Rawls 1971) considerations. Indeed, to be worse off than others is less depressing if and when absolute improvement is fast and can be expected to remain so.

4. For short-run phenomena affecting the trade balance, see Dornbusch and Krugman (1976).

5. Although it does not quite fit into the growth context, the reader may wish to keep in mind the classical case of a (current account) surplus country importing, and a deficit country supplying, gold and financial assets, including international money. It may be more than a mere coincidence that a catching-up country feels proud about earning its foreign exchange reserves, rather than borrowing them, and that, after having been successful in manufacturing, it also wishes to achieve international status in banking.

6. For a somewhat different "life cycle hypothesis" of trade balances, see Crowther (1957).

7. A decaying economy, if there should be one, would turn toward autarchy, including export restrictions.

8. In 1939 Schumpeter (p. 1050) foresaw a new Kondratieff upswing, which, if its beginning is dated in the mid-forties, seems to have lasted for about three decades.

9. Hourly wage costs in 1978 and 1968:

| | 1978 | 1968 | | | 1978 | | 1968 |
|---|---|---|---|---|---|---|---|
| Country | U.S. $ | U.S. = 100 | | Country | U.S. $ | U.S. = 100 | |
| Belgium | 10.59 | 129.0 | 45.1 | Canada | 7.53 | 91.7 | 77.4 |
| Sweden | 10.29 | 125.3 | 64.1 | France | 6.47 | 78.8 | 42.4 |
| West Germany | 9.79 | 119.2 | 45.4 | Italy | 5.65 | 68.8 | 34.0 |
| Netherlands | 9.57 | 116.6 | 45.7 | Japan | 5.45 | 66.4 | 19.3 |
| United States | 8.21 | 100.0 | 100.0 | U.K. | 4.07 | 49.6 | 32.1 |

Source: U.S. Department of Labor, Bureau of Labor Statistics.—Kiel Institute of World Economics.

10. The relationship between real and monetary influences of exchange rate changes has been shown by Dornbusch (1973), among others, with Bruno (1976) extending the analysis to problems of growth. An early exposition is Salter (1959), but see also SVR (1964–65, para. 35–36).

11. "Even a boom, however strong it might be, could not quickly bring the economy back to full employment in a form similar to that which prevailed before 1974. Because, during the process of structural change, much of the capital stock has been revalued, potential GDP in terms of physical capacity is less than potential GDP in terms of labor at the prevailing real wage level. In this sense, the German economy is confronted with a job gap, the counter-part of which is insufficient real capital formation" (Fels and Weiss 1978, 33).

12. In 1974–75 the LDCs increased their share of the German market for the first time during a recession (Fels and Weiss 1978, 42). Mounting competitive pressures of suppliers from LDCs and the newly industrialized countries affect major parts of whole industries like steel, textiles, shipbuilding, and metal manufacturing and hence the economic future of previously prosperous regions in which these industries are concentrated.

## References

Bruno, Michael, "The Two-Sector Open Economy and the Real Exchange Rate," *The American Economic Review*, Vol. 66, Menasha, Wisc., 1976, pp. 566–577.

Crowther, Geoffrey, *Balances and Imbalances of Payments*, The George H. Leatherbee Lectures, 1957, Boston, 1957.

DIW (Deutsches Institut für Wirtschaftsforschung), "Finanzierungsstruktur und Verteilungswirkungen einer nachfrageorientierten Strategie zur Wiedergewinnung der Vollbeschäftigung," *Wochenbericht*, 13, Berlin, 1979, pp. 139–147.

Dornbusch, Rudiger, "Devaluation, Money, and Nontraded Goods," *The American Economic Review*, Vol. 63, Menasha, Wisc., 1973, pp. 871–880.

———, and Paul Krugman, "Flexible Exchange Rates in the Short Run," *Brookings Papers on Economic Activity*, Washington, D.C., 1976, 3, pp. 537–584.

Eckstein, Otto, *The Great Recession, With a Postscript on Stagflation*, Data Resources Series, Vol. 3, Amsterdam, 1978.

Fels, Gerhard, and Frank Weiss, "Structural Change and Employment, The Lesson of West Germany," in: Herbert Giersch (Ed.), *Capital Shortage and Unemployment in the World Economy*, Symposium 1977, Tübingen, 1978, pp. 31–53.

———, K.-W. Schatz, and F. Wolter, "Der Zusammenhang zwischen Produktionsstruktur und Entwicklungsniveau, Versuch einer Strukturprognose für die westdeutsche Wirtschaft," *Weltwirtschaftliches Archiv*, Vol. 106, 1971 I, pp. 240–278.

Giersch, Herbert, "Economic Union between Nations and the Location of Industries," *The Review of Economic Studies*, Vol. 17, Cambridge, 1949/50, No. 2, pp. 87–97.

———, "Akzelerationsprinzip und Importneigung," *Weltwirtschaftliches Archiv*, Vol. 70, 1953 I, pp. 241–283.

————, "Probleme der regionalen Einkommensverteilung," in: Walther G. Hoffmann (Hrsg.), *Probleme des räumlichen Gleichgewichts in der Wirtschaftswissenschaft*, Tagung aus Anlaß der 175. Wiederkehr des Geburtstages von J. H. v. Thünen, Schriften des Vereins für Socialpolitik, N. F., Bd. 14, Berlin, 1959, pp. 85–118.

————, "Episoden und Lehren der Globalsteuerung," in: *Wirtschaftspolitik, Wissenschaft und politische Aufgabe*, Festschrift zum 65. Geburtstag von Karl Schiller, Beiträge zur Wirtschaftspolitik, Bd. 25, Bern, Stuttgart, 1976, pp. 277–296.

———— (Ed.), *Capital Shortage and Unemployment in the World Economy*, Symposium 1977, Tübingen, 1978.

Hayek, Friedrich A. von, *Individualism and Economic Order*, Chicago, 1948.

Heitger, Bernhard, and Frank D. Weiss, "Structural Change in a Two-Sector Open Economy, A View from West Germany," in: Herbert Giersch (Ed.), *International Economic Development and Resource Transfer*, Workshop 1978, Tübingen, 1979, pp. 315–332.

Hicks, Sir John, "'Revolutions' in Economics," in: Spiro J. Latsis (Ed.), *Method and Appraisal in Economics*, Cambridge, New York, 1976, pp. 207–218.

Krelle, W., "The Bonn-Econometric Model of the West-German Economy," in: *The Models of Project Link*, Contributions to Economic Analysis, 102, Amsterdam, 1976, pp. 199–217.

Latsis, Spiro J., "A Research Programme in Economics," in: idem, *Method and Appraisal in Economics*, Cambridge, New York, 1976, pp. 1–41.

Lehment, Harmen, "Lohnpolitik und Beschäftigung bei festen und bei flexiblen Wechselkursen," *Weltwirtschaftliches Archiv*, Vol. 115, 1979, pp. 224–241.

Leijonhufvud, Axel, *On Keynesian Economics and the Economics of Keynes, A Study in Monetary Theory*, New York, 1968.

Rawls, John, *A Theory of Justice*, Cambridge, Mass., 1971.

Sachverständigenrat zur Begutachtung der gesamtwirtschaftlichen Entwicklung (SVR), Jahresgutachten 1964/65: *Stabiles Geld—Stetiges Wachstum*; 1965/66: *Stabilität ohne Stagnation*; 1967/68: *Stabilität im Wachstum*; 1978/79: *Wachstum und Währung*, Stuttgart, Mainz.

Salter, W. E. G., "Internal and External Balance: The Role of Price and Expenditure Effects," *The Economic Record*, Vol. 35, Melbourne, 1959, pp. 226–238.

Schumpeter, Joseph A., *Theorie der wirtschaftlichen Entwicklung*, Leipzig, 1912.

————, *Business Cycles, A Theoretical, Historical and Statistical Analysis of the Capitalist Process*, Vols. 1, 2, New York, London, 1939.

Strigel, Werner H., "Fehlendes Vertrauen als Wachstumsbremse, Ergebnisse und Folgerungen aus qualitativen Unternehmerbefragungen," *Ifo-Studien*, Vol. 24, Berlin, München, 1978, No. 1/2, pp. 21–41.

Thünen, J. H. von, *Der isolirte Staat in Beziehung auf Landwirtschaft und National-ökonomie*, Hamburg, 1826.

U.S. Department of Commerce, *Foreign Direct Investment in the United States*, Report of the Secretary of Commerce to the Congress in Compliance with the Foreign Investment Study Act of 1974 (Public Law 93-479), Vol. 5: Appendix G—Investment Motivation, Appendix H—Financing, Appendix I—Management and Labor Practices, Washington, D.C., April 1976.

# 3 Problems of Adjustment to Imports from Less-Developed Countries

The group of less-developed countries (LDCs) has set as its target an increase of its share in world manufacturing production from around 7 to 8 percent now to 25 percent in the year 2000. Although the figure is probably too high to be realistic, it can be taken as a symbol of the LDCs' efforts to improve their position in world production and international trade. Advanced countries are called upon to support these efforts by freeing imports from LDCs.

The West German Government, in 1971, under Willy Brandt and in matters of economic policy dominated by a professional economist (Karl Schiller), gave a fairly unambiguous anticipatory response:

Structural changes which are triggered by the increasing integration of the developeing countries into the international division of labor must not be hampered; they must rather be supported, if necessary by adequate measures of structural policy. Especially the exodus of labor and capital from the industries where an adjustment of the changed market conditions becomes necessary, must not be obviated by preservation subsidies. (*Bundesregierung* 1971)

The response would have been less positive,

· had the country suffered from unemployment

· had trade associations and labor unions had a hearing, and

· had weak rather than strong growth prevailed in the decades before, so that it had not become popular to be optimistic in the liberal tradition of Anglo-Saxon political economy.

Reprinted with permission from *The World Economic Order: Past and Prospects*, edited by Sven Grassman and Eric Lundberg. New York: St. Martin's Press, 1981, 265–288.

## Free Trade and Real Wages

Neoclassical economics contains the message of the Stolper-Samuelson theorem: Labor in advanced countries will suffer a decline of real wages in terms of each and every commodity if free imports are permitted from countries where labor is not the scarce factor.[1] In a similar vein, the Lerner-Samuelson theorem implies that free trade will—under certain conditions—lead to an international factor price equalization even if no factor movements take place. To become equal through trade, real wages must rise where they are low, and fall where they are high, in the absence of free trade. Neoclassical economics thus shows free trade to be an issue of conflict between labor in capital-rich and in capital-poor countries.

Neo-Marxian economics attempts to reestablish the presumption in favor of a worldwide class conflict between capital and labor. The notion of "unequal exchanges" (Emmanuel 1972) is introduced to demonstrate that the rich in the North benefit by exploiting the poor workers in the South. Although Samuelson has shown that the argument is wrong (Samuelson 1976), it nevertheless has strong emotional appeal. Those who use it fail to ask themselves whether it would really be better for the workers in the South if the capitalist countries refused to employ them (Lerner 1976).

A similar reasoning starts from the proposition that advanced countries are so powerful that they can determine which international transactions and markets are to be free or restricted. They will opt for freeing the capital market and those segments of commerce which increase the demand for capital and reduce the demand for labor. This raises two points:

1. The first is an observation: In the 1960s European investors were not so much interested in free access to foreign countries but attempted—with the consent of domestic labor—to promote immigration from the South. Why was there no class conflict over this issue in the European North? The answer will be approached in more detail below.

2. The second point is a presumption: If the present relationship between freedom and protection is biased against labor and the LDCs, a removal of the remaining restrictions, upheld by capitalists in the advanced countries, should lead to higher real wages and/or employment in the world at large. However, we observe that moves toward freer imports from LDCs into advanced countries are not only resisted by capitalists but also by labor. This is in line with the Stolper-Samuelson theorem. It may, however, apply only to specific labor-intensive industries which have no chance for survival without protection. Here, labor and capital are—so to speak—com-

plementarily locked in. Nevertheless, labor in general may feel that it is at least indirectly affected and that there is a depressing effect which free imports from labor-rich countries will have on the full employment level of real wages.

The conflict between labor here and labor in the LDCs seems to be bridged by a newly emerging ideology. It recommends protection for more growth in the advanced countries—along the lines of the Cambridge (England) New Economic Policy Group. The LDCs are advised to concentrate on "basic needs" and on integration among themselves so that they need not rely so much on outward-looking policies and free access to the product markets of advanced countries. This type of thinking—implying a two-factor model and a worldwide class conflict between labor and capital —thus supports ideas of disintegration, delinking, or whatever the current terminology is. The fear of exploitation overshadows the hope that there are gains from trade to be exploited which could make everybody better off.

Such pessimism is perhaps warranted for some countries which are comparable to those weak persons, both young and old, who find the competitive struggle and the resulting division of labor anything but attractive. Lord Kaldor (1978) seems to hint at that with regard to an advanced country. A national economy may indeed have become so incapable of adjusting its internal structure to exogenous changes that it needs to be inward looking in order to survive, just as aged persons tend to become more inward looking. Without protection of even the least competitive industries and firms, there would not be enough profits to maintain capital intact or to generate some modest growth. Economists and political leaders in such countries (1) tend to stress the demand rather than the supply aspects of growth, (2) tend to call upon other countries to generate demand—rather than stimulate domestic private investment ahead of demand, (3) tend to complain about the country's commodity terms of trade as a bad fate—rather than stress the simple rule that improvement requires a change in the country's product mix in compliance with (or anticipation of) changing income elasticities of demand and prices, (4) tend to favor government policies—rather than emphasize the problem-solving capacity of private decision makers, or (5) tend to be sensitive to a strong popular quest for individual security and interpersonal equality. There are, of course, elements of a positive feedback mechanism in this. Economists, by giving advice that is sound only in the short run, can play an accelerating role. If this is the case one may call the country a "Keynesian economy" in view of Keynes's emphasis on the short run and his contribution to the stagnation thesis for the medium run.

As the problem of LDCs is not the subject or this chapter, there is no place to dwell upon the distinction between inward- and outward-looking economies in the Third World. It is sufficient to note that both types do exist and that outward-looking economies are growing more rapidly—or that rapidly growing economies tend to be more outward looking. The only inference to be drawn here is that inward-looking LDCs are more stagnant compared to fast-growing outward-looking countries which are in a process of catching up and which are likely to be the major beneficiaries of outward-looking policies in the West.

The counterpart of a Keynesian advanced country may be called a "Schumpeterian country." The model of such an economy may be conceived to have the following properties:

1. Firms and families have a high adaptive capacity; they consider exogenous disturbances to be challenges which have to be met with a forward-oriented response.

2. Their emphasis on a forward-oriented response corresponds with a high capacity to learn (research), to innovate, to experiment, and to imitate.

3. Institutional arrangements are not so tight and inflexible as to become a brake on forward-oriented responses.

4. Incomes (after taxes and transfers) contain high compensation for risk-bearing (profits), learning (human capital), and successful response to changes (relative factor prices sufficiently flexible interregionally and inter-industrially). Rewards for pure (unskilled) labor and capital are correspondingly less important. So is the fear that free imports from capital-poor and labor-rich countries might significantly worsen the distribution of income.

5. Most people's time horizons are long enough to transform the "Big Trade-off" between equity and efficiency (Okun 1975) into a trade-off between equality and growth, where prospects for high growth deemphasize the natural feelings of envy. The time horizon may be related to the age structure of the population.

6. Supply (and supply policy) is considered to be more important than demand (and demand management). Demand is taken for granted or is created in a process of innovation guided by the search for outlets with a high income elasticity of demand. The terms of trade are rarely of concern

as they tend to improve (on a Paasche basis) or quickly recover from exogenous shocks under the impact of adjustments in the product mix or the export basket.

7. Because of its high (actual or expected) human capital content domestic labor is complementary (rather than competitive) to both domestic capital and with immigrant labor. Domestic labor can specialize for job opportunities higher up in the hierarchy, which are less accessible to foreigners on account of the language barriers. This makes for a low resistance against foreign workers.[2]

8. Economists and other intellectuals still praise the virtues of openness vis-à-vis the future (indeterminacy) and the rest of the world; they consider competition not only as an allocative mechanism but also as a social instrument of discovery (Hayek) and believe that competition, in additional homeopathic doses, will strengthen rather than weaken the vitality or the socioeconomic system (which is seen as a catallaxy rather than a hierarchically coordinated entity). As long as economists entertain ideas akin to eighteenth-century Anglo-Saxon philosophy, the country can be assumed to be fairly young (as England during the Industrial Revolution).[3]

Keynesian and Schumpeterian countries can well coexist if the former do not insist on more than occasional help so that the latter remain free to render their best service to the rest of the world by making use of their relatively high capacity to adjust. This makes the outward-looking countries in the Third World the natural partners of advanced Schumpeterian countries.

If economic policies are to express people's preference and behavioral patterns, there is no good reason for the West to speak with one voice or to form a trade policy convoy. Those who are able to make greater progress in freeing imports from LDCs should be at liberty to do so. This raises the question as to whether the conditional most-favored-nation (MFN) clause should not be substituted for the unconditional clause. It would allow for progress at the expense of perfection. Once experiments of partnership between young developing countries have proved beneficial, they will be imitated or joined by others.

An important success condition is certainty about the inevitability of adjustment. Entrepreneurs tempted to look backward and to engage in defensive activities should not be given hope for political support, as such activities would entail costs for the domestic economy and the Third World.

## Beyond the Point of No Return

At this juncture a pause is necessary in order to survey some questions that need to be discussed subsequently.

Experience from European integration suggests that adjustment is facilitated if the decision to remove import barriers is irreversible and preannounced. Would this apply also to the present case?

If an irreversible decision is advantageous, one would like to know something about the size and the nature of the adjustment problem. What does past and current research tell us?

In European integration, the free trade commitment was made in combination with decisions opening the prospects for a common labor market, and firms seemed to like that. Do we have a similar complementarity here?

If intraindustry adjustment is unimportant in trade between countries with different levels of development and income, what does interindustry adjustment involve?

Interindustry adjustment might still be intrafirm adjustment, if the firm covers various industries. By the same token intrafirm adjustment call also be interregional and even international if the firm is a multiplant enterprise. Is intrafirm adjustment easier than interfirm (or market) adjustment?

To cope with the adjustment problem, where are governments better than markets and where are markets better than governments? What is the possible role of information and economic research in this field?

Policy certainty reduces information costs. If it is true that alternatives are not given but must be searched for, then even the elimination of one or several possible options must reduce the cost of decision making. This speaks in favor of making the free import commitment definite and irreversible. But any policy change, the more so if it is irreversible, ought to be preannounced, so that decision makers in the private sector know what they have to (or need not) take into account in far-reaching decisions. This is not in order to please the business sector, but to avoid inefficient decisions which involve a waste of resources, eventually at the expense of real wages. Moreover, an irreversible commitment must be credible, and in order to be so it must appear to be feasible and reasonable ex ante. A host of questions will be raised in the legislature during the ratification process. This is why we must assess, at least, the order of magnitude of the adjustment problem. Before doing so, it may be useful to ask who—on the political scene—is likely to challenge the estimates. Experience suggests that major opposition will not originate from firms and other profit maximizers. They may already anticipate the adjustment called for although they will testify against it if asked in official hearings. Strong opposition is rather certain to come from various trade associations, labor unions, and similar nonprofit institutions which pursue goals like membership maximization, growth for growth's sake, or mere survival. As will be seen later, sensitive industries are often regionally concentrated. Regional representatives in political decision-making bodies will, therefore, be among the hardest opponents.

## The Size of the Adjustment Problem

At the time when the West German government made the policy declaration quoted at the beginning of this chapter, the Kiel Institute started empirical work on the long-term problems of the economy, including its structure of protection, its structural anomalies, and its actual and potential problems of adjustment to imports from LDCs. It is on this work that this section most heavily draws. Figures and estimates relate to West Germany, but some findings are likely to have a wider application. The sector which will have to bear the brunt of the burden of adjustment to imports from LDCs is manufacturing. As a matter of qualification we should note at the outset that its share in the country's GDP and employment is so much beyond any norm derived from international cross-section analyses (related to per capita income) that there is reason to believe in a backlog adjustment process; this holds to the extent that the anomaly can be imputed to the long-lasting undervaluation of the currency which clearly benefited the international sector, mainly manufacturing.[4] The backlog hypothesis does not, of course, apply to that part of the anomaly which is due to permanent factors such as the raw material deposits and cheap river transportation in the Ruhr district and the waste disposal system of the Rhine. Less of the structural anomaly needs to be corrected, if the country should play a greater role as a capital exporter and hence also as an exporter of capital goods to LDCs.

With regard to the starting position and past trends we note:

1. The division of labor in manufacturing with the LDCs is explainable by human capital and raw material intensity: German industries tend to be the more competitive in trade with LDCs the more human-capital intensive and the less raw-material intensive they are (Fels 1974; Wolter 1977a).

2. The system of protection discriminates more against LDCs than against industrial countries (Fels 1974). Nevertheless, persistent protection could not reverse the declining industries' weak position, nor could it prevent the

developing countries from capturing additional shares of domestic consumption (Wolter 1977b).

3. In 1975, in most German industries, imports from developing countries accounted for less than 5 percent of domestic consumption. Exceptions are musical instruments, toys, and sporting goods (9.9 percent), clothing (9 percent), leather and leather manufactures (8 percent), nonferrous metals (6.6 percent), and textiles (5.4 percent). Nevertheless, low-wage countries exerted considerable adjustment pressure on a number of domestic industries. First, imports from these countries have increased at an unprecedented rate since 1970. Second, in several subbranches of manufacturing developing countries gained considerably larger market shares than is evident from overall industry figures. And third, due to their low wage level and concomitant price competitiveness in certain industries, the supply from developing countries induced strong price competition on domestic markets (Wolter 1977b).

4. In recent years imports of manufactures from LDCs grew annually between 30 percent and 100 percent—albeit starting from low levels—in goods such as plastic products, glass, electrical engineering, office machinery, light metal products, road vehicles, precision and optical goods, clocks and watches, fine ceramics, and ships and boats.[5]

5. The brunt of the adjustment burden is borne by economically weak groups, since it is the industries with a high share of low-skill (especially female) employment and the industries concentrated in backward regions which are under particularly strong adjustment pressure (Fels 1974; Wolter 1977b).

6. The industries so far most severely affected by adjustment pressure are characterized by a relatively large number of small and medium-sized firms. Nevertheless, within these industries, the medium-sized firms (100 to 1000 employees) tended to cope with the adjustment problem better than the larger and the small ones (Fels and Horn 1976).

7. Even in those industries of manufacturing which are characterized by relatively high R&D expenditures and above-average human-capital intensity such as chemicals and engineering, there continue to exist firms which (still) have standardized and labor-intensive products in their output mix (Dicke and Weiss 1978).

8. In general, it can be said that firms which spend much on research and development, planning and organization, and industrial designing, and firms which produce in small lots to customer specification have proved to be resistant to competition from LDCs.

Studies of the West German engineering industry which go further into detail lead to the following conclusions:[6]

1. Adequately defined skill variables—such as the relative importance of craftpersons, operators, and managerial personnel—go far to explain why some subsectors are more competitive vis-à-vis LDCs than others, but surprisingly enough certain proxies for the technology factor, like R&D intensity, did not yield significant results.

2. Standardized engineering products do not enjoy a comparative advantage in West Germany.

3. If the output is motor vehicles or metal products, competitiveness greatly depends upon proximity to competitive suppliers of component parts or other inputs from industrial sources.

4. The range of products under severe competition from LDCs is wider than was initially expected.[7]

5. The adjustment process in labor-intensive industries seems to have been aggravated by relatively sharp increases in wages for unskilled labor since 1970. A test of substitutability of craftpersons and physical capital for unskilled labor revealed a relatively high elasticity (Dicke and Weiss 1978). This finding is consistent with the recent relative increase in the rate or unemployment of unskilled workers.

A rather detailed study of the steel industry shows that producers in the United States and Western Europe are about to lose their international competitiveness in mass steel. Adjustment pressure is less strong in rolling mill operations where skill requirements are high and proximity to customers is important. The highly advanced countries remain competitive in new steel technology, in specialty steel products and their application, in new capital goods for the steel industry, and in the supply of whole steel plants. Mass steel production, which is too costly in advanced countries and for which there is not enough demand in poor countries, is moving toward semiindustrialized countries (Wolter 1977c).

As to the static effects of policy changes in favor of free imports, relevant studies for West Germany do not lead to dramatic results.

1. Eliminating MFN tariffs only would raise the welfare level in the Federal Republic of Germany by not more than DM (deutsche mark) 700 million per year (per capita: DM 12) (Glismann 1977).

2. If nontariff barriers to imports of textiles and apparel were abolished, real income would rise by about DM 1500 million per year (per capita:

around DM 25). These are the most highly protected products in the Federal Republic of Germany outside agriculture and coal mining (Glismann 1977).

3. Tariff liberalization would reduce employment in West Germany's manufacturing sector by about 1.2 percent, a figure which would become even lower if additional employment opportunities for increased exports were taken into account (Fels and Glismann 1975).

The overall static effects of trade liberalization on real income and employment were also estimated as of minor importance by other authors for other countries (for example, Magee 1972; Cline et al. 1976).[8]

This is not incompatible with more dramatic results for those branches of industry which were thought to be particularly sensitive to free imports from LDCs (Dicke et al. 1976).[9] The main conclusions, which refer to the extreme case that both tariff and nontariff barriers would be abolished, indicate that the leather and clothing industries would almost lose their bases of existence, unless they can succeed in concentrating on high income elasticity products subject to the vagaries of fashion—a possibility open to firms producing close to leading consumer markets.

On the assumption that the export potential of LDCs and their imports from Germany will increase more than in the past so that a 20 percent upward shift in the trend of imports from and exports to LDCs takes place, a research group of the Kiel Institute arrives at the following conclusions (Hiemenz and Schatz 1977):

1. Full liberalization of imports from LDCs will reduce the number of jobs in German manufacturing by another 0.8 million. This would be more than 11 percent of present employment in manufacturing (in 1976: 7.4 million).

2. Foreign *gastarbeiter* (guestworkers) will be more than proportionately affected since they are highly concentrated in lines of production and jobs where skill requirements are low. The effect will be particularly strong where foreigners compete with domestic female workers; it will be less so where foreign workers are—or have made themselves—complementary to domestic workers by accepting work which requires heavy physical effort or otherwise has high disutility.

3. Should foreign workers be discriminated against in the sense that they would not be offered a new job whenever they lost one in this process,[10] they would still bear not more than 20 percent of the job losses.[11] Even under such discrimination, therefore, employment of domestic workers in

manufacturing would still decline by 0.7 million or 9 percent of present employment in manufacturing (1976) (Hiemenz and Schatz 1977).

Foreign workers are presumably more mobile than their domestic competitors. This is why, in the first place, their influx contributed to the industrial agglomeration tendencies and to the growth of urban centers in the 1960s. Their return home in the adjustment process under the assumed discrimination strategy would minimize the employment problems in these regions. This applies to North Rhine—Westphalia and Baden-Württemberg where more than a quarter of all employees in manufacturing were foreigners in 1974. In all peripheral regions, however, the job losses due to increased imports from LDCs would far outweigh the present employment of guestworkers (Hiemenz and Schatz 1977, 55 and Table 3). A strategy to ensure that all employment effects would fall on guestworkers would, therefore, require either the migration of German workers from the periphery to the central areas (plus a change in industrial occupation) or some relocation of the unaffected branches of manufacturing into those peripheral areas that most resemble the LDCs in their industrial structure. The relocation would be preferable to migration for reasons of regional balance. It would prevent an overcongestion in central areas, should the decline of employment in manufacturing be compensated by a growth of the service sector which—in some respects—seems to have locational advantages in those central areas where the employment impact of more import competition would be small.

To form a general judgment on the size of the adjustment problem the following points relating to West Germany stand out:

1. If free imports from LDCs would not destroy more than 0.8 million jobs until 1985, as has been estimated, the task appears manageable as it affects only about 11 percent of employees in manufacturing over ten or more years, and hence not much more than 1 percent per annum.

2. These displacement effects are small if compared to past technological displacement.

3. Compared to the displacement effects of past imports from LDCs they are large.[12] The burden will be felt more than in the past when it was eased by high employment growth and the selective import of guestworkers, and when its impact was less concentrated in individual industries and regions.

Any general judgment at this stage can only be of a tentative nature and will therefore be colored by personal predilections. The author's feeling is that an advanced country of the Schumpeterian type could well consider adjustment to free imports from LDCs as a "salutary jolt" toward growth in new directions. A trade challenge may well compensate for the apparent weakening of the technological growth stimulus. But there is an unfortunate coincidence of a labor-saving bias in both trade and technological development, which is likely to require new and early responses if it is not to overstrain the labor market's capacity to adjust. This appears to be the sensitive point at a time when an increased desire for job security is raising the social costs of economic growth (as we measure it) to levels which make growth look less and less attractive.

**Toward a Forward-Looking Adjustment Policy**

If the advanced Schumpeterian countries dared to make an irrevocable promise to LDCs to remove all import barriers but to stretch adjustment over a period of, say, ten years, they need not, in the author's opinion, resort to industry-specific government assistance programs. The conversion potential of established firms in an advanced country should actually be large enough to cope with the adjustment problem without specific help.[13]

General, as opposed to industry-specific, measures to increase the conversion potential[14] would include:

1. Supply-oriented policies to promote economic growth, notably tax incentives for job creation, for making relative wages more responsive to market conditions, and for promoting product innovation—including product innovation in the investment goods sector, which will become process innovation once the new equipment is installed. (As a complement to supply-oriented policies, the society must be prepared to tolerate high after-tax incomes from innovative and entrepreneurial activities, not only because of the incentives they provide, but also because of their contribution to a growing test market for new high-income elasticity products.)

2. Investment grants for returning foreign workers if it is reasonably assured that they will take their job with them, perhaps under the guidance and with the know-how and market information of their previous employers.

3. Free information from independent competing research institutions to firms in sensitive industries about structural trends and available adjustment opportunities, including locational innovation—in other words, the transfer of production to low-wage areas within the country and low-wage countries in the world at large.

4. Removal of barriers to intranational and international locational innovation, including an offer to LDCs for forming a "free investment club" that
would serve to protect against expropriation without due compensation
and thus promote the flow of direct foreign investment.[15]

These propositions assume that markets, if well supplied with low-cost
(or even free) information, have the capacity of doing better than governments, which often ignore or distort information. The often-made suggestion of creating in West Germany or elsewhere a government agency to
control the structure of industrial investment has little appeal, except in an
economy which is so backward that a good investment plan could be
drawn up by imitating more advanced countries, which must and do rely
on decentralized entrepreneurial search processes. There is, however, a side
issue bearing directly on the adjustment problem: Should governments in
advanced countries veto investment which raises the capital-labor ratio in
defense against job destruction from LDCs (defensive investment)? A positive case can be based upon the argument that such investment means "job
abortion" in LDCs if the latter lose in the ensuing "investment war," and a
waste of resources if the latter win. It can also be argued that such defensive investments lead to an excessive capital intensity of world production
and hence to a capital-shortage type of world unemployment. The tendency for such defensive investment must be expected to be great in aging
economies, notably among businessmen, who have narrow technological
knowledge, so that incapability of product innovation adds to a natural
aversion to locational innovation. Labor unions, which also in any case
dislike international locational innovation, will reluctantly support defensive investment. However, even here the case for a government body to
veto specific investment is weak, since it requires a high degree of certainty
about the lack of medium-run prospects for product innovation or even
technological breakthroughs. In any case, government would be well advised to rule out positive acts, such as delaying the removal of import
barriers or subsidizing the (defensive) investment under the heading of
adjustment assistance. A principle for government behavior that takes this
consideration into account would be: no adjustment assistance without
product innovation or locational innovation.

While the market is superior to government in future-oriented decision
requiring information which has to be searched for, firms may be superior
to markets when it comes to adjustment. If firms are large and decentralized, they may be tantamount to integrated labor markets and integrated
capital markets. As multiproduct, multiplant, multiregional, or multinational

firms, they should be more efficient in coping with the adjustment problem than a polypolistic group of firms adding up to the same size. Otherwise, their survival in competition with smaller firms would merely rest on monopoly power. In this case, however, they would invite antitrust action. This could be suspended as long as the monopoly gains are used for an intrafirm transfer system designed to reduce the hardship of adjustment. If their existence is due to superior efficiency they should be able to handle the adjustment task without government assistance. Hence. no adjustment assistance to firms above a certain size. An exception may be made when they perceive a new diversification potential, the exploitation of which, however, will often require a new management.

The multinational firm has undiscovered virtues in an international adjustment process.[16] It can gradually shift production to LDCs when import barriers are lowered and it can serve its old market from the new source of supply. Job destruction here and job creation there are synchronized by central decisions. The market could hardly do better because of subjective uncertainty, that is, imperfect information on what the competitors do: Someone has to start—either a producer in an LDC, who seizes the opportunity of more free entry into an advanced country and acts in the expectation that he can crowd out some competitor there, or a producer in the advanced country gives up in an act of anticipatory adjustment, thus making room for more imports and production in an LDC. Thus, the market essentially copes with the international adjustment problem by ex post coordination only.

The best alternative to international intrafirm adjustment is anticipatory adjustment. Outcompeting is worse from a cosmopolitan point of view, since it absorbs entrepreneurial resources in LDCs where they are particularly scarce. Advocates of anticipatory adjustment have heard all of the more or less respectable arguments for import protection and a few new points relating to uncertainty about the future (see, for example, Scheid 1974). The uncertainty arguments are not dissimilar to the popular belief that it is advisable not to engage in speculation and hence to refrain from portfolio adjustment. However, nonaction constitutes action when the system is changing, and perhaps the most fatal action when the government has decided about the direction. All the uncertainty arguments against anticipatory adjustment are, therefore, based on the assumption that the point of no return will not be reached.[17] This is why preannouncement and irreversibility are so important. LDCs have good reasons to press for them.

Seen in this context, anticipatory adjustment might deserve assistance out of taxpayers' money.[18] Funds for this purpose could be diverted from foreign aid or from maintenance subsidies, which must be phased out if adjustment is the prime objective. Recipients could be:

1. workers, if the purpose is retraining, migration, or self-employment;

2. firms, if they perform the task of retraining and job relocation;

3. regional authorities, if they can show that adjustment in the region's industry mix is vital, that it requires the replacement of economically obsolete parts of the infrastructure by the new industry-specific investments, and that the new industries or firms are at the doorstep.

As process innovation is excluded, being a defensive action, and as product innovation is a continuous process and can easily be financed by bank loans and bond or stock issues, the adjustment assistance could concentrate on locational innovation, interregional and international.

The domestic locational restructuring of the viable part of manufacturing must be expected to meet with the following difficulties:

1. To the extent that the firms are based on raw material deposits and cheap access to waterways, they will have to incur higher transportation costs or switch to other inputs or other sources of supply.

2. To the extent that skilled labor is industry specific, labor will have to move together with the locus of production from the central areas to the periphery. But where shall the incentive come from, if the periphery has absolute locational disadvantages which are not compensated in the form of lower real wages?

3. The political process favors policies to keep costs from rising in the central areas, either in the form of rent control or in the form of public infrastructure investments in the transportation system. Both respond to strong short-run pressures in constituencies which are thought to be decisive in general elections.[19]

Far-sighted regional policies, which seem to be wasteful in the short run, could be a way out of the dilemma.[20] Other solutions would be a sharp decline of rents in peripheral areas and the introduction of labor-saving innovations to raise labor productivity when firms move their production sites to the periphery of the domestic economy. The latter case requires an elaboration of the principle established above: process innovation should not be subsidized unless it is part of a locational innovation program.

Subsidies to locational innovation can be tied to the condition that the recipient firm offers an undiminished—or increasing—number of jobs to domestic workers at prevailing wage rates. In this case a product innovation or a change in the product mix would be a prerequisite. A clear-cut government announcement to grant such adjustment assistance could induce hesitant firms to leave the protectionist camp and to join the free trade league. Such adjustment assistance, indirectly linked to product innovation and scaled to job creation for new products, could be viewed as a general form of structural policy in support of the growth sector.

Apart from anticipatory adjustment assistance, there may be a case for compensating the owners of specific resources for the losses they suffer in the adjustment process. The case may be based upon equity considerations: nobody should suffer from policies which were introduced after specific resources were acquired. Political considerations may suggest that such compensation is the easiest way of removing resistance to change. While compensation would thus encourage change on the one hand, it will also be a burden—in the form of higher taxation on those who happen to earn transitory high incomes as rewards for (successful) innovative activities. This negative effect on spontaneous economic growth, which by itself is a factor facilitating adjustment, calls for qualifications of the compensation principle. Possible forms of qualification, in addition to those already mentioned, could be:

1. No compensation to capital owners, since they should have started speculating about changes in government policies in the continuous learning process going on in financial markets.

2. No compensation for the loss of human capital, unless the owner has a low conversion potential due to his old age.

3. No compensation to immobile skilled workers, unless they are prepared to accept part of the adjustment burden by moderating wage claims as a possible means of slowing down the adjustment process.

Instead, means and efforts to raise the professional and locational conversion potential of the labor force at large are called for. As hope for specific compensation impairs interest in raising the conversion potential, false hopes should be destroyed as early as possible by making the compensation rules known, together with the irreversible decision to move toward free imports from LDCs and whatever principles of adjustment assistance society deems to be the acceptable compromise between equity and efficiency.

## Notes

I am grateful to Hugo Dicke, Gerhard Fels, Frank Weiss, and Frank Wolter for helpful comments on an earlier version.

1. This sentence disregards the qualification which the authors make with reference to the multifactor case. However, the purpose of the theorem is to show "that there is a grain of truth in the pauper labor type of argument for protection" (Stolper and Samuelson 1941, 356).

2. Domestic capital benefits from a selective immigration because the labor makes it easier for the firms to invest where they are. Selective immigration reduces the otherwise existing pressure to invest in peripheral areas or in the places where the foreign workers come from.

3. It appears tempting to make these conjectures operational, so that the relative economic age of countries or regions could be identified, but this would require a fairly comprehensive research program. A guess may, however, be appropriate with regard to West Germany on the basis of the author's personal observation and intuitive interpolation: that country still has some features of a Schumpeterian economy despite definite signs of aging not yet visible from a distance.

4. See Fels, Schatz, and Wolter (1970); Fels and Schatz (1977/1); Dicke and Heitger (1977).

5. In nominal terms; the Statistical Office does not publish price index for regional trade flows.

6. See Dick (1978), Dicke (1978), Heitger (1978), and Weiss (1978).

7. It includes: most metal products; in electrical engineering: switchgear, wiring devices, household appliances, lighting fixtures, and radio and television sets and their components; among road vehicles: the bicycle; in mechanical engineering: mountings and fittings, sewing machines and standardized tools.

8. It has to be noted that these studies and those mentioned before in this paragraph do not quantify dynamic effects of liberalization.

9. The study referred to assumes inter alia that the removal of import barriers will not affect the real exchange rate. The reason given (p. 106, footnote) is that the study is limited to the impact effects of liberalizing imports from LDCs only and that so far these imports had little weight in the import bill.

10. Such discrimination against guestworkers if conceived as a policy would, of course, have to be accompanied by fair compensation payments. It could be supplemented by a grant or a loan that allows the recipient to take the job with him when he returns, perhaps also temporarily assisted by his firm. It should not be impossible to find adequate institutional forms.

11. This compares to 80 percent for a discrimination strategy applied to a total trade development in conformity with past trends. The difference is due to the fact that the assumed 20 percent shift in trend would more severely affect indus-

tries in which guestworkers are not so heavily concentrated or have already been laid off.

12. Roughly eight times as large, according to Wolter (1977b, 120, 128).

13. A firm's or a country's conversion potential can be defined as its potential capacity to change the product mix. It is related (1) to size, since size is a proxy for the diversity of resources, and (2) to the availability of nonspecific factors which can be turned to alternative uses.

Old vintages in the stock of physical capital and human capital permanently employed indicate a high conversion potential at the time of replacement. The postulate of raising a firm's conversion potential includes the recommendation

a. to drop low-income elasticity products from the product mix at an early stage;

b. to add new products (Schumpeter-goods) to the output mix, even if this lowers profits, as a safeguard against the dangerous situation that would arise if old products were to be dropped under competition from LDCs without having discovered the high-income elastic goods which could fill the gap and without having acquired the experience to produce them in line with traditional quality standards;

c. to hire workers with a great learning capacity as a form of investment;

d. to replace management when it turns out to suffer from product fetishism ('We are steel makers, not profit maximizers');

e. to start joint ventures and even merger negotiations as measures of a last resort to import new technology or an imaginative management.

A country's conversion potential depends upon: (1) the conversion potential of its firms in the international sector; (2) the information and transaction costs of interfirm adjustment; and (3) the costs of regional and professional adjustment in the labor market.

14. Apart from benefiting the country itself, such measures help LDCs because (1) they lead to higher real wages in advanced countries, thus making it easier for LDCs to compete; and (2) they promise a quick withdrawal of advanced countries from the supply of standardized products with a high content of unskilled labor and hence raise the income elasticity or world demand for the same products from LDCs. That is what matters most to prevent the LDCs from adopting costly strategies of unbalanced growth and delinking, and from wasteful efforts to develop a growth pole of their own—with emphasis on heavy industries, which are very capital intensive and create dangerous dual-economy problems.

15. Such an arrangement would have to go beyond existing bilateral agreements. It should include a set of rules for the behavior of large multinational firms and a negative list of what governments would refrain from regulating and controlling. The negative list is necessary to reduce uncertainties emanating from the general fear that governments might interfere with markets in various ways that would destroy confidence and start a vicious circle that might either end with the emigration of the form and its capital or the expropriation or the reduced capital value left at a token compensation. The major point, however, would be the creation of a common fund for paying compensation, in the case of outright expropriation, according to international rather than national law. Claims to future allocations of

Special Drawing Rights would be the capital-poor countries' contribution in the form of collateral. If we assume that an advanced country and a semideveloped country made such an arrangement as an open club to which others could accede if they were prepared to accept the rules of the game, the enterprise—if successful at the start—might grow due to the promises it holds out (1) to those capital owners and entrepreneurs in advanced countries who have to resort to international locational innovation; and (2) to all factors complementary to foreign investment in the participating LDCs.

For both countries—or groups of countries—it would raise allocative efficiency and smooth the adjustment process to the extent that trade and factor movements are complementary in a Schumpeterian growth scenario.

16. As a conglomerate it can cope with structural change and adjustment within its own confines: importing from foreign subsidiaries, improving the quality of the imported products so that they better fit the tastes of the domestic market, supporting R&D, changing the emphasis in its product mix toward new goods, retraining the employees, pensioning off workers with obsolete skills, utilizing plant sites and retrainable workers in domestic problem areas for new lines of production, and coping with the resistance of labor unions and local communities against import-induced structural change. Being usually more powerful than a small firm under severe competition, the large conglomerate with its wider profit margins is less under the exigencies of short-run survival. It can be less averse to short-run risk and lake a longer view in its decision-making process. While it will respond more slowly to short-run changes in the incentive structure (as all big animals) it can afford to devise and maintain intrafirm transfer payments which help to mitigate the impact of change on individuals. In this respect it is—in its extreme form—a substitute for the social functions of both the family and the state. Public pressure is certainly strong for large firms to pursue intrafirm redistribution policies. Representative in this respect is the large Japanese firm.

Note that it is the conglomerate rather than the textbook big one-product firm that can internalize the adjustment costs; and it must be a conglomerate sufficiently decentralized in its decision-making process so as to offer scope for Schumpeterian managers. Needless to add, it must be active as an innovator and subject to competition from LDCs. These pressures seem to have been a strong factor making large enterprise more multifarious, "as they often must develop into conglomerates in their search for survival opportunities" (Namiki 1973, 252).

17. Anticipatory adjustment is criticized by means of familiar protectionist arguments and statements to the effect that

a. it is too difficult to identify the sensitive products and industries well in advance by conventional methods (time-series, market share analyses, country-by-country cross-section analyses);

b. the factor-proportions theorem on which predictions could be based disregards the productivity of human skill and ingenuity, notably in circumstances where need is likely to be the mother or invention;

c. neither product innovations nor process innovations can be ruled out as legitimate means to rescue the status quo (although defensive process innovations may enhance the labor-augmenting bias in the techniques adopted and may exacerbate the world job gap and capital deficiency);

d. surveys conducted among engineers give reason to believe that a technological breakthrough for an industry subject to competition from LDCs is just around the corner and that, therefore, the correct policy is temporary protection or maintenance assistance rather than accepting the burden or adjustment;

e. domestic production offers positive external effects, such as support for peripheral regions, marginal male workers and married female workers, or renders nonpecuniary benefits to customers, like the military system, or to the whole population in case of war or periods of trade disruption.

To these points one can reply (in reverse order):

f. external economies or the permanent and reversible type are a matter for permanent direct subsidies and have nothing to do with the adjustment problem;

g. defense consideration can often be better met by stockpiling than by protection; they should, therefore, be kept out of consideration when nonweapons are at stake;

h. income tranfers to peripheral regions, old workers, females, and other disadvantaged groups can be divorced from the production of sensitive goods. The transfers may then be granted only under the condition that product protection is being phased out. The amount could be made dependent upon the recipient's active participation in anticipatory adjustment;

i. it is up to the individual recipient firm to decide whether support for anticipatory adjustment is needed or whether it is advantageous to wait for a technological breakthrough or to embark on defensive investment for process innovation;

j. it is the firms themselves, rather than any research institution or government, that has to identify sensitive products. How sensitive a product is to competition from LDCs will be discovered in the market while import protection is being phased out under the preannounced plan.

18. Assisting anticipatory adjustment can be justified along the following lines:

a. Above-average effective protection is prima facie evidence for a lag in the adjustment process. Unless it has already become redundant, it merits replacement by adjustment assistance.

b. However, assistance for anticipatory adjustment in exchange for above-average protection is not justified if the recipient uses it either for simply maintaining capital intact, or for defensive process innovation, or even for product innovation. Hopes for survival based on product innovation are a suitable subject of communication with commercial lenders and investors rather than with government authorities. Hence, practically only inter- and intranational locational innovation are left as possible bases for anticipatory adjustment assistance.

19. In these circumstances there is reason to fear that some of the peripheral regions of West Germany are bound to suffer a decline in manufacturing production and employment. The decline may, where possible, be compensated by promoting tourist activities and by concentrating the allocation of federal funds for research in these areas in the hope that a center for the production of knowledge

may attract people who are capable and venturesome enough to make use of new knowledge in the production of commodities which are likely to find a market.

20. It can be presumed that the advanced countries in Europe are similarly structured and face similar regional adjustment problems. In the framework of its regional policy, the EEC may experiment with the creation of three or four new growth poles in areas which (1) have severely suffered in the past from the existence of national economic frontiers; (2) have gained a higher development potential from the removal of former national economic frontiers; and (3) suffer from a severe decline in manufacturing employment due to increased competition from LDCs.

The argument for support rests on the assumption that the decline in economic activity is temporary in view of the lift in the region's development potential. For a similar proposal see Cairncross et al. (1977), Chapter 3, notably p. 88, recommendation 17.

## References

*Bundesregierung, Presse- und Informationsamt der*, "Entwicklungspolitische Konzeption der Bundesrepublik Deutschland für die Zweite Entwicklungdekade', Bulletin (Bonn, 1971). Translated in R. Scheid, "The Export Needs of Developing Countries and the Need for Adjustment in Industrial Countries," in H. Giersch (ed.), *The International Division of Labor—Problems and Perspectives* (Tübingen, 1977).

Cairncross, A., Giersch. H., Lamfalussy, A., Petrilli, G. and Uri, P., *Economic Policy for the European Community* (London, 1977).

Cline, W. R., Kawanabe, N., Kronsjo, T. O. M. and Williams, T., *Trade, Welfare and Employment Effects of Multilateral Trade Negotiation in the Tokyo Round* (The Brookings Institution, 1976, unpublished).

Dick, R., *Der Einfluss der Industrialisierung der Entwicklungsländer auf den Maschinenbau der Bundesrepublik Deutschland und anderer Industrieländer* (Kiel, 1978 (ms)).

Dicke, H., *Aussenhandels- und nachfragebestimmter Strukturwandel des westdeutschen Strassenfahrzeugbaus*, Kieler Studien 152 (Tübingen, 1978).

Dicke, H., Glisman, H. H., Horn, E.-J. and Neu, A. D., *Beschäftigungswirkungen einer verstärkten Arbeitsteilung mit den Entwicklungsländern*, Kieler Studien 137 (Tübingen, 1976).

Dicke, H., and Heitger, B., "Der Zusammenhang zwischen Aussen- und Binnenwirtschaftssektor im Entwicklungsprozess," *Die Weltwirtschaft* (1977).

Dicke, H., and Weiss, F., "Angebotsbedingter Strukturwandel in der westdeutschen Investitionsgüterindustrie," *Die Weltwirtschaft*, 1 (1978).

Emmanuel, A., *Unequal Exchange* (London, 1972).

Fels, G., "The Export Needs of Developing Countries and the Adjustment Process in Industrial Countries," in H. Giersch (ed.), *The International Division of Labor— Problems and Perspectives* (Tübingen, 1974).

Fels, G., and Glismann, H. H., "Adjustment Policy in the German Manufacturing Sector," in OECD, Adjustment for Trade (Paris, 1975).

Fels, G., and Horn, E.-J., "Kleine und mittlere Unternehmen im Prozess des weltwirtschaftlichen Strukturwandels," in K. H. Oppenländer (ed.), *Referate und Diskussionsbeiträge der Tagung vom 8. bis 10. Oktober 1975*, veranstaltet vom Ifo-Institut für Wirtschaftsforschung (Munich, 1976).

Fels, G., and Schatz, K.-W., "Sektorale Entwicklung und Wachstumsaussichten der westdeutschen Wirtschaft bis 1980," *Die Weltwirtschaft* (1977).

Fels, G., Schatz, K.-W., and Wolter, F., "Sektoraler Strukturwandel im weltwirtschaftlichen Wachstumsprozess," *Die Weltwirtschaft*, 1 (1970).

Glismann, H. H., Die gesamtwirtschaftlichen Kosten der Protektion, Kieler Diskussionsbeitrag No. 35 (Kiel, 1977).

Heitger, B., Strukturelle Anpassungsprobleme der Metallverarbeitung in den Industrieländern als Folge der Industrialisierung der Entwicklungsländer (Kiel, 1978 (ms)).

Hiemenz, U., and Schatz, K.-W., "Internationale Arbeitsteilung als Alternative zur Ausländerbeschäftigung," *Die Weltwirtschaft*, 1 (1977).

Kaldor, N., "Seul le protectionnisme peut sauver l'angleterre," Le Figaro (18–19 February 1978).

Lerner, A., Comment on G. Kohlmey, "World Trade and Intraregional Trade, Trends and Structural Changes," in Fritz Machlup (ed.), Economic Integration Worldwide, Regional, Sectoral (London 1976).

Magee, S. P., "The Welfare Effects of Restrictions on U.S. Trade," Brookings Papers on Economic Activity (Washington, D.C., 1972).

Namiki, N., "The Japanese Economy—An Introduction to Its Industrial Adjustment Problems," in K. Kapina (ed.), Structural Arrangements in Asian-Pacific Trade, Japan Economic Research Center Paper No. 01 (1973).

Okun, A., *Equality and Efficiency: The Big Tradeoff*, The Brookings Institution (Washington D.C., 1975).

Samuelson, P., "Illogic of Neomarxian Doctrine of Unequal Exchange," in David A. Belsey et al. (eds.), Inflation, Trade, and Taxes (Columbus, 1976).

Scheid. R., "The Export Needs of Developing Countries and the Need for Adjustment of Anticipatory Structure Adjustment," in H. Giersch (ed.), The International Division of Labor—Problems and Perspectives (Tübingen: J. C. B. Mohr, Paul Siebeck, 1974).

Stolper, W., and Samuelson, P., "Protection and Real Wages," The Review of Economics and Statistics (1941). Reprinted in American Economic Association, Readings in the Theory of International Trade (Philadelphia, 1949).

Weiss, F. D., Electrical Engineering in West Germany—Adjusting to Imports from Less Developed Countries, Kieler Studien 155 (Tübingen, 1978).

Wolter, F., "Factor Proportions, Technology, and West German Industries' International Trade Patterns," *Weltwirtschaftliches Archiv* (1977a).

Wolter, F., "Adjusting to Imports from Developing Countries," in H. Giersch (ed.), *Reshaping the World Economic Order* (Tübingen, 1977b).

Wolter, F., "Perspectives for the International Location of the Steel Industry," Kiel Working Paper No. 60 (Kiel, 1977c).

# 4

# The Role of
# Entrepreneurship
# in the 1980s

## The Economic Situation in the 1980s

In thirty years of fast economic growth, large parts of Europe and Japan
have succeeded in catching up with the United States. Since the early
seventies, however, all industrialized countries, including North America,
have entered a phase of slow growth and slow productivity advance. This
has reduced the scope for raising real wages much below what had been
customary, notably in Europe. Wage pressures induced by past experience
turned out to be excessive. This is why many firms and millions of jobs and
workers were squeezed out of the market and why structural unemployment has reached levels which appear unbelievably high to all those who
do not remember the thirties.

At the same time, firms in Europe's advanced economies suffer from a
profit squeeze and from increasing pressures of competition among themselves, but also under increasing pressures of competition from the United
States and Japan and from those newly industrialized countries which have
successfully started a catching-up process of their own. In this new era of
competition and slow growth we must be on guard against the dangers of
increasing protectionism. After governments have gone so far as to promise full employment at almost any costs and to guarantee a reasonable
minimum income to almost everybody at taxpayers ' expense, it is all too
likely that they will find themselves under increasing pressures to extend
the welfare state to the business community and to protect and subsidize
more and more firms which have lost their viability and their capacity to
adjust. But we know for sure that this would be the wrong direction.
Whatever you subsidize, you make it grow in numbers. If you subsidize

Address given in Helsinki on May 6, 1982, at the spring meeting of the Finnish section of
the International Chamber of Commerce. Reprinted with permission from Kiel Discussion
Paper No. 88, August 1982. Copyright 1982 by Institut für Weltwirtschaft, Kiel.

unemployment, you will have more unemployment; if you subsidize students you will have more students; if you start subsidizing less developed countries you will soon have more of them; and if you extend the welfare state to firms, you will quickly have more firms needing this welfare state to survive. At the end of the road we see everybody relying on everybody else in a society which has lost its internal strength and which is bound to suffer a decline in its standard of living. This is why more and more ordinary people with sound judgment start to look for a turnaround. But the road toward prosperity and growth through more reliance on self-help and innovative competition is long and steep, not very attractive to politicians who need spectacular results well before the next elections. The turnaround will, therefore, be delayed until the situation has become worse and worse and until more and more people understand that there is no alternative. In these circumstances, Europe will probably not have returned to substantially faster economic growth before the end of the eighties even if we can persuade ourselves to quickly agree why we are where we are and where we have to go from here.

It all started with the Keynesian idea that the objectives of high employment and economic growth could be socialized and handed over to the governments. Monetary-fiscal policy based on Keynesian expert advice was thought to provide enough effective demand and to be smart enough for fine-tuning the economy in such a way that the old business cycle with its recessions or depressions would no longer retard economic development. When fine-tuning of this sort produced more and more inflation—and even more unemployment in the medium run—incomes policies in various forms were introduced. Their purpose was to repress inflation, but as they were bound to involve more and more direct control of prices and wages they distorted the allocative mechanism of the market and diverted attention and activity from competition, investment, and innovation. The Schumpeterian entrepreneur who is engaged in forward-looking, dynamic competition lost ground to the Keynesian business manager who is closer to the government than to the market and who pays more attention to demand created by governments than to demand created by its own supply. This—together with the march into the welfare state—was bound to result in a slowdown of economic development and productivity growth. If the trend is to be reversed, the driving force needs to be changed from demand pressures to supply incentives, from government to private business, from the rear wheels to the front wheels of the system.

The new policy concept from which we can expect a turnaround after a difficult transition period corresponds to old-fashioned but sound classical economic thinking. It entrusts the central bank with the sole and exclusive responsibility for preventing monetary inflation and that kind of unemployment which may result from unanticipated monetary deflation (Keynesian unemployment). But such monetarism is not enough, at least in the context of the European labor market. To cope with the evil of classical unemployment which results from excessive wages, we may have to experiment with new forms of unemployment insurance (making this insurance more similar to a private insurance system) or with measures to reduce the monopoly power of organized labor. Details cannot be discussed here. What then remains is the fundamental question, who would be responsible (1) for the growth of potential output and hence for economic development and (2) for that productivity advance that allows real wages to rise without creating classical unemployment. This question has a simple answer: the group of genuine economic entrepreneurs in the business community.

**The Supply of Economic Entrepreneurs**

Mainstream economics has almost nothing to say about the supply of genuine entrepreneurs. The entrepreneur is a decision maker, this is true. But everybody has to make decisions; and if the resources are given, and if all relevant information is readily available and processed, rational decision making even in complex situations can be entrusted to a computer. It is most remarkable to note that, in the great debate about economic calculation in the interwar period, economists thought that a socialist system could easily solve the economic problem by imitating the pricing system of the market and by letting civil servants do the job of adjusting inputs and outputs to changes in relative prices according to some easily comprehensible maximization formula. To be sure, such a system can work. But it is modeled to resemble perfect competition, a peculiar market form which we may find—in some approximation—in the potato market or the hog market, where decision makers have to take prices as given. In this case, quasi-automatic decision making is all that is required. It leads, by the way, to a deterministic solution which may satisfy social engineers, but hardly anybody interested in freedom of action, human development, and economic evolution. This system excludes the economic entrepreneur by leaving no room for the discovery of hitherto unknown facts about better products and processes, new inputs and locations, and unrevealed buyers' preferences. It imitates the market economy as an allocative mechanism but not as an engine of discovery and evolution. Even Schumpeter, who stressed the role of the entrepreneur and to whom we owe so much for understanding economic development (Schumpeter 1912) missed this essential point when he discussed the feasibility of socialism (Schumpeter 1943).

No theory can explain economic development if it assumes that alternatives or options are given and then proceeds to concentrate on formal maximization techniques. I suggest that we do almost the opposite: Leave the solution of maximization problems to a mathematical slave and computer and concentrate on

- search activities and search strategies, and on
- criteria for options which deserve exploration and for avenues that should be left aside because they are most likely to prove to be dead ends.

These two points imply:

1. An entrepreneur has to be alert so that he or she can observe every signal which indicates new opportunities. Such opportunities may arise from changes in relative prices, from scientific development, from rising incomes or consumers' saturation, from the failure of close competitors, or from new laws and political shocks.

2. The entrepreneur must evaluate these signals by raising the following questions:

- Is there an opportunity for profit?
- How long will the opportunity exist, given the alertness of old and new competitors?
- How much capital is needed?
- What other complementary resources will have to be obtained at what cost to exploit the opportunity?

As always, every tentative answer will give rise to new questions, and every further search for answers will involve costs, including the exhaustible resource of human time.

3. As time is short for an entrepreneur, the exploration must somehow be finished by means of judgment which is still full of intuition. Good intuition is based on knowledge about the outcome in similar cases. This is the experience stored in one's long-term memory. Those who are too young can ask for other people's experience in the form of impartial advice. But they should not ask experts who have fallen in love with specific ideas.

4. Good advice is particularly needed if the envisaged opportunity is the result of one's own imaginative thinking. It is only if one can convince others that one can feel protected against deluding oneself.

5. The alert entrepreneur, in order to remain alert for new signals, must often discard old options under the pressure of time and new information. Everybody needs spare capacity for absorbing and evaluating new signals; leisure in this sense is a kind of investment. It can help against single-mindedness or obsession—something which a researcher or inventor may need, but which an entrepreneur cannot afford until he has taken a considered decision in favor of one single option.

6. While the researcher can afford to go on thinking and pondering (because this may be the activity he is being paid for) the entrepreneur in competitive positions must realize that his income is derived from the results of doing something, and often from doing it earlier than his competitors.

7. There are risks involved in seizing an opportunity but the good entrepreneur will judge them in relation to the forces he can mobilize in the event of an imminent danger. Adrenaline will be produced in his own body, and assistance can be obtained from relatives, friends, and collaborators and from the suppliers of risk capital who already have a stake in the venture. It is this mobilization of forces in the fight against risk and uncertainty that is more important than anything else to distinguish the entrepreneur from a gambler and to make him so different from a passive participant in a lottery game (McClelland 1961). But situations in which additional forces must be mobilized will arise very frequently when discovery and innovation take place under competition and free entry—as opposed to monopoly with high barriers to entry.

8. Competition is thus also an important element in speeding up the decision-making process (by the way: in research as well as in business). Economists have considered competition mainly as a device for reducing costs and prices and as a means for improving quality. But the true dynamic implication of competition is that it forces things to be done more quickly.

9. Opportunities need not be discarded but can be shelved; a "wait and see" attitude is advisable if hazardous competitors are in the game; they are likely to fail at an early stage in exploring and exploiting an opportunity. Their failure produces valuable experience which can greatly help one in launching the second attack.

10. Any new combination—to use Schumpeter's words for what the entrepreneur is to carry out—is likely to meet with resistance from opposing forces in political circles, public opinion, labor unions, or among customers, whether the new combination is a new product, a new production process, or a shift of the production process to a new location, perhaps in a foreign

environment. Some of these resistances are likely to be based on fears that will prove unwarranted in the end, but which will be emotionally strong in the beginning. To minimize such emotional resistance requires the creation of confidence, an early explanation of what is going on and what is to be achieved, and an assurance that negative side effects will be limited and will, if necessary, be compensated. A sharing of profit with those who are prepared to share the risk can be a useful device. Apart from this, emotional resistance will be minimized if the innovation can be presented as a series of steps rather than an indivisible huge venture. Comparison between microelectronics and nuclear energy suggests that more people are prepared to accept change when it comes piecemeal, so that they can evaluate each new step on the basis of past experience and feel free to reject or modify it should the negative side effects appear too large. Apart from this, a step-by-step introduction of new technologies allows people to learn to live with progress. This is why the automobile turned out to be such a success in the history of socioeconomic development: Generations of people learned to drive and to handle technologically more advanced cars—and they enjoyed it.

Now that we have enumerated all the qualities essential for successful entrepreneurial behavior the question arises, whether we have enough good entrepreneurial talent, and if not, whether we can produce more of it by forming teams. Let me start by giving a tentative answer: there is no shortage of entrepreneurial talent, but institutional resistances and technical requirements may create so complicated situations that no single person, but only a combination of persons, can successfully perform the entrepreneurial role.

Let me first deal with the first part of the answer. My belief that there is no basic shortage of entrepreneurial talent is derived from the observation that most of the qualities that we have described as essential for entrepreneurial activities are exhibited by good car drivers in crowded, but fairly unregulated streets. Choose any number of young people, give each of them a car, teach them the essentials of driving, and most of them will become good, and perhaps quite often aggressive, drivers after the period of time required for gathering experience and for developing good judgment and instincts in potentially dangerous situations. In a process of learning by doing, most candidates will become experts in anticipating other people's behavior, in discovering opportunities for overtaking, and in judging the potentialities of their equipment. Of course, there will be differences in performance; and a process of competition and natural selection (which some will consider too costly) is likely to raise the state of the art. Having been carried in taxi cabs and chauffeur-driven cars in numerous countries all over the globe, I cannot imagine that there is a shortage of talent in this field; and as driving seems to be so similar to entrepreneurial activity I would need strong evidence to become convinced that entrepreneurial talent is genetically determined and could, therefore, be a limiting factor in economic development even over the long haul. The analogy of driving can be well extended to include other forms of human activity which require similar sorts of instinct and skill and which can be observed everywhere in the world.

Not every person is a driver all the time. Similarly, effective entrepreneurship in its more pronounced forms may be limited to a certain phase in a person's life cycle, when alertness and aggressiveness are still strong while enough experience and predictive power have already been accumulated. Since the late sixties, I have strongly felt that the West must sooner or later suffer from a loss in potential economic driving power due to the fact that it failed to transform a rebellious youth into a vigorous cohort of achievement-oriented entrepreneurs. How much (potential) entrepreneurial talent has been wasted in futile and unproductive attacks on the establishment, and even in law-breaking, in hijacking and in all the other forms of outright terrorism? It would be useful to enumerate all those barriers to entry that contributed to diverting young entrepreneurial forces into the dead-end avenues of anticapitalist revolt. In this connection, it should not be left out of account that formal education, including academic training, may reach far too long into adult life or may, given its length, be too passive or reflective in character for too many people who are disposed to become active decision makers in their prime of life. For these reasons I also fear that in less developed countries (LDCs) intellectual training—as opposed to apprenticeship and professional education—receives more attention and emphasis than is good for economic development.

The entrepreneur so far described is an ideal type (attitude, state of mind, form of behavior) rather than a person in real life. What he needs in the world as it is are complementary factors, such as managerial skill, technical knowledge, and capital. Whether entrepreneurs can acquire enough capital or whether capitalists hire entrepreneurial managers is not important as a matter of principle, but given the abundant supply of entrepreneurial talent and the probability that it is easier for a person to acquire managerial skills than to accumulate capital, it appears evident that capitalists will normally hire entrepreneurs. In this case, capital becomes the limiting factor and a barrier to entry.

After all, what we have in this world as fields of operation for entrepreneurial talent are firms. They exist because subordination under organizational structures with strong hierarchical elements is often more efficient than a system of horizontal contracts in the market—with independent agents who cannot easily be induced to adjust their contracts as may be necessary from time to time (Coase 1937).

• One source of the firm's relative efficiency is flexibility: a change need not be renegotiated with all contracting parties but can be ordered since the cooperating persons are under service contracts (for a certain or indefinite period) which leave it up to the firm's discretion what is to be on their daily agenda. This advantage is being greatly reduced now by stiff work rules and regulations, by elements of workers' codetermination, and by legal and institutional difficulties in case the firm has to terminate the service contract.

• In these days we observe that hierarchical efficiency is, indeed, being lowered by government interference and workers' resistance (union resistance), whereas the relative costs of communication and hence of horizontal coordination over the market are on a decline.

This suggests that the balance is likely to tip more toward a higher degree of decentralization in large firms. This change may lead to the factual dissolution of bureaucratic systems into conglomerates of a large number of profit centers. Casual observation suggests that persons at the top of such profit centers feel and behave more like entrepreneurs and consider the firm as something like a separate capital market. There is a sharing of profit and (uninsurable) risk between the capitalist and the manager-entrepreneur which could be a model for similar arrangements with the lower strata of hitherto strictly hierarchical systems. Here, I suppose, is a vast field of opportunities for making better use of the abundant supply of entrepreneurial talent within existing firms. Even small steps in this direction can help in the important task of raising workers' motivation. They can help to reduce the great danger that bureaucratic management methods, like bureaucratic government with high taxation, force more and more entrepreneurial talent to emigrate into the underground economy.

In such a complex institutionalized society, as we have it now, few potential entrepreneurs can become effective without acquiring sufficient knowledge about legal and political constraints and without developing a feeling for the mentality of organized labor. But what about immigrant entrepreneurs who are quick to penetrate the restaurant business in advanced countries? They just prove the point since they mainly employ family members and are quick to withdraw once they get into conflict with existing laws and regulations. By the way, these immigrant entrepreneurs and their success in many countries, including LDCs, support the hypothesis that pure entrepreneurship is abundant everywhere, not only in advanced countries, and that one of the most important inhibitions for its becoming virulent at the source must be the deterrent effect of rules and regulations which tend to criminalize the pathbreaker and his transitory reward for changing the existing state of affairs. While the domestic entrepreneur is handicapped by his grasp of the deterrent, the immigrant is ignorant and feels courageous and innocent. But one has also to consider that the immigrant entrepreneur has (almost) no option of rising in the social hierarchy by joining those who want to conserve it. Thus he has to do things differently in order to succeed, and to succeed as an entrepreneur is perhaps the only avenue open to him in an otherwise closed arteriosclerotic society. This was the fate and the entrepreneurial role of the Jews in Central Europe, and anti-Semitism developed in response to their success. Now it is the Chinese in South Asia and the Indians in East Africa who perform the role of the immigrant entrepreneur. And much of the emotional resistance against the subsidiaries of foreign multinational companies in America outside the United States must have something to do with the fact that they are foreign, that they behave differently, and that they prove to be successful and hence profitable.

If an individual is too one-sided to be successful as an entrepreneur in a complex institutional environment he or she can decide to cooperate with complementary persons in what—for brevity's sake—I should like to call a team. This is a group formally or informally coordinated by leadership. What leadership is supposed to produce is—in my opinion—a plan for concerted action that turns potential conflict into hopeful harmony by making every participant believe that he or she will be better off (in both absolute and relative terms) in comparison to any option open to him or her as an individual. Self-confidence and charisma—to produce hope among the partners—may be sufficient at the beginning, but after some time it is only success that can succeed in keeping the team together in a mutually stimulating cooperation. Failure, disappointment, and skepticism produce internal conflict and—eventually—disintegration. As so much emotion is involved, the team may produce very good results but also disastrous mistakes. From time to time, either the leader or the membership will have to change if the team is to survive critical situations as a coherent group. Although the team is superior to an individual decision maker when the latter cannot acquire all the skills needed for successful action in complex situations (or if he cannot hire the skills on a permanent basis or from case to case), the team's ability to take wise decisions must not be overestimated. A serious drawback stems from the difficulty of synthesizing (more or less analytical) knowledge relating to different fields. If a common denominator has to be found—as in committee decisions for which unanimity may be standard practice—it will be on a low level and will—as a rule—imply much neglect of relevant special knowledge. This is at least my experience in committee work. A better solution may emerge when the chairman listens—and tries to extract as much knowledge from the participants as he can—and then makes up his mind in full individual responsibility (or tries to write the committee report by himself). What matters in dealing with a complicated subject is the feeling of an indivisible responsibility for the outcome. Teams may do excellent work in the performing arts, but the performance has to be orchestrated by someone. If the task is to acquire and integrate new information, the team leader will also act as a filter, using his own experience and the knowledge stored in his long-term memory. Here we have an optimization problem. Too much experience and knowledge of past cases may reduce the capacity to listen and to learn. This raises the serious question of the optimum age of retirement from a decision-making job. To this I have no impartial answer. But to remain curious and to maintain the capacity to learn is certainly also a worthwhile subject for systematic self-training.

**A Socioeconomic Environment for Productive Entrepreneurship**

As the supply of entrepreneurial talent seems to be practically unlimited, the number of actual entrepreneurs will be determined by conditions (limitations) on the demand side, i.e., by the demand permitted, induced, or actively provoked by the socioeconomic structure and the political and cultural environment. To make it short, I should like to submit the following hypotheses for consideration, discussion, and possible refutation:

1. Almost no demand for economic entrepreneurs is permitted in centralized systems without private property (centralized socialism). Here the economic entrepreneur is crowded out by the socioeconomic imperialism of a powerful centralized political elite.

2. A similar situation exists in a centralized theocracy based on religious beliefs that the future is not open (after the last of the prophets disclosed what life and society are to be about). Entrepreneurship in this case—as in

the previous one—can flourish only in the underground economy or in tolerated enclaves.

3. Market socialism, defined as a system of decentralized decision making without private property in firms, permits a given number of entrepreneurs to operate established firms but does not encourage entrepreneurship in the creation of new firms. However, there may be, as in Yugoslavia, private property in firms below a certain size and thus a field of operation for petty entrepreneurs. In any such case where entrepreneurship finds only a limited field of action in the economy, entrepreneurial talent will be attracted by politics or will tend to emigrate.

4. The mixed capitalist economy offers attraction to entrepreneurial talent not only in the private sector but also in government, including state-owned enterprises, regulatory agencies, the social security system, bureaucracies for policy making, and the system of competing political parties. Due to the satisfaction obtainable in the political power structure, the public sector must be considered to absorb much entrepreneurial talent which then adds to the driving force behind the expansion of the state. Nineteenth-century imperialism (which was expansive beyond the geographical frontiers) has turned into the imperialism of the social state and the welfare state in the twentieth century. However positively this may be judged in many respects, there is one grave disadvantage: entrepreneurs in the system of state bureaucracy tend to be counterproductive by reducing the scope for entrepreneurial action in the private economy. Now we observe the tendency for public sector bureaucracy to expand in the field of international economic cooperation. Proposals for a New International Economic Order (NIEO) and for a worldwide welfare system would lead, if adopted, to a similar bureaucracy as has developed in Brussels to serve and to complicate European economic integration (European Community). Business has certainly contributed to this development by asking government institutions to bring about equal (or fair) competitive conditions by all kinds of rules and subsidies. But now the time seems to have come for genuine entrepreneurs in business to join forces with those observers of the scene who emphasize the counterproductive activity of entrepreneurs in public bureaucracy and the political system. A counterrevolution is not likely to be successful unless strong beneficial effects can be demonstrated to flow at a rather early stage from the one or two experiments underway at the present time.

5. Paul A. Samuelson (1980) made the gloomy prediction that market capitalism may survive only under fascist regimes. What he means are not

corporativist societies (as Mussolini's Italy), but military dictatorships as they exist in some Latin American countries or in parts of the Far East. His language is confusing and alarming, but as a German I must emphasize that tremendous entrepreneurship was set free when the military governments of the Allied Forces enforced a currency reform in 1948 and allowed Ludwig Erhard, who was then merely an economic expert educated in a libertarian tradition, to remove most of the controls that had their historic roots in National Socialism. Having lived through that period I must admit that it would have been extremely difficult for any democratic party in power —with a strong opposition at work and elections on the horizon—to perform that type of surgery. And the idea of a domestic (rather than foreign) military dictatorship performing such a tremendous task would be unthinkable in retrospect and horrible in present circumstances. All this is much food for thought and detached discussion; but to make a long story short, I will state two propositions:

a. For rejuvenating an economy there is perhaps no substitute for unconditional surrender after defeat in war (Kindleberger 1978).

b. The issues of political democracy versus authoritarian government cannot be usefully discussed without reference to the relative size of government and its functions in social and economic life.

6. The optimum size of government in this respect is a minimum government which concentrates on the protection of life and property, on external defense, on the enforcement of private contracts, and on the supply of socially valuable goods that neither the market nor free associations of individuals (clubs) can be expected to provide (public goods). The dividing line between what the government will do and what it will not do must be clearly drawn and must remain fixed so that entrepreneurial activity can fill the area left for the market without fear of nationalization, interference, or predatory competition by public authorities. If such fears exist, the market will neglect the areas close to the dividing line, so that government, or the public at large, sees a vacuum which could be taken to be a market failure calling for government action. (This is comparable to a national frontier which also tends to push away economic activity into geographical areas closer to the center.)

7. The idea that government must feel responsible for the supply of entrepreneurs (and for the growth of potential output) has no analytical basis, except under second-best conditions when government has done serious damage to economic life. But even in this second-best case the solution lies in the removal of uncertainty, barriers to entry, or excessive taxes on

income from entrepreneurial activity and in the restoration of confidence between government and the public. Positive action would probably do more harm than good and would create—among the more successful entrepreneurs—an unnecessary feeling of gratitude toward government, and perhaps corruption. Instead, economic entrepreneurs should be and remain proud of their personal achievement and should not think that even part of their skill—and their human capital at large—were due to the benevolence of political entrepreneurs who have always been ingenious in redistributing other people's money.

8. To complete the picture, a word should be said about organizational entrepreneurs who find a living between the government and the market by forming pressure groups. Their personal satisfaction and their social product lies first of all in the defense of the market against government intervention. But political power vested in government is also being used to offer subsidies. If organizational entrepreneurs are tempted to extract subsidies or to lobby for any kind of protection against domestic or foreign competition, they become more and more part of the government machinery. Genuine economic entrepreneurs should be alert against this danger.

9. Every group wants protection, at least in the form of barriers to entry. And every potential entrepreneur, who is eager to see such barriers removed, will feel strong internal pressure to change his mind once he has succeeded in entering. If this is a general tendency, freedom of entry becomes a public good and should be protected by a general law of constitutional dignity. Such a law should include free imports of goods and services, free inflow of capital and—on the basis of reciprocity—free immigration. In the long run, reciprocity with regard to free immigration might be irrelevant, because free immigration into really open societies will mainly attract entrepreneurial talent and will thus cause a drain on the supply of entrepreneurs in less open societies. If the latter behave rationally —but this is a matter of time—they will compete by becoming more open themselves. Short-term experience may contradict this optimism, but there is a chance for the trend to change.

10. As a political economist I am all in favor of experiments. The experiments relevant here might be "zones of free economic activity." There is much entrepreneurial talent even in declining regions and cities. Instead of subsidizing these problem areas under the heading of regional policy, it would be much better to invigorate them by removing all controls and barriers to entry for a trial period of time—say ten years—sufficiently long to bring about positive results. The major difficulty is perhaps that

interest groups will mobilize public opinion against such experiments. But as the underground economy seems to expand everywhere, more and more people may wish to see it come to surface. In any case, wherever the underground economy is the training camp for entrepreneurs (as the black market was in West Germany after 1945), there is growing need for creating outlets which enable these entrepreneurs, young or old, to operate in the open market so that even the fiscal entrepreneurs (running the tax system) and the political entrepreneurs (who must think about balancing the budget despite their expenditure promises) can discover that they depend upon entrepreneurial activities in the economy.

To conclude and summarize, let me make some general observations:

1. All Western industrialized countries find themselves in a phase of slow growth and slow productivity advance. Average rates of progress are lower than they used to be in the late sixties. Wage pressures, based on past performance and not yet fully reduced to the poor conditions of the eighties, have proved to be excessive and have led to very high rates of unemployment all over Europe, Profit rates are depressed.

2. There are no immediate prospects for a quick return to the good old days of the golden sixties. We should not even try to go back to the policies of demand pressure and monetary-fiscal expansion which gave us the inflationary growth of the sixties. This is because we still have to pay the bill for what went wrong:

– accelerated growth produced the counterrevolution of the environment;

– the march into an oil-intensive civilization, fostered by fast growth and relatively low energy prices, produced the counterrevolution of mankind's exhaustible resources in the form of an oil shock; and

– cheap money was only for a while cheap money in real terms, when inflation had not yet reached its tolerance level. During this period of depressed real rates of interest:

  • governments ran into high debt and wasted money in unproductive expenditures;

  • households ran into debt and invested in owner-occupied houses as the best hedge against inflation, thus making an investment which does not raise the capacity to produce and the number of productive jobs;

  • firms were misled to run into debt as interest rates were so low, and as the wage push was so strong—reducing profits to very low levels —firms failed to raise enough equity capital;

- the productive investment that firms actually undertook in the seventies was artificially capital intensive, as one must expect it to be when the interest rate is too low and the wage level too high;

Now, after inflation has reached tolerance levels and is being fought everywhere, we observe the counterrevolution of savers and lenders: interest rates corrected for inflation are excessively high, and they will remain higher than in the seventies and higher than normal until we have corrected the distortions produced by cheap money and inflation in the seventies; i.e.,

- the shortage of productive capital in the business sector,

- the public deficits,

- the low propensity to save and to lend for productive investment, and

- the labor-saving bias in technical progress, induced by excessive wages and excessively low real interest rates.

3. In contrast to the golden sixties when governments could produce growth by exploiting

− the money illusion among savers and

− the tax illusion among citizens,

we now have not positive but negative money illusion, not positive but negative tax illusion.

Governments therefore cannot lead us into a phase of new economic growth. This task has become again the challenge for business and for the entrepreneurial potential in our societies.

4. My position with regard to the entrepreneurial potential is twofold. First, the potential supply of entrepreneurship is unlimited. Second, we can make use of this supply by raising the demand for it. This demand has been suppressed by

− the growth of bureaucratic rules and regulations,

− the domestic imperialism of the welfare state,

− the growth of bureaucracy within industry, greatly but only partly induced by government bureaucracy, and

− excessive wage pressures from organized labor.

The general conclusion then is: If we want more growth and productivity advance for the benefit of our populations we will have to exploit the huge potential supply of entrepreneurship, and the only way of doing it in this phase of correcting distortions is to enlarge the scope for free action, self-reliance, and individual responsibility.

## References

Coase, Ronald H. 1937. "The Nature of the Firm." *Economica* 4:386–405.

Kindleberger, Charles P. 1978. *The Aging Economy*. Bernhard-Harms-Vorlesungen, no. 8. Kiel: Institut für Weltwirtschaft.

McClelland, David C. 1961. *The Achieving Society*. Princeton: Van Nostrand.

Samuelson, Paul A. 1980. "The World Economy at Century's End." Lecture delivered at the Sixth World Congress of Economists, Mexico.

Schumpeter, Josef A. 1912. *Theorie der wirtschaftlichen Entwicklung*. Leipzig: Duncker & Humblot.

Schumpeter, Josef A. 1942. *Capitalism, Socialism, and Democracy*. New York: Harper & Brothers.

# 5 Comment on Professor Samuelson's Paper: "The World Economy at Century's End"

Professor Samuelson deserves the applause he has received for his address about Keynes, Schumpeter, and "The World Economy at Century's End." However, my role is not to praise him, but to criticize. Let me try to discharge my duty:

1. by searching for a bias and for faults in Samuelson's picture; and

2. by indicating where the picture does not fill the frame given by its title and the more general context of this congress's theme, "Human Resources, Employment and Development."

There are two main characters in the picture—Keynes and Schumpeter —and one favorite subject matter—the mixed economy. Samuelson is in sympathy with Keynes who, half a century ago, predicted the high standard of living—and the boredom—people would enjoy at the century's end in a Swedish-type society. The material foundation of this society is the mixed economy. Keynes himself seems to have given birth to it; at least he nursed it. For without the Keynesian Revolution there would not have been protection against deflation and persisting slump (p. 66), and the world would not have experienced the miracle decades of the 1950s and the 1960s (p. 66). As the mixed economy has humane qualities (p. 66) we are left with the impression that Keynes's real historical role was to be something like the alma mater (in its original sense) of the good society.

The second main character is Schumpeter, who happened to be Samuelson's teacher. He does not look like a good mother, but like an unsympathetic dominating father. Samuelson calls him cynical (p. 58, p. 66),

Reprinted with permission from *Human Resources, Employment and Development, Vol. 1: The Issues*, edited by Shigeto Tsuru. London: The Macmillan Press, 1983, 78–87. Copyright 1983 by the International Economic Association. The page numbers in parentheses refer to the article by Paul Samuelson in the same volume.

schizophrenic (p. 60), and half a mountebank (p. 63). Methodologically, he must have been fairly authoritarian: with a wave of his hand he airily dismissed post-Keynesian apprehensions instead of invoking theoretical arguments (p. 62); his thought was confused (p. 68); and he broadened definitions when it suited him, for example, the definition of a socialist to include Samuelson and others who are objective about capitalism (p. 68).

As a forecaster Schumpeter earns a C in Samuelson's eyes (p. 65) because he substantially underestimated the postwar performance of Germany and Japan, Sweden and Switzerland, and of the whole world economy (p. 66). He even believed in Hitler's victory (p. 61). Politically, he was a conservative (p. 70) and—if you read between Samuelson's lines—an advocate of the fascist solution (p. 75). Taken together this comes close to an overkill, cunningly hidden in a marvelous exposition devoted to the future of the world economy. Final judgment must be left to future historians, if not psychologists, of economic thought who have lower opportunity costs than we at this congress.

To turn to the subject matter, we note that Samuelson's main concern is the mixed economy, set in sharp contrast to Schumpeter's unfettered capitalism. For lack of definition, we have to gather that this type excludes both classical socialism and all countries where the market operates under the umbrella of a one-party dictatorship. It is unclear where he puts Mexico, but as to the Organization of Economic Cooperation and Development (OECD) countries, they all seem to be included, with the possible exception of Yugoslavia. Samuelson's favorite example of a successful mixed economy is Sweden, which is mentioned far more often than Keynes's own country. What is so exciting about the mixed economy, apart from its vitality which seems to contradict Schumpeter's horoscope or Hayek's horrorscope of an inevitable march into socialism? Is it an ongoing election campaign in the United States or a hazardous Thatcher experiment in Britain? In my opinion the real issue of the mixed economy is—apart from stagflation—the unhappy choice between equity and efficiency, so aptly described by the late Arthur Okun.

If the characteristic feature of the mixed economy is the mix between market efficiency and a determined government policy in pursuit of equity and social security, I fail to see its relation to Keynes. Its roots can be traced further back to Bismarck's social security legislation of almost a hundred years ago and to those German economists who called their professional society founded in 1872 Verein für Socialpolitik or "association for social policy." I also see a close link to the West German postwar concept of a "social market economy."

However, Samuelson is preoccupied with effective demand and with fiscal policy propelling the multiplier-accelerator mechanism. Thus private autonomous investment is left out of the picture, and the Schumpeterian entrepreneur, hardly alluded to by Samuelson, has no role to play as a driving force of economic development. I admit that the dynamic entrepreneur is now a rare animal, after more and more businessmen in mixed economies have become Keynesians waiting for the government to provide them with effective demand for induced investments; but the postwar economic miracle, at least of West Germany, mentioned by Samuelson, had a different engine. This development is not at all miraculous when seen through Schumpeterian rather than Keynesian glasses. If you want an explanation even more closely related to human resources than Schumpeter's you had better try to extract it from David MacClelland's pioneering book, *Achieving Society*.

As regards West Germany in the 1970s Samuelson maintains that her performance was worse than that of the United States. When on an earlier occasion he supported the point with statistics of industrial production I explained why this was not admissible in a period of accelerated decline in the share of the industrial sector. Now the reference is to GDP. Here the growth rate in the 1970s is indeed higher for the United States (3.2 percent) than for West Germany (2.8 percent). However, West Germany clearly outperformed the United States in terms of the growth rates of GDP per capita, GDP per employee, and GDP per hour worked, not to mention the fantastic productivity growth in West Germany's relatively shrinking industrial sector. Sweden, which receives so much praise for not slowing down the rate of growth of its social pie (p. 66), exceeded West Germany's postwar performance (p. 66) in no decade in terms of GDP, or GDP per capita, or GDP per person employed.

Sweden, which Samuelson believes to have shown annual productivity improvement of 8 percent, is in actual fact not advancing at a record pace. Trusting Denison's figures, we see Swedish productivity growth from 1950 to 1973 below that of many other countries, though above that of North America and the United Kingdom. From 1973 to 1978 productivity growth in manufacturing was lower than before, but particularly in Sweden; Sweden even fell behind Canada and the United States. Only Britain was a worse performer than Sweden among the countries selected by Denison (Denison 1979, 146).

One of the central points in the present mixed economy debate is the question whether government expenditure as a percentage of trend GDP will continue to rise, as it did until recently in all major OECD countries, led by the Netherlands, the Scandinavian countries, and the United Kingdom (OECD 1977, 211). The answer may well be yes, in accordance with Adolph Wagner's law formulated in 1861. This law is plausible to those who see Parkinson's law operating in "bureaucracies without bankruptcy" and who observe how politicians compete for special groups of voters by making promises at taxpayers' expense.

But history has seen reverse swings, like the "retreat from mercantilism into laissez-faire in the nineteenth century" (Cairncross 1976, 113), heralded by philosopher-economists of Scottish and English origin. These intellectuals in Schumpeter's sense had a workable alternative to government regulation—the market. This is why they were more successful in their drive toward a withering away of the state than Karl Marx and those who followed him in this respect. Intellectuals of the same spirit were at work in Prague in 1968. Economists seem to contribute to such swings with the fashions of the profession. When the market has a wide scope to operate we concentrate our efforts on supposed market failures, assuming a perfect government which ideally could do better. And when we accumulate experience under real world governments—mercantilist, fascist, and socialist—we rediscover and preach the virtues of the market like those German economists around Walter Eucken who had opposed and yet survived Hitler. What Schumpeter possibly failed to see is that intellectuals tend to be dissidents in either polar system. Economists are intellectuals in the "state versus market" controversy and are bound to overshoot as long as the profession is incapable of defining rules for the optimum division of labor between governments and markets which are sufficiently operational and can be applied in different sociopolitical circumstances.

As long as we have not done serious work in this field we have to rely on personal impressions. For the sake of further discussion let me draw on forty years of experience in the German civil service and state the following presumptions:

1. Civil servants are relatively efficient and usually do their best. Yet serious coordination inefficiencies do arise from overcentralization, lack of relevant information in the bureaucratic communication system, institutional rigidity, and a systematic incapability of using and expanding the learning potential of the human resources employed.

2. Most serious is the lack of rewards for economizing, risk taking, and innovating. As a director of a government-financed and bureaucratically controlled research institute, I have to spend most of my effort on main-

taining and defending natural human motivations against external pressures to substitute control for confidence and regulation for incentives.

3. Decentralization of responsibility helps in many respects, but it cannot be tolerated in wide limits if the output is not subject to external evaluation and competition. Internal competition is merely a substitute; and it can mislead people who receive freedom for decision-making into becoming mere budget maximizers.

Fortunately for GNP growth, the government sector can rely upon the Central Statistical Office to estimate its output as equal to its input and to impute to its servants an annual productivity increase of 2 percent or whatever the top secret guesstimate just may be. So much about X-efficiency in the public sector in countries like West Germany.

Outside the public sector, detailed regulations and controls have similar depressing effects on motivations and productivity improvements in the market. However, we in Germany observe many foreigners becoming petty entrepreneurs. The question of how they can cope with all the regulations formulated in an involved German that they can hardly read, let alone understand, has a plausible answer: they have the privilege of ignoring these regulations and of returning to southern Europe once they get into difficulties due to this ever-growing literature. Another striking observation is that the international sector of the West German economy which is exposed to the storms of Schumpeterian competition shows a much higher productivity growth than the overregulated and cartel-ridden domestic sector. Thus the open economy comes to the rescue of the mixed economy.

An alternative way of getting around the high state content of the mixed economy is disloyalty: tax avoidance through shortening of the working week and retreat into tax-free activities during leisure time. Together with a subsidization of search for employment by relatively high unemployment benefits and the pensioning off of the unemployed close to retirement age, this gives plausibility to presumptions that the modern mixed economy suffers from the emergence of a substantial underground economy. Those who want to learn more about this phenomenon are advised to study what is becoming known as Italy's "new economic miracle."

For Samuelson the real problem of the mixed economy is stagflation. My explanation for this disease is that politicians have been made to believe in the existence of a stable nonvertical Phillips curve. When unemployment is low, they discover inflation, and when inflation is low, they consider unemployment as public enemy number one. The outcome is a politically determined go-and-stop business cycle. Its go part (in terms of output) requires the existence of money illusion (supported if possible by exchange rate illusion) or adaptive expectations which bring about a time lag in the upward adjustment of wages and prices. An illusion which is thus exploited disappears. It then needs to be restored. This happens in recessions. The less effective this restoration, the greater must be the subsequent inflation if it is to produce the expected output effect. Thus, by walking up and down the Phillips curve politicians shift it—and worsen the trade-off. The problem in my view requires extensive reform. The two conflicting targets of low unemployment and price level stability need a separate institution or instrument for each and a division of labor between them that matches the norms of comparative advantage. This is not the place to describe the ideal solution; but some consensus societies (in the context of an open economy) seem to be on the right track when they gradually learn that there is more classical unemployment in this world than Keynesians believe and that such unemployment must be tackled on the wage front rather than by monetary acceleration.

Let me now talk about the world economy rather than Samuelson's paper. The main topic left out of his picture for the road to 1999 is the lack of productive jobs compared with the hundreds of millions of people in less developed countries (LDCs) who need and deserve them. How can the advanced economies in the First World most effectively contribute to a mutually advantageous solution of this serious problem?

My answer, apart from development aid, is: make the mixed, advanced economy as open as possible for those LDCs that wish to take advantage of export-led growth and an international transfer of capital and knowledge. Resistance against liberal imports from countries with an abundant supply of labor is likely to be strong in countries where labor is well organized and politically influential. This proposition is based on the Stolper-Samuelson theorem, on the existence of adjustment costs, and on the fact that governments usually have little maneuvering room for paying adjustment assistance as a temporary device. The proposition is borne out by abundant experience. This seems to indicate that the real class conflict of our age is between labor in less developed countries and labor in advanced countries. The mixed economy may have humane qualities, as Samuelson emphasizes, but its organization in a nation-state limits humanitarian activities essentially to compatriots, and perhaps even only to those who belong to pressure groups.

Unfortunately, the rich mixed economy solves some of its domestic problems at the expense of poorer countries in the Third World. Here is a short list of examples:

1. A premature reduction of wage differentials—interindustrial, interregional and between unskilled and skilled workers—attempted in the name of equity, aggravates adjustment problems in structurally weak industries and regions, and contributes to heavy unemployment among youths, females, and elderly persons. To mitigate this effect on the poor at home, a system of import protection and subsidies is built up which largely discriminates against the poor abroad.

2. Domestic labor unions, notably under codetermination, protest against direct investment in LDCs unless the investment is complementary to domestic labor and can be justified as securing domestic employment at higher real wages. This limits direct investment in LDCs to projects which are either sales oriented or ensure cheap raw material supplies.

3. High real wages for unskilled workers are a strong inducement to labor-augmenting innovations which raise the capital intensity built into the capital stock, including the capital intensity built into investment goods which are delivered to LDCs under development assistance programs. The growing unemployment in the world economy has thus little to do with effective demand, but very much with technology and capital shortage.

4. Artificially low energy prices, notably in the United States, maintained under populist pressures, worsen the position of oil-importing LDCs.

5. Government deficits in advanced countries, often recommended for preventing domestic unemployment, have a crowding-out effect not only on domestic firms but also on foreign firms and governments, including governments of LDCs.

In search of a common cause for such malfunctions, I dare to submit a hypothesis that could help us to understand, if not predict or prevent, some likely developments in the world economy during the next two decades:

1. The tendency to overvalue present goods relative to future goods (observed by Böhm-Bawerk) leads to an increased shortage of capital unless the real rate of interest is allowed to be positive and high enough.

2. Under the impact of policies devised to fight classical unemployment by Keynesian methods, the mixed economy shows a tendency to depress the real rate of interest, sometimes below zero.

3. Mankind tends to overvalue human resources not only in relation to physical capital but also in relation to natural resources, including exhaustible raw material deposits and in relation to human capital.

4. Once the shortage of natural resources and of capital exceeds threshold levels, human resources will accept, although reluctantly, a devaluation. This will be felt as a crisis. It will probably last until mankind has adjusted to a sufficiently high real rate of interest on both capital and exhaustible resources.

5. The mixed economy in advanced countries is abused to prevent market forces from enforcing quick adjustments to changes in the world economy. The main reason is that the objective of social justice is vague and that, in the absence of generally accepted norms, traditional relative prices and traditional income differentials are often taken as the best possible approximation. This social conservatism is likely to lead to increasing protection against LDCs. The Stolper-Samuelson theorem demonstrates how the relative value of human resources can be maintained in advanced countries, albeit at the expense of LDCs and world welfare.

6. In advanced countries, such protectionism reduces economic growth by slowing down structural change; and in LDCs it strengthens political pressures in favor of delinking and import-substitution policies. Defensive investments in advanced countries defeat LDC attempts at earning the foreign exchange needed for job-creating investments. Taken together this is likely to exacerbate the capital shortage and unemployment in the world economy in this century.

Let me conclude on an optimistic note. Like Samuelson, I have a dream. It is about the open rather than the mixed economy. To be specific, I shall formulate several wishes addressed to the European Community, of which my country of citizenship is a member.

First: replace the Common Agricultural Policy by a system of income subsidies so as to end the vicious circle of producing, protecting, storing, or dumping that arises from excessive "target prices," "intervention prices," and "threshold prices" (Cairncross, Giersch, Lamfalussy, Petrilli, and Uri 1974, 91–115). The waste that the mixed economy produces in this area, while large parts of the world suffer from starvation, is a bad precedent and a human tragedy.

Second: enlarge the European Community (EC), but make sure that the new entrants will support commercial openness as if they were still excluded.

Third: make a unilateral and irreversible pledge that all imports will be fully liberalized from duties and controls in a series of steps before the end of this century.

Fourth: member countries should be induced to cut all permanent subsidies in a parallel series of steps in order to obtain financial means for granting adjustment assistance on a temporary basis; capital losses, however, need to be compensated for only if and to the extent that windfall profits have been subject to taxes and provide the financial means.

Fifth: capital outflows will follow free commodity imports once domestic entrepreneurs have learned that it is both possible and cheaper to serve the domestic market for standardized products by producing in countries where labor is abundant. LDCs wishing to participate in this resource transfer should be invited to form investment agreements which clearly define the frontiers between government and enterprises and which give assurances against whatever political risks are seen as an impediment.

Sixth: technology follows investment and trade, but rich EC countries can do much to encourage the export of investment goods that incorporate technologies appropriate for LDCs. Fears about unemployment in rich countries can easily be dispelled by demonstrating the vast demand for investment goods that is bound to develop once LDCs can earn more foreign exchange and become viable capital importers. There is no Keynesian liquidity trap in the Third World.

Seventh: rich EC countries, which import more and more standardized Heckscher-Ohlin goods and will also have to pay relatively more for resource-based Ricardo goods, can maintain their position on the world income scale by concentrating resources on the research and the development of new and better products which, in honor of Samuelson's teacher, I like to call Schumpeter goods.

Eighth: the developing advanced rich economy must be open vis-à-vis the future as well as vis-à-vis less advanced countries. Openness vis-à-vis the future requires a free market in ideas as well as in goods. This practically excludes fascism and other forms of dictatorship. Hence there is no fascist solution that could be imagined for a Schumpeterian economy, whatever Schumpeter may have thought a couple of decades ago.

Ninth: perhaps the most important good for the world economy is good money, money with a fairly stable value in terms of goods and services. The dollar, after having been used to produce the environment for the miracle decade of the 1960s, no longer qualifies for that role. Those central banks in Europe which produce close competitors to the dollar should quickly learn how to become the supplier of the $n^{th}$ currency and how to earn the compensating seignorage gain.

Tenth: Europe will remain one of the three centers of the world economy outside Comecon. Having largely caught up with the United States in the last three decades, the strong countries in the European Community should feel responsible for a Community policy that would help other countries to catch up with them. It is in this way that international income differentials can be reduced in a worldwide positive-sum game.

Although these wishes are addressed to policy-makers I am not without hope. This hope is based on the belief that people in a society which is open vis-à-vis the rest of the world and open vis-à-vis the future cannot but learn from failures and success.

## References

Cairncross, A. 1976. "The Market and the State." In T. Wilson and A. S. Skinner, eds. *The Market and the State: Essays in Honour of Adam Smith*. Oxford: Clarendon Press, 113−134.

Cairncross, A., H. Giersch, A. Lamfalussy, G. Petrilli, and P. Uri. 1974. *Economic Policy for the European Community: The Way Forward*. London and Basingstoke: Macmillan.

Denison, E. F. 1979. *Accounting for Slower Economic Growth—The United States in the 1970s*. Washington, D.C.: The Bookings Institution.

MacClelland, D. 1961. *The Achieving Society*. Princeton, N.J.: Van Nostrand.

McCracken, P. et al. 1977. "Towards Full Employment and Price Stability." A Report to the OECD by a Group of Independent Experts. Paris: OECD Publications.

# 6

# Towards an Explanation of the Productivity Slowdown: An Acceleration-Deceleration Hypothesis

## with Frank Wolter

### Facts and Hypotheses

After two and a half decades of prosperous postwar development, Western industrialized countries recently experienced a slowdown of economic growth and productivity advance together with an increase in the rates of inflation and unemployment. In trying to explain this malaise we are looking at a diagnosis that could help us to identify early indicators of a future turnaround or some policy variables which deserve to be included in a therapeutic program. Although we shall focus on what can be measured, complying with the standards of the guild,[1] we shall not refrain from considering complex relationships which can be grasped only intuitively, even if they include phenomena which lie beyond the limits of official statistics.[2] The outcome may be "soft economics," but we find some consolation in the dictum that it is better to be vaguely right than to be precisely wrong.

We start with statistics on the advance of labor productivity[3] in fourteen Organization of Economic Cooperation and Development (OECD) countries between the late 1950s and the late 1970s, subdivided into five periods to average out cyclical effects (Table 6.1).[4] This is sufficient to show that the productivity slowdown is a phenomenon common to all advanced countries.[5]

As the slowdown in productivity advance occurred after a long phase of rapid economic development it seems to reflect the erosion of many of the favorable conditions which contributed to the long spurt of economic development in the West after World War II. This general presumption raises

**Table 6.1**
The growth of labor productivity in selected OECD countries, 1955–1980 (peak to peak, %)

| Country | Total Economy | | | | |
| | Late '50s | Early '60s | Late '60s | Early '70s | Late '70s |
|---|---|---|---|---|---|
| United States | 1.8 | 3.0 | 1.0 | 1.4 | 0.3 |
| Canada | 1.7 | 2.5 | 2.0 | 2.8 | 0.2 |
| United Kingdom | 2.2 | 3.1 | 2.8 | 3.1 | 1.1 |
| Sweden | n.a. | 4.5 | 3.1 | 2.0 | 0.4 |
| Denmark | 5.2 | 3.7 | 3.3 | 2.8 | 1.3 |
| Norway | 3.8 | 4.5 | 3.5 | 1.5 | 2.5 |
| Finland | 3.6 | 4.7 | 5.1 | 4.7 | 2.5 |
| Netherlands | 4.0 | 3.1 | 4.4 | 4.4 | 1.9 |
| Belgium | 2.5 | 5.2 | 3.9 | 4.4 | 2.4 |
| Germany | 4.6 | 4.9 | 4.6 | 4.1 | 3.2 |
| Austria | 5.0 | 4.6 | 6.4 | 5.2 | 2.8 |
| France | 4.3 | 5.0 | 4.5 | 4.7 | 2.9 |
| Italy | 4.6 | 5.0 | 6.2 | 4.2 | 1.7 |
| Japan | 8.4 | 12.5 | 8.6 | 6.3 | 3.0 |

Sources: Calculated from OECD, *National Accounts Statistics*, Paris, various issues. OECD, *Labour Force Statistics*, Paris, various issues. IMF, *International Financial Statistics, Yearbook 1981* (Washington, 1981). *Sachverständigenrat zur Begutachtung der gesamtwirtschaftlichen Entwicklung, Mut zur Stabilisierung, Jahresgutachten 1973/4* (Stuttgart und Mainz: Kohlhammer, 1973). *Economic Report of the President: Transmitted to the Congress February 1982* (Washington, 1982). ILO, *Yearbook of Labour Statistics, 1965*.
Notes: Gross domestic product in constant prices per employee.
For country-specific benchmark years, see the Annex at the end of the chapter.

numerous questions. Here is a tentative list of hypotheses, based on theoretical consideration and casual empiricism:

I. From the increasing concern about the underground economy we suspect that output statistics for recent years may underestimate the real performance of advanced economies.

II. The productivity slowdown as we measure it may be due to the development toward a postindustrial society.

III. Or workers reduced their effort in order to increase it in leisure activities.

IV. Or what we observe is a slowdown in the demand for income in terms of effort,[6] perhaps supported by an increasing preference for job security.

V. And it may have been the acceleration of income growth that raised the income elasticity of demand for security.

VI. Or rapid growth was so much taken for granted, that societies developed an increasing demand for equity and equality,[7] perhaps without realizing how much it would cost in terms of growth performance later on.

VII. For Europe and Japan the productivity slowdown may have marked the end of a technological catching up process.

VIII. And firms in the United States have perhaps suffered so much from the loss of their technological monopoly positions that they felt no longer capable of taking innovative risks at the previous rate.

IX. Can the slower productivity advance merely be a return to normality after a phase of artificial acceleration, perhaps combined with some overshooting on the low side?

X. As the growth of labor productivity slowed down more than the growth of the capital/labor ratio,[8] it can well be that the gross additions to the capital stock have become less efficient, perhaps due to inflation and an inflation-induced decline in the real rate of interest.

XI. Or did capital efficiency suffer from the drastic changes in relative prices which occurred in the wake of rapid growth in the early 1970s—higher costs for the environment, exhaustible resources, and energy, including oil?

XII. Another presumption could be a misallocation of investment due to new government interventions.

XIII. As to the efficiency of labor, it may have deteriorated with declining educational standards or with a massive increase of the share of inexperienced labor in total employment.

XIV. Finally, there are marked international differences in the slowdown of productivity advance. Could this be related to differences in wage behavior and concomitant changes in the level and structure of employment?

These hypotheses are not mutually exclusive. In fact, we submit them with a view to considering them as elements in a process of mutual causation.

**Evidence and Evaluation**

Evidence presented in table 6.2 makes it quite clear that the conditions governing the growth of labor productivity have drastically deteriorated since the early 1970s.[9] Whether we relate the growth of labor productivity per employed person—on Cobb-Douglas account—to the growth of the capital-labor ratio or—on Verdoorn account—to the growth of real out-

**Table 6.2**
The growth of labor productivity related to the growth of the capital labor ratio and real
output in industry, international corss-section, 1960–1979

| Period | Industry[a] | $n$ | $\bar{R}^2$ | $F$ |
|---|---|---|---|---|
| 1960–73 | $\pi E = 1.520 + 0.810\ CL$<br>$(0.150)^a$ | $10^b$ | 0.76 | 29.30 |
| 1973–78 | $\pi E = 0.675 + 0.435\ CL$<br>$(0.255)$ | $10^b$ | 0.17 | 2.91 |
| 1960–73 | $\pi E = 1.338 + 0.649\ OUT$<br>$(0.140)^a$ | 14 | 0.61 | 21.33 |
| 1973–79 | $\pi E = 1.638 + 0.548\ OUT$<br>$(0.253)^a$ | 14 | 0.22 | 4.70 |

Sources: Calculated from OECD, *National Accounts Statistics*, Paris, various issues; OECD,
*Labour Force Statistics*, Paris, various issues; OECD, 1980.
Notes: Mining and quarrying; manufacturing; electricity, gas and water; construction.
  Symbols: $\pi E$ = real output per employee; $CL$ = capital labor ratio (nonfarm business
sector); $OUT$ = real output. All variables are expressed as average rates of growth over
the period under inspection.
  Austria, Belgium, Canada, Denmark, Finland, France, Germany, Italy, Japan, Netherlands,
Norway, Sweden, United Kingdom, United States.
a. Significant at 5 percent level; standard errors in parentheses.
b. Except Austria, Denmark, Netherlands, Norway.

put, a fit which is highly satisfactory for the period from 1960 to 1973,[10]
fails to be so since then. The correlation with the capital-labor ratio even
ceases to be statistically significant.

In explaining this phenomenon with reference to facts and figures we
have to put Hypothesis I aside because too little is known about how the
underground economy[11] affects recorded input on the one hand and recorded output on the other. To the extent that the factors behind the
underground economy contributed to the productivity slowdown they will
come up in connection with other hypotheses.

Shifts in the intersectoral composition of output and employment (Hypothesis II) are well measurable and turn out to be a significant factor here
for the following reasons:

1. In the 1950s and 1960s, in all countries under review the highly productive industrial sector had developed rapidly at the expense of less productive agriculture (GW 1982, Table 4). Apart from raising the average, this
shift had forced agriculture to speed up its own productivity advance. This
process slowed down in the 1970s.

2. At the same time, we observe an acceleration in the growth of employment in government services, a sector which exhibited a below-average

level of productivity already in the 1970s in all countries investigated except in Finland and Japan (GW, ibid.).

3. Private and public services which turned out to be the only sectors which expanded their share in employment in the 1970s exhibit a growth of measured productivity slower than that in industry or agriculture (GW 1982, Table 5).[12]

Although these structural shifts must indeed have contributed to the decline of measured productivity advance, they are far from being capable of explaining it entirely as we conclude from shift and share analyses (OECD 1980, 33–44; Fels and Schmidt 1981, 109–11; United Nations 1982, 46) and from the observation that the productivity slowdown is a phenomenon common to all sectors (GW 1982, Table 5). What we cannot uncover—for statistical reasons—as a phenomenon common to all countries are changes of a similar nature among firms and within firms: more services and slack (static and dynamic) everywhere because of less accountability or less competition where the service content is higher.

Hypotheses III to VI attribute the slowdown to shifts in preferences. To the extent that these shifts were the explanation and could at the same time be taken as an expression of the unconstrained will of people to substitute leisure or security for income or consumption, the productivity slowdown would be nothing to bother about. Against this we tend to hold that strong wage pressures, despite rising unemployment, indicate a high demand for income; that increasing underground activities reveal an elastic supply of effort in exchange for income net of taxes; that the notion of consumer saturation has always become fashionable in recessions (just as Keynes's "psychological law" became prominent in and after the Great Depression) only to be forgotten in subsequent recoveries; that the saturation concept has meaning only with regard to quantities at given qualities[13] and evaporates when it is extended to new goods and services or to wants like private health care and private security against insurable risk. Hence, although all countries under consideration expanded their transfer system relative to GNP (GW 1982, Table 6),[14] this was not the consequence of demand at prices reflecting social opportunity costs. Instead we conjecture that it was more due to strong competition among suppliers in the political arena, supported by a combination of facts and fictions, including fast growth that could be extrapolated under appropriate demand conditions, populist belief in underconsumption and oversaving, and confidence in the ability of government to always carry the burden of the debt.

If it had been a preference for more security and equality that produced the relative growth of the welfare state, the underlying implicit assumption must be taken to have been twofold: accelerated growth would not be checked by external constraints; nor would growth be impaired by an induced change in people's mentality. With the benefit of hindsight we consider both assumptions to be unwarranted in principle.[15] Once growth has started to slow down for any of these reasons, a negative effect on productivity advance is a strong possibility. Revenues automatically generated while growth was fast had to be raised by higher taxes and social security contributions. The wedge between gross and net incomes for both labor and business was bound to increase. This is likely to have impaired work incentives, the incentives to control costs in firms, and—with a lagged effect on productivity—investment performance. As to the latter we know that it worsened in the 1970s in all our countries, except in Canada, the United Kingdom and Norway, the "nouveaux riches de l'énergie" (GW 1982, Table 7). But we doubt that investment performance alone fully explains the productivity slowdown.

Yet a slowdown in the flow of product or process innovations (Hypotheses VII and VIII) may have impaired the quality of the additions to the capital stock.[16] In fact, there are indications to back the hypothesis of a technological stalemate:

1. As is evident from table 6.3, firms in Europe and Japan greatly benefited from the possibility to import and adapt best-practice technology developed in the United States until the early 1970s, but later on this source of economic growth and productivity advance had dried up.[17]

2. At the same time, the speed at which the technological frontier is shifting outward may have declined. For North America the fact that other countries had caught up must have implied a partial erosion of quasi rents derived from superior technology and organization, notably in the markets for capital intensive and skill-intensive manufactures. Indeed, United States R&D expenditures increased more slowly than gross domestic product in the period from 1964 to 1979; while some countries like Japan, Germany, and Sweden are in a process of catching up also with regard to R&D expenditures, this has not yet been sufficient to stem the decline for the West as a whole (table 6.4).

On the other hand, casual evidence suggests that we are not in the midst of a technological impasse. Microelectronics, biotechnology, new industrial materials, among others, have opened up new wide avenues for technolog-

**Table 6.3**
The technology gap hypothesis, international cross-section, 1964–73 and 1973–79

| Sector | Period | Equation[a] | $n$ | $\bar{R}^2$ |
|---|---|---|---|---|
| Total economy | 1964–73 | $\pi E = 31.122 - 6.564 \ln GAP\ 64$ <br> $(1.047)^a$ | 13 | 0.78 |
| Total economy | 1973–79 | $\pi E = 9.491 - 1.779 \ln GAP\ 73$ <br> $(1.714)$ | 13 | 0.09 |
| Industry[b] | 1964–73 | $\pi E = 25.330 - 4.868 \ln GAP\ 64$ <br> $(1.692)^a$ | 13 | 0.43 |
| Industry[b] | 1973–79 | $\pi E = 3.004 - 0.019 \ln GAP\ 73$ <br> $(2.244)$ | 13 | 0.00 |

Sources: Calculated from OECD, *National Accounts Statistics*, various issues; OECD, *Labour Force Statistics*, various issues; R. Summers, I. B. Kravis and A. Heston, "International comparison of real product and its composition: 1950–1977," *The Review of Income and Wealth*, series 26, no. 1, March 1980.
Notes: Symbols: $\pi E$ = average annual growth rate of real output per employee over the period under inspection; ln = natural logarithm; *GAP* 64 or 73 = per capita income of individual sample country in percentage of per capita income of the United States in 1964 or 1973 (country-specific peak year; see the Annex at the end of the chapter) valued at purchasing power parities.
 Austria, Belgium, Canada, Denmark, Finland, France, Germany, Italy, Japan, Netherlands, Norway, Sweden, United Kingdom.
 Country-specific peak years are 1973–79. See the Annex at the end of the chapter.
a. Significant at 5 percent level; standard errors in parentheses.
b. Mining and quarrying; manufacturing; electricity, gas and water; construction.

**Table 6.4**
R&D performance of selected industrial countries, 1964–79

| Country | Gross domestic expenditure on R&D as % of GDP | | |
|---|---|---|---|
| | 1964 | 1973 | 1979 |
| United States | 3.14 | 2.50 | 2.41 |
| Canada | 1.07 | 0.99 | 0.94 |
| United Kingdom | 2.32 | 2.13[a] | 2.20[b] |
| Sweden | 1.20 | 1.60 | 1.89 |
| Netherlands | 2.03 | 2.01 | 1.98 |
| Belgium | 1.05[c] | 1.43 | 1.40 |
| Germany | 1.41 | 2.09 | 2.27 |
| France | 1.84 | 1.78 | 1.82 |
| Italy | 0.67[c] | 0.88 | 0.84 |
| Japan | 1.47 | 1.87 | 2.04 |
| All ten countries | 2.40 | 2.12 | 2.08 |

Sources: OECD, *Science and Technology Indicators, Basic Statistical Series*, Volume B, *Gross National Expenditure on R&D (GERD) 1963–1979* (Paris, 1982).
a. 1972.
b. 1978.
c. 1965.

ical development and are continuing to do so. Empirically, Griliches (1980) could not detect a major impact of recent R&D performance on the productivity slowdown in the United States. His conclusion that R&D performance was a consequence rather than a cause of the worsening of the growth climate is quite plausible to us. It supports the notion of mutual causation in the framework of an acceleration-deceleration hypothesis.

This carries the discussion to the question whether the productivity slowdown cannot be best explained by the exhaustion of a policy potential (Hypothesis IX). In this respect, the poor performance of the 1970s has to be seen against the background of a policy-induced acceleration of economic growth and productivity advance in the 1960s. It may be the deferred price for it.

The productivity advance which the United States economy exhibited between 1962 and 1966 was indeed faster than during the two preceding business cycles and also very rapid by standards set in the first half of this century (GW 1982, Table 9). We attribute this acceleration to the implementation of the Keynesian policy program. With the claim that the economy is manageable, the Kennedy administration generated optimistic expectations for the returns on investment. This worked well for several years, supported by positive feedbacks. These included:

1. the favorable influence of investment on overall demand, capacity utilization, the age structure and the productivity of the capital stock, and on profits and profit expectations;

2. the favorable influence of relatively fast productivity advance on unit labor costs, given adaptive expectations in wage negotiations (a wage lag);

3. the favorable influence of a high effective demand for labor on attitudes toward technical progress, the interindustry and intraindustry division of labor in the world economy, and the degree of specialization among firms in general.

When efforts to repress price inflation failed and price inflation accelerated under the impact of the Vietnam war, the scope for an accelerated productivity advance was exhausted; and mutual causation with a negative sign (vicious circle) can easily be envisaged to have reduced productivity advance below the long-run trend.

In Europe productivity growth in the 1960s benefited not only from catching up but also from an export-led growth process, supported by the high import demand in the United States and an overvaluation of the U.S. dollar vis-à-vis European currencies which accelerated the transatlantic flow of direct investment to Europe. Economic growth was further fueled by elements of mutual causation as in the United States

But all this was unsustainable. The acceleration of growth on both sides of the Atlantic boosted the demand for labor and/or raw materials and energy, including oil, throughout the 1960s. When supplies became inelastic, the accumulated upward pressures in the bottleneck areas—limits to growth—were to explode in a variety of shocks.[18] This happened during the business cycle which began at the end of the 1960s and ended with the worldwide boom of 1973. As a lagged consequence of the demand-induced growth process, which had helped to bring about the productivity acceleration, the Western world saw itself faced with high and volatile rates of inflation, a burst of raw material prices, and a quadrupling of oil prices.

The acceleration of inflation since the late 1960s[19] may have contributed to the slowdown in measured productivity advance at least indirectly: by pushing workers into higher tax brackets, it may have impaired work incentives; by leading to the taxation of phantom profits, it probably had negative effects on the quality and volume of business investment; by making inflation more volatile, it must have raised the level of business uncertainty, and—in the absence of index-linked bonds—it diverted funds from productive investment to the production of assets which were thought to be a good hedge against it ("concrete gold," structures, and real estate).[20]

More important in our view were the effects that the inflationary or accommodating monetary policy had on the level of real interest rates and hence on the relation between real interest rates and real wages (Hypothesis X). Table 6.5 shows for the United States and West Germany that real interest rates dropped by 2–3 percentage points when inflation accelerated after 1969 and that they further fell when the oil price shock was accommodated between 1973 and 1975. Throughout the whole decade they were markedly below what had been customary in the 1960s in both countries, obviously due to expectations which were strongly influenced by the experience of a less inflationary past (adaptive expectations producing a time lag on the capital market). This coincided with opposite movements on the wage front in Europe. Table 6.5 shows for Germany that in the early 1970s real wages increased much faster than output per hour, even if the positive terms of trade effect is fully taken into account,[21] and that unit labor costs in real terms further increased from 1973 to 1975 when, in addition, the terms of trade effect became negative.

This must be seen as a fundamental distortion in the relation between the two most important factor prices: depressed real rates of interest and excessive real wages. Depressed real rates of interest obviously helped to

**Table 6.5**
Employment, wages, productivity, interest rates, consumer and producer prices, and terms of trade effects in the United States and Germany, 1962–81 (%)

| | Manufacturing | | | Rate of inflation | | Average real rate of interest[b] | Terms of trade effect[a,c] |
|---|---|---|---|---|---|---|---|
| | Hours worked[a] | Real hourly compensation[a] | Output per hour[a] | Consumer prices[a] | Wholesale prices[a] | | |
| *United States* | | | | | | | |
| 1962–66 | 3.3 | 1.8 | 4.2 | 1.8 | 1.3 | 2.8 | 0.0 |
| 1966–69 | 1.6 | 2.1 | 1.7 | 4.1 | 2.2 | 3.4 | 0.0 |
| 1969–73 | 0.0 | 1.6 | 3.2 | 4.9 | 6.0 | 0.4 | 0.0 |
| 1973–79 | 0.7 | 0.9 | 1.4 | 8.5 | 9.8 | −1.7 | −0.7 |
| 1973–75 | −4.6 | 1.2 | 0.0 | 10.0 | 14.0 | −6.0 | −2.0 |
| 1975–79 | 3.5 | 0.7 | 2.1 | 7.8 | 7.7 | 0.5 | 0.0 |
| 1979–81 | −1.9 | −2.9 | 1.3 | 11.9 | 11.7 | 0.7 | −0.5 |
| *Germany* | | | | | | | |
| 1962–65 | 0.8 | 4.7 | 6.2 | 2.8 | 1.3 | 5.1 | −0.1 |
| 1965–69 | 0.0 | 5.5 | 5.7 | 2.2 | 0.5 | 6.6 | 0.0 |
| 1969–73 | 1.3 | 8.3 | 4.8 | 5.3 | 4.6 | 3.8 | 0.2 |
| 1973–79 | −2.1 | 5.6 | 5.3 | 4.6 | 5.0 | 2.4 | −0.2 |
| 1973–75 | −4.7 | 7.5 | 5.4 | 6.5 | 9.0 | 0.3 | −0.2 |
| 1975–79 | −0.8 | 4.3 | 5.2 | 3.7 | 3.1 | 3.4 | −0.2 |
| 1979–81 | −0.8 | −0.2 | 1.2 | 5.9 | 6.7 | 2.6 | −1.3 |

Sources: U.S. Department of Labor, *Handbook of Labor Statistics 1979*. U.S. Department of Labor, *Monthly Labor Review*, vol. 103 (1980), no. 12, pp. 32–9. IMF, *International Financial Statistics*, various issues. OECD, *Main Economic Indicators*, various issues. Sachverständigenrat *zur Begutachtung der gesamtwirtschaftlichen Entwicklung, Jahresgutachten 1979/80 und 1981/82*. U.S. Government, *Economic Report of the President*, February 1982.

a. Average annual rates of growth.

b. Geometric average of government bond yields deflated by wholesale prices (Germany: prices for industrial products).

c. $TTE = [(1 + GNI_r) \div (1 + GDP_r) - 1]$ where $GNI_r$ = rate of growth of real gross national income (defined as gross domestic product in constant prices minus net exports in constant prices plus net exports in current prices deflated by implicit import prices); $GDP_r$ = rate of growth of real gross domestic product (geometric average of yearly rates of growth over the period under inspection).

keep more firms in business, taking the pressure of rising unit labor costs as given. Or they permitted real wages to rise faster and to stay higher than would have been possible—in given circumstances—without creating (even) more unemployment.

In the United States, no such distortion developed before 1973.[22] It was only after the first oil price hike that a drop in the real rate of interest could have a function to support real wages, which indeed continued to rise despite a decline of distributable output per hour. Over the whole period from 1973 to 1979 the real rate of interest was negative on average (and was lower in every subperiod than in the 1960s) whereas real wages rose slightly more than distributable output. From this we conclude that a similar distortion of factor prices in favor of labor and against capital gradually developed in the United States as it had in those parts of Europe for which Germany can be taken to be representative.

When price signals have time to work out their full effects on the supply side, such a distortion resulting from inflation (demand pull or accommodated cost push) must be considered to have several or all of the following side effects:

1. a decline in the propensity to save;

2. a tendency of potential savers to accept and even support a policy of substituting social security for private capital accumulation (Hypothesis V);

3. a tendency of governments to run deficits which—in the absence of index linked bonds—can be financed by borrowing at low real rates of interest and a tendency among governments to spend too much even for infrastructure investments (Hypothesis X);

4. a tendency to invest savings in real assets rather than financial assets, but not in shares of companies which require much cooperation of—excessively expensive—complementary labor;

5. a tendency, therefore, to neglect capital formation for use in production processes, notably where much complementary labor is required, and hence a slower rate of growth of the productive capital stock;

6. a bias in favor of labor-saving techniques that offer a reduction of excessive unit labor costs without a corresponding increase in—artificially low—capital costs;

7. a tendency in R&D to pay excessive attention to labor-saving inventions and innovations and to unduly neglect capital saving paths of technical progress.

An accommodating monetary and fiscal policy designed to absorb negative supply shocks will eventually lose its effect when inflationary expectations catch up with actual inflation. This is likely to happen when inflation reaches its political tolerance level and is no longer allowed to accelerate. In the subsequent process of bringing down inflation rates, inflationary expectations tend to be higher than actual inflation: the public exhibits distrust, i.e., the reverse of money illusion. The result is—in the absence of widespread financial indexation—an excessive level of real rates of interest. Together with excessive real wages, they are characteristic for the early 1980s. At the same time our diagnosis leads us to suspect

1. that the stock of physical capital is inadequate in size and distorted in structure: with too large a consumptive part (e.g. housing) and much too small a productive part which contains too small a number of sufficiently productive jobs to permit an adequate level of employment at given (excessively high) real wages;

2. that the stock of knowledge is distorted in the sense that it offers more labor-saving opportunities and fewer capital saving opportunities than a return to an adequate level of employment would require.

The first point indicates that we believe to observe capital shortage and—at least in Europe—capital shortage unemployment;[23] the second point substantiates our general fear of technological unemployment. To the extent that the additions to the capital stock were distorted one must expect them to have had a lower productivity on the average. Unfortunately, we do not see how this complex diagnosis, which may be an important clue to the problem, can be supported by available statistical information.

The two oil price shocks must also have directly impaired the economic value of the existing stock of capital in the business sector (Hypothesis XI) as this stock embodied a technology which was adjusted to much cheaper oil and energy inputs. One way of accounting for this is to depreciate the value of the stock, considering the more oil-intensive bits and pieces as greatly obsolete to the extent that labor is not prepared to accept the burden (for the sake of maintaining its former level of employment). Available statistical information on the size of the capital stock, or its capacity to produce, must therefore be suspected of overestimating the magnitudes that matter. The alternative way of looking at the problem is to realize fully that the flow of economic services from the existing stock has been reduced and hence the latter's contribution to total factor productivity and hence also to labor productivity as we measure it.[24] Adjustment—of book values as well as of techniques—takes time. Accelerated inflation and depressed real rates of interest provided more of such time, but, apart from distorting the information about relative factor scarcities, they probably also delayed the adjustment itself. This is perhaps why the post-1980 world recession turned out to be so severe. More important in this context: considering that the abrupt oil price hike most probably was the lagged effect of more than a decade of accelerated growth, we are led to interpret the recent productivity slowdown as a process of repair. In a more historical perspective, the advanced countries are now repaying in terms of slower growth what they borrowed from land and nature in the period of accelerated growth before.

A similar case is environmental protection, which became urgent roughly at the same time. It meant absorbing inputs without increasing measured output (Hypothesis XII),[25] and as the professional discussion in the vast literature on the theory and practice of environmental control indicates,[26] the inputs were not as efficiently used as they could have been, had governments not intervened with direct regulations, but with close substitutes to market signals that would have allowed the full use of knowledge available on the spot, and a careful balancing of costs and benefits in the great variety of given circumstances.[27]

A misallocation of investment resources may also have resulted from other forms of government interference, including measures to promote R&D, and controls and subsidies to protect senile industries (Hypothesis XII):

1. As to R&D activities it has been asserted that their social returns tend to exceed the private returns by a significant margin,[28] but it is impossible to determine what size, what structure, and what evolution of public R&D promotion would be appropriate. What the data show (table 6.6) is that countries with negligible (direct) government support (like Japan, Finland, the Netherlands, Belgium) do not necessarily suffer from a corresponding poor productivity performance. After all, governments can only give at other people's expense, and what they give to promote R&D may well reduce business funds which would otherwise be partly devoted to R&D at the source. Also, heavy government involvement seems to be biased in favor of single large firms. Such a bias is likely since bureaucracies prefer to deal with bureaucracies. For Germany we have evidence that public R&D promotion is heavily concentrated on a small number of companies which are known to be large ones (table 6.7), although in recent years criticism

**Table 6.6**
Government funds for R&D in the business enterprise sector in selected advanced economies, 1970 and 1979 (%)

| Country | Shares of business enterprise sector in total R&D performance | | Share of government funds in gross expenditure on R&D performed by the business enterprise sector | |
|---|---|---|---|---|
| | 1970 | 1979 | 1970 | 1979 |
| United States | 66.4 | 67.6 | 43.1 | 32.8 |
| Canada | 38.9 | 44.2 | 15.4 | 14.5 |
| United Kingdom | 63.6[a] | 64.2[b] | 31.9[a] | 29.3[b] |
| Sweden | 70.1[c] | 69.7 | 18.7 | 12.8 |
| Denmark | 47.3 | 51.1 | 3.9 | 11.2 |
| Norway | 45.6 | 49.4 | 18.9 | 24.1 |
| Finland | 54.5[d] | 54.8 | 5.0[d] | 3.1 |
| Netherlands | 55.9 | 51.5[b] | 6.1 | 5.1[b] |
| Belgium | 54.9[e] | 69.6 | 8.4[e] | 4.9 |
| Germany | 63.7[d] | 65.1 | 18.2[d] | 21.2 |
| Austria | 54.6 | 50.8[f] | 8.1 | 9.3[f] |
| France | 55.6 | 59.5 | 32.4 | 21.7 |
| Italy | 54.5 | 57.6 | 4.6 | 6.3 |
| Japan | 60.7[g] | 57.8[h] | 1.3[g] | 1.4[h] |

Source: OECD, *Science and Technology Indicators*, Basic Statistical Series, volume B (Paris, January 1982).
a. 1969–70.     e. 1973.
b. 1978–79.     f. 1975.
c. 1969.        g. 1970–71.
d. 1971.        h. 1979–80.

**Table 6.7**
R&D grants to industry by the German Ministry of Research and Technology, by number of recipients, 1973, 1975, 1977 (%)

| Number of recipients by grant size | Share in total grants | | |
|---|---|---|---|
| | 1973 | 1975 | 1977 |
| 5 largest recipients | 50.9 | 37.6 | 33.9 |
| 25 largest recipients | 85.4 | 71.2 | 63.1 |
| All other recipients[a] | 14.6 | 28.8 | 36.9 |
| Total | 100 | 100 | 100 |

Source: Deutscher Bundestag, 8. Wahlperiode, Drucksache 8/3024, Bonn, 28 June 1979.
a. 1973 : 241; 1975 : 445; 1977 : 674.

against this has induced government to provide more R&D assistance to small- and medium-sized firms.[29]

2. In the 1970s, in North America and Europe new nontariff trade barriers were erected to protect sectors like steel, shipbuilding, textiles, clothing, leather, shoes, or consumer electronics against increasing import competition from suppliers located in Japan and newly industrializing countries.[30] Societies thus deliberately refrained from fully exploiting the productivity potential offered by international trade (Giersch 1970, 11–12).

The protection of senile industries became, of course, more relevant with the emergence of structural or classical unemployment:[31] when labor is overvalued in the market, workers observe a dearth of employment opportunities, and they feel—and are—threatened not only by labor-saving technologies but also by what may be called Stolper-Samuelson unemployment (Giersch 1980) so that they (and their employers) call for protection to maintain employment at given (excessively high) real wages.[32]

Real wages became crucial for employment where they failed to accommodate negative supply shocks flexibly, i.e., the higher costs for energy, raw materials, and the environment, thus enforcing the economic obsolescence of capital mentioned above. While positive supply shocks—like falling real prices for oil, the technological rent captured in Europe's catching-up process, or the productivity potential exploited by trade liberalization and European economic integration—raise employment when real wages do not adjust sufficiently quickly in collective bargaining, negative supply shocks translate themselves into less employment to the extent that the level of real wages is inflexible downward. And, while a higher level of employment makes the economy more flexible, a stiffening of the labor market makes it less capable of exploiting its productivity potential. On this account, productivity advance is likely to have slowed down the more where negative supply shocks met with real wage resistance.

However, the flexibility effect is perhaps only temporary and likely to be swamped by the reverse effect of employment on productivity. Average labor productivity—which we measure—will increase (faster) when marginal labor and capital which are least productive are eliminated from the production process; it will fall (increase less fast, show a faster decline in its growth rate) when relatively much labor—notably unexperienced labor—is being added to the work force. This hypothesis finds support in table 6.5. It shows for the period 1973–79:

1. that the United States had a low increase in distributable output per hour, much lower than in any period since 1960, combined with an in-

crease in real wages not outpacing it; this went along with an increase in employment;

2. that Germany had a much faster increase in distributable output, as fast an increase as in the early 1970s, but combined (a) with an increase in real wages clearly outpacing it, and hence (b) with a sharp decline in employment.[33]

From this we conclude:

1. that U.S. manufacturing would have shown a faster productivity advance, combined, however, with massive job losses—instead of gains in employment—had real wages responded less flexibly to the supply shocks;[34]

2. that manufacturing in Germany would have experienced a similarly strong slowdown in measured productivity advance as it had in the United States, had real wages not outpaced the rise of distributable output—the lower rise, of course, that would have shown up in the statistics if employment had not declined;

3. that the absorption of unemployment on this side of the Atlantic is conditioned by a fall of real wages—relative to the slower productivity advance that will be measured when employment has started to increase.

The hypothesis for West Germany—wage movement inertia pushing up measured productivity at the expense of employment—is plausible to us on account of casual observations. We believe

1. that it was marginal (less efficient) labor which was either released or which remained unemployed because it was thought to be too expensive for what it did or could produce, a point which, however, may indicate that it was the overpricing of marginal labor rather than of labor as such which produced the effect (Hypothesis XIII);

2. that it was often marginal firms not applying best practice techniques which were crowded out of production;

3. that firms and workers who remained in the process felt more insecure under the impact of fiercer competition and made increasing efforts to restructure the production process with a view to reducing X-inefficiency;

4. that firms under heavy cost pressures and a profit squeeze concentrated on process innovations, perhaps at the expense of product innovations which appeared less urgent and more risky and more difficult to finance;

5. that in making process innovations firms placed major emphasis on

techniques which promised to reduce labor cost pressures, a practice criticized by union officials as investment for job killing (*Wegrationalisieren von Arbeitsplätzen*);

6. that Germany has not experienced the birth and survival of so many new firms—relative to the number of existing firms—as the United States did according to Birch (1981).

Of course, we have to bear in mind that real wages are the result of (1) upward pressures on nominal wages and (2) policies to constrain inflation. How strong upward pressures were can be seen from table 6.5: nominal hourly compensation in 1973—75 rose not less than in 1969—73.

The proposition that there was a trade-off between a productivity slowdown and an increase of unemployment when the terms of trade of labor and capital deteriorated vis-à-vis the suppliers of energy (and the environment) can be generalized for the countries under review (Hypothesis XIV).[35] As table 6.8 indicates we find that the international differences in the productivity slowdown strongly correlate with corresponding differences in the increase of unemployment.[36] These differences were in our opinion also largely conditioned by the degrees of real wage rigidity or real wage inertia.

**Table 6.8**
The productivity slowdown in industry related to the capital labor ratio and unemployment, international cross-section, 1973—79 over 1964—73

| Capital-labor ratio | $n$ | $\bar{R}^2$ |
| --- | --- | --- |
| $D\pi E = 0.280 + 0.245\ DCL$ | 10 | 0.08 |
| (0.186) | | |
| ...and structural unemployment | | |
| $D\pi E = -0.089 + 0.266\ DCL + 0.176\ DUE$ | 10 | 0.62 |
| (0.119)[a] (0.049)[a] | | |

Sources: Calculated from OECD, *National Accounts Statistics* (Paris), various issues; OECD, *Labour Force Statistics* (Paris), various issues; OECD, *Economic Outlook* (Paris) 12/1980; UN, *Monthly Bulletin of Statistics* (New York), various issues.
Notes: Mining and quarrying; manufacturing; electricity, gas and water; construction.
    Symbols: $D\pi E$ = ratio of productivity advance (real output per employee) 1973—79 over 1964—73; $DCL$ = ratio of growth of the capital-labor ratio 1973—79 over 1964—73; $DUE$ = ratio of (weighted) average unemployment in the periods 1973—79 over 1964—73.
    Belgium, Canada, Finland, France, Germany, Italy, Japan, Sweden, United Kingdom, United States.
    Country-specific: peak to peak; for exact benchmark years, see the Annex at the end of the chapter.
a. Significant at 5 percent level; standard errors in parentheses.

**Conclusions**

The fourteen hypotheses which we reviewed in the light of available evidence suggest themselves for being consolidated into a medium-term acceleration-deceleration theorem of the following type.

1. An accelerated productivity advance could be achieved in the 1960s when long-term business investment in plant and equipment—the leading factor in productivity advance—was boosted by an improvement in the relation between expected profits (the marginal efficiency of investment, the natural rate of interest) and the interest rate prevailing on financial markets (the money rate of interest), both corrected for expected inflation.

2. This improvement was due to:

a. Keynesian demand management policies in the United States and, somewhat later, in Europe, which kept the money rate of interest in check, supported by adaptive inflationary expectations;

b. favorable supply conditions with regard to energy and exhaustible environmental resources, but also labor (in Europe: notably immigrant labor);

c. economic rents from the technological catching-up process (in Europe and Japan) and from an increasing intraindustry division of labor within Europe and among Europe, the United States and Japan;

d. a favorable attitude toward technical progress, as can be expected when labor is underpriced and scarce;

e. scale economies combined with low costs of structural change under conditions of straightforward quantitative growth.

3. Like a short-term cyclical boom, this medium-term acceleration of growth and productivity advance was unsustainable; it was checked for the following reasons:

a. Straightforward quantitative growth was bound to fall into disrepute after it had raised general welfare in some fields and could no longer hide its deficiencies and costs in other fields; what the public legitimately demanded after a period of fast quantitative growth was a new public good called "qualitative growth."

b. For Europe and Japan the opportunities of technological catching up were finite.

c. Export-led growth in Europe and Japan had to come to an end as it was based on an overvaluation of North American resources and currencies that flooded the rest of the world with dollars.

d. Supplies were limited and had to become less elastic at given relative prices in the fields of energy, exhaustible resources, and—for Europe— skilled manpower.

e. Accelerating inflation, due to (futile efforts of) fine-tuning and the fact that declining supply elasticities were accommodated by monetary policy rather than wage policy, had to be stopped at some point.

4. Elements of mutual causation which had positively affected the acceleration process turned negative:

a. While straightforward quantitative growth—with scale economies and minor changes in relative prices—had boosted investors' confidence, qualitative growth—requiring more structural adjustment in response to greater changes in relative prices—made business uncertain and pessimistic.

b. After fast productivity advance had enabled a fast increase in real wages without impairing employment opportunities, organized labor held extrapolating (or adaptive) wage expectations when the transition to qualitative growth occurred; instead of accommodating the greater investment uncertainty, organized labor in large parts of Europe rejected taking into account the sharp deterioration of its full employment (or equilibrium) terms of trade vis-à-vis energy and the natural environment and started a fiercer struggle over the income distribution, which weakened the social consensus, induced governments to embark upon populist reform policies, strengthened protectionist attitudes, and led to more unemployment or to a lower productivity advance and possibly to both.

c. While monetary acceleration *cum* adaptive expectations on financial markets had kept real rates of interest in check during the 1960s and while it helped once more when it was used again to accommodate the higher level of energy prices after 1974–75, a stop of monetary acceleration was bound to raise the real rate of interest to its long-run equilibrium level, perhaps with some overshooting; and a monetary deceleration to bring down inflation rates—again *cum* adaptive expectations—finally produced the exotic real rates of interest we had in the recent past.

As to conditions on the labor market that would bring us back to satisfactory levels of employment, we can state: if a norm for real wage increases in the future were to be established on the basis of past trends, the measured increase of labor productivity in the base period must not only be corrected for changes in the terms of trade and in the costs of other inputs, it must also be corrected for changes in employment. The equilibrium productivity advance, i.e., the advance consistent with constant employment, must be judged to have been lower (higher) than what is actually measured if employment has fallen under the pressure of excessive wage costs (if wages have been lagging behind the growth of distributable output). If the target for the future is not constant employment but rising employment, the wage norm has to be further reduced by a margin whose size will depend upon the speed at which employment is to be increased. A level of employment which was too low for too long a time is likely to have generated wage-induced capital obsolescence and a corresponding job gap. In order to close this gap a long and strong lag of real wages behind productivity advance may be necessary for sufficiently boosting profit expectations, profits, and investment. Wage restraint also has the function of accommodating the high real rates of interest which are required for raising the propensity to save and for inducing investors to change their technological bias from labor-saving to capital saving methods of production.

An acceleration of investment in plant and equipment (promoted by lower wage costs), a better allocation of this investment, and a more efficient use of the existing stock of capital (enforced by relatively high real rates of interest) would in combination gradually close the structural job gap. By raising the medium-run level of employment, this would reduce resistance against exploiting the gains from specialization, freer trade, and faster technical progress, and pave the way toward a more rapid productivity advance, faster wage increases at given levels of employment, and a renewed social consensus, perhaps with less reliance on collective action. But the process of transition may be tough, comparable to what the world experienced half a century ago. The catharsis could be facilitated by

1. an intellectual consensus on the fundamental distortions that have to be corrected,

2. institutional changes in the labor market to make wage behavior more responsive to unemployment,

3. a removal of barriers to entry for new firms and entrepreneurial talents, and

4. efforts to reduce uncertainty in the relationship between governments and markets.

Measures to boost demand may be necessary should mutual confidence collapse in a critical phase, but mutual confidence and confidence in government can be best trusted to revive and to induce a sustainable expansion of effective demand, in compliance with a renewed growth of factor productivities and aggregate supply, if relative factor prices reflect relative factor scarcities.

## Annex

If not otherwise stated, throughout the chapter, the following years have been used as benchmark years in the countries under investigation:

| | | | | | | |
|---|---|---|---|---|---|---|
| Austria | 1955 | 1960 | 1964 | 1970 | 1973 | 1979 |
| Belgium | 1955 | 1961 | 1964 | 1969 | 1973 | 1979 |
| Canada | 1955 | 1962 | 1966 | 1969 | 1973 | 1979 |
| Denmark | 1955 | 1960 | 1964 | 1969 | 1973 | 1979 |
| Finland | 1955 | 1960 | 1965 | 1970 | 1973 | 1980 |
| France | 1955 | 1960 | 1964 | 1969 | 1973 | 1979 |
| Germany | 1955 | 1962 | 1965 | 1969 | 1973 | 1979 |
| Italy | 1955 | 1963 | 1967 | 1970 | 1973 | 1980 |
| Japan | 1955 | 1961 | 1964 | 1970 | 1973 | 1980 |
| Netherlands | 1955 | 1960 | 1964 | 1970 | 1974 | 1979 |
| Norway | 1955 | 1960 | 1965 | 1969 | 1974 | 1980 |
| Sweden | — | 1961 | 1965 | 1970 | 1974 | 1979 |
| United Kingdom | 1955 | 1960 | 1964 | 1968 | 1973 | 1979 |
| United States | 1955 | 1962 | 1966 | 1969 | 1973 | 1979 |

## Notes

We would like to thank colleagues at the Institut für Weltwirtschaft, in particular Claus-Friedrich Laaser, Klaus-Werner Schatz and Frank Weiss, for helpful comments on an earlier draft. For an extended version of this chapter, see Giersch and Wolter (1982), in the following quoted as GW (1982).

1. For a critical view see Barbash (1982).

2. This comes close to Hayek's notion of the limits of measurement in the analysis of "phenomena of organized complexity." See Hayek (1964, 1975).

3. Throughout this chapter, we must limit the analysis to labor productivity for lack of a comprehensive set of data on capital stock available to us.

4. To eliminate the effects of labor hoarding in mild recessions and better utilization of the stock of employed labor in upswings, the advance or labor productivity is measured from peak to peak. For country-specific benchmark years, see the annex at the end of the chapter.

5. For an empirical test which underlines the significance in the break in the productivity trend see United Nations (1982, 49). The productivity puzzle has

provoked a plethora of empirical research. The most comprehensive efforts employ a growth accounting framework (e.g. Denison 1979, 1982; Kendrick and Grossman 1980). Growth accounting, however, may be misleading as Nelson (1981) pointed out because it cannot cope adequately with (1) the issue of complementarity among the factors of production (Mayer 1921/2); (2) the influence of variables not incorporated in the underlying theoretical model; and (3) the nature of economic growth as a disequilibrium process. We have the feeling that Nelson is essentially right and have come to believe that the disequilibrium point is most relevant in the present context.

6. This concept goes back to Robbins (1930) and the literature quoted on p. 123, ibid., which includes passages from Dalton, Robertson, and Wicksteed.

7. See Okun (1975).

8. For evidence see OECD (1980, 48).

9. We obtained similar results from corresponding calculations for the nonfarm business sector, performed on data given in OECD (1980) for samples of up to twelve countries; for these calculations labor productivity was alternatively measured in terms of the number of persons employed or of the number of hours worked.

10. In the case of the Cobb-Douglas function, the estimated coefficient obviously reflects the influence of more factors than capital, such as embodied technological change. Therefore, from the above regressions one can only conclude that the set of all forces which is proxied by the growth of the capital-labor ratio has lost its influence in the late 1970s.

11. For magnitude and implications see Langfeldt (1982); Feige (1980); Tanzi (1980); Contini (1981); Frey et al. (1982).

12. This may well be a statistical illusion due to estimating real output in various services from input indexes or constructing the real output series as Laspeyres indexes. But it is also true that larger parts of the service sector are sheltered from international competition and, therefore, under less pressure for reducing costs and improving productivity. Furthermore, many services in fields like health, insurance, banking, or transport, which exhibit features of cartelization, partly due to guild ethics and partly to public regulation, and services in the public sector, which are not exposed to the penalties and the rewards of the market, have grown particularly fast. On the other hand, new technologies based on microelectronics make the notion questionable that productivity advance in services is by necessity weak because of the technological structure of these activities (Baumol 1967; Baumol and Oates 1975, Chapters 16, 17).

13. See Schmidt (1977).

14. We note in this context a political catching-up process: across thirteen of the fourteen countries under investigation, the "income elasticities" of the transfer system tend to be the higher the lower the initial ratio of public transfers to gross domestic product (Spearman coefficient of rank correlation: 0.71; in this correlation

the Netherlands are excluded because in their case the period of observation is not comparable to that for the other countries). For basic data see GW (1982, Table 6).

15. For external constraints see further below. For evidence on behavioral differences under alternative welfare regimes see e.g. Maddison (1912, 13); Grubel (1982, 25).

16. This notion brings us back to the stagnationists of the 1930s who believed that the dearth of major new industries was one of the main reasons for the economic malaise of their time (Hansen 1941) and presumed a theory of the mature economy which was completely refuted by the fast economic growth of the 1950s and 1960s. For early criticism of the stagnationists see Terborgh (1945) and the literature cited therein (ibid., p. 9). In a recent study, Nordhaus (1981) identifies technological depletion as one of the major factors behind the recent productivity slowdown.

17. See also Christensen, Cummings, and Jorgenson (1980); Kendrick (1981, 156–166).

18. Rigidities, producing relatively long lags in price responses to changing factor scarcities, may be due to institutional inertia. See Glismann et al. (1978, 1980).

19. Later on, inflation was further fueled by efforts to accommodate the drastic oil price rise through monetary and fiscal expansion.

20. See Giersch (1974, 7–8); Feldstein (1982, 8–13).

21. In an open economy this adjustment is necessary to arrive at "distributable output."

22. A highly plausible explanation can be found in the acceleration of productivity advance which followed the devaluation of the U.S. dollar and the Nixon wage-price controls program, an acceleration that shows a striking similarity to developments under the Kennedy-Johnson administration. The decline of the real rate of interest (by 3 percentage points as calculated in table 6.5) must therefore be related to the rising prices of food and raw materials. In addition to cushioning a negative "supply shock" from this area it contributed to a strong rise of corporate profits in U.S. manufacturing, independently brought about by the acceleration of productivity advance and a wage lag.

23. See Malinvaud (1977, 1982); Giersch (1978, 1979).

24. The relevance of the oil and raw material price increase for the productivity slowdown in the advanced economics has been shown in empirical studies by Jorgenson (1978), Nordhaus (1980), Bruno (1981), Baily (1981), and others. We can add the observation for North America and Europe that the slowdown was much more pronounced in heavy manufacturing than in light manufacturing where energy consumption per unit of output is significantly lower, and that in the United States the productivity of mining activities sharply decreased when the oil price shock offered incentives to reopen already exploited wells and to increase production from marginal oil, gas, and coal fields (GW, 1982, Table 12).

25. For example in 1977, in German industry an average share of 4 percent (manufacturing 4.9 percent) of total investment was devoted to environmental protection. Of course, there is a wide spread among individual industries, where clothing (0.6 percent) and mineral oil refineries (22.2 percent) mark the extremes.

26. Haveman and Christainsen (1981, 74) attribute 8 to 12 percent of the slow-down in U.S. productivity advance to environmental regulations. See also e.g. Tietenberg (1982).

26. In retrospect it may be said that measured productivity advance in the 1960s was boosted by not accounting for environmental inputs or that the public had illusions about environmental costs just as it had illusions about other costs of quantitative economic growth.

28. See, for example, Mansfield et al. (1977).

29. How important it is for dynamic economic development to have a good climate for small firms and the creation of new ones can be inferred from a study by Birch (1981) who covered a sample of 5.6 million businesses in the United States. He concludes for the period 1969–76 (1) that regional differences in the growth of employment had been due to differences in the rate of creation of new jobs while the rate of loss of existing jobs was the same across all regions; (2) that two-thirds of the net new jobs created were established by firms with twenty or fewer employees; (3) that about 80 percent of the replacement jobs were created by establishments four years old or younger, and (4) that almost 90 percent of job replacers can be characterized as providers of services.

30. For details see Institut für Weltwirtschaft (1979).

31. This term was coined by Malinvaud (1977), but the phenomenon was already well known in classical economics.

32. See Stolper and Samuelson (1941).

33. The reason why the U.S. economy showed more real wage flexibility than the German economy (Sachs 1979; Branson and Rotemberg 1980; Gordon 1982) is perhaps that the U.S. labor market has a less oligopolistic structure containing more elements of (monopolistic) competition. One may speculate whether three-year contracts with cost of living adjustment provisions as they prevail in the United States are much worse for employment (or an inflationary employment policy) than the yearly wage rounds without indexation, as they prevail in Germany in an environment which is very sensitive to inflation, but still has adaptive expectations implying real wage inertia.

34. This takes account of the observation that in the United States in the 1970s effective labor services seem to have declined relative to measured labor input (Hypothesis XIII). Its impact on the productivity slowdown, however, is controversial. See Perlman (1978, 1981) and Baily (1981); see also Prais (1981).

35. However, Austria, Denmark, Norway, and the Netherlands had to be excluded from the analysis for lack of data on the change in capital-labor ratios.

36. In the same way we tested the relationship between the increase of structural unemployment and the productivity slowdown also for other aggregates (nonfarm business sector, manufacturing). The relationship turned out to be robust.

# References

Baily, Martin Neil (1981). "Productivity and the services of capital and labour." *Brookings Papers on Economic Activity*, no. 1, pp. 1−50.

Barbash, Jack (1982). "The guilds of academe." *Challenge*, March/April 1982, pp. 50−54.

Baumol, William J. (1967). "Macroeconomics of unbalanced growth: the anatomy of urban crisis." *American Economic Review*, vol. 57, no. 3, pp. 415−26.

────, and Oates, Wallace E. (1975). *The Theory of Environmental Policy*. Englewood Cliffs, N.J.: Prentice-Hall.

Birch, David L. (1981). "Who creates jobs?" *The Public Interest*, no. 65 (fall), pp. 3−14.

Branson, William, and Rotemberg, Julio (1980). "International adjustment with wage rigidity." *European Economic Review*, vol. 13, no. 3, pp. 309−32.

Bruno, Michael (1981). *Raw Materials, Profits and the Productivity Slowdown*. National Bureau of Economic Research, Working Paper no. 660. Cambridge, Mass. (April).

Christensen, L. R., Cummings, D., and Jorgenson, D. W. (1980). *Relative Productivity Levels, 1947−1973: An International Comparison*. Harvard Institute for Economic Research, Discussion Paper, no. 773 (June).

Contini, Bruno (1981). "Labour market segmentation and the development of the parallel economy—the Italian experience." *Oxford Economic Papers*, vol. 33 (November), pp. 401−12.

Denison, Edward S. (1979). *Accounting for Slower Economic Growth: The United States in the 1970s*. Washington, D.C.: Brookings Institution.

──── (1982). *The Interruption of Productivity Growth in the United States*. Paper prepared for the Conference of the Royal Economic Society, London, July 22.

Feige, Edgar L. (1980). *A New Perspective on Macroeconomic Phenomena: The Theory and Measurement of the Unobserved Sector of the United States*. Netherlands Institute for Advanced Studies, Wassenaar (August) (mimeo.).

Feldstein, Martin (1982). *The Conceptual Foundation of Supply Side Economics*. Harvard University and NBER (mimeo.).

Fels, Gerhard, and Schmidt, Klaus-Dieter (1981). *Die deutsche Wirtschaft im Strukturwandel*. Kieler Studien Nr. 166, Tübingen: J. C. B. Mohr (Paul Siebeck).

Frey, Bruno S., Weck, Hannelore, and Pommerehne, Werner (1982). *Has the Shadow Economy Grown in Germany? An Exploratory Study*. Zürich (April) (mimeo.).

Giersch, Herbert (1970). *Growth, Cycles and Exchange Rates—The Experience of West Germany*. Wicksell Lectures, Stockholm: Almquist and Wicksell.

—————— (1974). "Index clauses and the fight against inflation." In *Essays on Inflation and Indexation*, pp. 1–23. Washington: American Enterprise Institute.

—————— (1978). "Preface." In *Capital Shortage and Unemployment in the World Economy* (ed. H. Giersch), Symposium 1977. Tübingen: J. C. B. Mohr (Paul Siebeck).

—————— (1979). "Aspects of growth, structural change, and employment—a Schumpeterian perspective." *Weltwirtschaftliches Archiv*. Band 115, Heft 4, pp. 629–52.

—————— (1980). "Die Rolle der reichen Länder in der wachsenden Weltwirtschaft." *Schweizerische Zeitschrift für Volkswirtschaft und Statistik*, vol. 118, 3, pp. 301–20.

——————, and Wolter, Frank (1982). *On the Recent Slowdown in Produtivity Growth in Advanced Economies*. Kieler Arbeitspapiere (Kiel Working Papers), no. 148, Kiel: Institut für Weltwirtschaft (July).

Glismann, Hans H., Rodemer, Horst, and Wolter, Frank (1978). *Zur Natur der Wachstumsschwäche in der Bundesrepublik Deutschland—Eine empirische Analyse langer Zyklen wirtschaftlicher Entwicklung*. Kieler Diskussionsbeiträge (Kiel Discussion Papers), Nr. 55. Kiel: Institut für Weltwirtschaft (June).

——————, (1980). *Lange Wellen wirtschaftlichen Wachstums—Replik und Weiterführung*. Kieler Diskussionsbeiträge (Kiel Discussion Papers), Nr. 74, Kiel: Institut für Weltwirtschaft, December 1980. Reprinted in Dietmar Petzina, and Ger van Roon (eds.), *Konjunktur, Krise, Gesellschaft. Wirtschaftliche Wechsellagen und soziale Entwicklung im 19. und 20. Jahrhundert*. Stuttgart: Klett-Cotta, 1981, pp. 66–106.

Gordon, Robert J. (1982). "Why U.S. wage and employment behaviour differs from that in Britain and Japan." *Economic Journal*, vol. 92, no. 365, pp. 13–44.

Griliches, Zvi (1980). "R and D and the productivity slowdown." *American Economic Review*, vol. 70, no. 2, pp. 343–48.

Grubel, Herbert (1982). "Reassessing the costs of social insurance programs." Paper presented at the Conference on *Reassessing the Role of Government in the Mixed Economy*, Kiel, June 23–25.

Hansen, Alvin H. (1941). *Fiscal Policy and Business Cycles*. New York: Norton.

Haveman, Robert H., and Christainsen, Gregory B. (1981). "Environmental regulations and productivity growth." In *Environmental Regulation and the U.S. Economy* (ed. Henry W. Peskin, Paul R. Portney, and Allen V. Kneese), pp. 55–74. Baltimore: Johns Hopkins University Press.

Hayek, Friedrich August von (1964). "The theory of complex phenomena." In *The Critical Approach to Science and Philosophy. Essays in Honour of K. R. Popper* (ed. M. Bunge), pp. 332–49. New York.

—————— (1975). "The pretence of knowledge." Nobel Memorial Lecture held December 11, 1974, *The Swedish Journal of Economics*, vol. 77, no. 4, pp. 433–42.

Institut für Weltwirtschaft (1979). *Ursachen und Formen des neuen Protektionismus.* Kiel (mimeo.).

Jorgenson, Dale W. (1978). "The role of energy in the U.S. economy." *National Tax Journal,* vol. 31, no. 3, pp. 209–20.

Kendrick, John W. (1981). "International comparisons of recent productivity trends." In William Fellner (Project Director), *Essays in Contemporary Economic Problems: Demand, Productivity and Population.* Washington and London: American Enterprise Institute, pp. 125–70.

————, and Grossman, Elliot S. (1980). *Productivity in the United States: Trends and Cycles.* Baltimore: Johns Hopkins University Press.

Langfeldt, Enno (1982). "The unobserved economy in the Federal Republic of Germany: A preliminary assessment." *Seven papers presented at the International Conference on the Unobserved Sector,* Institute for Advanced Study. Wassenaar, June 3–6.

Maddison, Angus (1982). *Leading Countries in Capitalist Development: Their Secrets of Success.* Paper presented at the 45th Meeting of the Association of German Economic Research Institutes, Bonn, May 13–14 (mimeo.).

Malinvaud, Edmond (1977). *The Theory of Unemployment Reconsidered.* Oxford.

———— (1982). "Wages and unemployment." *Economic Journal,* vol. 92, no. 365, pp. 1–12.

Mansfield, Edwin, Rapoport, John, Romes, Anthony, Wagner, Samuel, and Beardslay, George (1977). "Social and private rates of return from industrial innovations." *Quarterly Journal of Economics,* vol. 91, no. 2, pp. 221–40.

Mayer, Hans (1921, 1922). "Untersuchung zu dem Grundgesetz der wirtschaftlichen Wertrechnung." I und II, *Zeitschrift für Volkswirtschaft und Sozialpolitik,* Wien, NF 1 und 2, pp. 431–58.

Nelson, Richard R. (1981). "Research on productivity growth and productivity differences: Dead ends and new departures." *Journal of Economic Literature,* vol. 19, no. 63 (September), pp. 1029–64.

Nordhaus, William D. (1980). "Oil and economic performance in industrial countries." *Brookings Papers on Economic Activity,* no. 2, pp. 341–88.

———— (1981). *Economic Policy in the Face of Declining Productivity Growth.* Cowles Foundation Discussion Paper, no. 604, Yale University (September).

OECD (1980). *Productivity Trends in the OECD Area.* CPE/WP, vol. 2 (79), p. 8, first revision (Paris).

Okun, Arthur (1975). *Equality and Efficiency. The Big Tradeoff.* Washington: Brookings Institution.

Perlman, Mark (1978). "Discrepancies of supply and demand in the labor market: sectoral, regional, and professional—causes and cures." In *Capital Shortage and*

*Unemployment in the World Economy* (ed. H. Giersch), pp. 139–69. Symposium 1977, Tübingen: J. C. B. Mohr (Paul Siebeck).

————— (1981). "Some economic consequences of the new patterns of population growth." In William Fellner (Project Director), *Essays in Contemporary Economic Problems: Demand, Productivity and Population*, pp. 247–79. Washington and London: American Enterprise Institute.

Prais, Sigbert J. (1981). "Vocational qualifications or the labour force in Britain and Germany." *National Institute Economic Review*, no. 98 (November), pp. 47–59.

Robbins, Lionel (1930). "On the elasticity of demand for income in terms of effort." *Economica*, vol. 10, pp. 123–29.

Sachs, Jeffrey (1979). "Wages, profits, and macroeconomic adjustment: A comparative study." *Brookings Papers on Economic Activity*, no. 2, pp. 269–319.

Schmidt, Klaus-Dieter (1977). "Die Bedürfnisse der Menschen in den achtziger Jahren." In Deutsche Gesellschaft für Betriebswirtschaft. 30. Deutscher Betriebswirtschafter Tag, Berlin 1977. *Strukturwandel, Neue Chancen für die Unternehmen*, Bd. 1, pp. 141–55.

Stolper, Wolfgang F., and Samuelson, Paul A. (1941). "Protection and real wages." *Review of Economic Studies*, vol. 31, no. 3, pp. 545–52.

Tanzi, Vito (1980). "The underground economy in the United States: Estimates and implications." *Banca Nazionale del Lavoro Quarterly Review*, no. 135 (December), pp. 427–53.

Terborgh, George (1945). *The Bogey of Economic Maturity*. Chicago: Machinery and Allied Products Institute.

Tietenberg, Thomas H. (1982). "Market approaches to environmental protection." Paper presented at the Conference on *Reassessing the Role of Government in the Mixed Economy*, Kiel, June 23–25.

United Nations (1982). *Economic Survey of Europe in 1981*. Prepared by the Secretariat of the Economic Commission for Europe (Geneva), New York: United Nations Publication Sales No. E.82.II.E.1.

# 7            Labor, Wages, and Productivity

This year [1982] Mannheim University is celebrating its seventy-fifth anniversary. Next year, in 1983, economists will remember the one hundredth birthday of John Maynard Keynes and Joseph Schumpeter, who were born at the time when Marx died. Also in 1983, they will celebrate the two hundredth birthday of Johann Heinrich von Thünen. These are important occasions for economists. Unfortunately they coincide with a period of slump reminding us of the global economic crisis 50 years ago that we call the Great Depression, or the period 150 years ago that inspired Marx and Engels to predict the collapse of capitalism. Such times are characterized by unemployment. How unemployment can be eliminated is the major challenge of economic policy. In trying to understand this challenge, we shall make use of what Thünen, Keynes, and Schumpeter contributed to economic science.

The headstone to Thünen's grave—who died in 1850, exactly one hundred years before Schumpeter—carries an equation for what Thünen thought to be the fair or natural wage, $A = \sqrt{a \cdot p}$, where $a$ stands for the conventional minimum income necessary for consumption and $p$ for what a worker produces net of capital depreciation and other inputs. Workers are considered to save and therefore also earn income from the ownership of capital. Wilhelm Krelle (1961) further advanced this interpretation when he observed that Thünen's wage formula postulated a society in which all assets belonged to workers, so that the returns from all factors of production accrued to labor. But in that case, as can readily be seen, the question of just shares in total income becomes irrelevant (as Krelle himself says). More relevant is the reverse question of what workers would have to pay

The German original appeared under the title "Arbeit, Lohn und Produktivität" in *Weltwirtschaftliches Archiv* 119 (1983): 1–18. Copyright 1983 by Institut für Weltwirtschaft, Kiel. Translated by Wolfgang Kasper, Canberra, Australia.

to the other factors of production if labor had to hire capital and land services, if capital and land were to be used in the most productive way, and capital was to grow so as to ensure full employment in the future, preferably with rising wage rates.

The formula on Thünen's grave does not answer such questions. But some answers can be derived—at least indirectly—from the model that Thünen developed in his book, *The Isolated State*, which was published in 1826, half a century after Adam Smith's *Wealth of Nations*. In order to analyze the spatial order of an economy, Thünen assumes a homogeneous plane where transport costs are determined by distance, the weight of products, and their rate of spoilage. A central city is in the middle of the plane. All production activity will then orient itself toward this central place. From the center toward the periphery, there will emerge as a production pattern a system of rings characterized by a decreasing intensity of land use. Far away from the center the plane becomes wilderness. This pattern is only brought about by transportation costs. Land near the city has a locational advantage that is reflected in a differential rent—a higher land value. People, and hence labor, are completely mobile. They locate in such a way that their real wage—the purchasing power of their nominal wage—is equalized throughout. Thus on Thünen's plane, the population density will steadily decrease from the center to the periphery. The forces that make for this equalization operate partly through interregional trade and partly through interregional migration. The same principle applies to capital, which is also completely mobile and able, unlike land, to avoid the disadvantage of high transportation costs by gravitating toward the center, so that the capital/land ratio declines toward the periphery in the same way as the labor/land ratio. The interest rate, or yield on capital, will be the same everywhere, just like the real wage. At the periphery, where no capital is used and land is free, the entire product accrues to labor. At the edge of the wilderness, economic activity just generates the marginal product of labor. This marginal product represents, in all locations, the value that the last (the marginal) unit of labor adds to total output. The same applies to capital. The interest rate is the same throughout and equals the marginal product of capital. Wherever in Thünen's system there is productive activity, the product is shared in such a way that capital and labor receive a return equal to the value of their marginal product. The differential rent of land is capitalized in land prices; they rise from zero at the periphery toward the center, reflecting the advantage of lower transportation costs.

We can use this model to ask a few questions of present-day relevance.

First, if the population grows and with it the supply of labor, new land will be colonized on the periphery and land rents will rise everywhere. If everything else remains the same, more labor is used per unit of land and combined with a given capital stock. The product generated at the edge of the wilderness where land is free is worth less than before because it is produced farther away from the center and has to bear higher transportation costs. And the marginal product of labor goes down not only at the periphery but throughout. The increase of the labor supply thus leads to a wage reduction. Without it, the additional labor would be unemployed.

This case covers demographic changes such as a baby boom or the influx of labor from abroad. In the case of a population decline, as fewer join the work force or as immigration is cut back, workers can expect a rise of wages and employment opportunities. The same would occur if population pressure were relived by emigration, as in Germany during the Great Depression one hundred years ago or in the middle of the nineteenth century when misery drove Silesian weavers into insurrection (Thomas 1973).

Second, what happens if Thünen's state introduces legal minimum wages or permits the formation of trade unions, which act as supplier cartels to obtain wages higher than otherwise? The answer is clear: Wage compression ceases from competition among workers, except perhaps in the underground economy. It could be an improvement, though only if the supply of labor showed a negative elasticity, for example, if depressed wages had forced women and children to work in order to survive. This pressure will be relieved. On the other hand, wages reduce the volume of labor demanded. No one can indefinitely employ workers who claim more than what the market judges to be the value of their marginal product. Wage and marginal product must be equal in Thünen's model. If fewer workers are employed, the marginal product rises. Thus, with wages above the market clearing level, the wage determines what the marginal product has to be. Job destruction and labor saving will ensure that the marginal product rises in reaction to higher wages. Those who retain their jobs receive higher incomes, whereas the others lose their natural right to work at a wage rate that is equal to the market value of their marginal product.[1] The outcome of excessive wages is classical unemployment.

Third, let us assume now that statutory or union-imposed minimum wages are valid only in the center—not elsewhere—and that the unions create unemployment insurance or get the city authorities to dole out unemployment benefits. The model predicts that there will be unemployment in the city and maybe also outmigration. Those willing to work will migrate to the flat land. And there will also be immigrants from rural areas into the city. The latter will search more or less intensively for higher paid work in the city but with the fallback of social security. They may live in slums or other temporary quarters waiting and tolerating temporary penury because they hope for a job with a higher marginal product than they could obtain outside the city. What they hope for is a rent for labor that the labor cartel has created. The element of rent induces those with jobs to defend them as if they were a property right. Worries about job security will therefore be on everyone's mind. This contrasts with the hopes of those who are waiting for a job vacancy (like those lecturers who used to wait, a generation ago, for a vacant chair and who calculated retirement dates using "Who's Who in Academia").

Jobs with artificially raised minimum or union wages are not only threatened by wage compression from immigrants. They are also threatened by the competitive pressure of products from outside the city, and possibly—if we equate Thünen's city with the affluent industrial countries—from the newly industrializing countries (NICs) and the Third World.

How does such import competition come about? When city wages are suddenly raised, a few jobs (at the edge of the city) lose their competitiveness in relation to comparable jobs in the periphery—that is, outside the high wage zone. To some extent these jobs can be protected if firms switch to production methods that economize on labor that has become artificially expensive. Such practices will be criticized for their alleged destruction of jobs. Eventually, some jobs will have to migrate to locations outside the high wage zone. In the city, there will be talk of the exportation of jobs. But job exportation is the consequence of the fact that producers of imports from across the border enjoy a wage advantage. Workers who do not wish to wait for employment at excessive city wage rates will migrate to locations across the border where they compress wages, as competition dictates, in the production of goods that in the high-wage city happen to be already under import pressure.

What can be done against such competition by cheap labor from outside? The answer is straightforward: support minimal wages by import protection. The market distortion of high wages can be neutralized by a second distortion. One will probably engage in selective protectionism, though not against imports from places with similar conditions, that is, other industrial countries. Rather, protection will be aimed at those imports that contain much labor—and labor without artificially raised wages at that. Within the Thünen model, these are the imports from the plane surrounding the city; in the world economy, they are imports from countries with a comparative advantage from the plentiful supply of cheap labor, that is, labor-intensive products. Those who suffer from the protection of excessive wages at the center are therefore the poorer nations outside, the NICs, and the poor countries on the periphery of the world economy. What will the victims have to say about these protective measures, which are founded on the Stolper-Samuelson theorem—protectionist measures that amount to the abortion of embryonic jobs in the Third World? We know the answer. The accusations are of "exploitation," "imperialism," and "class warfare." But as the Thünen model shows, it is not evil capitalists who are behind this but forces in the labor movement who try to make labor in the center sufficiently scarce, by import controls, to match the artificially raised wage level. These connections are not readily understood by the outside world, because the Marxist intellectuals of the periphery view the center and all disturbances it creates exclusively as the result of capitalist evil. We also know their reactions to all this: import substitution or even autarky, "independencia," or at least actions to cut oneself off from world markets and to retaliate with import controls. Such reactions, of course, impair the worldwide division of labor. All countries and locations—and humanity as a whole—are then deprived of the great advantages that international trade confers. All are impoverished by a counterproductive trade war. Thus, it is highly likely that the world economic crisis of the 1930s would have taken a less dramatic turn had the United States not raised trade barriers so dramatically by passing the Smoot-Hawley Act.

Before discussing real-world issues more closely, it may be useful to pause for a brief methodological digression. Models like that of Thünen are greatly simplified images of reality, a kind of caricature. They permit us to draw conclusions about reality, though only insofar as the model's properties represent the essence of reality. An exact replication of reality is impossible and unnecessary, as it is in the case of a map that has to abstract from much detail in order to show clearly or predict the roads and service stations for motorists or the hiking trails for walkers. To the extent that a model can answer queries and can sharpen diffuse and often confusing observations, the model becomes a paradigm (in the sense given to it by T. S. Kuhn), a considered vision of the world, a basis for fruitful reflection and research, perhaps a scientific research program (in the sense of J. Lakatos).

Thünen's model belongs to classical economics. It aims to understand long-term interactions and therefore abstracts from details of adjustment and from temporary disequilibriums. Classical equilibriums under laissez-faire conditions are also good approximations to efficient optima, except where property rights have not been established—as in the case of the ecological environment—or where external costs and benefits cannot be internalized without public intervention. Understandably, the search for deficiencies of the model (or of market competition in reality) will be more intensive if the equilibrating forces run counter to powerful vested interests. In the case of unemployment, there has always been a debate over whether it is caused by excessive wages, as the classical Thünen model suggests, or inherent market failure. This sets the stage for one of the two great economists who were born exactly one hundred years after Thünen, John Maynard Keynes.

Keynes's *General Theory*, published in 1936, aims at proving the possibility, even the probability, of an equilibrium with underutilized resources, including involuntary unemployment. Keynes denies that automatic, spontaneous corrections will occur. One reason is that the unemployed workers will not actively bid down wages when the money wage is too high. A second reason is that even with falling wage rates, employment could not be expected to increase. It is no wonder that economists close to labor unions refer to Keynes when they deal with unemployment. Moreover, Keynes fails to ask where the unemployment, which is to be eliminated, stems from in the first place. Classical economists will not deny that wages, even if they remained constant, may well have become excessive, if the money supply has been reduced to an unanticipated extent or has risen by less than expected. Classical economists then speak of unemployment due to disinflation or deflation or a shortage of money or a temporary stabilization crisis that could be overcome by increasing the money supply (reflation) or by returning to a steady path of monetary expansion.

Keynes admits that less transaction money is required when wages and prices fall, so that the real money stock increases (Keynes effect). But this increase in real money disappears in his famous liquidity trap, which opens when the nominal interest rate is near zero so that it cannot decline further (Tobin 1980).

Real interest rates are, of course, higher than nominal rates when prices fall, as was the case in the 1930s. They can then well be higher than the marginal efficiency of investment. But once prices and wages have fallen enough to reach a new equilibrium level, then underemployment would require the marginal efficiency of investment (of the investment volume needed for full employment) to be close to zero—lower than the level of interest rates could be.

If one asks how a situation could possibly occur in which investment opportunities are not sufficiently great to generate positive rates of return, the general answer can, again, be only that wages are excessive. This takes taxes and risks as given. Indeed, if wages cannot or must not drop further, then there is no alternative to asking the government to cut taxes or to reduce political uncertainty and risk by adopting a steadier economic policy, including a liberal multilateral trade regime. Seen from today's perspective, there is not only Keynes's liquidity trap, which could be filled, if necessary, by monetary expansion; there can also be a "confidence trap," which is perhaps more relevant and represents a general problem. As far as the government is concerned, we have to conclude that the wage level required for full employment will have to be the lower, the heavier is the net burden that the government places on the private sector. The government burden can be readily incorporated into the Thünen model if we introduce, as the equivalent for a negative production factor, a general value-added tax whose incidence is proportional on all factor incomes, including real wages, and which, like a tribute paid to a foreign country, benefits no one within the system. If labor refuses to pay this tribute, then in the short run, there will be underemployment of all factors of production due to inadequate investment. In the longer run, there will at least be underemployment of labor.

In search of a program to reduce current unemployment, Keynesians suggest an increase of the nominal money supply. Under certain circumstances, when a deflation has to be corrected or a stabilization process can be terminated after having achieved its purpose, they will meet with other economists who temporarily share their belief that more money will generate more real demand. The common ground is the presumption that prices will not rise for the time being because more output will raise labor productivity by allowing firms to exploit hidden productivity reserves. Such a productivity push has the same effect on profits and profit expectations that a cut in real wages would have with constant productivity. This, then, is the most favorable case: a reflation to correct a deflation or to discontinue a disinflationary policy that is going too far.

Non-Keynesians, however, part way with Keynesians where the increase of the money supply is to cut excessive real wages. To achieve this, prices would have to rise permanently. The strategy is modeled on the concept of the Phillips curve, which reflects the proposition that more employment can be attained if society is prepared to tolerate a certain rate of inflation. In the public policy debate in Germany, the concept was echoed in the slogan that with 5 percent inflation, the country would be better off than with 5 percent unemployment. However, this trade-off exists only over the short run. Over the longer term, it is likely to fail because unions will soon realize that inflation is cutting real wages. They will then attempt to catch up with inflation and will try to anticipate, and even outpace, it. If inflation is still to have an effect on real wages, it must accelerate over time. To avoid a collapse, inflation has to be discontinued from time to time; at least a slowdown is indispensable as a pause. During this interval, jobs will be eliminated in a stabilization crisis. Genuine Keynesians consider such breaks as inappropriate and costly. In the short run, they appear to be right. But they overlook two things. First, a "confidence trap" is bound to arise, if not sooner then later, when inflation becomes "enemy number 1." Second, an inflation intended to accommodate excessively high real wages by lowering interest rates distorts the ratio between real wages and real interest rates. It therefore causes permanent damage.

The second point needs to be elaborated, because little has been said about it in the literature (but see Giersch 1982). The strategy of fighting unemployment by inflation succeeds best when money illusion is prevalent or, put another way, when many people still hope for stabilization. Illusory stabilization hopes are harbored by workers who believe that higher wage rates resulting from the collective bargaining process amount to a corresponding increase in their purchasing power, ignoring that the higher pay will largely be nullified by higher prices. Those hopes are reinforced if price rises can be blamed on evil entrepreneurs rather than a deliberate expansionary policy. Illusory hopes are also harbored by savers who take the nominal interest rate at face value, failing to calculate the real interest rate, that is, the nominal rate minus inflation.

Real interest rates compressed by inflation make life easier for government and allow firms to bear excessive real wages. But interest rates can be kept artificially low for quite a while only if indexation is prohibited so that creditors cannot easily protect themselves against unanticipated inflation. And government—in the absence of indexation—gains from inflation not only as a debtor but also as a tax collector, from both bracket creep and the taxation of phantom profits. All this boils down to mortgaging the future. Why?

The answer is simple. If loans and capital are artificially cheap in real terms, borrowers and investors do not economize as much as real scarcities would dictate. Capital is wasted everywhere. The government sector, which is less under cost control than the private sector and more under the pressure of vested interests, tends to become too large. It grows at the expense of the private sector due to bracket creep and the taxation of phantom profits. Private households, in the face of low returns on bonds, look for assets that hedge against inflation: consumer durables like carpets, art, antiques, second homes, and luxurious apartments ("concrete gold"). And business firms, in an attempt to avoid the taxation of phantom profits and hence of the companies' own real capital base, try to borrow more than they would otherwise do. Hence the ratio of debt to equity tends to go up. In order to evade excessive real wages, firms use the funds they manage to borrow despite reduced supplies of savings, mainly for labor-saving investment. They economize on employing labor and deploy excessive amounts of capital per worker. Have these developments occurred in Germany? The answer has to be yes. What we observe after a couple of years is a capital stock that contains too few productive jobs in relation to the supply of labor. The resulting unemployment is classical unemployment, a "capital-shortage unemployment," as it was called after World War II. It is a classical unemployment of the second degree. Many other parts of Europe appear to suffer from it, and perhaps also some Latin American countries that have used soft credits to invest in very capital-intensive, roundabout ways of production.

Depressed real rates of interest and excessive real wages must also have consequences for the direction of technical progress. They can be less easily observed. The pace of technical progress as such need not slow down when wages are too high and—as a partial compensation—real interest rates are too low. But such a distorted factor-price ratio, if it persists, will induce firms to look out for options that are predominantly labor saving, that is, more labor saving than capital saving, and possibly capital deepening.

This holds predominantly for process innovations: excessive wages and depressed interest rates tend to favor new technological options that substitute capital for labor. The result is technological unemployment. We may call it classical unemployment of the third degree. It is not due to new knowledge that fell like manna from heaven but due to a selective use of knowledge (and a selective search for knowledge) induced by a distorted factor-price ratio. Anglo-Saxon post-Keynesians tend to ignore the dangers of both capital-shortage unemployment and technological unemployment, in contrast to economists familiar with the German-Austrian literature and with the economic malaise in the Weimar Republic. In Weimar Germany, wage-push pressures, capital shortage, and technological unemployment were quite familiar terms.

Keynes did not address himself to these longer-term consequences. His advice is therefore appropriate for short-term emergencies—that is, for a liquidity crisis, when a liquidity trap opens, or for a stabilization crisis when monetary policy is in too sharp a conflict with wage policy. It may also apply to an endogenous cyclical downturn when real wages are temporarily too high relative to a level of labor productivity that has been depressed by a fall in output. In such circumstances, something may be gained if the central bank—perhaps supported by the government—temporarily raises demand by supplying more money. But such a therapy fails to offer a long-term relief. It carries the danger that the economy gradually becomes addicted to the "inflation drug" and eventually succumbs to it. Keynes effectively forestalled any criticism by those with a longer time horizon in mind with his dictum that "in the long run, we are all dead." Yet Keynes died three and a half decades ago, far too early. We and, even more so, our children and grandchildren whose economic prospects are our concern, live in what Keynes considered the long run. In his last essay before his death, he expressed doubts about the efficacy of his medicine as administered by his disciples. Would he still call his theory, if he were alive today, the General Theory? Many who were familiar with his capacity to learn from experience do not believe so.

Classical theory, by contrast, has its focus on permanent problems and effects: on classical unemployment of the first degree as shown in the framework of Thünen's model and on classical unemployment of the second and third degree as they can be observed now after the Keynesian medicine of depressed real interest rates has been used in Germany and elsewhere in Europe. Instead of curing the causes of unemployment, that is, excessive wage levels, the medicine of low interest rates as recently applied alleviated only the symptoms. A Keynesian solution was adopted to solve a classical problem; a new distortion was introduced to neutralize the original one. This had secondary consequences that outlasted Keynes's short run.

When in the immediate postwar period the Keynesian message arrived in Germany, German economists—with the inflation experience in back of their minds—were very skeptical. They sensed the dangers from diagnosing unemployment invariably as the consequence of a lack of demand and a shortage in the money supply and were quite irritated when, after 1945, they listened to American Keynesians who failed to recognize that the German economy suffered not from a lack of demand but from a shortage of physical capital in the sense that the capital stock, heavily damaged by bombing, did not provide a sufficiently large number of jobs for the working population, including the armies of demobilized soldiers and the millions of refugees from the eastern territories.

The current unemployment is also due to a shortage of physical capital, though in a somewhat modified sense: the capital stock does not contain a sufficiently large number of jobs that are sufficiently productive to allow the firms to pay the prevailing real wages without eroding the capital base. For this, the appropriate therapy cannot simply be more demand. What is needed is more and harder work for a higher rate of saving and investment, for more capital formation without a decline in living standards. The additional savings will contribute to creating new jobs or improving the existing ones. This is the same formula that proved successful in overcoming the capital shortage unemployment of the reconstruction period immediately after the war.

So far we could largely ignore that there is an upward trend in labor productivity due to technical progress and the growth of the capital stock per worker. We now have to incorporate this productivity advance into our analysis, as it is being blamed for the strong surge in unemployment during the recent past. Indeed, it is said that the pace of productivity advance is too fast for allowing everybody to work full time; therefore the work week should be shortened. This may sound plausible, but it is not if one looks at how productivity and wages influence employment.

Assume an unbiased (neutral) productivity advance of (say) 3 percent per annum. It has no effect on the volume of employment if it is accompanied by a rise in real wages of 3 percent. Unit labor costs then remain unchanged, as does the margin that is needed to meet capital costs and risk. But if wages rise by 4 percent, profits are squeezed. A wage increase going beyond the productivity advance implies a redistribution of incomes from profits to wages, that is, an increase in the wage share. In the past, unions have justified excessive wage increases with the argument that they would serve as a whip to productivity or as something like a tonic for those entrepreneurs whose competitive drive has flagged. Overall productivity increases, as we measure them, may indeed be speeded along by such wage pressures. But a parallel effect will be unemployment from job losses. It occurs when the pressure from rising unit labor costs reduces the margin available for capital costs and profits to such an extent that marginal enterprises have to close down, that intramarginal enterprises must eliminate marginal jobs, or that enterprises in general are induced to substitute capital for labor.

We saw in the Thünen model that labor productivity adjusts to the prevailing wage if the wage is exogenously given. In a growing economy, just like in the stationary model, the additional productivity per unit of labor is brought about at the expense of employment. It implies that pro-

duction rises by less than productivity. On average, more is being produced per hour or worker because the less productive hours and workers
have been cut out. As far as the resulting wage increases are concerned, it
is clear that while those people who have retained their jobs get more pay,
the others are left with unemployment benefits instead of a wage payment.

Statistics readily illustrate this. Productivity gains in West German industry accelerated between 1969–73 and 1973–79 from an annual 4.8
percent to an impressive 5.3 percent, while the volume of hours worked,
which had previously increased by 1.3 percent per annum, now fell by 2.1
percent annually. International cross-section analyses show that this is not
a mere coincidence. Let me quote one telling example. While the German
manufacturing sector achieved the remarkable gain in productivity of 5.3
percent with a falling volume of hours worked, the American manufacturing sector managed just a meager 1.4 percent; but the work volume increased (by 0.7 percent annually).[2]

How can one ensure that more people find jobs at a time when everyone
claims that there is a shortage of work? The answer must begin with the
cause of unemployment. Since the student revolt in the late 1960s, labor
has been able, at least in Europe, to obtain ever higher rewards. These
increases exceeded the growth in labor productivity; as a consequence, jobs
were destroyed. The first wage push at the end of the 1960s coincided with
the dollar's depreciation against European currencies. The second wage
push in the early 1970s occurred at a time when the terms of trade deteriorated due to the first oil shock. Moreover, the wage increase compatible
with low unemployment would have had to be below the rise in labor
productivity (as we measure it) for a second reason: the baby boomers were
about to enter the labor market. This posed a problem similar to the influx
into West Germany of returning soldiers and refugees after 1945. The
question as to who failed in the existing situation is a touchy one for both
employer and employee organizations, but possibly also for economists
who believe they have an educational function in society.

Increasing evidence supports the hypothesis that unemployment is indeed related to wages. Gutierrez-Camara and Vaubel (1981), Roth (1982)
and Kirkpatrick (1982) have produced solid econometric work to test and
support the dependence of employment on real wages. Lehment (1982),
also from the Kiel Institute of World Economics, has produced a time-series
analysis for West Germany in support of the wage hypothesis. In contrast,
public discussion tends to exclude wages from the possible causes of unemployment. Perhaps it is the great economist who in his model assumed
rigid money wages who has to bear some responsibility for it.

Thus, the shortest way out of the current malaise seems to be blocked off. This can also be seen from the confused reaction of German employers' associations to the proposal of a temporary halt in the rise of money wages. Instead, the idea of a shorter work week is increasingly accepted. It means that the right to work is to be rationed so that everyone gets a fair share in a volume of work that has become too small. On the surface, the argument seems quite plausible: if the "whip" of excessive wages has led to a percentage rise in labor productivity that exceeds the percentage increase of the national product (which is, after all, the output of all hours of work), then the number of hours "needed" is apparently becoming smaller. Social engineers, having observed this for the past, tend to extrapolate the relationship into the future. They speak of a "wage-productivity scissors" and turn their "theory" into a prescription for policy. Nothing needs to be revised or corrected on the wage front, provided everybody is induced to work fewer hours. This sounds convenient to people at the wage bargaining table. Ordinary people led by common sense may intuitively question the cure on the ground that so far, rather few problems could actually be solved by resting or doing less rather than by pulling up one's sleeves. The common sense is right: more rather than less work has to be done to form more capital and, through this, to create new and more productive jobs. Unfortunately economists have not been particularly well trained for revealing pseudo problems and pseudo solutions for what they are.

Just as in the 1920s when conditions in Germany were similar, false diagnoses and therapies for labor market problems are aided and abetted by involving the so-called purchasing-power theory of wages. This theory conveys a message simple enough to be carried on banners at demonstrations: higher wages lead to more consumer demand (provided no jobs are lost), and they increase total demand (provided the velocity of circulation of a given money volume increases). But both provisos are critical:

1. Whether jobs are maintained or lost depends on whether investment activity responds positively (to more consumer demand) or negatively (because of a profit squeeze). Investment behavior is the key. Consumer spending may help, though only for a short while, but investment that creates permanent jobs is likely to be impaired.

2. Should the velocity of circulation fail to increase, there is a quick remedy: increase the money supply. In this perspective, the purchasing power theory of wages just calls for more money to be brought into circulation—not by banks or through fiscal deficits but through wage increases.

It is tantamount to proposing that the government might simply hand out the money needed to finance higher wages to employers directly.

Yet when it comes to giving more money to people with a high propensity to consume, the central bank might simply throw the money out the window. Such an increase in the money supply would be once and for all, while higher wage rates, once agreed and awarded, may de facto be irreversible as a minimum. The problem is familiar from fiscal pump priming: after it has incurred a deficit to fight a recession, the government has a permanent burden that reduces its fiscal flexibility in the future. From this we draw the general conclusion that even if monetary expansion is justified (if that is the message of the purchasing power theory of wages), it should never involve methods that introduce irreversibilities. Apart from this, it is worth recalling that monetary expansion has effects on output and employment only if and to the extent that it is not neutralized by an induced increase in nominal wages, interest rates, and prices (Hume effect).

In the present circumstances [1982], it may well be appropriate for Germany to end the disinflation process and to speed up monetary expansion. Such a strategy, however, would be justified only if we could be sure that the expansion really had its full effect on output and not fuel inflation. For this, a voluntary wage pause is needed, a consensus not to raise wages in response. Wage restraint, on the other hand, needs to be coupled with an expansionary policy package in order to produce its full employment effect. Given the extent of the unemployment problem, nominal wages should be kept constant for a considerably longer time than the half-year that is currently considered in the public discussion. I would plead for turning the pause for nominal wage increases, once the upswing has started, into a longer-term pause with regard to real wage increases. This means that automatic indexation should be permitted in collective bargaining contracts wherever there is a voluntary agreement not to raise money wages for other reasons. In that case, all improvements in labor productivity would directly or indirectly contribute to job creation.

Given the scarcity of physical capital from which the German economy is suffering, it would be desirable for workers to participate in the process of capital formation. The pause in real wage increases should therefore be followed by real wage increases that are channeled into capital formation: workers who earn more should be induced to save more, and they should save more for improving the capital stock of their workplaces. Profit participation of workers to promote capital formation, as an alternative to overall increases in real wages, could serve to eliminate poor worker motivation as it is observed here or there. Some unions, which are very centralized, will, of course, raise objections. But if in the course of time collective wage bargaining and industrial relations should become more decentralized, as must be expected, it will be at the level of the firm or the plant that workers will discover their true interests. It is at that level anyway where it will be decided whether work opportunities arise or disappear, whether productivity increases or not, and whether the wage is genuinely earned or merely received. Those who are skeptical about the capacity of organizations and their members to learn should not forget that people's thinking and behavior will sooner or later adjust to be in conformity with the necessities of their real situation.

Productivity gains that permit a rise in real wages without destroying jobs (that is, the employment-neutral or genuine productivity progress) flow from improved skills and a better quality of capital goods. Compared to technological leapfrogging into nuclear technology or the space age, as it has been pushed by governments and defense-related research lobbies, the advance brought about in the market at the level of the innovative firm appears more humane. It is certainly more acceptable because it occurs in incremental steps, which people can comprehend. Although piecemeal technical progress or piecemeal engineering (to use Karl Popper's term) is beneficial to economic as well as social welfare, it often suffers from the general criticism that is aroused by that progress which, according to Lenin, springs from the barrel of the gun.

The true agent of economic progress is the entrepreneur, whom no one placed more at center stage in economics than Joseph Schumpeter, the other great economist of this century who was born one hundred years ago. While Keynes, his macrotheory, and its application in the form of global demand management were the guiding visions for the 1960s and early 1970s, until their policy potential was exhausted, the 1980s and 1990s appear to be closer to Schumpeter and his vision of entrepreneurship. The entrepreneur of the future will have to cooperate more closely and for mutual benefit with workers who are themselves enterprising and capital forming.

This means that the progress needed to bring about a sufficiently rising volume of employment at constant or rising real incomes may also have to be propelled by those who are still conventionally called workers. This group includes not only employees in research and development positions but employees everywhere, provided they work in sufficiently decentralized systems, are fairly free to learn from experiments, and may apply new

insights and knowledge on the job. The incentive for entrepreneurial behavior on the job may come from profit participation. Enterprising employees could greatly help us to break out of the great stagnation of the
1970s and 1980s.

In contrast to Thünen's society, which was rural-feudalist and based on
land as the main factor of production, and in contrast to the society that
Marx and Keynes analyzed with an emphasis on conventional capital, the
society that will give the economy new impulses in the coming decades
will, if I am not totally mistaken, be a society in which human capital counts
for more than physical capital. We may call it a learning society or a
knowledge-forming society. It could be human capitalism in the Schumpeterian tradition.

In this perspective, Thünen's answer to the question of the fair wage
refers not only to the pure wage for labor but also to the renumeration for
human capital offered by employees and for the risks that enterprising
people are allowed to accept at their workplaces. When time has come to
speak in those terms—perhaps at the one hundredth anniversary of Mannheim University, and I hope in happier circumstances—someone may
again place wages, labor, and productivity into the center of interest. He or
she will then be able to cite—and I trust, with more justification than I
am—the formula on Thünen's headstone.

## Notes

This chapter is slightly amended version of an address given on November 26,
1982, on the occasion of the seventy-fifth anniversary of the University of Mannheim. At the same time, the address was intended as an attempt to demonstrate the
fertility of Johann Heinrich von Thünen's scientific approach on the occasion of his
two hundredth birthday.

1. These are hard facts against which one may wish to protest. It is not surprising
that the protestations are, in the first instance, directed against the model that
makes such predictions. But in reality these protestations are directed against the
circumstances that the model represents—a competitive order.

2. The figures are taken from Giersch and Wolter (1982, Table 5), reprinted here as
chapter 6.

## References

Giersch, Herbert. 1982. "Ausbruch aus der Stagnation. Chancen für neue Arbeits-
plätze." In Risiken und Chancen der künftigen Wirtschaftsentwicklung. Institut für
Weltwirtschaft, Kiel Discussion Papers, no. 84, March.

Giersch, Herbert, and Frank Wolter. 1983. "Towards an Explanation of the Productivity Slowdown: An Acceleration-Deceleration Hypothesis." *Economic Journal* 93, no. 369:35–55.

Gutierrez-Camara, José L., and Roland Vaubel. 1981. "Reducing the Cost of Reducing Inflation through Gradualism, Preannouncement or Indexation? The International Evidence." *Weltwirtschaftliches Archiv* 117:244–261.

Keynes, John Maynard. 1936. *The General Theory of Employment, Interest and Money.* London: Macmillan.

Kirkpatrick, Grant. 1982. "Real Factor Prices and German Manufacturing Employment: A Time Series Analysis, 1960I–1979IV." *Weltwirtschaftliches Archiv* 118: 79–103.

Krelle, Wilhelm. 1961. "Lohn: (I) Theorie." In *Handwörterbuch der Sozialwissenschaften,* 7:1–16. Edited by Erwin v. Beckerath et al. Stuttgart: Gustav Fischer.

Lehment, Harmen. 1982. *Der Einfluß der Lohnpolitik auf Produktion, Beschäftigung und Preise in der Bundesrepublik Deutschland seit 1973.* Institut für Weltwirtschaft, Kiel Discussion Papers, no. 82, February.

Roth, Jürgen. 1982. *Mehr Beschäftigung durch Reallohnzurückhaltung—Zum Streit zwischen kosten- und nachfrageorientierter Lohnpolitik.* Institut für Weltwirtschaft, Kiel Discussion Papers, no. 85, March.

Schumpeter, Joseph A. 1942. *Capitalism, Socialism, and Democracy.* New York: Harper & Brothers.

Thomas, Brinley. 1973. *Migration and Economic Growth: A Study of Great Britain and the Atlantic Economy.* 2d ed., Cambridge: Cambridge University Press.

Thünen, Johann Heinrich von. 1826/1850/1863. *Der isolirte Staat in Beziehung auf Landwirthschaft und Nationalökonomie.* Vol. 1, Hamburg: Friedrich Perthes (1826); vol. 2, part 1, Rostock: G. B. Leopold (1850); vol. 2, part 2, and vol. 3, Rostock: G. B. Leopold (1863).

Tobin, James. 1980. *Asset Accumulation and Economic Activity: Reflections on Contemporary Macroeconomic Theory.* Yrjö Jahnsson Lectures. Oxford: Basil Blackwell.

# 8                           The Age of Schumpeter

The centenary [in 1983] of Schumpeter's birth coincides with a revival of Schumpeterian economics. Could the third quarter of this century justly be called the "age of Keynes" (Hicks 1974), the present fourth quarter has a fair chance of becoming the age of Schumpeter. Before giving some substance to this proposition, I shall present a short introduction to Schumpeter's life, work, and paradigm.

## I

Schumpeter was born in a small place in Moravia, the only child of an Austrian couple. When his father, a cloth manufacturer, died four years later, his mother moved to Graz (Austria) where he attended elementary school until the age of ten. Then his mother married a retired general. For Schumpeter this meant access to Austria's foremost school, where he passed with flying colors. At Vienna University (1901–6) he was inspired by Böhm-Bawerk and Wieser, Carl Menger's students. After taking his doctorate in 1906 he spent the summer term in Berlin, was a research student at the London School of Economics, and accepted a position at the International Court in Cairo, from where he returned to Vienna to submit his habilitation thesis. Shortly afterward (1909) he became associate professor in Czernowitz (now in the Soviet Union) and, two years later (1911), full professor in Graz, where he taught until 1919, except for 1913–14. During that year he was visiting professor at Columbia University, which gave him an honorary doctor's degree at the age of thirty-one. His last six years in Austria (1919–25) were devoted to nonacademic ambitions which he could not realize, neither as an Austrian minister of finance for less than

Reprinted with permission from *The American Economic Review* 74 (May 1984): 103–109. Copyright 1984 by the American Economic Association.

eight months in 1919, nor as the head of a private bank, which eventually collapsed in 1927, leaving him with a high personal debt to be paid off. It was with great relief that he received offers from two universities in Japan and Germany, accepting the one from Bonn where he was professor of public finance for seven years. Shortly before Hitler came to power, Schumpeter went to Harvard. He was a cofounder of the Econometric Society, served as its president from 1937 to 1941, was elected to the office of president of the American Economic Association (1948), and was designated to be the first president of the newly founded International Economic Association. In January 1950, Schumpeter died in his home in Taconic, Connecticut.

## II

Schumpeter's main work as a scholar has three strands: an evaluation of past and current economic theory, starting with his postdoctoral book on the state of economic theory (1908) and ending with the posthumous *History of Economic Analysis* (1954); the elaboration of a theory of economic evolution, starting with *The Theory of Economic Development* (1912) and culminating in *Business Cycles* (1939); and the advancement of a theory of social and institutional change, starting with *Crisis of the Tax State* (1918), culminating in *Capitalism, Socialism and Democracy* (1942), and ending with a paper at the AEA meetings, "The March into Socialism" (1950).

## III

Obituaries and later biographic essays[1] allow offering a stylized picture of Schumpeter's fascinating personality.[2]

Schumpeter was highly sensitive to aesthetic values. He always remained the aristocratic gentleman of the late Austrian Empire who loved elegant clothing, refined meals, polished manners, cultivated conversations, and, above all, beautiful women. His style of writing was baroque, with frequent excursions into seductive side issues, occasionally ending up in mere l'art pour l'art. Even as an economist he seems to reveal an aesthetic bias: in his admiration for Walras and in his enthusiasm for the art of formalizing complex phenomena, an art which lay beyond his own reach.

Schumpeter was a staunch individualist. He loved to "épater les bourgeois," that is, to express shocking minority views even at the risk of isolating himself from the mainstream of political and economic thinking. Always ready to display a wide range of sparkling ideas he excited

a large number of students who later became famous economists—
Samuelson, Schneider, Smithies, Stackelberg, Stolper, and Sweezy, to
mention only those whose names begin with S like Schumpeter. However,
his impact was inspiration rather than indoctrination: in Schumpeter's
Socratic view of scholarship, there was no legitimate place for the mis-
sionary zeal and the fighting spirit of intellectual sectarianism. Furthermore,
his work was too original to permit easy paradigmatic simplification: he
advanced into dynamics when mainstream economics was grappling with
static optimality; he stuck to microeconomics when the tide of Keynesian
macro theory supplied a new generation of economists with a fertile intellectual playground; and he turned to historical methods when econometrics
—under Schumpeter's own intellectual sponsorship—began to swamp
economics.

In accordance with his social background Schumpeter was inclined to see
the world from an elitarian perspective. He regarded clusters of talented
people as the driving force behind economic and political history: entrepreneurs who push forward society's technological frontier; a nobility to protect the capitalist system by performing the political functions which are
alien to the commercial outlook of the bourgeoisie; and the intellectuals
who help to destroy capitalism by undermining its ethical basis in an
almost tragic process of critical subversion. Even Schumpeter's unfortunate
decision to enter politics in 1919 seems to be in accordance with the role
which he saw for himself as a member of the old elite in a period of
transition.[3]

## IV

The essentials of Schumpeter's thought can best be inferred from his relation to Keynes and the economics of Keynes. Apart from a streak of
jealousy which may have distorted his judgment, Schumpeter's apparent
dislike of Keynes's gospel had deep roots in basic differences of a paradigmatic nature. Consider his penetrating critique of the *General Theory*
which focuses on four crucial points. First, he objected to what he called
"Keynes' practice of offering, in the garb of general scientific truth, advice
which ... carries meaning only with reference to the practical exigencies of
the unique historical situation of a given time and country" (1936, 791),
namely, England in the 1930s, a practice which Schumpeter—then a detached observer of worldly events—regarded as appropriate for a politi-
cian, but not for a "scientific" economist. Second, Schumpeter objected to
Keynes's lighthearted use of economic aggregates, most of all "the exten-

sion of the Marshallian cross" (1936, 793) to aggregate demand and supply functions, a procedure which the microeconomist Schumpeter deemed to be highly suspect. Third, Schumpeter criticized Keynes's assumption of a given technology with a lack of investment opportunities, which appeared absurd to the man who had declared the dynamics of technology, the process of creative destruction, as the very essence of the capitalist system. And finally, there was Keynes's message that unemployment could be attributed to underconsumption and, hence, to private thrift and an unequal income distribution, a message which, according to Schumpeter, enabled the disciples to destroy "the last pillar of the bourgeois argument" (1951, 289). To Schumpeter, the historian of intellectual and institutional change, this message made up the essence of the Keynesian revolution.

Behind this fundamental critique we find a social vision which in some crucial respects is diametrically opposed to that of Keynes. Schumpeter's vision takes shape when we recognize how he characterized his great contemporary in a later essay: "He was surprisingly insular, even in philosophy, but nowhere so much as in economics" (1951, 274). "He was not the sort of man who would bend the full force of his mind to the individual problems of coal, textiles, steel, shipbuilding. Least of all was he the man to preach regenerative creeds" (pp. 274ff). This point about "regenerative creeds"—made in 1946—highlights Schumpeter's postwar optimism. The point is gaining more and more relevance in our present phase of slow world economic growth, a phase with cumulating pains of delayed adjustment. In such a phase, the faith in the regenerative forces of a decentralized market system has once more become critical for the choice of the appropriate socioeconomic paradigm. Let me take this presumption as a justification for considering now a possible—non-Keynesian—paradigm along Schumpeterian lines of thought, hoping that it may help us to better interpret the present quarter century following the "age of Keynes."

## V

Such a post-Schumpeterian paradigm may be stylized in the form of ten basic postulates.

1. The approach is micro rather than macro, socioeconomic (if not socioecological) rather than mechanistic. In the spirit of Schumpeter's "methodological individualism" it concentrates on processes rather than outcomes, on voluntarism rather than determinism. Being addressed to current world economic development, it stresses relevance rather than rigor, movement rather than static optimality.

2. Steady-state equilibriums may be attractive aesthetic devices, but economic life and history show cycles and discontinuities as a normal feature: sunspot cycles, life cycles, product cycles, election cycles, fashion cycles, seasonal cycles, business cycles, growth cycles, technological revolutions, and all sorts of lagged adjustments and overreactions to unanticipated events in the markets for factors and products, for assets and monies. With an unknown future, civilizations can only learn by trial and error; equilibriums can only be identified by passing them from the other side, just as the pendulum finds its point of rest only in a process of damped oscillations.

3. What matters most in present circumstances are the driving forces of economic development in advanced countries. Emphasis, therefore, is on the growth and dissemination of knowledge, on pathbreaking entrepreneurs who create new markets and successful "intra-preneurs" who rejuvenate old firms, on credit creation for the supply of venture capital, and on Schumpeterian competition (i.e., on innovative monopolistic competition rather than sterile perfect competition, on oligopolistic rivalry rather than collusive equilibriums, on aggressive trading rather than mere arbitrage transactions).

4. In the international economy which Schumpeter mostly neglected—despite an occasional sympathy for U.S. protectionism in what Schumpeter called a "mercantilist, nationalist, bellicose world" (1940, 7)—the emphasis for the advanced countries is on free trade rather than fair trade (trade minus competition); for the less advanced countries it is on offensive export orientation rather than protective import substitution, and for North-South relations it is on product cycle goods, private resource transfer, and catching-up processes.

5. Elasticities, and notably adjustments involving the supply side, are primarily a function of time because of institutional and technical rigidities and inflexibilities in behavior patterns. The relevant time span is longer than the Keynesian short run (which Schumpeter equated with a forty-month cycle), but shorter than the Marxian long run (which includes the eventual breakdown of the system). In terms of calendar time, we may estimate this medium run to cover two to three decades, so as to include at least one turning point of a Kondratieff cycle in Schumpeter's three-cycle hypothesis.

6. In such a cyclical setting, and with an unlimited potential for the growth of knowledge, stagnation can be taken as a temporary phenomenon unless the economy is overregulated. Even in the absence of new technological revolutions, stagnation will last only until relative prices of factors and goods have sufficiently adjusted to restore the incentive structure: profits

and profit expectations must be high enough to induce entrepreneurs to overcome barriers to entry erected in favor of existing suppliers.

7. The real rate of interest may be zero in the model of a stationary state, as the young Schumpeter asserted; in a dynamic world it can turn out to be negative, as in the recent phase of unanticipated inflation but will thereafter be correspondingly higher as it is now in the subsequent period of correction, when (a) monetary disinflation is not fully anticipated, (b) saving habits in the private sector and spending habits in the public sector are slow to adjust to an increasing demand for loanable funds, (c) investors are slow to shift from excessive capital-deepening to more capital-saving technologies, or (d) investment is clouded with too much uncertainty due to a reorientation in the development process.

8. Uncertainty and limits to growth also result from political attempts at impairing property rights and, if intellectuals are the propelling force, from their influence on the social atmosphere, including the public's attitude toward technical progress, entrepreneurship, self-help, and Schumpeterian competition on a national and international plane. The "march into socialism," however, is not inevitable, as intellectuals in their monopolistic competition are also innovative in producing and propagating alternative models of society or even learn from experience as they often do when they enter practical life or when they live under real socialism.

9. In an open world economy, Schumpeterian competition also prevails among governments and central banks. Such policy competition—as competition elsewhere—is efficient in the medium run as a process of discovery and learning although—or because—it offers unpleasant short-run lessons to the misbehaving countries and central banks. In a (Keynesian) short-term paradigm—so close to the heart of politicians in office—these lessons are denounced as beggar-thy-neighbor policies, thus yielding popular arguments in favor of policy cartels called "coordination."

10. Entrepreneurial talent is in almost unlimited supply, but in some countries it finds productive outlets only abroad, or less productive (or even counterproductive) use in politics and government, in public and private bureaucracies or in the military.

## VI

A post-Schumpeterian paradigm has to cover the whole world economy with all its diversity. In accordance with the strength of the (re)generative forces we may distinguish

1. "Advanced Schumpeterian areas" which have plenty of innovating firms and people to act as growth locomotives (for example, parts of the United States and Japan);

2. " Less advanced Schumpeterian areas" which are populated by firms and people who as imitators are active absorbers of foreign technologies and capital (for example, Taiwan, Singapore, South Korea, Hong Kong);

3. "Advanced Keynesian areas" which suffer from distorted factor prices depressing the marginal efficiency of capital and from institutional rigidities impeding the entry of new entrepreneurship so that government deficits and foreign demand are needed as substitutes for autonomous investment (for example, large parts of continental Europe);

4. " Less developed Keynesian economies" which for similar reasons rely on import substitution strategies, government deficits financed by inflation, and hopes for a "New International Economic Order" (for example, Latin America and parts of Southern Europe).

This typology is, of course, not complete; we may further identify "Ricardian economies" which exploit their natural resources and convert them into consumption or other forms of wealth, "Malthusian regions" which find themselves in the population trap, and "Marxian countries" which conduct central planning and state trading.

## VII

The geographic base of this post-Schumpeterian paradigm can be systematized by making use of a theory of location derived from the writings of a German economist who must be mentioned today together with Keynes, Marx, and Schumpeter, as he was born 200 years ago: Johann Heinrich von Thünen. In a book published in 1826 Thünen not only prediscovered marginalism (which earned him high praise from Schumpeter) but also developed a center-periphery model for the spatial division of labor on a homogeneous (i.e., non-Ricardian) plane surrounded by a wilderness. Thünen took the central market as given, but the center can well be explained by (1) the provision of a public good called law enforcement or defense which is—as Adam Smith has taught us—a prerequisite for the division of labor, or by (2) assuming a point of superior resource endowment with high-quality land, raw material deposits, or favorable climatic conditions which yield a Ricardian rent, or by (3) introducing external economies of agglomeration which generate knowledge to be used by entrepreneurs and which, therefore, produce the Schumpeterian transitory rent which we call profit. In the real world we can depict many centers and a hierarchical order of them, but the major center-periphery systems in the world economy have turned out to be supranational like the Pax Britannica of the nineteenth century, the Pax Americana of the twentieth century, or the present triple center system of North America, Western Europe, and Japan (leaving aside the Marxian center in Eastern Europe). As economic development essentially consists of exploiting knowledge, a social atmosphere conducive to knowledge production must be taken to be the most important element in the formation of growth centers. This is why MIT and Stanford have become the Mecca and Medina of achievement-oriented thinkers and operators; why some countries like Japan and France strive hard on the technology front; and why large parts of Europe where equality was considered to be more important than (Schumpeterian) excellence presently tend to fall behind in world economic development.

## VIII

The present quarter of the twentieth century is likely to become Schumpeter's age, since autonomous investment—at least in Europe—has become so weak during the past decade that the sociopolitical focus is shifting toward regenerative forces which seem to have been weakened by extensive reliance on monetary-fiscal management. The medicine of boosting demand surely helped in the short run. Where it was periodically withdrawn for the sake of fighting inflation, it even helped over a number of business cycles. In the medium run, however, it was bound to weaken the patient's motivations and his overall physical strength. This is so because any kind of unconditional support to suppliers—from full-employment guarantees, fine-tuning promises, and programs of industrial policy right down to specific subsidies and sophisticated protective devices against import competition—must be presumed to produce a dependence effect and gradually weaken the need to adjust, and with it the need that is proverbially considered to be the mother of invention and innovation. In more general terms, it can be said that permissive policies promoted the march into the soft society which, for lack of a hard constitutional dividing line between social goals and individual responsibilities, became overwhelmed by populist pressures. Moreover, permissive policies offer incentives for rent seeking, thus distracting entrepreneurial talent from future-orientated activities to lobbying and distributional issues. Eventually, governments find themselves at the limits of the tax state which the young Schumpeter clearly foresaw.

The post-Schumpeterian paradigm proposed here includes the vision of a turnaround to be brought about by regenerative forces. Where can they be found? (1) We observe disillusionment with government policies, including the welfare state, and an increasing sensitivity to fiscal issues. (2) We witness the growth of the underground economy which has a good chance of becoming a school for entrepreneurship, similar to the black market in Europe's initial postwar phase before the miraculous reconstruction, and also a spectacular growth of self-employment and job creation in new firms for new products in some parts of Europe as well as in the United States. (3) We visualize how severe lapses from full employment are about to weaken rigid labor market institutions even in syndicalist Europe where a tendency toward greater balkanization and flexibility has developed. (4) And we take it that further progress in telecommunication will not only boost investment by itself but also by facilitating decentralized decision making. Should these new technologies promote decentralized production, they can be expected to further improve the incentive structure by making the old factory system obsolete and with it the rigid labor market institutions inherited from the past.

The turnaround may be firmly expected but it can come about only gradually. At least in Europe, dynamic forces are hampered by encrusted institutions. Perhaps technical progress alone will suffice to overcome institutional obstacles by carrying innovative activities into unregulated fields. But in many regions and industries on both sides of the Atlantic, a temporary crisis may be both inevitable and necessary to bring about the destruction which Schumpeter considered to precede creation or to go along with it. By widening the spread in earnings between forward-looking and backward-looking persons, firms, industries, and countries, the turnaround will strain widespread feelings for equity and the so-called social-democratic consensus. And there will be no reward for tolerating inequality until the turnaround has actually led to faster growth. Rawlsians will, therefore, have to stretch their implicit time horizon beyond the Keynesian short run, so as to include the medium run which is the time horizon required for starting and successfully completing adjustment processes on the supply side. Hence time will remain a resource in short supply, but in high demand.

As an indicator of how much the time pattern of preferences diverges from the time pattern of opportunities and necessities, I submit taking the dramatic change from excessively low to excessively high real rates of interest in the world economy. In my view this change reveals how much society in the past has allowed itself to live at the expense of its future. Lower real interest rates will eventually come back, albeit not by decree or a different monetary regime but only after the world has again learned to pay its tribute to the laws of efficiency for the benefit of capital formation. In the international context the turnaround will not get underway before a Schumpeterian perspective has gained widespread support in the industrialized and newly industrialized countries of the North. Only after more northern entrepreneurs, firms, and governments have adopted forward-looking strategies that anticipate the changing international pattern of comparative advantages, will southern entrepreneurs, firms, and governments feel encouraged to link themselves more closely to the northern growth locomotives. When this has happened, an accelerated world dynamics will raise the marginal efficiency of capital in the South, and thereby will—in a virtuous circle—promote a sustainable private resource transfer to the South and also diminish the high level of uncertainty currently prevailing on international capital markets.

Once world economic growth has reaccelerated—say toward the end of this decade [1980s] or in the 1990s—Schumpeter in his Valhalla can step back from the intellectual leadership which this chapter attributes to him in the succession of Keynes. But for today the question is whether the man who wanted to be the greatest economist of his time could be imagined to agree with the preceding attempt at bringing his version in line with the course of economic history after his death. A competent answer must be reserved to those who were lucky enough to know him personally. So I have to be quiet. What remains is the wider question whether any Schumpeter-based paradigm has relevance at all for this quarter century, but here the judge can only be future history itself.

## Notes

I am grateful to Karl-Heinz Paqué for valuable comments on earlier drafts.

1. See the seminal contribution by Gottfried Haberler (1950) and the remarkable paper by Christian Seidl (1982), who succeeds in discarding some old myths about Schumpeter through careful analysis of the historical evidence.

2. For a more detailed analysis along the following lines, see Karl-Heinz Paqué (1983).

3. Of course, personal ambitions played their part as well. On the whole issue, see Seidl (1982, 38).

## References

Haberler, Gottfried, "Joseph Alois Schumpeter 1883–1950," *Quarterly Journal of Economics*, August 1950, *64*, 333–72.

Hicks, John R., *The Crisis in Keynesian Economics*, Oxford 1974.

Paqué, Karl-Heinz, "Einige Bemerkungen zur Persönlichkeit Joseph Alois Schumpeters," Kieler Arbeitspapier No. 193, Institut für Weltwirtschaft, Kiel, December 1983.

Schumpeter, Joseph A., *Das Wesen und der Hauptinhalt der theoretischen Nationaloekonomie*, Leipzig 1908.

————, *Theorie der Wirtschaftlichen Entwicklung*, Leipzig 1912 (English: *The Theory of Economic Development: An Inquiry into Profits, Capital, Credit Interest, and the Business Cycle*), Cambridge, MA, 1934.

————, *Die Krise des Steuerstaats*, Leipzig, 1918.

————, book review of Keynes, J. M., *The General Theory of Employment, Interest and Money, Journal of the American Statistical Association*, 1936, 31, 791–95.

————, *Business Cycles*, Vols. I, II, New York; London, 1939.

————, "The Influence of Protective Tariffs on the Industrial Development of the United States," an address before the Academy of Political Science, April 11, 1940.

————, *Capitalism, Socialism and Democracy*, New York, 1942.

————, "The March into Socialism," *American Economic Review Proceedings*, May 1950, 40, 446–56.

————, "John Maynard Keynes 1883–1946," *American Economic Review*, September 1946, 36, 495–518; reprinted in *Ten Great Economists, From Marx to Keynes*, London 1951, 260–91.

————, *History of Economic Analysis*, Vols. I, II (from manuscript by Elisabeth Boody-Schumpeter), New York 1954.

Seidl, Christian, "Joseph Alois Schumpeter in Graz," Research Memorandum No. 8201, Universität Graz, August, 1982.

von Thünen, Johann Heinrich, *Der isolierte Staat in Beziehung auf Landwirtschaft und Nationalökonomie*, Hamburg, 1826.

# 9                      Openness and Incentives

Openness vis-à-vis the world and an improved incentive system at home are the key requirements for a lasting reacceleration of economic growth in Europe, the United States, and indeed most other parts of the world. More specifically, the policy-oriented message to be propounded in this chapter is essentially twofold: (1) Europe could already learn much from the United States to improve its incentive system and to make its internal markets more open. (2) Openness vis-à-vis the world economy is a task to be pushed onto the policy agenda in the United States, as well as in Europe and Japan. Such international openness involves more competition among governments and central banks, a competition that can support our hopes for limited government and sound money in future decades.

Forty years ago, the outlook was much less bright; for many people in Europe, it was almost desperate. My own country, Germany, although no longer on the road to serfdom, was still in a shambles. Millions lived as displaced persons lacking food and shelter in a centrally administered economy that left them no other room for self-help than the black market. But night changed into day almost suddenly when two measures were taken that had long before been advocated by liberal economists like Walter Eucken and Wilhelm Röpke: a currency reform and the quick removal of many controls. The currency reform was made by the Allied authorities; the removal of controls was the heroic decision of one man, Ludwig Erhard. Sound money and the restoration of incentives by reopening the market system produced a miracle that few had dared to expect. Without Erhard, who later succeeded Adenauer as chancellor of the Federal Republic, the Marshall Plan, as useful as it actually was, might just have been another case of inefficient aid.

---

This is a slightly modified version of the presidential address given at the regional meeting of the Mont Pèlerin Society in Indianapolis, September 6, 1987.

The lesson to be drawn is worth preserving. The controversy around the events was essentially about supply elasticities. Market pessimists and socialists stressed the existence of bottlenecks that would produce huge rents and unacceptable inequalities should controls be lifted. In contrast, members of the Mont Pèlerin Society (MPS) and other economists of our persuasion argued that supply elasticities would turn out to be high after a short while provided individuals and firms were free to adjust. They were right. GNP growth rates in Germany averaged 8 percent in the 1950s and 4.5 percent in the 1960s. Mass unemployment, essentially due to a shortage of physical capital, disappeared in the 1950s. In the early 1960s the capital stock grew so fast that immigrant labor had to be pulled in. Surely there were unique factors at work: the economies of reconstruction and catching up. But a comparative look at socialist East Germany demonstrates how much the Federal Republic owes to the opening of markets and the restoration of the incentive system.

This lesson is in danger of being forgotten; memories are short, and the miracle has been fading since the late 1960s. Fortunately, recent history has new examples to offer. European countries can learn from the miraculous employment performance of the U.S. economy in the difficult period after 1973, from the success stories of the small and open countries in the Far East, from the improved economic performance of Britain in recent years, and from experiments with free enterprise zones in several countries. We also see our case supported by the astounding effects of domestic market liberalization on agricultural production in less developed countries and by the hopes that millions of people attach to the promises of greater openness and better incentives in China and the Soviet bloc.

On the European continent, we observe encouraging signs at the polls. They testify to sound instincts of the population in most countries. But economic policies and performances lag behind. The unemployment rates are far too high—11 percent on average in the European Community, 8 to 9 percent in West Germany. In comparing unemployment figures in Europe and the United States, we have to keep in mind that most European countries have lower female participation rates and much more disguised unemployment among formally enrolled students than the United States. Europe's unemployment has hardly a Keynesian content. A mere demand boost would soon accelerate inflation. This is why such advice from the American East Coast finds little response. Europe's deficiency is on the supply side. Just as the German currency reform of 1948 would not have produced a miracle by itself, but did so spectacularly in conjunction with a removal of controls, so does a better employment performance in Europe require a dismantling of those restrictions that make the labor market inflexible. It is this inflexibility that is meant by the term *Eurosclerosis*, not any deficiency in high tech, as some politicians and engineers believe. The focus is to be on the whole employment system, including barriers to entry for new entrepreneurs (Giersch 1985).

The inflexibilities blamed by the term *Eurosclerosis* are likely to develop everywhere, but they prevail less in the United States than in Europe, and they are more deeply rooted in European traditions. One root is the medieval guild system. It rested on the privilege of producers to organize themselves in cartels and to protect these cartels against outside competition by institutional barriers to entry. The apprenticeship system, as it still exists in Germany, is an essential part of it. This system is good for the formation of human capital but separates insiders and outsiders. To be sure, the propensity to form cartels always exists among producers of the same trade, as Adam Smith's famous dictum underlines. This holds for services just as well as for goods markets, as we know from professional organizations, craft unions, and labor unions. But without government protection, the rents that keep these cartels together would be washed away. The mere threat of competition from cheaper sources of supply abroad or from the technological frontier may be sufficient to make participants behave "as if" there were actual competition. In the past, potential competition from abroad was strengthened by technical progress in international transportation; as to the future, we can anticipate great benefits for international competition from progress in telecommunication. No wonder that governments have been—and will be—under protectionist pressures most of the time.

Europe's guild and cartel heritage had and still has its protective belt, also in the world of ideas. Let me mention the ideas of nationalism and autarky, paternalism and solidarity, syndicalism and guild socialism, French planning and German codetermination, of industrial democracy and a third way between capitalism and socialism. They all contributed to a corporatist ideology as the Catholic church did and still does with its socioeconomic teachings and its influence on the Christian-democratic parties on the Continent. The common denominator is a deeply conservative longing for a specific and limited order that promises fair results to those who form part of it. This conservatism contrasts with such apparently horrible things as cosmopolitism, Manchester liberalism, laissez-faire capitalism, or anarchy. Corporatist conservatism, in Europe and elsewhere, has on its side

• the belief in old, established professional ethics,

• the plausibility of quality and skill requirements for the paternalistic protection of supposedly uninformed consumers, and

• the emotional appeal of patriotism, xenophobia, and other forms of separating insiders from outsiders, including anti-Semitism.

Outsiders are always suspected of practicing dumping or other forms of beggar-thy-neighbor policies. They are seen to disturb the solidity of the specific order, the functioning of corporatism as a system.

It is my conviction that corporatism in the labor market bears the main responsibility for Europe's rising unemployment after 1973. At that time a wage wave (against which labor had been warned in at least one country) culminated to collide with a cost push arising from energy prices and environmental concerns. It produced a squeeze of profits and investment and thus a capital shortage at the very time when the baby boom generation entered Europe's labor market. Corporatism is an inflexible system. Earlier on, in the 1950s and 1960s, this system was slow to catch up with productivity advances when Europe's product markets developed surprisingly fast. The system at that time permitted an excess demand for labor—without an excess demand for goods: classic overemployment. Now, in the 1970s, the same inflexibility has produced the opposite result: excessive wages and, hence, classical unemployment. Full employment promises from governments made the wage negotiators insensitive to the negative employment effects they produced. And governments yielded when they were pressed to pay subsidies or to grant import protection wherever jobs came under the pressure of foreign competition. Corporatism gives birth to protectionism, domestic and international. This danger is great on both sides of the Atlantic.

Before making generalizations, there is a puzzle to be solved. Austria and Sweden, though often considered the most corporatist countries, used to have the lowest unemployment rates in Europe, together with Switzerland. To a large extent, the explanation is openness. Being small countries, they are almost bound—so to speak—by the force of nature to be open to international competition. And their neutrality prevented them from joining the European Community. Such natural and historic openness has two economic consequences. One is that outside competition is difficult to ignore or to shield off. Thus, the need to adjust is inevitable. The second positive effect is that openness due to smallness promotes consensus—as it does in the small group, in the club, in the family, in the corporation. Corporatism with consensus is more viable than corporatism without it or corporatism with class struggle. A corporatist consensus may even facilitate a necessary adjustment: in the Swedish case, real wages could be brought down by a currency devaluation in a social-democratic consensus. But in a longer perspective, we see Austria and Sweden facing heavy adjustment problems. Their celebrated "active labor market policy," which mainly consists of artificially cutting the supply of labor by administrative schemes like government training programs, amounts to little more than a strategy of hiding the unemployment that results from excessive wages and wage rigidities. Clearly, this cannot be a viable long-run solution.

The cure for Europe's disease, in my opinion, is a comprehensive strategy of openness with a three-fold emphasis on privatization, deregulation, and liberalization. As to the labor market, it seems to me to be most urgent to establish—on a constitutional level—a "citizen's right to work." It is to be understood as the right to sell one's services at any wage an employer finds acceptable, independent of what is stipulated in collective bargaining agreements. Such a right, if it existed, would need public protection, given the prevailing corporatist mood in Europe. Otherwise, unemployed workers might be afraid of exercising it; and potential employers might resent the danger of being accused of exploitation.

A supplementary right to unrestricted market entry appears to be equally necessary in Europe. The public debate about such a right would already be helpful by revealing where such barriers have been erected to exclude outsiders and thus to limit the supply of entrepreneurship. Once such an entrepreneurial right had been established, or were even only under serious discussion, a genuine process of discovery would soon gain momentum. It would make us aware of all the obstacles that have been erected over the years by legislative bodies and courts but also by administrative acts, a myriad of obstacles that hardly anybody can be completely aware of now.

These citizens' rights are abstract rules similar to those advocated by MPS members against public debt, big government, and increasing government interventions. Once established in statutes or only in people's minds, such abstract rules help to preserve the free society. But with regard to the right to work and the right of free entry into goods and service markets, we are far behind, even in public discussion, at least in Europe. A new awareness seems to be required on the old continent, a kind of citizens' movement for openness. Why has such a movement not started long ago? One possible answer lies in the proposition that "exit" is an alternative to "voice" and that for centuries a migration movement across the Atlantic was enough of an outlet to calm down voice and protest in overregulated Europe. Those who built the free society under the U.S. Constitution can now conserve it. Europe is far behind in the process of liberalization; it still has a largely unfinished agenda of openness. Consider only that *openness* is merely another word for *capitalism* and that in corporatist Europe, *capitalism* is still a dirty word.

Openness also means competitiveness. In fact, there is hardly any better way of defining competitiveness in an economically meaningful sense. Nobody who charges an excessive price is competitive; and every country can be competitive in an overall sense if it allows the exchange rate to be freely determined in a competitive market. A truly competitive country excels in attracting mobile resources from the rest of the world: human capital and physical capital, knowledge and technology. By being open and hence competitive, North America attracted human resources from feudalist and corporatist Europe. In recent years the United States has again attracted capital by running a current account deficit. In contrast to European politicians and many other observers, I do not mind these capital flows. Those who lend resources to the United States must know what they are doing since they have been warned by so many economists (and journalists) who tell them on the basis of macroeconomic data what precisely an imbalance is and how long it can last. What European politicians who worry have to realize is that capital flows across the Atlantic can surely be reduced and even reversed. But the condition is that Europe becomes more competitive on the world capital market. There is only one way to achieve this: Europe must offer better opportunities for entrepreneurship and investment by making its markets more open and its employment system more flexible. If capital imports are of great concern in the United States, the answer to my mind is not protectionism in goods markets—that is a great danger to the free world—but a correction of those government distortions that depress the U.S. savings rate.

Europe's disease of high unemployment and slow growth is not due only to its corporatism. It must also be attributed to the excesses of the welfare state and the negative incentive effects they produce. What is primarily at stake in present-day Europe in this context is (1) the incentive to search for a regular job—instead of being unemployed or doing occasional work in the shadow economy, and (2) the incentive to earn exceptional profits—instead of doing mere routine business.

There is no doubt that the welfare state in Europe has been greatly expanded over the past two decades. This is even more true if one includes government subsidies to agriculture and ailing industries and other forms of domestic and external protection. The impairment of the incentive system that such a comprehensive welfare state is bound to entail did perhaps not become so obvious when the economy was rolling along at full speed on the straight road of quantitative growth, as it did until the early 1970s. But when growth involves rapid structural change, as it does today in Europe under the impact of increasing competition from some newly industrializing countries, all this featherbedding is likely to be a severe brake on economic progress. Protection is a public bad because it destroys the public good of an enterprising social atmosphere.

Most of those who feel this way welcomed the American sharp turn toward reducing taxes under the Reagan administration. But our hopes that Europe would feel inspired to imitate the U.S. example quickly were spoiled by the noise about the emerging budget deficit and by the Keynesian interpretation given to it in prominent circles. Nevertheless, some steps in the right direction have been taken in Europe; other steps are under consideration. But they will be far from sufficient to restore fully the enterprising spirit in European countries. This is why we have to go on pleading not only for deregulation but also for the restoration of the incentive system through cuts in marginal tax rates.

Once a breakthrough has been made, success can be trusted to breed success in a virtuous circle similar to West Germany's postwar miracle. But even in a population that holds on to some memories of that successful experiment, it has proved impossible to arouse public emotions strongly enough to make politicians aware of a great opportunity for action on the tax front. Given this background, Erhard's 1948 reform under General Clay looks truly gigantic. Nothing remotely similar appears to be realistic for the time being. Even the simple and appealing rule that the government should let us have at our disposal at least half of the additional income we earn by rendering additional services to others was defeated in the German public debate about the modest tax reform scheduled for 1990. Thus, the principle of limited government will have to be continuously urged on the political agenda time and again, not only in the years but in the decades to come. Competition among national governments for internationally mobile resources will help.

The third postulate of constitutional importance, apart from free entry and low marginal taxes, is sound money. Here again the best guarantee for citizens is openness. It involves free competition among central banks, which amounts to a denationalization of money in practice. We are not as far from it as it may appear in abstract theory. One of its preconditions is free currency convertibility, for capital transactions as well as for trade. As a citizen, I think that everybody who wants to protest against her or his government should have an inalienable right to emigrate and to transfer her or his claims and property rights to the new place of residence abroad.

A second requirement is fully flexible exchange rates; they are necessary to avoid the high social cost of political misalignments and as indicators of good and bad behavior of central banks and governments.

In a regime of free international currency competition, national central banks have strong incentives to serve their customers loyally. Inflationary policies to boost demand artificially or to raise an inflation tax have quick boomerang effects. They induce capital flight and thus increase the real rate of interest at the expense of all immobile domestic resources, notably labor, as Mitterand had to learn when he made his socialist experiment in 1981. Such boomerang effects are the reason that Keynesians are so eager to propose, and some politicians are so fond of, international monetary cooperation or new gimmicks to tax the inflow and outflow of capital.

In contrast, sound money pays dividends in international currency competition. These dividends are received not by the central bank but by the owners of domestic resources. Savers can feel safer and investors can trust in stable financial conditions with rather low real interest rates. The examples of Switzerland and, to some extent, Germany indicate the importance of this point. The case of Switzerland also proves that small countries can do as well under flexible exchange rates as large countries. Only when unsound policies are to be pursued is a small country's openness felt as a constraint. Equally, large countries such as the United States can earn the premium of monetary stability. But their greater power is more likely to induce their authorities to adopt more permissive policies. This is the lesson of the late 1960s, when currencies tied to the dollar were effectively compelled to inflate as a contribution to financing the Vietnam War. Liberal economists who at that time effectively fought for flexible exchange rates (for example, in Germany) have no reason to regret this.

In an open world economy, countries are bound to compete for internationally mobile resources. This should be an incentive for national governments to be more efficient and less populistic and to limit themselves to the supply of those goods and services for which they have a comparative advantage relative to private enterprise, relative to voluntary associations, and relative to local governments in their domain. This lesson of international competition among governments may not have come through yet. But it is imperative and impelling. Competition for lowering tax burdens will remain on the agenda in advanced countries competing with the United States. And deregulation is bound to spread from the United States to other countries, though it will take more time than we wish. Yet we also hear increasingly strong calls for international cooperation and coordination, and in Europe, also for harmonization. In fact, these calls amount to pleas for the formation of government cartels. Apart from the General Agreement on Tariffs and Trade, such cartels are cartels for intervention, cartels to reduce openness and incentives. The term *cooperation* just clouds the issue.

Behind the calls for coordination and harmonization, I believe I recognize the pretense of knowledge and the voice of constructivist rationalism. Economists specializing in matters of international economic policy feel tempted to offer their advice to policymakers who are eager to show that summit meetings are more than show business. These economists make politicians believe that the world economy will perform better if it is run by a visible hand. Targets are being suggested for various policy variables, not only for monetary expansion, where they have some useful information content, but also for national GDP growth rates, for current account balances, and for fiscal deficits. The emphasis is, of course, by necessity on the demand side, where macro economists have their domain, not on the supply side where the real work has to be done for faster spontaneous growth. In this sense, the demand bias and the coordination talk is potentially counterproductive, a red herring. Sufficient demand will come forth in the world economy—in the absence of a monetary contraction—if individuals and firms are free to increase their supplies and to learn how to adjust quickly to changing conditions on a worldwide market. But the freedom to adjust needs to be given to them, so that the required adjustment and the learning that has to go on all the time can take place in competition. The politicization of the world economy through coordination is not helpful in this respect. It can only have the consequence that the word *crisis* is heard and read disturbingly often in the news: balance of payments and foreign exchange crises, trade wars, breakdowns of commodity markets, beggar-thy-neighbor accusations. The politicization symptom most horrible to an international economist of the classical persuasion is the increasing tendency to focus on bilateral trade relations and to assert with strong moral overtones that they have to be balanced.

All this could be extensively developed into a lecture on methodological individualism in international economics. Let me merely say in conclusion that it helps greatly in the classroom to see the world as a catallactic system divided by national borders of diminishing importance, with competing national governments and monies, competing tax systems and business firms, internationally mobile and immobile owners of human capital and property rights. Such a view can prevent the student of economics from uncritically internalizing holistic concepts like economy and country or statistical constructs like GDP or bilateral trade flows, which, unfortunately, feature prominently in the rhetoric of politicians and of economists close to the political scene.

An individualistic openness of the mind is perhaps the best protection against collectivism. In matters of economic policy, national and international, openness is intimately tied in with competition and incentives. The communication revolution that is going on was once thought to lead to an Orwellian nightmare. It may well turn out to work for decentralization and individual responsibility instead. This supports the confidence that we have passed the watershed and that the way before us will lead to a truly open world economy.

**Reference**

Giersch, Herbert. 1985. *Eurosclerosis.* Institut für Weltwirtschaft, Kiel Discussion Papers, no. 112.

# 10    Individual Freedom for Worldwide Prosperity

In the past few years, it has become increasingly evident that needs and opportunities follow parallel trends in the East and in the West. While liberal Western economists speak out for more openness and better incentives, the Soviet Union strives for "glasnost" and "perestroika," which, in Russian, means little more than an improved incentive system. This is encouraging. To be sure, some of us in the West feel that we were too optimistic a few years ago about the development in the foreseeable future. Such setbacks are perhaps inevitable everywhere, notably in countries that are in the vanguard on the march toward an open world order. But we can derive hope from the fact that a loss of steampower at the front of the train does not necessarily lead to its slowing down if the brakes happen to be loosened elsewhere, for example, at the end of the train. Socialism is in a deep crisis. This has an effect on social democrats all over the world. The Mitterands of today are far more open-minded than they were a decade ago. And so is the general public in many countries.

One may question whether the world is as interlocked—or interdependent—as to warrant the metaphor of a train. My answer is positive for the purpose at hand. The world's recent history shows that there are worldwide movements in thought and practice. Let me give some examples.

World War I brought an end to the liberal world order of the nineteenth century. It gave rise to economic centralization and comprehensive planning in many countries and led to Marxist and fascist dictatorships in Eastern and Western Europe right through World War II. Lenin and Stalin, Mussolini and Hitler were cynical dictators with a deep disrespect for the individual, urging the masses to sacrifice personal liberty and even life for the collective good of some class or party, nation or race that was claimed

This is a slightly modified version of the presidential address given at the opening session of the general meeting of the Mont Pèlerin Society in Tokyo on September 5, 1988.

to be superior to others and to be destined for victory by some imagined laws of history. In the interwar period, the world was being closed in every respect: historical determinism reigned over openness, government planning over individual choice; autarchy and protectionism gained over nineteenth-century multilateralism and free trade; exchange controls replaced the gold standard.

This closing of the world order continued after 1945 in those parts of the world that became known as the "South" (in the so-called North-South conflict) or the "Third World": Mao's China, Kim Il Sung's North Korea, the Indochina of Ho Chi Minh and Pol Pot, Ne Win's Burma, Sukarno's Indonesia, Nasser's Egypt, black Africa mostly under one-party dictatorships. The list can be lengthened by many more names, including Castro's Cuba and the countries suffering from "proxy" wars. At the end of the list we would have Khomeini's Iran and Soviet-occupied Afghanistan.

The counterrevolution after World War II started in the defeated nations of Europe and Asia, notably in General Clay's Germany and MacArthur's Japan about four decades ago. While the Third World came under the influence of Harold Laski, Friedrich A. Hayek's socialist counterpart at the London School of Economics and Political Science, the intellectual battle in the advanced countries of Europe and Asia was won by Hayek. The idea of freedom for prosperity quickly spread in the West thanks to the German miracle, which we owe to Ludwig Erhard and the advice and support he received from Wilhelm Röpke and Walter Eucken.

Books such as Hayek's *Road to Serfdom* surely carry conviction, mostly among readers who have been conditioned by their experience to feel instinctively that the thought they absorb must in fact be true. But equally convincing is the experience from the successful experiment that invites imitation. The liberalization of trade in Europe, fostered by Marshall aid, was one form of transmission; Germany's early move toward convertibility on capital account in 1958 was surely another. Countries lagging behind in the liberalization process turned out to be laggards in income growth as well. The naive political assertion that government planning rather than economic freedom is required to overcome poverty was refuted by experience. In the late 1970s Britain closed a historical circle by losing faith in Fabianism and by rediscovering liberalization as the only appropriate cure for the British disease—about two centuries after one of her greatest sons had shown the way toward the *Wealth of Nations*.

In Asia it was the example of Japan's outward orientation that invited imitation. The small Asian countries that could not afford the luxury of a closed economy followed the same track. Economic liberalism brought about spectacular growth in the Pacific Rim, though not always accompanied by a parallel process of political liberalization.

But there is hope for political pluralism in the future. It rests on the notion of politicoeconomic interdependence. This interdependence may be conceived as consisting of a vicious circle and a virtuous circle. Both can be illustrated by reference to recent history.

A vicious circle was at work in the interwar period when the rise of dictatorships and central planning reinforced the disintegration of the world economy and when this disintegration in turn made it easy and almost costless for dictators and planners to strengthen their power by closing the economy. The folly of the Smoot-Hawley tariff in the United States was surely a contributing factor in political practice, just as in the intellectual debate Keynes's writings on "the end of laissez faire" and on "national self-sufficiency" (Keynes 1926, 1933) were perceived to support an inward-looking interventionism. Central planning and autarchy became, of course, less objectionable and even quite popular, given the mass unemployment in the wake of the Great Contraction and in the absence of appropriate measures to cure it quickly. There is a big question on which I have been pondering for more than fifty years: would Hitler have come to power without mass unemployment and the disintegration of the world economy? My answer is no. Had prosperity prevailed rather than distress, my father's generation would have opted for freedom. But my judgment is perhaps biased by the striking experience during the last four decades when I was lucky to observe how individualism and worldwide prosperity provided a firm basis for democracy in the western part of my country and in many parts of the free world.

The change from the vicious circle to the virtuous circle might have come about spontaneously, albeit with some delay, if it had not been for the war. In actual fact, the economic turnaround was prepared for the world by the Western Allies at their conference in Bretton Woods (1944) and could start only after the war had ended with the liberation of Western Europe in 1945. I do not think that Bretton Woods was decisive, but it formulated and expressed the political will to restore a more open world order, at least for trade in goods. The crushing of dictatorships, however, was decisive. It opened the door toward a free market in ideas as well as in goods. When Friedrich Hayek gave his opening address to the first Mont Pèlerin Society (MPS) meeting at Mont Pèlerin on April 1, 1947, he observed,

The farther one moves to the West ... where liberal institutions are still comparatively firm, and people professing liberal convictions still comparatively numerous, the less are these people prepared really to reexamine their conviction and the more are they inclined to compromise.... I found on the other hand that in those countries which either had directly experienced a totalitarism regime, or had closely approached it, a few men had from this experience gained a clearer conception of the conditions and value of a free society.... The actual decay of a civilization has taught some independent thinkers on the European Continent lessons which ... have yet to be learnt in England and America. (Hayek 1967a, 149–150).

Hayek's message can be compressed into a brief statement: bad experience gives rise to lasting lessons. Let me add: societies must be free in order to be able to transmit such lessons and to apply them in practical life. Eastern Europe lacked such freedom. When Western Europe became free, it learned the lessons in almost no time. It learned them lastingly from the prosperity that economic liberalism was quick to produce in Europe's most devastated and impoverished parts. The transmission of experience was certainly facilitated by the relative cheapening of medium-range transportation and communication. This holds also for Eastern Europe. Without the decline of information costs, we would hardly have had the uprisings in East Germany in 1953, in Hungary and Poland in 1956, in Czechoslovakia in 1968. And in the Soviet Union, would there be perestroika without glasnost and hence more information, and would there be the loosening of Moscow's grip in the former Baltic states in the north and the transcaucasian states in the south? My answer is no. Cheap communication and up-to-date information may often surpass our capacity to absorb, thus impairing, for example, our sense of history; but we have to be grateful that it has telescoped our geographic awareness with at least one important consequence: cheap communication is making freedom more contagious.

In his book Nineteen Eighty-four, George Orwell warned us of the danger that cheap communication would turn out to promote centralization and dictatorship. In this way, he contributed to immunizing the world against this danger. But if my reading of recent history is correct, I have come to be sure that, in the present circumstances, cheap communication on balance works in favor of a decentralization rather than a centralization of decision making. The opportunity exists in all dimensions of decision making: within firms as well as in the worldwide division of labor. Cheap communication has a potential for serfdom as well as for freedom, but, given the prosperity that freedom and capitalism have produced in recent history in large parts of the world, the net effect in the future is likely to be in favor of individual liberty.

Setbacks on the march toward an open world order should not discourage us. Looking back we can gain optimism from the fact that the revival of Marxism and the emergence of the New Left that we have observed—in the wake of the baby boom, the expansion of higher education, the Chinese Cultural Revolution, and the Vietnam War—did subside in little more than a decade. This intellectual fashion stirred up the atavistic emotions of young people who had learned to see the world through ideological glasses and were not acquainted with the traditions and the lessons of social history; but it left few traces in the social fabric of today (putting aside left-wing terrorism in parts of Europe). We can also derive comfort from the observation that the idea of a New International Economic Order did not survive the 1970s and quickly died when the international debt problem came to the fore. This debt issue showed that an international resource transfer is of no use when the recipient countries fail to make productive use of the imported capital or when they pursue policies that necessarily lead to a capital flight.

In the advanced countries, a new serious threat to the free market is arising from ecological concerns. We know that the social costs of using the environment are not taken care of by the price mechanism because our system of property rights does not include public goods like fresh air and clean water. For us, this ecological gap highlights the importance of private property; for the other side, this gap is a failure of the market system, inviting all sorts of government regulations and controls. No wonder that socialists and ecologists often join forces with bureaucrats and politicians eager to exercise controls and that they are supported by intellectuals in the media who address themselves to people's emotions. We know that bureaucratic solutions, apart from limiting freedom, are economically wasteful in this as in other fields. The adoption of direct controls for environmental purposes has certainly contributed to the slowdown in productivity advance that the industrial countries have experienced since the late 1960s. In many cases this negative effect was not understood and was, therefore, not anticipated in collective bargaining on the wage front. Therefore, environmental dirigism has contributed to the rise of unemployment, at least in Europe. The lesson for the future is that environmental problems should better be dealt with in ways that are more compatible with the market. What Hayek wrote in 1960 about town planning equally applies to environmental policy: "The issue is ... not whether one ought or ought not to be for ... [it] but whether the measures to be used are to supplement and assist the market or to suspend it and put central direction in its place" (Hayek 1960, 350).

In the new field of environmental policy, economists can demonstrate in very specific terms that market-oriented solutions are least costly. One need only compare the direct emission controls (command and control measures) with the auctioning of emission permits. The auctioning method has the clear advantage that it leads to scarcity prices, which give all polluters a general incentive to mobilize the available knowledge and to search for innovative solutions. In Hayek's terms, they ensure a better use of knowledge in society. Moreover, specific controls that impose state-of-the-art technology usually provide some period of grace for existing firms, while requiring full compliance by newcomers. This is why the business establishment likes them. Auctioning prices, on the other hand, do not discriminate against newcomers. By keeping the market open, they are not only efficient but also fair.

New technologies, one often hears, deserve the financial support of national governments if, as some economists add, the new ventures promise economies of scale that are large enough (relative to world markets) to be worth capturing for the domestic economy. This interventionist argument is similar to that for an optimum tariff designed to exploit the country's monopoly power. And it is also similar to some superficial version of the old infant-industry argument for protection. As government support takes the form of a subsidy—rather than a tariff—retaliation leads to competitive subsidization. For the world economy, the outcome is likely to be an excessive pace of technological advance in one direction, at the expense of an alternative use of resources, including alternative paths of technological progress. I suspect this to involve a waste of resources in most cases. Technological mercantilists derive their enthusiasm from the notions of increasing returns or scale economies. In my view, their position is as unfounded as the old physiocratic myth that agriculture was the only really productive sector or as the subsequent enthusiasm for industry that assumed long-term economies of scale to be associated with manufacturing and its inherent indivisibilities. In contrast, I maintain that we can have— or will happen to have—fast productivity advance in any line of production for which we can produce—and in which we can apply—new knowledge.[1]

It is true that the leading sector attracts human brains, but this is not to be confused with increasing returns. Moreover, the leading sector often enjoys government support for import substitution or export promotion. Entrepreneurial politicians in power can be quite quick in joining the bandwagon to promote a sector that is likely to show gains in the foreseeable future anyhow. This is technological mercantilism rather than increasing returns. As to the opportunity costs of government support for certain lines of applied research, we can only confess that nobody knows them. Hence, they will be neglected in the political market. This bias leads to a speeding up of certain technological developments, with two serious consequences. One is the danger of running up against unforeseen bottlenecks, that is, unbalanced growth with cycles in investment activity. The second danger is an increasing public animosity against technical progress as such. What the public seems to be afraid of is the great leap forward, which is the exact opposite of those piecemeal improvements on a broad front that are brought about in the market by innovative competition on the supply side subject to continuous testing by consumers on the demand side. Big governments bring about bigger events, some of which may well be disasters such as the wars of the past, or future ecological catastrophes, as feared by so many. What is strange, then, is that ecopacifists, especially in Europe, are often so close to collectivist ideas instead of becoming libertarians.

Whenever something is going wrong, a choice can be made between more government or less government. Most people still feel that more government is the natural solution. They even do so when big government was the problem to begin with. In the international field, many observers deplore that we have a world order without a world government. In the absence of a world government, they would say we need at least policy coordination to avoid chaos. These observers equate competition among governments with a beggar-thy-neighbor game or even an approximation to war in the extreme case. Coordination thus appears as a self-evident necessity requiring—like motherhood—no intellectual defense whatsoever. But there is an open question: coordination—what for? If it is to preserve the earth's ozone layer or for other genuine world public goods like peace, hardly anyone would fail to support it. But if, on the other hand, coordination is tantamount to an intergovernmental cartel, I would strongly object because I consider the emerging competition among governments for internationally mobile resources to be the best protection for the saver and the consumer, for the holder of money and financial assets, and for the taxpayer and the individual as a citizen. Government cartels to eliminate competition for internationally mobile resources would destroy the best hopes we can have for an emerging open world order.

Even in the more technical field of monetary policy, the case for coordination is not very convincing. Proponents of coordination are full of praise about how coordination helped to avoid the severe consequences that the stock market crash of October 19, 1987, might have had on worldwide prosperity. Yes, the outcome could have been worse than it was. But why should we attribute the functioning of the capitalist system to policy coordination? Was it not in the enlightened interest of every large country and central bank anyhow to let the demand for money find an elastic supply when liquidity preference was expected to increase in the wake of the crash? Was this not the lesson we have learned from Milton Friedman's research in monetary history? The answer is yes. Moreover, there was and there always is a good reason to inform and perhaps also to consult each other, mainly to avoid intervention at cross purposes. Yet behind this, there is the awkward question whether the "crash" itself was not the consequence of previous coordination efforts and their interpretation by the market. Martin Feldstein offers an answer: "The expectation that [U.S.] monetary policy would tighten to defend artificial exchange rate levels can destabilize financial markets. The fear that the Fed would push rates even higher than they were in early October—to offset the downward pressure on the dollar that resulted from the unfavorable trade news of October 14th—was one of the key factors that triggered the stock market crash." (Feldstein 1988, 5–6).

The general lesson is clear: If in an open order some values or prices are made less flexible as a result of coordination, something else, be it prices or volumes, will suffer greater fluctuations. The normative conclusion is simply: governments and central banks should allow markets to operate freely and should themselves proceed in a fairly predictable way so that markets are not disturbed and can operate more smoothly. This would be coordination for nonintervention. Whether policy coordination for activism makes the economic universe more predictable is open to fundamental doubts.

Despite last year's stock market crash, the world economy is in a good cyclical position. The upswing that started in late 1982 has completed its sixth year. The figure for GNP growth has been around 3 percent in the industrial countries and in the world as a whole for more than a decade. A slowdown in the Organization of Petroleum Exporting Countries area was compensated by faster growth elsewhere; and shortfalls in Africa and the Middle East were outweighed by extraordinarily fast growth in Asia, notably in the Asian newly industrializing countries.

Looking back at the whole period since World War II we may safely say that capitalism has shown an extraordinary vitality, giving us the fastest economic development the world has ever experienced in its history. Compare this with the gloomy picture that was painted for us 140 years ago by Marx and Engels in their Communist Manifesto or by the stagnationists around Keynes and Alvin Hansen 50 years ago.

To take only the stagnationists, it is hard to avoid the conclusion that they were wrong on all accounts.

1. Did a saturation of consumer wants and oversaving become a limit to economic growth? It did not in the past, nor will it in the future, because people have unlimited desires, not limited wants. And if there is anything wrong with present savings, it is that they are too low in large parts of the world.

2. Was there—as the stagnationists feared—a decline in investment opportunities because of American capitalism approaching geographic frontiers? The answer again is no. Instead, we observed the rise of international corporations operating on a worldwide scale. This rise was unforeseen by the stagnationists and thus demonstrates how wrong one can be if one sticks to the traditional closed-economy assumptions.

3. Was there—or will there be—a dearth of investment opportunities arising from a slowdown of invention and innovation activities as the stagnationists thought? The answer again is no. More people than ever are living on this planet who are capable of doing research, of inventing, and of transmitting new knowledge at ever lower communication costs. The people who are ingenious may be limited as a percentage of total population, but the absolute numbers have been growing all the time due to overall population growth; and a larger part of the world's population has come or will come into closer contact with knowledge production due to declining communication costs.

Keynes in his growth pessimism once predicted that full employment policies would bring the long-term interest rate down to zero in one generation. Instead, we observe that the real interest rate (which is what he apparently meant) is at a historically high level. This is a signal for the world's population and for governments to save more so that more of the vast investment opportunities that the future seems to offer can be exploited in a shorter period of time. The high interest rate is also a signal to make better use of existing resources, to exploit fully the productivity potential that free trade offers through a worldwide division of labor, and to augment this productivity potential by letting capital, and capital-intensive human resources, flow freely across national borders.

This brings me to the agenda for accelerating the move toward an open world order. The productivity and growth potential that we could exploit by free trade is anything but small. It could even be enlarged by deregulation so that competition from outside sources could fully penetrate the sheltered domestic sector. In that case I would trust an estimate, derived from cross-section analyses of effective protection in the 1960s and 1970s (Heitger 1987), that free trade would not only bring a once-and-for-all increase in the world's productive potential, but a permanent increase in output growth by about 2 percentage points. Thus, a really open order could well reproduce the high growth rates the world had in the 1960s.

Resistance comes from organized interest groups. They lobby for protection against cheap imports that make the income prospects of domestic producers deteriorate. But such deterioration is necessary to push resources into alternative uses where they are more valuable at world market prices. The resulting protectionism has nothing to do with the theoretical arguments for import tariffs based on monopoly power or some presumed market failure. On the contrary, such defensive protectionism arises because markets are seen to work properly, though in a fashion that is regarded as cruel. Those negatively affected feel hurt, but what they want to have protected is usually nothing but the rent element in their incomes. In their rhetoric they make us believe that they just need support to smooth the adjustment process. In a similar way they want protection against what they call dumping—price cutting by foreign suppliers that is often not more than one has to expect from new entrants into an open market. The protectionist rhetoric is designed to appeal to xenophobia or fairness. John Rawls is called in to help close the economy.

But such a closing amounts to a destruction of income opportunities elsewhere. Those hurt include not only people at home—consumers and producers in the domestic export sector. Those most severely affected are likely to be the much poorer people in the export sector of some less developed country, poorer people eager to catch up. Harming such poorer people is certainly not fair in the Rawlsian sense. The fact that insiders invoke the fairness principle immediately raises the question about outsiders: Whose interests are (implicitly or deliberately) impaired by those who claim fairness for themselves? In international trade, the outsiders include foreigners; in the similar case of protection against new technologies, the outsiders include future generations. In this wider perspective, the whole idea of fairness, including fair trade, becomes highly suspect as a violation of Kant's categorical imperative. It is free trade, not fair trade, that meets Kant's norm.

Protection or subsidization, even if introduced on a temporary basis, nearly always becomes permanent in practice. Sunset provisions for phasing out such support may be a rational remedy, but not in permissive societies. Such societies show a tendency to being closed more permanently, often behind an ideological veil. This largely applies to Europe. In Europe, politics still has a more romantic or ideological flavor than public choice theory would allow for. Without this romantic element in European thinking and politics, I could not possibly explain the public support that Europe's protectionist agricultural policy still has, although employment in agriculture is down to a small percentage of total employment (for example, 5 percent in West Germany by 1986). In addition to the romantic notions of fairness and permissiveness, there is an important role being played by mere tradition. Even the very notion of fairness is—in a historical context—heavily determined by the past. In the absence of a specific criterion for fairness, people are inclined to take the relative income positions of the recent past to which they have become accustomed as a kind of benchmark for judging the fairness of relative incomes today. This tends to create implicit property rights, quasi-entitlements in income maintenance notions. They play a role in some European market economies that their proponents call "social." The outcome is defensive protectionism, international and domestic—that is, the closing of markets for the preservation of previous relative positions of income and status.

Consider again agriculture. Numerous suggestions for liberal reform have been made in Europe, without much appeal in practice. The radical solution I support and prefer would be to abolish all agricultural support systems at one stroke and to give farmers a once-and-for-all compensation for the loss in earnings (and land values) that would result from this move to world market prices. The compensation given to farmers would be interest-bearing government bonds. Nobody directly affected would lose, but those who have to foot the bill now and then—as consumers and taxpayers—are certain to gain. Surplus production would disappear, and all the wastes would go, including the ecological damages resulting from overfertilization. Farmers could reinvest the compensation they receive, and lower farmland prices would provide an incentive to reforestation and other forms of land use, which would then become profitable. To be sure, there are technical difficulties as with every reform. But so far the idea as such has hardly caught any attention. Why is this so? One answer is that we may be up against atavistic irrationalities in moral judgments. The farmer is taken to provide us with the bread that used to be asked for in prayers; and it has to be the nearby farmer—as in previous times when high transportation costs and tribal wars prevented the emergence of an extended order. It is this extended order in which people do not yet instinctively trust. Agricultural protection is perhaps the extreme case of resistance against the emerging open world order. In the current Uruguay

Round of General Agreement on Tariffs and Trade negotiations, it may turn out to be the major stumbling block.

As far as the European Community (EC) is concerned, Europe has embarked on a program of completing the internal common market by 1992. This involves the removal of all border obstacles to the free movement of goods and services and of capital. The static gains have been estimated to lie between 4 and 7 percent of GDP. Additional dynamic gains can be expected from more intense competition if the move is accompanied by deregulation and privatization and by a parallel external liberalization that most free market economists would consider essential. We hope that the European label and the magic number that 1992 may become—half a millennium after the discovery of America—will accelerate the work for reforms that have been on the agenda of some countries for a long time but have so far been repressed by what we call "the tyranny of the status quo" (Friedman and Friedman 1984).

A real breakthrough—at least in doctrine—was achieved by the EC Commission's 1985 White Paper. This document was largely written by the British commissioner, Lord Cockfield. In the same vein, there was a decision by the European Court establishing the principle of the country of origin in matters of regulation. This principle amounts to the rule: what is legal in a product's country of origin must not be an import impediment in the country of destination. This principle of the country of origin could also apply to value-added taxes, as was suggested a long time ago (Giersch 1962). These indirect taxes would then be treated like direct taxes—as a cost equivalent for the public goods consumed at the location of production. What the country of origin principle thus generally implies is free competition among different locations where taxes are locational factors like land prices and where rules and regulations are part of the locations' infrastructure. Such free interlocational competition, therefore, really is competition among governments; it is the competition of governments for internationally mobile resources such as capital and entrepreneurship and also labor with a high content of human capital. This competition, if not regulated by harmonization agreements, would force governments to improve their price-performance ratios, that is, to reduce their X-inefficiencies, in attempts to attract valuable resources. Such attraction, in the end, would also benefit local land and labor. A harmonization of regulations and taxes would come about as a result of such competition, but in a stepwise process leading to a much lower level of regulation. The outcome would be more to the taste of those mobile resources that are the object of competition.

And they happen to be the resources that need openness as a condition for making their best contribution to future progress.

Such competitive harmonization—in a process similar to natural selection—of course goes against the grain of what Hayek called constructivist rationalism (Hayek 1967b). Such rationalism—or constructivism—has so far dominated postwar European thinking under the French influence from Jean Monnet to Jacques Delors. In this respect Lord Cockfield's White Book of 1985 was a revolution, a Waterloo for Descartes, so to speak. But the struggle between constructivism and evolutionary selection goes on. It is not yet decided in practice (for example, in the field of regulation), and it may be the constructivists who will win, at least in the area of European monetary unification.

Tendencies we observe on the world level—toward fixed exchange rates, target zones, monetary coordination—are even more clearly visible in the form of monetary constructivism in Europe. The Common Market is said to need a common currency, which is to emerge from the present cooperation of central banks. What many politicians want is the emergence of a monetary monopoly from a central bank cartel. If the need for such a European currency were real, there would also be, to draw a parallel, an even greater need for a common European language, equally to be constructed, perhaps by an academy of linguists, as a compositum mixtum of ingredients from all national languages. But instead of Esperanto, English has turned out to be the winner in the linguistic market. In the monetary market, the European currency unit (ECU) as a composite money so far has not won in intra-European transactions, neither against the dollar nor against the Swiss franc or the deutsche mark. And it is open to doubt whether any artificial money will ever win against a currency that, over a long history, has gained great credibility as a stable store of value—and more credibility than a composite money, with many less credible currencies as constituent elements, can immediately offer. The only solution, apart from natural selection by competition among existing currencies, would be to supply an index-linked ECU as a parallel currency. If governments and central banks failed to make such an innovation, private banks could do so—of course not only for asset holding and transactions in Europe but also worldwide.

Individual freedom would bring about such an innovation if freedom were specified to include, as a citizen's right, the free choice of currencies. Other citizens' rights are also essential for the move toward an open world order. They include

- the right to low marginal income taxes,
- the right to work—in the sense of being allowed to sell one's services at any wage an employer finds acceptable, and
- the right to unrestricted market entry into goods and service markets.

The right to work is, of course, directed against syndicalism and the discrimination against outsiders that syndicalism often entails; whereas the right to free market entry is the leverage needed to mobilize citizens—as workers against domestic corporatism, as consumers and exporters against international protectionism.

The right to low marginal income tax rates—and, in a sense, the other rights too—would be less urgent points on the agenda if there were full freedom of capital movements and free migration, particularly for human capital. Governments would then feel much more constrained by the pressures of locational competition and would be forced, as already indicated, to offer more freedom to the suppliers of mobile resources.

Locational competition—or competition among governments—is perhaps the decisive criterion for the openness of the world order. Under competition and openness people have more and greater opportunities for "exit" as an alternative to "voice" in expressing protest. This gives hope for a depoliticization of life. The constraint for government arises not only from actual competition; it may also arise from potential competition, that is, from credible threats of emigration by future-oriented, and hence particularly valuable, resources. Will governments become more sensitive to such threats? I suppose the answer is yes—however, under the proviso that governments do not find it opportune to form cartels under such headings as cooperation, coordination, harmonization, or political integration. Without such cartel arrangements, individual freedom will also find allies among the owners of immobile resources, including labor. The latter are bound to realize sooner or later that their future earning prospects largely depend on the presence of mobile resources, which are likely to be entrepreneurial, innovative, or merely future oriented like investment capital. While there may be antagonism between labor and old capital in a closed society, an open society that competes for mobile resources is bound to learn the medium-term lesson of positive complementarity between labor and new capital. My anti-Marxist hope is that declining communication costs, including border controls, will make old class conflicts more and more obsolete and strengthen the tendencies for productive cooperation within competing units.

In this perspective, the poor will increasingly realize that they have better income prospects in the neighborhood of the rich than in the neighborhood of the poor. In some parts of the world, like corporatist Latin America, much will depend upon whether public opinion, including the church, is prepared to learn this medium-run lesson of openness quickly enough. Otherwise, these countries—being uncompetitive in world capital markets—must face the danger of falling into the poverty trap in a vicious circle of overpoliticization and overindebtedness, political unrest and economic decline, administrative corruption and hyperinflation, in sharp contrast to the open and competitive countries, as we find them in Asia, that have good opportunities to demonstrate the working of the virtuous circle of individual freedom and increasing prosperity.

**Note**

1. And for the time being, I take the position that the notions of increasing returns, scale economies, synergy, unbalanced growth, and so on either refer to indivisibilities that are partly man-made and short-run phenomena or are a myth based on the mechanistic assumption that growth means quantities rather than quality, size rather than satisfaction.

**References**

Commission of the European Communities. 1985. *Completing the Internal Market. White Paper from the Commission to the European Council.* Brussels: Commission of the European Communities.

Commission of the European Communities. 1988. *Research on the Costs of Non-Europe: Basic Findings.* Vol. 1. Brussels, Luxemburg: Commission of the European Communities.

Feldstein, Martin. 1988. "Thinking about International Economic Coordination." *Journal of Economic Perspectives* 2, no. 2:3−13.

Friedman, Milton, and Rose Friedman. 1984. *The Tyranny of the Status Quo.* London: Harcourt Brace Jovanovich.

Giersch, Herbert. 1962. *Zur Frage der Anwendung des Ursprungs- oder Bestimmungslandprinzips bei der Umsatzsteuer im Gemeinsamen Markt.* Schriftenreihe der Wirtschaftsvereinigung Eisen- und Stahlindustrie zur Wirtschafts- und Industriepolitik, no. 1. Düsseldorf.

Hayek, Friedrich A. 1944. *The Road to Serfdom.* London: Routledge & Kegan Paul.

Hayek, Friedrich A. 1960. *The Constitution of Liberty.* London: Routledge & Kegan Paul.

Hayek, Friedrich A. 1967a. *Studies in Philosophy, Politics and Economics*. London: Routledge & Kegan Paul.

Hayek, Friedrich A. 1967b. "Kinds of Rationalism." In Friedrich A. Hayek, *Studies in Philosophy, Politics and Economics*. London: Routledge & Kegan Paul.

Heitger, Bernhard. 1987. "Import Protection and Export Performance: Their Impact on Economic Growth." *Weltwirtschaftliches Archiv* 123:249–261.

Keynes, John Maynard. 1926. *The End of Laissez-Faire*. London: Woolf.

Keynes, John Maynard. 1933. "Nationale Selbstgenügsamkeit." *Schmollers Jahrbuch für Gesetzgebung, Verwaltung und Volkswirtschaft im Deutschen Reiche* 57:561–570.

Orwell, George. 1949. *Nineteen Eighty-four*. New York: Harcourt.

Rawls, John. 1971. *A Theory of Justice*. Cambridge, Mass.: Harvard University Press.

# 11 EC 1992: Prospects and Problems

Five hundred years after Europeans discovered North America, Europe is to form an integrated market by removing all border controls between the twelve members of the European Community (EC). This is what project 1992 is about. It can be interpreted as the last and most important step in a series that started four decades earlier with the formation of the European Coal and Steel Community under French leadership in 1952. The last step is to bring about the removal of all obstacles to cross-border trade in goods and services and to the free mobility of capital and entrepreneurship, including the human capital of professionals.

The intermediate steps were: (1) the formation between 1958 and 1968 of the EC customs union, which covered industrial products and mainly promoted intraindustry trade; (2) the accession to the EC of Britain, Ireland, and Denmark in 1973; (3) the arrangements for free trade in industrial goods with the European Free Trade Association (EFTA) countries (Austria, Finland, Iceland, Norway, Portugal, Sweden, and Switzerland) in 1973; and (4) the entry to the EC of Greece in 1981 and Spain and Portugal in 1986.

The movement toward freer trade has so far been limited to industrial goods, and it has suffered from protectionist setbacks. Nontariff barriers against imports from third countries were imposed by individual member states; they would have been circumvented had they not been supplemented by intra-EC border controls. They were applied to textiles and steel, but, for instance in the case of France, also to cars and machinery. Moreover, there are—or were—quantitative restrictions or import prohibitions on pharmaceuticals, alcoholic beverages, and products that do not meet national standards and norms.

Reprinted with permission from *Rivista di Politica Economica* 79 (December 1989): 185–197.

Two different views or paradigms of Europe's integration movement have been in conflict from the beginning. One paradigm is what Hayek calls "constructivism" or "constructivist rationalism." Its focus is on institution building, bureaucratic integration, political unification, and centralism —some form of French planning. Its philosophical roots go back to Descartes and have been nourished up to the time of Delors by what Hayek termed the "pretence of knowledge" (Hayek 1974). As central planning is out of the question nowadays, the paradigm favors regulation and the harmonization of institutions, taxes, and norms before the removal of border controls. This policy paradigm comes close to Europe's corporatist traditions, which, of course, go back to the medieval guild society. When applied to the EC in the beginning, these corporatist and centralist tendencies were severely attacked by the German neoliberals of the 1950s, including Wilhelm Röpke and Ludwig Erhard, who was the Bonn government's first economics minister and second chancellor (Giersch 1988).

These critics held the opposite view, in recent years most openly pronounced (though unfortunately with some nationalistic overtones) by Margaret Thatcher in her famous Bruges speech. This view holds that markets know better than bureaucrats, that productivity arises from diversity rather than uniformity, and that harmonization will come about, to the extent that it is useful, by the pressures of evolutionary competition, which is interpreted as a process of discovery (Hayek 1968). Competition helps to identify the cheapest supplier of a product or service, the best location for a firm, the most suitable means of communication or payment, the institutional arrangements most suitable for productivity growth, and the combination of taxes and public goods preferred by the relevant public. Instead of politicians and bureaucrats, the last word in the choice of money and norms, of institutions and goods, can and should go to the consumer, who is to be seen as needing no paternalistic guidance. "Exit" rather than "voice" is the means of voting that will become predominant once the obstacles to the free movement of goods and services, people and capital have been removed. Currency competition would be the best means of finding out to what extent the Common Market needs a common currency, just as participants decide by themselves what language to use in contracts. Esperanto, by the way, would not suggest itself as a viable solution to the linguistic part of the communication problem, and from this a parallel could be drawn to money.

Exceptions to the rule of market superiority are obvious: they concern market failures in the form of negative external effects, such as on health or the environment. On the other hand, increasing returns to scale are no such externality, as we know, so technical norms will gain ground in a competitive process without needing any government support or coercion. Centrally imposed technical norms are even dangerous; they are easily used as a basis for administrative protection against imports from third countries.

In the present German policy discussion, one term has emerged that describes the comprehensive nature of institutional competition well: *Standortwettbewerb*—"competition among locations." Cities compete with cities, regions with regions, countries with countries. And they compete for the mobile resources: for investment and human capital, for entrepreneurs and good taxpayers. We also see central banks competing with each other for the holders of their money. All of these institutions can improve their competitive positions—for the benefit of the immobile resources—by offering good services and public goods at low cost. The mobile resources will vote with their feet. And governments that behave irresponsibly by running deeply into debt will observe in the capital market how their ratings as borrowers go down. This experience will improve fiscal discipline. Workable competition for mobile resources, however, requires that governments be prevented from setting up common funds and forming cartels under such appealing names as unification or harmonization.

According to this view—which I happen to share—the best that Europe can expect is that the harmonization agenda will remain unfinished on December 31, 1992, and that border controls will nevertheless be removed the next morning, just as governments have promised.

The European Court achieved a breakthrough for harmonization under the pressure of market competition when it ruled against the German government in deciding that domestic regulations fixing the ingredients of liquor, beer, and sausages must not be abused to prevent the import of such products from other EC members (Court of Justice 1979). Consumer protection had, of course, been invoked as an argument for what was actually producer protection. The ruling of the European Court means a shift from the principle of the country of destination to the principle of the country of origin. What is legally produced in the country of origin must be accepted as legally produced in the country or destination. EC members have now agreed to respect each other's norms in the Single European Act. But they are still reluctant to put the country-of-origin principle into practice; they leave it to the court to decide in specific cases.

Competition is the key to faster productivity growth. If EC Europe should have more competition—in the goods and factor markets, among regulatory systems, and in the field of public goods and taxes—then the old continent can look forward to a reacceleration of economic growth in the 1990s. Calculations published by the EC Commission promise a once-and-for-all gain in Europe's potential output of 2 to 3 percent from the removal of border controls alone and another gain of the same order of magnitude from the improvement in the general competitive climate (Commission 1988). To put it differently: with a trend rate of growth of potential output in the range of 2.5 percent, EC Europe could have growth rates of actual output ranging between 3 and 4 percent for half a decade. But this is not the upper limit.

My guess is that Europe has a good opportunity to lift the rate of growth of potential output from 2.5 percent at present to 3.5 percent in the foreseeable future and to add a once-and-for-all gain of 5 percent on top of it over half a decade, so that actual growth rates in the mid-1990s would be in the range of 4 to 5 percent, as they were in the golden 1960s.

The general reason for my optimism is that, in matters of long-run growth, we can rely on some forms of mutual causation. There are virtuous and vicious circles. Europe had an induced productivity acceleration during the postwar process of decontrol and liberalization, of reconstruction and catching up with the United States. A productivity deceleration, still largely unexplained by traditional economics, followed when the long upswing came to an end after 1968—with a wage revolt in Europe, with the oil price shocks, and with the awareness that owing to environmental damage rapid growth could no longer be permitted. Instead of making the market system more flexible to permit quick adjustments, European governments expanded in size at the expense of the private sector and took refuge in a protectionist policy, international and domestic. This whole process can now be reversed. If it is not reversed on the occasion of the 1992 supply shock, Europe will have missed her greatest opportunity in decades. To repeat: The growth rate of trend productivity (per man-hour) can well be raised from 2 to 3 percent. With some increase in employment, the trend rate of growth of output could be 3.5 percent instead of 2.5 percent. Europe's rates of actual output—for a few years—could then well be in the range of 4 to 5 percent.

Let me briefly sketch some specific reasons for my optimism:

1. twenty years of relative stagnation since 1968 have mitigated the real wage pressures that brought the long postwar upswing to an end;

2. oil prices have declined;

3. we have digested the new costs associated with environmental concerns, at least to a considerable extent;

4. inflation, which during the 1970s permitted the accommodation of the great cost push, has now abated;

5. real interest rates have been high enough long enough to make investors aware once again of the need to choose projects with a high capital productivity;

6. returns on investment in Europe are no longer below what firms can earn form investing in financial assets;

7. wage moderation has helped to make current growth employment intensive again;

8. an increase in the demand for labor has made the labor market more flexible, encouraging employers to engage in search activities and in investment in human capital. A positive hysteresis effect is, therefore, possible in the future;

9. the pressure of (investment) demand against existing capacities should reduce protectionist pressures;

10. governments may learn that current inflationary dangers can best be fought by removing restrictions on the supply side, in contrast to producing a recession by suddenly restricting monetary growth. European prosperity, supported by domestic liberalization, would also improve the prospects of worldwide liberalization and of a successful outcome of the Uruguay Round of the General Agreement on Tariffs and Trade (GATT) provided that Europe can solve its agricultural problem as outlined below.

There are already signs that European businesses are preparing for more intense and innovative competition after 1992—a development that should increase the trend rate of labor productivity in Europe. Some of these signs are as follows: (1) casual empiricism suggests that firms are already speeding up investment in preparation for 1992; (2) competition is increasingly interpreted as innovational competition and time competition: speed up innovation, shorten the product cycle; (3) more and more firms recognize innovation to improve the location of production—locational innovation—as a new element in evolutionary competition: if you cannot reduce costs for old products where you produce them now, you had better either purchase them from low-cost producers elsewhere or produce them yourself in low-cost locations. This approach will make better use than is made now of the catching-up potential of low-wage areas or countries in Europe and elsewhere; (4) time competition will press for better use of the computer and its productivity potential, both for innovation and for the decentralization of decision making; (5) organizational innovations are high on the agenda of firms. Although I deeply distrust the synergy arguments brought forward in discussions about mergers, I must mention them here as a potential source of temporary productivity improvements that could be made permanent in combination with organizational efforts to decentralize routine decisions.

The general point about productivity advance in this context is that productivity can once again start to rise faster than real wages in order to produce a wage lag similar to what Europe had in the 1960s. Monetary policy should, of course, accommodate better growth prospects or even anticipate them if the 1992 supply shock turns out to be accompanied, as I hope it will be, by deregulation that raises Europe's supply responsiveness.

Though many fellow economists would disagree with me, I would be quite happy if Europe were to make itself so attractive on world capital markets after 1992 that it would import capital from the rest of the world and run a current account deficit, at least for a couple of years. In fact, the marginal efficiency of business investment in Europe has already improved, a development that is likely to reverse the outflow of capital and to attract capital from abroad. Foreign direct investment in Europe will be induced by the trade diversion effect of Europe 1992 as well. And under the pressure of locational competition, regional and local communities in Europe will increase the volume of infrastructural investment and thus add to the demand side of the capital market.

The capital inflow will help to reduce Europe's capital shortage unemployment (by creating jobs that are sufficiently productive to match prevailing minimum wages and that also provide learning opportunities to less experienced workers), and the worsening of Europe's current account will, one hopes, mitigate protectionist pressures abroad and encourage a better international division of labor worldwide.

The decline of unemployment and the overall prosperity after 1992 should make it easier to combat internal protectionism in the form of excessive regulations, job protection, and preference for nearby suppliers in public procurement. A demand pull on the labor market would greatly reduce—or even overcome—Eurosclerosis.

This scenario is the opposite of the vicious circle that was observable in Europe in the 1970s; indeed, it looks like a parallel to Europe's long upswing in the 1950s and 1960s, which was similarly supported by decontrol and deregulation, liberalization, and the completion in 1968 of the EEC customs union.

Europe's new prosperity should make it easier to solve the Continent's agricultural problem. A switch to world market prices is not unrealistic. It could be facilitated by giving farmers full compensation for the net income loss they are likely to suffer; future income transfers for this purpose could be capitalized by offering landowners or farmers interest-bearing government bonds that they could sell to finance investments for better land use, including reforestation. These arrangements would improve resource allocation and growth in Europe and could contribute to the success of the Uruguay Round of GATT negotiations.

The greatest risk emanating from constructivist thinking has to do with what has been termed "the social dimension" of Europe 1992. The phrase implies prior harmonization of labor regulations in order to avoid "social dumping," as the German unions call it. Such harmonization would deprive backward areas and countries of their catching-up potential. Instead of attracting capital and productive jobs, these regions would demand subsidies from common funds and would offer fewer opportunities for the young, who would then emigrate and create a guestworker problem in the advanced parts of the EC. Finally, the less developed parts of the EC, such as Portugal, would demand—and certainly receive—protection against imports from less developed countries in the Third World. Corporatism and constructivism are thus likely to promote tendencies toward a "fortress Europe."

Some fifteen years ago, I was afraid that a common currency, by offering a common denominator for wages, would lead to excessive wage equalization in Europe (Giersch 1973). This possibility need not be feared any longer, since the EC has become much larger and labor unions are not as strong as they used to be. In this respect, Europe has become more like an optimum currency area.

Does Europe need a common currency? Constructivists say yes. They are right in asserting that a single currency for a single market would save transaction costs, thus facilitating market integration. They join with corporatists who think that the best means toward this end would be a merger of central banks arising from increasingly closer cooperation under the rule of fixed exchange rates. This cartel solution is likely to be adopted, perhaps with a view to giving the emerging EC central bank an independent status similar to the Bundsbank's independence from the Federal Republic's government.

Opponents of constructivism and corporatism do not deny the argument of lower transaction costs. Money is a means of exchange just as language is a means of communication. But it is for market participants to decide what money and language they want to use in their contracts (Vaubel 1978). A monetary Esperanto might not prove fit to drive out competing means of exchange or communication even if it were imposed as the exclusive instrument for legal transactions. The reason is that contracts have a time dimension; hence money must also serve as a standard of deferred payments. Lower transaction costs will not be desired if their advantage is outweighed by uncertainty about the future value of the means of payment and the unit of account. This uncertainty arises if the issuer of money has monopoly power that it can exploit in the pursuit of a maximum seignorage gain or inflation tax. Nonconstructivists who are opposed to such monopoly power are, therefore, highly skeptical about any money that is not subject to the controlling forces of currency competition. Free trade in money should, in their view, supplement free trade in goods. And if there is a case for a separate European currency, this currency ought to conquer its market as a parallel currency, which it would do only if it promised to be more stable than the national currencies it was supposed to replace.

Such a currency could be a cocktail of currencies like the European currency unit (ECU). The ECU's definition can and should be improved so that this unit of account promises stability in terms of goods and services. The formula would be quite simple: whenever the price index in France, measured in French francs, went up by $x$ percent, the number of French francs in the currency cocktail or basket would have to be increased by $x$ percent. The same formula would apply, of course, to any other currency constituting the ECU. Holders of ECUs would thus not be subject to any inflation tax, and the demand for ECUs would rise at the expense of national currencies unless the latter, on their part, became stable in terms of goods and services. This simple idea has, of course, no appeal whatsoever to European central bankers, who prefer the (presently discussed) path from an exchange rate cartel to a monopoly by merger.

Another red herring in the European debate is the supposed need for tax harmonization. Most governments want it because they are afraid of tax competition as a form of competition among locations. And the business community instinctively favors it because it instinctively hopes that it will contribute to the harmonization of costs as a basis for price cartels.

My earlier plea for locational competition among governments prevents me from supporting tax harmonization as a citizen. A tax cartel is likely to impair fiscal discipline and lead to higher tax rates since there will still be locational competition among governments on the expenditure side. Moreover, we do not know what the optimum tax system that tax harmonization should approximate is. In fact, the optimum system certainly varies from place to place and from time to time.

An argument recently put forward by a spokesman for the German ministry of economic affairs was that without tax harmonization we could not move toward a system with lower direct and higher indirect taxes. Such was the agreed objective, he said, based on agreement among economists. How does he know this? Who can assert that a consensus, even among experts, comes close to the truth about a matter that is basically normative and must be left to people's preferences? Perhaps the issue of direct versus indirect taxes will turn out to be irrelevant, since both are taxes on efficient behavior, whereas our concern has shifted to inefficiencies, including an inefficient use of the environment. A harmonized system is as inflexible as a cartel, whereas fiscal competition offers wide scope for experiments as a source of new knowledge.

Most people think that value-added tax (VAT) levels ought to be harmonized in order to avoid distortions when it becomes impossible, after 1992, to levy VAT on imported goods and to reimburse VAT when goods are exported. This is an erroneous proposition. The VAT is not a paternalistic consumption tax introduced to compensate for distorted preferences of domestic consumers, but rather a tax like the income tax or any other direct tax raised to finance the supply of public goods that, are inputs in domestic production. Yet no one has suggested that direct taxes be refunded when a product is exported and that domestic direct taxes be levied on goods imported from abroad. It is the present VAT system that has a bias.

This system discriminates against tourism in countries with high VAT levels, since it allows these countries to have an overvalued exchange rate. The exchange rate can be overvalued because exports are promoted by a heavy refunding of VAT as they cross the border, whereas imports are hampered by the levying of the (relatively high) VAT. This refunding and levying is not applied to tourist services that foreigners consume within the country; hence the discrimination.

If border controls are removed and refunding and levying is stopped, countries with excessive VAT levels will have to devalue to make exports (almost) as competitive as they were with refunding. On the other side, import prices will go up to compensate for the fact that the protective VAT is no longer levied. At the same time, the country will become more competitive in the field of tourist services.

Instead of devaluing, a country with relatively high VAT levels can compensate for the switch by wage moderation or by a fall in land values. Either alternative would leave real factor remuneration unchanged and would benefit the domestic tourist sector as well.

The business community is concerned with taxes on corporate profits. In this field, tax competition is likely to bring about, fairly quickly, a kind of harmonization on a lower level. Governments are sensitive in this respect because firms are likely to become more multinational and to shift the tax base, and even the locus of production, to countries with lower profit taxes. This downward harmonization need not be of concern in the longer run. Firms do not really bear taxes; they merely raise them from their customers or, if they cannot shift them forward, from the factors of production employed, notably from landowners and immobile labor. Indeed, it is the immobile factors of production that have the greatest interest in an efficient fiscal system, local, regional, or national. The mobile factors exert the competitive pressures.

In the last analysis, the case against fiscal harmonization rests on the diversity of cultural traditions in Europe. Tastes and habits are different; and so is tax loyalty. These factors may become more uniform as time goes on, but we cannot predict the pattern that will evolve. Hence there is no way to define it in advance, as would be necessary for ex ante harmonization.

Western Europe's historic contribution to modern civilization arose from its diversity, as we can gather from a comparison with the homogeneous empires on the less diverse land masses in the eastern parts of the Eurasian continent (Weede 1988). The fertile diversity of Western Europe, supplemented by the smallness and openness of its states in the prenationalist period, is worth being preserved and should not be sacrificed in the name of some continental unity.

### References

Commission of the European Communities. 1985. *Completing the Internal Market. White Paper from the Commission to the European Council.* Brussels: Commission of the European Communities.

Commission of the European Communities. 1988. "The Economics of 1992." *European Economy*, no. 35 (March).

Court of Justice of the European Communities. 1979. *Urteil vom 20.02.1979. Rechtssache 120/78.*

Giersch, Herbert. 1973. "The Case for a European Regional Policy." In Study Group on Economic and Monetary Union, *European Economic Integration and Monetary Unification*, 67–78. Brussels: Commission of the European Communities. Reprinted in Giersch, Herbert. 1991. *The World Economy in Perspective: Essays on International Trade and European Integration*, 179–185. Aldershot: Edward Elgar.

Giersch, Herbert. 1988. "Liberal Reform in West Germany." *ORDO* 39:3–16.

Hayek, Friedrich August. 1968. *Der Wettbewerb als Entdeckungsverfahren.* Kieler Vorträge, N.F., no. 56. Kiel: Institut für Weltwirtschaft.

Hayek, Friedrich August. 1974. "The Pretence of Knowledge." Nobel Memorial Lecture, December 11, Stockholm. Reprinted in *American Economic Review* 79 (December 1989): 3–7.

Vaubel, Roland. 1978. *Strategies for Currency Unification.* Kieler Studien, no. 156. Tübingen: J. C. B. Mohr.

Weede, Erich. 1988. "Der Sonderweg des Westens." *Zeitschrift für Soziologie* 17: 172–186.

# 12

# On the Transition to a
# Market Economy:
# Lessons from
# West Germany

This chapter consists of two parts: a highly selective story of Germany's postwar experience and an evaluation of the conclusions that can be drawn from it for the countries in transition from socialism to a market economy.

## Stylized Facts

Between 1936 and 1948 Germany had a centrally administrated capitalist system.[1] Until 1945, this system had reasonably well served its purpose of extracting resources for the buildup of the armaments industry by (1) the fixing of prices, wages, and rents at their 1936 level, (2) the rationing of consumer goods and foodstuffs and the tight regulation of housing, (3) compulsory delivery quotas for farmers, and (4) the central allocation of labor, raw materials, and major commodities.

This system broke down in the period of "postwar misery" from 1945 to mid-1948, due to (1) the collapse of communications and transportation, (2) the administrative disruption in the wake of the military occupation and denazification, (3) the demilitarization of soldiers, the return of prisoners of war, and the influx of refugees from the (former) Eastern provinces, and (4) an increasing money overhang.

As the prices of new goods were not (and could not be) regulated, resources were channeled into producing such fancy "new goods" as ashtrays, lamps, and dolls. On the other hand, "Each day, and particularly on weekends, vast hordes of people treked out to the country to barter food from the farmers. In dilapidated railway carriages ... hungry people travelled sometimes hundreds of miles at snail's pace to find something to

This is a slightly revised version of a paper presented at an Organization & Economic Cooperation and Development–World Bank conference on *The Transition to a Market Economy in Central and Eastern Europe* in Paris on November 28, 1990.

eat" (Wallich 1955, 659). The food rations issued frequently fell below the target of 1550 calories a day. The industrial capital stock in 1948 was 18 percent below its 1944 level and 7 percent below its 1945 level.

In Washington, the administration gradually realized that such economic distress in the Continent's traditional industrial heartland played into the hands of the communists and the Soviet Union. In March 1948, the Western Allies established a central bank in preparation for a currency reform. At the same time, a staunch liberal by the name of Ludwig Erhard was elected as director of the Economic Administration. Somewhat before, this administration had established an Independent Advisory Council of Academic Economists in which the leading "Ordoliberals" of the country played a prominent role and gained the majority (Böhm, Eucken, Miksch, Müller-Armack). With this intellectual support, Erhard obtained a vote in the parliament for the British-American occupation zone (Bizone), authorizing him to liberalize markets in connection with a currency reform.

On June 20, 1948, the currency reform was enacted. At a 1:1 exchange rate, individuals received 40 deutsche marks immediately and 20 two months later; firms received an amount of 60 deutsche marks per employee and public authorities the equivalent of one month's revenue. Cash balances, bank deposits, and savings accounts of private holders were scaled down; the effective conversion rate turned out to be 10:0.65. For the bonds issued by the former Reich, banks were granted low-interest "equalization claims" equivalent to 4 percent; almost all other debts were devalued by a factor of ten. The liquidity of the banks was restored by granting them deposits with the central banking system (amounting to 15 percent for demand deposits and 7.5 percent for time deposits and savings accounts). For all recurrent payments (wages, rents, and so forth) and for all official prices, the conversion rate was 1:1.

The central bank, empowered to be the sole provider of legal tender, became independent of the government and all political bodies, and the expenditures of public authorities had to be covered by current income or by credit in anticipation of future revenues.

Although the guidelines that the Bizonal parliament had passed on June 18 were not yet approved by the Allied Control Office, Erhard implemented them, on his own responsibility, by lifting the price controls for some foodstuffs and for almost all manufactured goods. He also did not renew the directives on the rationing of goods and the central allocation of resources.

A "little tax reform," enacted by the military government, improved the incentive system. It brought down income tax rates by roughly one third, cut the corporate income tax rate from 65 to 50 percent, and offered important tax exemptions for income saved and invested. Local taxes were raised, and a high excise tax on coffee was introduced.

On the morning after the currency reform, the shops were full of products that had been unavailable, except on black markets. This dishoarding of goods had a tremendous psychological effect. Moreover, industrial output started to soar; the 1936-based index rose from 50 in June to 77 in December, brought about by a lengthening of the work week (42 hours) and a rise of the industrial work force (13 percent). Most of this was achieved in textiles and shoes, electrical equipment and vehicles—that is, in sectors for which price controls had been lifted. The capital stock started to grow—in the second half of 1948 at an annualized rate of 5.6 percent, largely financed out of high business profits, foreign aid, and the public sector surplus.

The objection that the official statistics understate the economic activity before the reforms and hence overstate the spurt after June 20 has some merit. But the real importance of the economic reform—as opposed to the currency reform—can be gathered from the fact that the rapid progress observed in the Bizone was accompanied by a much slower pace of recovery in the French occupation zone, where the control measures were not enacted before early 1949 (see Ritschl 1985, 164).

Inflationary dangers emerged in the fall of 1948 after the second installment of the initial personal allowance had been paid out and the generous initial endowment with the central bank deposits made the quantity of money ($M_3$) grow (by 100 percent between the end of July and the end of the year) and firms managed to get along with rather small cash balances. As a result, consumer and producer prices increased by annualized rates of 33 and 45 percent in the first four months after the reform. Although real wages had not declined, labor unions called for a one-day general strike to be understood as a call for the return to a controlled economy. The subsequent tightening of monetary policy eased inflationary pressures and even led to a decline of the price level (0.5 percent monthly in 1949 and 1 percent monthly in early 1950).

Despite this cooling of the business climate, industrial production continued to grow, though at a slower pace, by 24 percent in 1949 and another 12 percent in the first half of 1950. For GDP growth, a reasonable estimate for the twenty-four months after the reforms is around 15 percent per annum. Most of this is due to (1) gains in labor productivity (longer hours, less unemployment on the job), (2) genuine reconstruction in the sense that large parts of the capital stock that had been damaged during the war could be repaired at rather low investment costs, and (3) a heavy restructuring of employment, mostly at the expense of agriculture and to the benefit of (metal) manufacturing and production-related services.

Although labor productivity rose fast and although real wages lagged behind until late 1949, unemployment became the major problem. Its rate surpassed 12 percent in March 1950, after the year 1949 had brought a net employment loss of 150,000 jobs. The regional pattern of unemployment was very skewed. In the two northern states, unemployment rates surpassed 26 and 17 percent, compared to 4.5 percent in the West and Southwest (North Rhine–Westphalia and Baden-Württemberg). The reason is that the bulk of the refugees from the East (almost 9 million) had been allocated to the rural areas, where they could find temporary work and shelter on farms, and that employment in agriculture sharply decreased.

Structural unemployment has been estimated to exceed 50 percent of total unemployment at that time. In a broad sense, the term includes capital shortage unemployment. This means that with a larger capital stock, more people from the countryside would have found gainful employment outside agriculture in both agricultural and industrial regions. In other words, capital, rather than labor, mobility was seen to be the limiting factor.

When in February 1950 the unemployment figure surpassed the magic number of 2 million, the American body supervising the implementation of the Marshall Plan in Paris openly criticized the West German government for its passive (non-Keynesian) attitude toward unemployment. Apart from a counter-memorandum, the German government responded with a work-creation program and a housing program; they were expected to give a short-run boost to effective demand through a prefinancing commitment by the Bundesbank. The bulk of the implementation, however, fell into the period when the Korean boom and the subsequent balance of payments crisis had already set in. On the supply side, the government was interested in raising the efficiency of the capital market and in making its contribution to capital formation—with the government's share in total investment expenditure reaching one-quarter in the early 1950s, and this with a heavy emphasis on housing, transportation, schooling, and the subsidization of private industry.

In the course of the 1950s, the capital shortage unemployment gave way to an emerging labor shortage that pulled in workers from East Germany and, after the building of the Berlin Wall in 1961, from the south of Europe. The GDP growth rate in the 1950s averaged 8 percent, and the balance of payments crisis during the Korean boom was followed by a persistent current account surplus.

The key to this extraordinary growth performance must be searched on the supply side. As to the supply of labor, we have to recognize that

1. one-third of the unemployed were expellees from the former eastern provinces who were well educated and highly motivated, prepared to go to the places where they saw work and career opportunities, and that

2. the immigrants from the territory of the German Democratic Republic moved right into the industrial centers of North Rhine–Westphalia and southern Germany, where they raised supply elasticities.

This elastic labor supply helped to limit the wage drift (over and above the minimum wages fixed in collective bargaining agreements) and thus contributed to (1) the maintenance of high profits for investment and (2) a process of capital widening with a high marginal productivity of investment (a low incremental capital output ratio).

Throughout the 1950s, wages increased less than labor productivity and producer prices. Real unit labor costs went down strongly in the three boom periods (1950–51, 1954–55, 1959–60), with only slight increases in between. All major decreases of real unit labor costs had a counterpart in substantial increases in the ratio of producer prices to consumer prices, which means that wage policy permitted the firms to retain their terms of trade gains as profits for investment. The explanation for this lies in

1. an organizational weakness of unions, though only at the very beginning,

2. a distraction of unions by their political objectives,

3. a combination of moral suasion by Erhard and of social responsibility on behalf of the unions, and

4. a continuous underestimation of the potential for productivity growth and for terms of trade gains.

In order to widen the bottlenecks that had arisen from controlling prices in the mining, steel, and energy industries, a so-called Investment Aid Law was enacted in 1952 for the purpose of channeling funds from business at large to the bottleneck sectors. This incursion into investment planning was of a corrective nature and ended in late 1954.

Until the mid-1950s, the capital market was fairly controlled in order to secure enough funds for residential construction (at 5 percent interest) while housing rents were still fixed. A partial liberalization of the bond market removed the interest rate ceiling (6.5 percent for industrial bonds) in late 1952. At the same time, tax favors were given for interest on industrial bonds. Only at the end of 1954 was the market for long-term bonds basically free and undistorted.

The housing shortage lasted until the second half of the 1950s. On top of general tax privileges for housing investments, a public housing program was launched in 1950. From 1949 to 1959 more than half a million dwelling units were built every year. This was apparently a great success, though at the expense of low housing quality and a controlled capital market. Liberal economists (like Röpke) would have prefered a free capital market, with free rents and direct rent subsidies to low-income earners.

In 1957, a competition law was enacted after a long debate of almost ten years. Until then the old rules inherited from the Weimar Republic prevailed. As they were rather soft on cartels, it must be said that the real safeguard for workable competition in West Germany came from the pressure of imports. Foreign competition acted mainly on the manufacturing sector.

Codetermination had been introduced on the firm level in the iron and steel industry of the British zone in order to prevent the former owners from taking over control again, perhaps also for ideological reasons ("industrial democracy") and to please the unions. It worked quite smoothly, at least in the period of fast overall growth, as the commercial part of the firms' business was not affected. In 1952, it was extended in weaker form (with labor occupying only a third instead of half of the seats on the supervisory board) to the larger firms of other sectors. However, there are works councils whose task is restricted to matters of personnel. Whether these arrangements helped to increase the economy's productivity potential is an unsettled question. Before the background of the historical experience of the Weimar Republic, the answer may be yes, but in comparison to Switzerland, which had even more social peace without codetermination, this answer is doubtful.

The best supply-side policy turned out to be West Germany's integration into the international division of labor for the production of goods and services. After an initial jump from 1948 to 1950, exports were growing, in real terms, at an average rate of 16 percent throughout the 1950s. The figure for imports is slightly lower—15 percent. As a consequence, the Bundesbank's foreign exchange reserves multiplied. This went along with changes in the commodity structure—first toward the prewar pattern, later on toward an intensification of intraindustry trade. Compared to 1948, West Germany's share in world imports trebled; the share in world exports increased by a factor of nine.

Unfortunately for the starting period until 1950, the internal reforms were not supplemented by a sweeping external liberalization, comprising, for example, a devaluation to cope with the dollar shortage or a flexible exchange rate and the removal of import quotas and tariffs parallel to the removal of price controls and the rationing system in the domestic economy.

Instead, the realignment of exchange rates subsequent to the devaluation of sterling in September 1949 even brought a slight upvaluation of the deutsche mark on a trade-weighted basis, thus contributing to the balance of payments crisis of 1950. And the liberalization of imports was left to the coordinated efforts under the guidance of the Organisation for European Economic Co-operation (OEEC) established in connection with the Marshall Plan.

Marshall aid was helpful but not indispensable. The first major shipments under the Marshall Plan did not arrive until early 1949, when the inflationary wave of late 1948 had already subsided. The food deliveries they brought closed a supply gap that otherwise would have called for short-term credits and a quicker abolition of the red tape that hindered exports. Aid receipts in relation to the 1950 GNP (more precisely, total aid receipts divided by four times the 1950 GNP) were 1.4 percent for Germany, much less than for neighboring countries (Austria 7.2 percent, Netherlands 4.9 percent, France 2.5 percent), which had a weaker growth performance. Nevertheless, the European Recovery Program made it easier for the other participating countries to accept the economic reintegration of West Germany into the international economy. West Germany, by the way, suffered a net outflow of resources in the postwar period if war reparations and the costs of military occupation are deducted from the assistance received.

In the General Agreement on Tariffs and Trade, West Germany was granted most-favored-nation (MFN) treatment by its most important trading partners as early as in September 1948. In August 1949, Germany extended MFN treatment to all contracting parties without regard to their policies toward Germany. The tariffs emerging from an intense internal debate were reduced during the Torquay negotiations without substantial concessions from other countries. And in October 1951 West Germany unilaterally cut some of the bargaining tariffs that were left over.

As to the removal of quotas, West Germany became a pioneer of liberalization in Europe after 1953, when it took unilateral steps in periods of cyclical upswings to combat inflationary pressures. However, there were major exceptions for foods and feeding stuff imports and for textiles, foreshadowing both the Common Agricultural Policy of the European Economic Community and the Cotton Textile Agreement of 1961. An almost dogmatic adherence to fixed exchanges rates under the Bretton Woods system led West Germany to use unilateral tariff cuts as a substitute for a revaluation from 1955 to 1957. All these liberalization moves, whether unilateral or in cooperation, turned out to promote exports—through limiting price and wage pressures and through inviting foreign competition to act as a spur to faster productivity advance in the economy's international sector.

Between 1951 and 1958, West Germany took steps toward full currency convertibility (1) on current account within the European Payments Union (EPU), then (2) with hard currency countries, except the dollar area, and (3) finally with the latter as well.

After the EPU had been dissolved in 1958 and most OEEC members had restored external convertibility of their currencies into dollars for current transaction, Germany in late 1958 and early 1959 removed most of the remaining restrictions on capital flows. The way to full convertibility had been cleared by a settlement with Israel (1952) and by the London Debt Agreement (1953), which cut prewar and postwar debt (including obligations under the Marshall Plan) by more than half.

**Opinionated Inferences and Counterfactual Considerations**

Compared to the 3 percent growth rate that was considered to be normal for long-run economic development up to World War I, the 8 percent growth of the West Germany economy in the 1950s, after the initial reconstruction, appeared like a miracle and was often called so. A miracle it was indeed, as no respectable person had ever dared to expect, let alone to forecast, it. This is already an explanation. Could the productivity advance have been fully anticipated at the wage bargaining table, profits—and investment out of profits—would have been lower, and the capital shortage unemployment would not have given way so quickly to a labor shortage that pulled in immigrant workers. Social unrest might have developed from the tensions between the indigenous population and those who had come as expellees and refugees from the (former) eastern provinces. And with more persistent unemployment, the relations between labor and capital (or management) would also have been less peaceful. In fact, one can say that positive surprises produced positive surprises, thus supporting a virtuous circle of success breeding success.

The conclusions for the Central and East European countries of today are as follows:

1. The population should be told not to expect too much but to look forward with confidence toward a recovery under the market system.

2. An initial period of decline and misery, though deplorable, may help to lower expectations and then give rise to faster growth afterward.

3. The example of West Germany in the postwar period—and of Japan and the small "Tigers" in the Far East—should be explained by emphasizing the vast growth potential a population can create for themselves by a high savings rate and strong competitive efforts to integrate themselves quickly and fully into the international division of labor.

4. The terms-of-trade gains that Germany made and were not discovered as productivity gains at the wage bargaining table were not windfall profits but must be seen as the result of hard work, structural adjustment, and aggressive selling in world markets.

Looking back over more than four decades of postwar development, one can conclude that the population in West Germany acquired the wealth and attained the income levels they would have had in the absence of the two world wars—that is, the income levels as they appear to be determined by geography and the present state of technical knowledge. This has a number of implications for Central and Eastern Europe:

1. The longer the "economic" distance to the present centers of industrial activity and knowledge creation in Europe (say: the longer the distance to the River Rhine), the lower will be the attainable income level.

2. The "economic" distance can be reduced by improving long-distance transportation and by close contacts with the centers of knowledge creation all over the world.

3. Under free market conditions, there will be a tendency for the East-West migration of skilled and venturous people, amounting to a loss of human capital in Eastern Europe.

4. This migration can be upheld only by reverse capital flows.

After 1945 West Germany had an inflow of ethnic Germans with much human capital and valuable skills due to the separation of the former provinces in Eastern Europe and the German Democratic Republic (GDR). In a longer perspective, this turned out to raise West Germany's growth potential. The same holds for immigrant workers from the South who raised supply elasticities and the flexibility of the labor market. Eastern European countries, including the territory of the former GDR, face the opposite situation. The danger of losing such resources can, however, be minimized if public opinion is persuaded to acknowledge:

1. that a market economy, in order to attract investment capital from abroad, has to offer high profits and must, therefore, be prepared to tolerate rather low unit labor costs;

2. that professionals and skilled workers with much human capital who are very mobile across borders must be offered interest on human capital in the form of relatively high earnings and earning prospects so that they resist the temptation to emigrate to the West; and

3. that for these reasons, the income distribution will have to be rather unequal during the process of catching up: very low wages for unskilled workers, who are immobile, and high earnings for human capital and investment capital.

Human capital formation was no problem in West Germany after 1945. From present-day East Germany we know that much of the human capital is not up to date or has an unsuitable structure of skills. Retraining on a large scale will be necessary. It should include training on the job. To the extent that firms are to perform those tasks, similar to professional schools, they will have to be offered incentives, perhaps in the form of lower corporate taxes, wage subsidies, or a low wage level. Language difficulties may limit the use of teachers from abroad, except in the case of East Germany; but it is likely that over the years the use of English will become more widespread in Central and Eastern Europe.

The issue of convertibility and exchange rates was important in the German case. In general one can say that a country becomes attractive to internationally mobile resources when its currency is convertible at an undervalued exchange rate—measured in terms of the production costs of standardized products. It will then pay foreigns firms to relocate production and to serve their former home market from places in Central and Eastern European countries. The relocation process goes, of course, along with a corresponding import surplus on current account in the recipient country. This import surplus should be considered a sign of strength rather than weakness.

The persistent German export surplus was healthy only because it reflected a rate of growth of exports high enough for gaining market shares. The opposite case of an export surplus going along with a loss of market shares should be evident. It is likely to be a symptom of decay: the country loses resources.

Foreign aid, like Marshall aid, may crowd out private capital imports via the exchange rate. The overvaluation of resources in East Germany (by applying a one-to-one conversion rate in the process of the 1990 currency unification) entails a substantial transfer of public funds from West Germany to equilibrate the current account. In order to avoid crowding out, foreign aid should be given only for specific projects that have a high degree of complementarity to private investment.

West Germany was a capitalist country in the sense that property rights could be viewed as intact. Private property was guaranteed in the Basic Law of the Federal Republic. The country also regained confidence on the international capital market. It could, therefore, have quickly moved toward covertibility on capital account and fully participated in world capital markets immediately after the 1953 London Debt Agreement. There is no reason to conclude from German economic history that it takes ten years after the introduction of sound money to reach convertibility on all accounts. Central and Eastern European countries that desperately need foreign capital should not wait, as Germany did, until this move is overdue.

Some property in West Germany was in public ownership, but no privatization issue arose in connection with the 1948 economic reform. There is no doubt that the liberal economists at the time would have made radical privatization proposals. Their fear of monopoly and monopsony power would have been strong enough to make them suggest that foreign bidders should have free entry in privatization sales. And their vision of a capital shortage would have induced them to submit strong arguments to the effect that a transfer of property rights to nonresidents could only amount to a net inflow of capital. The country's absorption power in the early years seemed immense. In the 1960s, when American direct investment was viewed with fear in other parts of Europe, German economists and even businessmen welcomed it as an element of competition. Such a cosmopolitan outlook is even more common now and can, therefore, not be wholly imputed to defeat in war. (Economic nationalism, however, showed its head on one latter occasion when in the 1970s a prestigious automotive company was on the verge of being bought up by a member of the Organization of Petroleum Exporting Countries).

Under conditions of a capital shortage unemployment, the social productivity of capital is likely to be higher than the private marginal productivity. The reason lies in the free availability of labor at given wages. Therefore, but also for neutralizing capital market restrictions, West Germany promoted household savings (in addition to offering sound money) and adhered to fiscal conservatism (budget surplus). Central and Eastern European countries can learn from this, mutatis mutandis. What they have to consider as different from the German case is the fact that there is now a world capital market that offers funds to good debtors and to countries whose governments deserve to be trusted as guardians of private property rights. Workers and the unemployed are therefore likely to be those who gain most from a political setting that promises a stable and strong, though limited, government.

Total factor productivity in West Germany turned out to be very high during the initial repair period. Such a "repair wonder" is unlikely in Central and Eastern Europe now, except after a period of chaos and disruptions, which everybody would like to avoid, or after a severe stabilization crisis with mass unemployment. But a "specialization miracle" may occur. The reason is that under socialism, firms as well as regions and countries tend to be underspecialized; they pursue autarchic policies. Once markets are functioning—with sound money, free prices, and vivid competition—firms as well as individuals will intuitively discover the truth behind the theory of comparative advantage and will spontaneously exploit the productivity potential offered by the intranational and international division of labor. This includes the gains from the application of new knowledge with which people become acquainted when they engage in trade with more advanced countries.

Almost every adjustment takes time, usually more time on the supply side than on the demand side. Elasticity pessimism is, therefore, not warranted, except in the short run. As in the German case, mobility and flexibility will turn out to be important for success. Note in this respect that economic growth in West Germany slowed in the 1970s when, at the time of the first oil shock, the immigration of foreign workers was stopped. The "social market economy" thereafter showed clear signs of "Eurosclerosis." The removal of barriers to entry (regulations of all sorts) is therefore essential in the eastern as well as in the western parts of the European continent. Less bureaucracy is likely to enhance supply responsiveness.

Entrepreneurship was not a scarce factor in West Germany's postwar growth. Demilitarization and denazification helped. A capitalist spirit soon developed—or, better, reemerged. After all, the bureaucratic system of central administration had existed for only a dozen years, from 1936 to 1948. In Central and Eastern Europe, the situation appears to be entirely different after forty and even seventy years of bureaucratic socialism. The teaching of business administration, though important, is not enough for the quick emergence of a dynamic business climate. Foreign managers may have to be hired for a limited period, and young persons will have to be encouraged to spend some time abroad to become acquainted with modern management methods—and to return, making a career at home.

In this perspective, the catching up of Central and Eastern Europe with the West may require a whole generation—twenty-five years. But there is also ground for a more optimistic assessment. The reason lies in the potentially low costs of transportation and communication. If in Europe the East and the West can be brought more closely together, the learning process in the East will speed up and will narrow the gap. Investment in communication may therefore offer high social returns.

Transportation and communication costs are partly institutional, rather than physical. West Germany greatly benefited from the formation of the European Community (EC). Without it, the slowdown of growth would have been more pronounced and have come earlier. Central and Eastern Europe should be quickly admitted to Western markets and Western institutions for economic cooperation. If this should force the EC to become more open, it would help both parts of the Continent.

**Note**

1. This part draws on Giersch, Paqué, and Schmieding (1992).

**References**

Giersch, Herbert, Karl-Heinz Paqué, and Holger Schmieding. 1992. *The Fading Miracle: Four Decades of Market Economy in Germany.* Cambridge: Cambridge University Press.

Ritschl, Albrecht. 1985. "Die Währungsreform von 1948 und der Wiederanstieg der westdeutschen Industrie." *Vierteljahreshefte für Zeitgeschichte* 33:136–165.

Wallich, Henry C. 1955. *Mainsprings of the German Economic Revival.* New Haven: Yale University Press.

# 13                 The Progressive Order

What are the conditions best suited to economic progress? What will determine the speed of this progress? My subsequent attempts at answering these questions will lead to the proposition that the rate of growth of knowledge production—and perhaps also of innovation—in the world is likely to increase in the next quarter century, as it obviously has done in the past during the last five hundred years. This is the potential. Actual outcomes will depend upon the extent to which we implement the conditions of a progressive order.

A progressive order is meant to be an arrangement that permits and brings about economic progress. Such an order can be conceived to consist of a "creative order," an "innovative order," and a "productive order." New ideas emerge to be tested and to be added to the stock of knowledge. This stock has the properties of a common pool and should grow as fast as possible. It includes inventions that can be turned into innovations that help to increase the value of output from a given flow of inputs. The innovative order is the link between knowledge creation and the growth of total factor productivity. I shall concentrate first on the creative order, then pass on to the innovative order, and subsequently deal with the productive order. This sequence and the conclusions will, I hope, make the treatment of the subject gradually more specific in economic terms.

## The Creative Order

The growth of the stock of knowledge is likely to depend on

• the number of people forming the world's scientific community in the broad sense,

---

This is a revised version of a paper presented at Scanning the Future, a conference organized by the Netherlands Central Planning Bureau in cooperation with the Ministry of Economic Affairs in The Hague, June 4–5, 1992.

- the density of communication among the members of this community,
- the resources available for research, and
- the rewards offered for scientific efforts and achievements.

Another factor conducive to the growth of knowledge is academic freedom, including tolerance toward the commission of errors and the absence of taboos and of devices to protect obsolete doctrines. However, members of the scientific community sometimes behave quite protectionist—perhaps just as protectionist as well-organized professions, guilds, and pressure groups. As they are inclined to limit freedom of entry not only to exclude lunatics or crazy ideas but also to reduce competitive pressures from foreigners or from the young, academic freedom has to be combined with openness so as to make the world's creative order efficient.

The size of the scientific community will continue to grow in each country as a share of a given population, though with some decline in average productivity. In advanced countries, it will also grow by immigration. Migration promotes communication and will thus contribute to raise research output and research productivity in advanced recipient countries and probably also in the world as a whole. Migration improves the allocation of the world's research resources. With or without migration, there is a high probability that more and more people and countries will join the Western civilization. They will contribute to knowledge creation, innovation, and worldwide productivity growth, as did Japan during the last hundred years.

The density of communication within the world's scientific community is an important factor in determining research productivity. This productivity can be expected to increase in the future as in the past due to:

- the migration of people from the peripheral areas to those central places that offer economies of agglomeration;
- the lowering of transportation and communication costs;
- the saving of transaction costs in the market of ideas by social innovations (language, rules of conduct, property rights, acknowledgments).

The prototype of a creative community is a research team—a group of persons with different talents but similar ambitions. Such a team may evolve spontaneously in a process of trial and error, but the process can be shortened in deliberate action by leaders (entrepreneurs) who have the knowledge, or the vision, or the intuition needed to form new and superior combinations. The team benefits from low transaction costs in the interpersonal division of labor due to proximity, familiarity, informality, credibility, and friendship. Teams are like families or firms. Scientific centers are agglomerations of teams comparable to conglomerates of firms.

The efficiency and coherence of teams is enhanced by pressures from a competitive environment. Competition among teams is likely to raise the importance of leadership. The team leader can obtain public esteem in return for feeding his or her ideas into the process of cooperation. And team members are prepared to supply additional inputs if they can gain reputation for better career prospects in the future. Low communication costs will ensure worldwide competition of research teams in the future.

The allocation of research funds and researchers among the various disciplines and among research teams and research centers in the world will remain left to the invisible hand of competition among researchers and donors, respectively. No central authority can have the knowledge required for central planning without making grave mistakes. Nor can a central authority fulfill the cost control function that is exercised by the (nearly) anonymous forces of worldwide competition. Governments may try to exert some influence, but without a significant effect.

In financing basic research, government involvement is almost indispensable. Enough public funds can be expected to come forth due to the prestige value the public has been taught to attach to scientific achievements. Moreover, private foundations will increasingly emerge, as private wealth is growing with rising incomes.

The financing of basic research by governments is probably not suboptimal in large confederations like the United States and the European Community (EC). While small individual countries cannot adequately internalize the benefits of such research (which makes them spend too little), large countries have reason to feel that they are better able to internalize than small countries. In the same vein, small countries will spend too little on basic research since they can hope to be free riders. Among the larger economic units, Japan is probably on balance a free rider in this respect. As countries cooperate, and even merge, they tend to spend more on basic research. The driving force is a political ambition to create an "identity," to demonstrate an achievement (as in the Olympic Games or in world exhibitions), to compete successfully for world championship in scientific achievement. This is often supported by the (deceptive) feeling that being only number 2 or number 3 in scientific competition comes close to an economic disaster. As a whole, competition for prestige can currently be counted on to compensate for any deficiency arising from the spillover and free-rider effects. Moreover, the scientific community has been very successful in lobbying. Harry Johnson (1975, 28) brought this point into sharp focus when he observed that "scientific research has become the secular religion of materialistic society."

The growth of knowledge is not likely to run into diminishing returns, though there is reason to believe that the easier discoveries have already been made. To be sure, bottlenecks are likely to arise in all directions, and in the Great Depression of the 1930s, there was much resonance for the apprehension that the world faced a dearth of inventions and innovations. But today, there is talk in almost all advanced countries about technological competition or about falling behind in a race under conditions of increasing returns. Others are alarmed by too much knowledge creation, fearing possible negative effects. This indicates that we can assume at least constant returns in the production of economically useful knowledge.

Increasing returns can be expected from specialized learning—up to a point. When diminishing returns are experienced, it is time for exploiting the opportunities of interdisciplinary cooperation, cross-fertilization, and alternative avenues. For this to be possible, the system needs some slack: tolerance toward errors, newcomers, outsiders, invaders, and entrepreneurs. Heterogeneous competition, monopolistic competition, and Schumpeterian competition are more conducive to the advance of knowledge (and productivity) than the rigorous determinism portrayed by "perfect" competition. Specialization makes for heterogeneity and product differentiation as a natural phenomenon.

In the spatial dimension, peripheral places must be able to take advantage of the potential for catching up, and centers of excellence must realize that their position can be challenged. A rating of research centers would give a boost to such competition, though heterogeneity may require the adoption of several value scales. No such rating has yet become practice on a European level, although the EC could easily stimulate competition among research centers by awarding degrees of distinction.

The optimal spatial allocation of creative resources must be left to free choice and the forces of competition. The outcome will not be very different from the locational pattern of other service activities. However, activities closer to the market will often outcompete the centers of research and learning in rivalry for housing sites and land. Apart from this, research needs the "social atmosphere" of a local community that is somewhat isolated from commercial activities. But being in spatial contact with modern industrial and service activities is helpful for financing research and for improving postdoctoral career prospects outside research. In the reverse direction, proximity eases the transfer of new knowledge to its place of potential application. Research centers are therefore factors of locational distinction for innovative activities. This has repercussions for competition among governments and locations; it raises public support for research. A research agglomeration—in the form of an institution—is kept together by:

• mutual confidence and, hence, by low costs of transaction and communication,

• a common ideology or research program,

• a common reputation,

• a common pool or store of knowledge (databank, library).

Hierarchy and bureaucracy are not conducive to communication; they are limiting factors for an order that derives its creativity from horizontal cooperation (exchange of information and ideas). Such an order must be interpreted as a nexus of contractual relations. Opportunistic behavior is limited by mutual control and by the prospects of long-term employment. Disloyalty entails severe disadvantages: a loss of reputation and a worsening of career prospects. These considerations are also relevant for the innovative order and the productive order.

Knowledge is a nonrivalrous good; it is part of a pool that cannot be deplenished. But it is often accessible only at the cost of some efforts: the user of knowledge has to acquire it in a process of learning. In this sense, knowledge is embodied, and if an invention is to be transformed into a profitable innovation, sizable complementary activities (adjustments) have to be performed and quite substantial outlays to be made. Knowledge thus becomes a private good. Nevertheless, the user activities are implicitly subsidized to the extent that the costs of basic research are borne by public institutions or private foundations.

Strategic alliances among big firms serve the legitimate purpose of creating new knowledge basic for certain lines of applied research that are believed to lead to new marketable products or services. These alliances can be taken to indicate that the public funding for basic research is inadequate; but they also show that the market can cope with such inadequacies, though by somewhat softening rivalry or impairing competition. Governments may have to watch that strategic alliances are confined to what is being called the "precompetitive stage." The cooperation agreement is claimed to involve lower transaction costs than trade in patents or detailed information. Cooperation on the basis of relational contracts resembles the informal trade in ideas within teams.

Patents serve the purpose of promoting private research outlays by making the new knowledge a private good (giving it the feature of excludability) for a limited period. Nobody can say what the optimum period of patent protection is. But if it is justified to assume that knowledge creation is accelerating, the issue becomes less important: patent protection will be less needed for speeding up progress, and more patents may become worthless before legal protection expires.

The closest link between the creative order and the innovative order is the intrapersonal technology transfer. It occurs when scientists become investors in order to become inventors or to push their ideas into the production process. Such an intrapersonal technology transfer is much easier if the centers of knowledge creation are private rather than government institutions. A public bureaucracy tends to lock in the researchers as civil servants for lifetime appointment, thus establishing a barrier between the creation of knowledge and its application. The centers of scientific excellence happen to be located in the United States, where no such bureaucratic barriers exist. This supports the view that the United States is likely to remain first in the production of knowledge and its first-hand application.

The creative order that has evolved over the last five hundred years—following the European Renaissance and the invention of the printing press —offers much scope for further great advances in the accumulation of knowledge. More and more intelligent people and more peoples will be pulled into this order. Think of Eastern Europe! In Asia, more than 1 billion Chinese are eager to be integrated. Other peoples of Asia are in a process of transition. If we consider what the world in the second half of this century owes to the contribution to technical progress made by the peoples of Japan and South Korea and how successful immigrants from Asia prove in competition with graduate students of Western origin, we are led to believe that there will be hardly any limits to the exponential growth of knowledge in the coming decades. At least the potential supply of contributors to the pool of new knowledge appears to be unlimited.

**The Innovative Order**

The innovative order is an order of monopolistic competition where firms have an opportunity of earning (transient) monopoly gains to cover the initial costs of transforming ideas into marketable product innovations and cost-saving process innovations. The monopoly position is limited in time because others can catch up; they will do so unless the monopolist is eager to stay ahead in the technological race. The normal state of affairs is not something to be called equilibrium in the static sense but a speed of techno-logical advance that can be expected on the basis of recent experience—a path of progress. Consider only the shortening of product cycles in the recent past.

Monopoly positions are limited in space as well as in time. The fear that there could be a world monopoly for a given product or input, making whole countries or continents "dependent" on a foreign supplier, which will then—like an enemy—exercise some destructive practices is absurd. There will always arise a host of competitors that, thanks to their smaller size, possess the advantage of greater flexibility. Even the potential of such competition will tame the giant.

Large organizations cannot cope with diversities. Their decentralization or dissolution will become inevitable. Today we observe how a giant like IBM needs to transform itself into an association of fairly independent units because it would otherwise break down like a socialist system of central economic planning. The innovative order is not merely monopolistic; it is monopolistic competition. Monopoly without competition seems to re-quire state ownership or protection by a governmental regulating body. Without government protection, monopoly positions will be eroded by technical progress. This trend is likely to continue.

The advanced parts of the world, which form the centers of the innova-tive order, will always be under the pressure of competition from below, that is, from low-wage cost locations closer to the periphery. This competi-tion is price competition, often denounced as "social dumping." It affects the suppliers of labor-intensive products with standardized technology. In the absence of protection, they have at their disposal three strategies of adjustment and innovation:

1. product innovations for capturing new markets,

2. process innovations for defending old markets,

3. locational innovations for shifting production to places where local costs, including wages, are distinctly lower.

Wage formation is crucial for maintaining the volume of employment. Wage flexibility has to support labor-saving process innovations so as to avoid the emergence of technological unemployment. And wage modera-tion is needed to give firms enough scope for financing product innova-tions that are employment creating. There is a mix of product and process innovation that allows full employment at rising real wages, despite the fact that competition from below is impairing the (factorial) terms of trade of local labor. Relative factor prices determine the nature of progress. Excessive wages (and low real interest rates) speed up the use of robots to replace manual labor. High real interest rates and low wages are favorable for capital saving innovations. The combination of excessive wages and artificially lowered interest rates as it prevailed in Europe in the 1970s created an aversion against labor-saving innovation. Robots, which were introduced at an accelerated speed, were denounced as "job killers." This is not likely to recur in the West, but it can well play a role in East Germany.

There is a mixture of process innovations and locational innovations: lean production and worldwide sourcing. It amounts to substituting foreign for domestic suppliers or foreign suppliers for in-house production.

Locational innovation can be supported by interlocational competition. By this we mean efforts of public authorities—local, regional, or national —to attract future-oriented resources, that is, scientists, engineers, and other knowledgeable people, together with capital and entrepreneurship, for improving the supply of jobs for the immobile indigenous population. The means are tax incentives, cultural activities, environmental improvements, infrastructural investments, support to research, and the formation of human capital. Competition among locations in this sense leads to the competitive formation of an innovative atmosphere. This is almost the only kind of industrial policy I find fully compatible with a genuinely open society. It is "industrial" policy not limited to industry; it is industrial policy not based on the "pretense of knowledge" (Hayek) about the prospects of specific industries and firms; and it is a policy controlled by the forces of competition and the interests of those immobile resources that have to pay for the competitive efforts.

Locations have comparative advantages that can be formed and cultivated. A few professors of chemistry at one or two German universities are to be credited for having raised the supply of innovative chemists to such an extent that nineteenth-century Germany became important as an exporter of chemical products. Another example is Silicon Valley. Local and regional authorities will become more and more aware of this relationship.

A monoculture surely provides advantages of specialized learning, but it does so at the risk of a reduced flexibility and adaptability. At least under conditions of rapid structural change, heterogeneity should not be greatly sacrificed. This is in line with recent empirical research. Using data on the growth of large industries in 170 U.S. cities between 1956 and 1987, Glaeser et al. (1991) discovered evidence that employment growth is encouraged by local competition and by urban variety. The explanation for the variety effect is seen in knowledge spillovers between different industries as it has been stressed by Jacobs (1969). This spillover is credited with dynamic effects, in contrast to the Marshallian scale economies within individual industries (Marshall 1890), which result from the sharing of inputs, such as specialized labor, and account for the localization of industries.

An industrial policy that is limited to supporting specific economic activities will inevitably tend to be biased to favor what is known: people or voters who want to be protected, products that happened to be successful in the past, lines of innovation that have already proved to be successful in other countries. Future-oriented resources are too scarce to be diverted to rent seeking, and bureaucrats giving handouts cannot dare to run the risks of genuine innovation. Industrial policy as understood in Europe or Japan may be appropriate for followers rather than for countries that are ambitious to lead in the innovative race. The question is, of course, always one of the policy's relative merits: compared to what? Compared to open competition and nondiscrimination, industrial policy looks bad. But there are worse ways of spending taxpayers' money—for example, Europe's common agricultural policy. The elimination of wasteful policies should be high up on any agenda for improving the innovative order.

A country's or location's competitiveness (in a commercial sense) is a fallacious concept. It takes the exchange rate or the wage level as given. Europe is less competitive vis-à-vis the United States if the deutsche mark is overvalued; and a place within a country is not competitive if the immobile resources, like labor and land, insist on demanding wages and prices that are too high. Commercial competitiveness may be equated with an export surplus, but an export surplus means an outflow of resources, not an attraction of capital for faster growth on the spot. The political community needs to be better informed about the fallacies of mercantilism.

Technological competitiveness is more difficult to asses. The notion is useful only in a long-run perspective and then only to the extent that the present technological standard can be taken as an indication of future commercial success and, hence, of good prospects for improving the firm's or country's factorial terms of trade (in the form of productivity growth that is faster than elsewhere). Technicians are inclined to overrate the importance of technological competitiveness in lobbying for funds or protection. Economists must help the public to understand better the role of technology in international competition.

The innovative order is the link between the creative and the productive order, but the link need not be very tight. Britain, for example, is ranking higher than Japan in terms of creativity, but Japan has been able to make a better economic use of the world's supply of new knowledge. I consider this anomaly to be the result of Japan's catching-up efforts and expect Britain to show a better economic performance in the future as a result of an improved economic order.

The innovative order has to cope with the problems of obsolescence. Specific physical capital will become economically obsolete; skills will be depreciated in the market; and incomes and land values in specific locations may fall under the impact of innovations elsewhere. The gainers would certainly be able to compensate the losers, but the more they have to do so, the less will be their net reward for taking the risks of innovation. If the potential losers had a veto power, they might block the innovative order altogether. But gradually, the public will learn that obsolescence of human as well as physical capital is a part of normal life and that lifelong learning is the price of progress.

Socialists once thought that a centralized system and a regime of public ownership would have a greater absorptive capacity than a decentralized capitalist system with monopolistic or oligopolistic competition. The main reason put forward was that in a decentralized setting, innovations would meet with resistance from those private owners of capital who are afraid of (premature or unanticipated) technological obsolescence of capital goods (not yet written off). What these advocates of socialism overlooked was that:

• in a process of innovation, human capital is as much involved as physical capital,

• human capital cannot be socialized except under serfdom,

• the owners of human capital that is specific (product or process specific) may equally resist innovations for fear of obsolescence, and

• a centralized system is permeated by contacts between people who know each other as comrades and therefore form alliances against progress or engage in mutual protection of their vested interests as owners of specific human capital.

Alliances for the protection of human capital ultimately can be broken only by the forces of competition: outside competition, anonymous competition, graceless competition, Schumpeterian competition in the form of creative destruction. The enemy of progress is protectionism. There is even intrafirm protectionism: one department may block another department's product innovation if the latter is considered harmful. This is why mergers are no guarantee for faster progress and why synergy effects from mergers may not materialize. The right cure for an aging corporation is quite likely an internal regeneration, with decentralization leading to more intense intrafirm competition. Innovators who are competing within a firm are sometimes called "intrapreneurs." This species will have to grow, and will grow, in numbers.

New knowledge needs human capital on its way to inventions and innovations. Hypotheses call for empirical testing; the researcher is eager to use her or his findings in teaching. Students taught by researchers become inspired to improve or to apply the findings. This appears to be a good tradition of Western civilization. The same holds for the dual system of professional education in Germany, where apprentices learn to practice while being taught the essential background knowledge. This is not the place to discuss details of human capital formation but to make only one additional point: if flexibility matters, a general (theoretical) training that lays the ground for a variety of professional avenues in research and lifelong learning offers good prospects for high incomes in a progressive society. A basic understanding of related subjects and of languages is important for reducing career risks in an uncertain world with much structural change.

Education is of great individual value for communication and for the exchange of experience and know-how and knowledge. But it also has external benefits: it widens the market and contributes to enlarging the pool of knowledge. This is an argument for public support to basic education. It gains strength if there is also a public welfare system since educated people are better able to help themselves; they tend to be more mobile and more flexible than those who are illiterate or have only limited experience. The skill of the population is a basis for future growth. Personal experience in a British camp for German prisoners of war in 1945−46 made me aware of the skill potential that my country could benefit from in the subsequent years of economic reconstruction. In a somewhat exaggerated formulation, one can say that in a country with a high skill potential of its population and a creative and innovative order, a devastated stock of physical capital can be rebuilt in almost no time. Reconstruction without an intact stock of human capital would have been much slower. This insight and a positive judgment on Europe's system of professional education brighten the prospects for Europe's growth in competition with North America.

Stocks matter, history matters, and so does geography. This is so because geography is not homogeneous, and history happens to be discontinuous. A good location offers rents of land and thus attracts people, including innovative people who attract more innovative people. This leads to the consequence of innovative agglomerations with centers of knowledge production on top. The history of Europe and North America illustrates this point. What has started to grow will probably continue to grow in the future, again by attracting resources. The economic system has centripetal forces that are only checked by rising rents of land and costs of congestion. Migration to the centers of agglomeration and prosperity will go on—in Europe from East to West, in the world to the United States across the Atlantic and the Pacific. Both Europe and North America will benefit from this. But Japan, the third center of world economic growth, is probably not in a position to derive benefits from immigration. It has a rather closed society, high costs of congestion, and a dual economy in the sense that it is excessively export oriented. Exporting goods and capital is no long-run substitute for the driving forces of internal competition.

In Europe, and perhaps also in Japan, the acceleration I expect from the fast growth of knowledge may well be braked by political opposition to:

- biotechnological research,
- the building of new networks for surface transportation,
- land use for water dams,
- nuclear energy production,
- the use of fossil fuels,
- the production of plastics and nonrecyclable materials.

Who knows what else will become a taboo in the next generation? Considering the various possible obstacles, I am inclined to believe that people in the advanced and highly populated areas and countries east of the Atlantic will not want a higher rate of growth of output per employed person (as we traditionally measure productivity) than people became accustomed to in the third quarter of this century. What can be achieved over and above this rate may be spent on an increase in leisure, health, job security, and environmental goods. People in advanced countries will also waste part of their growth potential in job protection, rent seeking, bureaucratic regulation, legal disputes, and distribution quarrels. In order to appreciate the contribution of the creative order and the innovative order to the well-being of people, we may have to revise our social accounting system to bring it closer to the notions of prosperity and progress.

### The Productive Order

The productivity advance, as we observe and measure it now, largely depends on the productivity advance within firms producing marketable output. The emphasis in defining the productive order must therefore be on intra-firm behavior (X-efficiency). One possible explanation for the unsatisfactory productivity performance in the last two decades is that much of the potential productivity of the computer has been consumed on the spot, that is, by those who could absorb it in nontaxable form.

Allocative efficiency is of secondary importance for productivity growth in traditional capitalist countries but not yet in Central and Eastern Europe. However, markets must be open, and firms must be free to choose their customers and their suppliers of inputs. The main role of competition is not in the allocation of resources; competition is much more important as a pressure for cost-cutting (process innovation) and as a spur to product innovations. If governments would refrain from protecting and subsidizing less efficient sectors or activities, they would, of course, improve allocative efficiency. But more important is that entrepreneurs know in advance that they cannot count on government support in case of failure and bankruptcy.

Cross-subsidization impairing allocative efficiency, of course, also occurs within firms, notably within large conglomerates. But the extent to which even large corporations can afford such waste is limited by competitive pressures. The openness of markets is a powerful constraint.

In the same vein, the ensuing competition among governments for mobile resources (such as human capital or investible funds) can be expected to limit the scope for excessive taxation and wasteful subsidization.

The productive order requires openness also in the sense that those who can produce a good or a service at lower marginal costs should not be prevented from doing so. Dumping charges have no economic rationale in the productive order. Few suppliers will find it rational to make gifts to their customers for any lengthy period, except perhaps in the unlikely case of a duopolist who wants to destroy the only competitor left and is not at all concerned with potential competition later.

Whether governments should be prevented from subsidizing innovations or whole innovative industries is a complex question. As indicated above, the answer to some extent depends upon who in the end is made to pay for it. If funds are diverted from senile industries that are bound to die, the promotion of new, specific ventures will presumably be an improvement. On the other hand, if the burden is placed on anonymous taxpayers who are likely to be as innovative or productive as the industries having to rely on lobbying for government aid, then the redistribution of opportunities is clearly not advisable. In the real world, the political game is biased in favor of those who are known and small enough in number to be well organized and forceful; and it is biased against the anonymous taxpayers who can be made to believe that they will hardly notice any burden. The idea that the country can capture (transient) monopoly rents from the subsidization of specific industries sounds attractive (similar to the optimum tariff argument), but if a positive outcome were reasonably certain for the subsidizing country (or for any location within its borders), then private business would seize the opportunity without public support. Too much talk about industrial policy by itself may make business hesitate and divert activity toward lobbying for subsidies.

The best support a government can give to innovative activities in production firms is to aim at being efficient, that is, to refrain from making unnecessary expenditures and to collect taxes only to the extent that they are needed to finance the provision of genuine public goods. The more opportunity people have to spend on their own account, the more will the market in the area serve as a test market, which is likely to attract customer-oriented production facilities.

What, then, can be forcefully brought forward to justify government subsidies to production? Is it national prestige, technical pride, defense? Doubts shift the burden of justification onto the shoulders of those supporting industrial policy. In this respect, one need not be dogmatic in particular cases. In some countries, governments and government agencies may be quite efficient in performing industrial activities; the essential condition seems to be—as in France—that the government sector has been able to attract a sufficient number of efficient administrators and highly qualified technical personnel. But would the population not perhaps be better off if the best talents were in the private sector and would push ahead in a highly competitive world market? The eventual success of a public industrial venture is not enough. The same excellent human capital might have produced a higher return in alternative uses.

The basic rule for a productive order on the level of corporations is essentially the same as the rule for the creative order. What is needed is team spirit in a competitive environment. The team spirit is to enable a cooperative division of labor without formal trading and high transaction costs. It is based on shared values, such as:

• meeting competition from other teams or companies,

• using a common pool of knowledge,

• striving for common goals,

• pursuing a policy of openness to attract people with a high level of qualification and motivation.

The competitive environment is to exert a pressure to preserve and improve the stock of common experience and to raise the common targets for the cooperative division of labor.

Genuine leadership in a productive order requires that the elements and forms of explicit hierarchy (or bureaucracy) are subdued in favor of efficient forms of participation in the decision-making process. Workers as members of teams must gain the feeling that they have common concerns and ambitions and that their constructive advice is welcome and will play a role in the final decision-making process. Participatory procedures can certainly be very time-consuming; this is the case when they are formal in nature. But if they largely consist of an informal exchange of ideas and suggestions, they can be quite efficient in leading to a consensus and to what may turn out to be a corporate culture.

The team leader should never fail to inform the personnel directly about dangerous developments in the economic environment. Alertness is a prerequisite of success in competition. Potential competition from innovative old and new companies should never be ignored as a challenge to a comfortable market position. In an open world economy, such competition can also come from rival firms that take advantage of the possibilities of locational innovation, that is, of moving closer to important customers or to cheaper sources of supply, including low-wage countries at the periphery of the world economy.

Investing in human capital is usually as necessary as improving the stock of fixed capital. There is reason to think that it does not play the role it should since personnel are normally free to leave the company at short notice. This will, of course, rarely happen in periods of recession and high unemployment. But in recession, higher priority is given to cost cutting than to investment in human capital. A way out is the creation of a corporate culture that has lifelong employment as an essential element. It implies that the best people see a good chance of climbing up to top management positions. An expansion of the firm's total labor force widens the scope for upward mobility and lifelong employment in a virtuous circle. The dangers of a vicious circle are obvious and need not be described. In order to avoid them, companies may resort to gaining market shares by acquisition, certainly a second-best solution.

As human capital gained from experience is often product specific, mergers and acquisitions for the purpose of diversification have rarely been successful. If internal funds are plentiful, they could better be invested in firm-specific R&D. Mergers promise synergy effects only to the extent that the R&D units share a common technology and can become heterogeneous by further specialization. Otherwise, there is a great risk of friction from unproductive internal rivalry.

The larger the company is, the more important it is internally to create conditions simulating a competitive market—for labor, capital, management, and know-how. What such markets can most efficiently provide is information on costs and returns, product improvements and productivity advances, target achievement and new ventures.

Motivation depends on culture and incentives. Culture includes such elements as work ethic, mentality, or loyalty. They are worth preserving. Education and an appropriate procedure of selection for appointment appear to be essential for maintaining high levels of motivation. But it is also necessary to provide incentives. This requires a fairly differentiated system of rewards, pecuniary and nonpecuniary. In granting special rewards, some discretion will help to avoid distributional quarrels and frustrations. The more developed is the team spirit and the system of informal mutual control, the broader and less specific can be the base for any bonus that should be paid for valuable contributions to common success. A broad-based bonus system has the advantage of contributing to cost flexibility in periods of recession and also for maintaining employment in difficult times. The optimum seems to be a combination between a broad-based bonus depending on the company's productivity advance and profits and a system providing incentives for particular individual achievements. Any pay system based on individual performance requires an acceptable evaluation procedure.

In organizing production, a balance has to be struck between the economies of specialization that entail rigidity and the advantages of flexibility that are likely to have a high payoff under conditions of structural change and in sophisticated markets. We immediately recognize the parallel to the contrast between the mechanical and the biological approach to economic life.

Decentralization is an important means to maintaining flexibility and to check the tendencies toward hierarchy and bureaucracy. Subordinates must often explicitly be encouraged to make decisions on their own responsibility instead of waiting for precise orders from above. At least group leaders have to behave as "intrapreneurs." They should be confident that errors will be tolerated if they are quickly corrected and taken as a source of learning. The formation of profit centers is a step toward creating, within the company, an internal market. The computer operating in support of spontaneous market coordination is superior to an Orwellian system of central monitoring. Internal competition is not indispensable. Rivalry within the company, apart from involving waste and a lack of specialization, may be a source of friction and even disinformation. A superior substitute is external trade: make use of outside sources if they offer cheaper supplies; sell even to competitors if they pay more than internal customers!

An international conglomerate with decentralized production facilities for diversified output can well be merely an efficient capital market and a common corporate culture facilitating the (internal) transfer of management and technology. Heterogeneous competition for a common pool of funds can give rise to a race for better productivity performance and a fruitful exchange of experience that would be impossible in an open market without a common roof.

## Conclusions

Some general strands of ideas have come up in the preceding sections on the creative order, the innovative order, and the productive order, which can be interpreted as trends likely to predominate in the next decades. They can be expressed—and extended—in the following statements.

The present quarter century, which I once called "The Age of Schumpeter" (Giersch 1984), is characterized by:

• a greater role for knowledge creation, innovation, and productivity advance as compared to the 1950s and 1960s,

• a greater importance of entrepreneurship and intrapreneurship than in the decades of catching up and expansion,

• an increasing pervasiveness of competition in all forms: intrafirm, intraindustry, global, interlocational, from above (product innovation), from below (process innovation), and from outside (potential competition from newcomers),

• a greater emphasis on flexibility, in contrast to size and scale economies (except for economies of scope in research and marketing),

• a greater concern for the human factor—in contrast to fixed capital—and for general education, professional education, job rotation, quality circles, team spirit, and team leadership,

• lean production with worldwide sourcing,

• a decentralization of decision making (along the lines of the subsidiarity principle), and even,

• a decentralization of production,

• the transformation of big business into conglomerations of independent business units (perestroika in firms),

• challenges to big government by separatist movements in smaller regions with a greater ethnic homogeneity.

Much of this results from a lowering of transportation costs and, even more so, of communication costs. The market gains at the expense of central planing, horizontal cooperation at the expense of hierarchy (command system), flexible coordination in heterogeneous markets at the expense of bureaucracy. The optimum is a combination of cooperation and competition—sometimes called "co-opetition"—similar to what was described as a desirable grouping in the creative order.

No general trend is without countervailing tendencies. What is desirable in a cosmopolitan perspective and will eventually materialize in the long run in the interest of overall prosperity will from time to time be braked or even reversed, though only temporarily. Here are some relevant considerations:

1. The widening of the market through lower transaction costs and the forces leading to more competition may find a counterpart in political and bureaucratic integration, for example, a centralist and interventionist European Political Union, and a leveling of differentials in factor prices (wages) by powerful labor unions and employers' association supported by government under the heading of a "social dimension." Such leveling would induce congestion and spatial concentration combined with protectionism (Fortress Europe). Much of this has to be expected in Europe due to a "constructivist rationalism" (Hayek) that works from top to bottom and goes against the spontaneous evolution from the bottom, where individuals make use of their creative and innovative powers.

2. Centralist experiments, however, will be aborted once it becomes clear that they are failures (like the Mitterand experiment in the early 1980s). Policy competition is here to stay, despite the glorification of policy cartels organized under the name of coordination.

3. There is one policy cartel that is really useful: the agreement among governments not to yield to domestic protectionist pressures, known as the General Agreement on Tariffs and Trade (GATT). A failure of the Uruguay Round of GATT negotiations to lead to a more open world economy would be a serious setback. But it will not destroy the open world order. Less trade will induce more migration and more international investment; it will also call for more development aid. Substituting factor move-

ments for trade will be embarrassing for many protectionists, particularly if it takes the form of migration. But one cannot say that it will impair world economic growth. Surely, induced protectionism aggravated the Great Depression of the 1930s. But memories are still strong enough to prevent the reoccurrence of such disastrous events.

4. In the field of technology, setbacks in the production of nuclear energy teach us a lesson about the acceptance of large-scale innovations that cannot be introduced incrementally and that are, therefore, burdened with the risk of great disasters.

There are also factors that can be hoped to promote technical and economic progress in the coming decades:

1. GATT (and hence the multilateral international trading system) will not break down or, if it really does, will quickly be restored.

2. With agriculture becoming smaller and less important in its voting power, the prospects are improving for a liberal solution to Europe's agricultural problem. GATT could be rescued, and entrepreneurship locked in agriculture would be freed for future-oriented activities with better perspectives.

3. Any restriction on trade—in goods, as well as in services and in knowledge—will give a boost to the emergence and growth of multinational firms and then to intrafirm trade in materials and products and to intrafirm technology transfer. International firms will outcompete national governments if the latter behave in a protectionistic manner in the traditional sense.

4. National frontiers will become more obsolete with the rise of international corporations that are likely to become what "national economies" were thought to be in the past.

5. Industrial policy, even in its forward-looking form, is a losing proposition unless it is applied collectively on a worldwide level to promoting knowledge creation and innovation. Even Europe is too small an area to be separated from the rest of the world's creative and innovative order.

6. The appropriate policy for open countries is locational policy to attract mobile resources for the benefit of immobile resources: it includes deregulation for free entry.

7. Easy entry stimulates product and process innovations; it also increases diversity, a factor that improves the growth prospects of the location.

8. Free entry is a challenging counterforce to harmful tendencies of concentration and monopolization.

9. The conversion to civilian purposes of physical and human capital hitherto used for armament production can be expected to accelerate economic progress, though only after a transition period.

10. The accession to Western civilization and an open world economic order of large areas in Asia and in Central and Eastern Europe with vast numbers of talented people will improve the use of existing knowledge and greatly contribute to overcoming the resistances to faster economic growth in the world economy.

The ultimate question arising in this context aims at the optimum pattern of the progressive order. The preceding reflections suggest an answer in line with the center-periphery model first proposed by Johann Heinrich von Thünen in his 1826 book on the isolated state and developed a bit further in articles that have become chapters 2 and 7 in this book.

The term appropriate for describing the basic pattern appears to be *coopetition*. It stresses the existence of centers—ranging from households and firms to teams and clubs, to cities and regional clusters of economic units engaged in production, innovation, and research, up to summits of knowledge creation and scholarship with worldwide influence. Though there is rivalry within them, these centers benefit from the advantages of proximity, which show up in the low costs of communication, transaction, and transportation among people who know and trust each other in the application of specific moral standards (cooperation). These Customs and morals are—so to speak—the network connecting them, their tight railroad or telephone system, their relational culture.

Apart from their cooperative morals, these centers are kept together by outside competition—competition that becomes more and more anonymous with increasing economic distance, that is, with increasing transaction costs. It includes competition from the own field of dominance nearby and far away, that is, cost pressure competition from below; and it includes innovative competition from similar centers (from above) elsewhere in the world. There are, of course, numerous center-periphery systems that are interdependent. They overlap, and they cooperate or compete with each other in what is a highly complex order.

What makes centers grow is the use of static rents for producing dynamic rents. Static rents include (1) Thünen rents due to geographic and other locational advantages, (2) Ricardian rents from natural resources like climate and the quality of land, and (3) cultural rents, comprising the advantages of urbanization (that is, of living close to each other), and enjoying the supply of public goods that (in open centers) are essentially club goods financed by taxes and customs duties.

The transformation of static rents into dynamic rents is exemplified by what may be called the true nature of the infant industry argument for tariffs: Start with a (regional) deficiency in the market for human capital and hence with an unexploited potential for producing income and wealth. Assume the case that the area could attract a firm that would produce not only salable output but also—as a by-product—an improvement in the quality of its work force. A customs duty on its product (or a subsidy) would be an adequate means to cover the non-pecuniary external economies arising in this form. This measure could be withdrawn after a while when additional firms have been attracted, which then derive as much benefit from the improvement in the area's labor force as they themselves contribute to the common pool of skill. The advantages of conglomeration do not dissappear after the withdrawal of the public support. They are irreversible and might reinforce each other. The process can go on—up to a point. But it is not immune against the dangers of decay if protectionism develops, with the effect that dynamic rents are converted into static rents for the benefit of shortsighted insiders. Openness is thus an essential element of "coopetition."

The cultural rent is an elusive concept. In order to have dynamic properties, it must contain forward-looking elements, as they are part of the creative and innovative orders. Economists will have to model and measure them, perhaps in the context of the "new growth theory," unless they want to leave the most interesting part of their subject to other disciplines—or to interdisciplinary cooperation.

## References

Glaeser, Edward L., Hedi D. Kallal, Jose A. Scheinkman, and Andrei Shleifer. 1991. "Growth in Cities." NBER Working Paper No. 3787, July.

Giersch, Herbert. 1984. "The Age of Schumpeter." *American Economic Review. Papers and Proceedings* 74 (May): 103–109.

Jacobs, Jane. 1969. *The Economy of Cities*. New York: Vintage Books.

Johnson, Harry G. 1975. *Technology and International Interdependence*. London: Trade Policy Research Centre.

Marshall, Alfred. 1890. *Principles of Economics*. London: Macmillan.

# II

## Monetary Policy, Inflation, and Exchange Rates

# 14       Entrepreneurial
Risk under Flexible
Exchange Rates

The purpose of this chapter is to show that, under flexible exchange rates, entrepreneurial risk need not be greater than under a regime of rigidly fixed rates. Greater variations in exchange rates will not lead to greater variations of expected profits from activities involving foreign exchange transactions:

if the exchange rate varies such as to even out different trends in wage costs and price levels;

if the exchange rate varies such as to neutralize cyclical fluctuations of foreign demand;

if the exchange rate varies such as to make domestic monetary policy more effective, thus reducing the need for variations in interest rates.

We start by defining balance-of-payments equilibrium with particular regard to the international integration of markets: incoming payments and outgoing payments should be equal without:

restrictions on convertibility;

official interventions in the exchange market;

official transactions for balance-of-payments reasons;

other measures for balance-of-payments reasons involving discrimination between domestic and foreign producers or asset holders; and

perhaps also variations in exchange rates.[1]

Balance-of-payments equilibrium can, however, be brought about or maintained by changes in the rate of interest and subsequent private capital movements. Balance-of-payments equilibrium in this sense:

Reprinted with permission from *Approaches to Greater Flexibility of Exchange Rates: The Bür-genstock Papers*, edited by George N. Halm. Princeton, New Jersey: Princeton University Press, 1970, 145–149. Copyright 1970 by Princeton University Press.

offers individuals all opportunities connected with the international division of labor;

offers individuals full opportunities of exploiting international differences in capital yield;

excludes all official transactions designed to support an exchange rate that, by being too low or too high, distorts the international division of labor and the international allocation of resources.

A constant exchange rate is provisionally included in the definition because of the widespread belief that variations in exchange rates place an additional risk on all activities involving foreign-exchange transactions. This belief stems from the analogy with interregional trade and payments, where exchange rates are rigidly fixed "for eternity." Entrepreneurs believe that, in interregional trade, there is no government interference with private competition, so that the outcome of the game is likely to depend on the firms' relative efficiency. This belief is fairly correct, if one disregards discriminating measures of regional policy that may be introduced without notice. But for competition to be undistorted by government intervention, fixed parities are not a necessary condition.

What makes interregional competition under rigidly fixed exchange rates so attractive are two conditions, which can also exist under flexible rates:

an equality of interest levels that ensures that capital costs per unit of output are roughly the same for competing commodities produced with the same technique, disregarding transport costs to be included in the costs of capital goods;

an equality of labor costs per unit of output, apart from differences in wage rates required for compensating higher transport costs in those locations where labor, by being immobile, accepts lower wages.

The second of these two conditions points to one major difference between interregional and international competition: if there are interregional differences in the Phillips curves, they must result in different employment levels and not in different labor costs. Where unit labor costs go up comparatively fast, firms are forced to dismiss workers, and where labor costs go up too slowly, firms offer more jobs than they can fill at the prevailing wage rate. With or without migration, the market mechanism ensures a parallel development of wage costs, and since capital movements ensure the equality of interest levels and capital costs among regions, the fixed rate of exchange that was an equilibrium rate originally remains an equilibrium rate all the time. And all the time competitiveness is depending on performance rather than on differences in economic policy (including wage policy).

This certainty that governments cannot interfere with the competitive game in the interregional case is often contrasted with the sudden shifts in competitive strength arising from parity changes in international trade. But entrepreneurs can have the same confidence—that it is performance that matters—under a regime of flexible exchange rates:

if the exchange rate varies so as to even out international differences in cost and price trends arising from different Phillips curves or from different policies; and

if interest rates reflect international differences in the rates of inflation, so that real interest rates are about equal.

Both these conditions can be expected to rule in the medium run, if governments and central banks refrain from intervening in foreign exchange markets and from taking action designed to keep the exchange rate away from its equilibrium level. Assume that it has become evident:

that country $F$ can maintain full employment only with an inflation of 4 percent per annum; and

that country $G$ is determined not to let the price level rise by more than 1 percent per annum.

In these circumstances:

the $F$ currency will depreciate in terms of the $G$ currency by 3 percent per annum; and

the interest level for all credits to be repaid in $G$ currency will be 3 percentage points lower than the interest level for credits to be repaid in $F$ currency.

There will be no distortion in trade and resources allocation between $F$ and $G$, just as if both countries were members of a true common market and a single currency area. As long as both countries continue with their economic policy, the change in the exchange rate will be easily predictable. However, should economic policy in one or both countries change in an unpredictable way, the change in the rate of exchange will cease to be predictable; as an equilibrium rate it will, however, be a rate of exchange that neutralizes the impact of policy variations on the competitive game between the producers of F and G. The only risk that remains is the risk of bad internal monetary management.

To summarize: what matters if one talks about the risk in activities involving foreign exchange transactions is neither a fixed rate of exchange nor a predictable rate of exchange but a rate of exchange that neutralizes distortions arising from unpredictable changes in economic policy.

Can a flexible exchange rate, apart from evening out disparities in cost and price trends, equally neutralize international disparities in the business cycle? The answer, I believe, is yes. Assume a cyclical excess demand in F that is not matched by excess demand in G. The F currency then depreciates (additionally) in terms of G currency, as long as interest levels do not react. But in a framework of proper monetary policy, there is an interest mechanism to counteract this tendency for the F currency to depreciate. It works in a twofold way:

an inelastic credit system or a policy of tighter credit puts a brake on F's boom by means of higher interest rates;

higher interest rates in F attract arbitrage capital from G so that the F currency depreciates less, and it may even appreciate.[2] F's trade balance will show a tendency toward a deficit insofar as:

excess demand is not checked by higher interest rates;

the propensity to import is not reduced by higher import prices (due to the depreciation of the F currency);

higher imports are not balanced by additional exports (due to the depreciation of the F currency).

This deficit is financed by the arbitrage capital that is flowing into F as long as the investment boom in F calls for relatively high interest rates. From all this it follows that cyclical divergences give rise to variations in the rates of exchange but that these variations are heavily damped if interest rates respond to cyclical divergences as well.

The same holds true the other way round: interest rates need not vary as much in response to cyclical disturbances if exchange rates are free to vary as well.

Assume that exchange rates are rigidly fixed and that monetary authorities are not permitted to control transactions and to intervene in the foreign exchange market. Any disturbance in F that pushes up investments and, thus, imports must then show its full effect on the interest rate so that the rate of exchange can remain constant in spite of a deficit in the trade balance.

Take the other extreme, which is perhaps even more unrealistic: if interest rates in F and G are rigidly fixed, it is the exchange rate that has to bear the full burden of the adjustment process. The F currency must depreciate until imports become sufficiently expensive compared with import substitutes and until sufficient resources are drawn into the export industries to maintain balance-of-payments equilibrium.

In between the two extremes there are many combinations, so that variations in interest rates are a substitute for variations in exchange rates and vice versa.

If there is a combination of interest rate flexibility and exchange rate flexibility that could be called optimum, it is unlikely to lie at the extremes. Why should a country have exchange rate flexibility and fix the interest rate? And only the most ardent proponent of fixed exchange rates would be prepared to place the whole burden of balance-of-payments adjustment on interest rates, when governments create disturbances by trying to pursue their own economic policy. Entrepreneurs might be inclined to argue that their total risk could be minimized by official interventions in foreign exchange markets so that both interest rates and exchange rates would be more stable. Such a "socialization of risk," however, has the decisive drawback that then the exchange rate cannot be neutral. If the currency is not allowed to depreciate, it is the foreign competitors that are subsidized, and if the currency is prevented from appreciating, it is the domestic producers that get a premium. Any reductions in risk from unforeseen variations in exchange rates or interest rates are, thus, to be paid in terms of distortions in the competitive game.

In addition to risks resulting from variations in interest and exchange rates necessary for balance-of-payments equilibrium, there are risks from cyclical changes in demand. While large countries suffer from domestic cyclical problems and from their own policy errors, the small countries are likely to import the cycle from abroad. In spite of this, small countries are being frequently advised to "integrate" with their big neighbors by means of fixed exchange rates. The argument that this must be so because firms in small countries have such a big stake in exports, usually overlooks two points.

First, a flexible exchange rate is a stabilizer with regard to fluctuations in external demand, just as a flexible price policy is the best strategy for a firm to stabilize employment, production, and sales.

Second, and perhaps more important, a flexible exchange rate makes domestic monetary policy more effective. This implies that exchange rate flexibility is a substitute for, say, tax rate flexibility or flexibility of public expenditures. While it has become an accepted doctrine in a number of countries that fiscal flexibility is a good thing for stabilizing the economy and reducing entrepreneurial risk, it is argued at the same time that exchange rate flexibility, which would in effect help to stabilize the economy along "monetarist" lines, is a bad thing because it would increase entrepreneurial risk. Considering how inflexible fiscal flexibility actually is, it appears reasonable to presume that exchange rate flexibility is not merely a substitute but a superior instrument.

## Notes

1. Variations in exchange rates are only provisionally in the list on grounds to be mentioned later.

2. To be exact, only spot and short-term forward rates appreciate. In the longer-term forward markets, a tendency to depreciate prevails, since arbitrageurs will want to sell immediately the additional F currency in forward markets. As Sohmen has shown, it is, however, the appreciation effect that is dominant. One reason is that foreign trade, which is transacted through spot and short-term forward markets, precedes the transactions that are hedged in forward markets. This shift in the timing is, above all, relevant with a view to cyclical fluctuations. The other reason is that, as has been shown above, spot and all forward rates will go up as soon as the rise in interest rates starts to work on the internal economy by reducing demand, and, hence, cost and price rises. This general appreciation effect comes about the earlier and is the stronger, the more speculators anticipate the stabilization success of a rise in interest rates, and the more they try to profit through purchases of domestic currency. (See Egon Sohmen, "The Theory of Forward Exchange," Princeton Studies in International Finance No. 17, Princeton 1966, 33ff.).

# 15     On the Desirable Degree of Flexibility of Exchange Rates

## Why Flexibility?

The question whether exchange rates should be flexible between any two countries or regions has been extensively discussed under the heading of optimum currency areas. Starting from the presumption that fixed exchange rates are desirable per se, the participants considered exchange rate flexibility as a second-best solution, permissible to compensate serious market imperfections.

Robert Mundell[1] viewed changes in exchange rates as a substitute for imperfections in the process of adjustment to demand shifts, which affect different areas differently. Stressing factor mobility in the adjustment process, he argued that there is no need for exchange rate flexibility and hence a case for fixed rates and a currency area if and when labor is sufficiently mobile to move out of the adversely affected country or region. Since mobility is a function of time and hence very high in the long run, even over large distances, the logical conclusion seems to be that in the long run the optimum currency area must be the whole world.

I find myself in disagreement with Mundell's criterion. Outmigration may sometimes be an appropriate answer to a balance of payments problem, but one cannot be sure about it, before the alternatives have received a fair trial in the market. The alternatives work through devaluation or a downward float. When real wages are reduced—in comparison to productivity—domestic employment opportunities are opened up, perhaps at the expense of competing employment opportunities abroad. With lower wage costs, investment opportunities become more attractive for foreign capital, notably in the export and the import competing sector. Moreover,

Reprinted with permission from *Weltwirtschaftliches Archiv* 109 (1973): 191–213. Copyright 1973 by Institut für Weltwirtschaft, Kiel.

there is a kind of real balance effect emanating from devaluation: domestic assets like land, shares, and whole companies become cheaper for foreign buyers (relatively cheaper for residents who are potential capital exporters). Outmigration may actually be the worst of all possible solutions to a balance of payments problem, since it is likely to be irreversible and to lead to a waste of capital invested in the infrastructure and a destruction of the environment through depopulation and overcongestion.

In the longer-run process of economic growth, exchange rate flexibility may be a means to prevent unsound agglomeration tendencies in some parts of the world. Such tendencies are likely to develop in a currency area with one unit of account, as soon as interregional wage differentials are artificially reduced below interregional productivity differentials in the name of equality. They impede the extension of currency areas and exchange rate unions beyond the boundaries of a common regional policy that is needed to make a currency area and even an exchange rate union a viable arrangement.

McKinnon conceded exchange rate flexibility only for fairly closed economies with a small foreign trade sector.[2] If very open economies devalued, they would face a great risk of induced internal price rises and subsequent wage increases: their attempts at changing the real rate of exchange might be defeated.

However, the argument that exchange rate flexibility is better for countries with a small foreign sector than for open economies seems to overlook that while it is more difficult in an open economy to reduce the real rate of exchange by a given amount, a smaller reduction of real wages in relation to productivity is needed in an open economy to correct or prevent a given amount of unemployment.

Moreover, open economies may need more exchange rate flexibility than closed economies for two reasons:

• they are more exposed to cyclical and other disturbances from outside and need more exchange flexibility as a buffer;

• while closed economies can more effectively use monetary policy to fight inflation with fixed exchange rates, open economies are more dependent upon price trends abroad, unless they change the transmission mechanism of the exchange rate.

In general, closed economics have more domestic problems and open economies more difficulties of adjustment to disturbances from abroad. If it were agreed that domestic problems should not be solved by exporting them and that countries should be permitted to mitigate or neutralize disturbances from abroad, then the more open economy should be allowed to have more exchange rate flexibility than the (bigger) closed economy. Peter Kenen argues that countries with a diversified export structure need no exchange rate flexibility, since shifts in foreign demand from one product to another are in this case less likely to have adverse effects on the terms of trade and the trade balance that would result in domestic unemployment.[3] This is probably correct. Turning it around, the argument implies, that countries of the banana republic type need (more) exchange rate flexibility. If export demand fell off (increased), devaluation (revaluation) would help

to support (dampen) exports,

to encourage (discourage) import substitution, and

to induce (reduce) capital imports by making domestic assets cheaper (more expensive).

More generally, flexible exchange rates would reduce the need for domestic measures against unemployment and would prevent them from leading to losses in foreign exchange reserves and to import restrictions on balance of payments grounds.

Upward as well as downward flexibility is needed if one considers inflation as much of an evil to be compensated as unemployment due to the downward inflexibility of wages. Herbert Grubel, Pascal Salin[4] and some participants of the 1970 Kiel Symposium on Integration through Monetary Union?[5] stressed the importance of exchange rate flexibility as a means of adjustment to different price trends resulting from internationally different positions of the so-called Phillips curve. A one-sided flexibility in the upward direction was suggested between 1964 and 1971 by the German Expert Council, mainly as a means of insulating the West German economy against the impact of insufficient price level stability abroad.

Most comprehensive is the argument that exchange rate flexibility, which returns to the Central Bank the power over the domestic money supply, makes monetary policy so potent that a country cannot only mitigate but also neutralize the impact of the foreign trade cycle on the domestic economy. The implication is that the domestic economy is fundamentally stable in isolation and that countercyclical demand management can keep it on an even keel, even if the exchange rate can only mitigate and not fully neutralize the effects on the trade balance of rising or falling foreign demand and of falling or rising foreign supply. If monetary policy is indeed so powerful under flexible exchange rates, one can go even a step further and envisage the case of a country that pursues an unstable fiscal policy and exports its domestic fluctuations through compensatory changes in the trade balance. Whether this would be beggar-my-neighbor policy and should be ruled out remains to be discussed.

In the ideal case flexible exchange rates are kept constant by the competent monetary authorities without controls of transactions and without intervention in foreign exchange markets, merely as a result of well-coordinated policies to regulate the money supply.[6] This, however, would imply that the countries concerned have the same policy preferences and the same trade-offs between employment and price level stability, which is certainly not the case. Nevertheless, if harmonization of policies is a goal in itself, it could presumably be achieved much more quickly and accurately under flexible than under fixed rates. Flexible rates would immediately reveal any lack of harmonization in actual fact by means of the very sensitive signal of exchange rate changes. Distortions arising from speculation would gradually become less important, if and when central bank coordination improved and became more easily predictable in a cumulative learning process. Flexible exchange rates which are being made constant through a coordinated monetary policy would, of course, also lead to a synchronization of business cycles. There is reason to believe that with a more sensitive coordination system "inside lag" of monetary policy would be shorter than with a system of coordination that requires large international conferences. Shorter lags might reduce cyclical fluctuations and hence the need for beggar-my-neighbor policies.

There is scope for the harmonization of countercyclical monetary policies even if the trend problem of international differences in inflation rates remained unsolved for the time being. In this case, the coordination targets under flexible exchange rates were not constant rates but more or less predictable crawls, associated, of course, with differences in interest rates that match the differences in the inflation rates on the one hand and the differences in forward premiums (or discounts) on the other. Agreements on the rate of increase in the quantity of money over increasing periods of time might be of help in the process of crawl coordination and would reduce the risks of serious beggar-my-neighbor cases.

Exchange rate flexibility without harmonization of monetary policies would at least open the way for competition among currencies. The idea of the optimum currency area can be dissociated from geography. What defines a currency area in economic terms is the total of transactions in which the respective currency is being used as a unit of account and as a means of payment. A currency that better serves its economic function will be used more extensively at the expense of less efficient currencies. The quality which matters is the stability of the value as seen by the users. It is up to them to decide. And we could trust in the survival of the fittest currency

• if exchange rates are sufficiently flexible to invalidate Gresham's Law and
• if initial differences in economies of scale did not matter (or were compensated).

The central bank issuing the preferred currency must, of course, be free to sell it against competing currencies. The good money driving out the worse money will be rewarded by a seigniorage gain. The better money need, of course, not be a money of national origin.

**How Much Flexibility?**

The desirable degree of exchange rate flexibility in a given situation depends upon the change in the exchange rate which is required per unit of time to remove (or to prevent) a dilemma between the policy requirements of external and internal equilibrium, a dilemma that exists (or would develop) under a constant exchange rate. Relevant in this context are:

• the size of the disequilibrium in the balance of payments that exists or that will develop if domestic policy objectives receive priority or, alternatively,
• the size of the divergence from domestic policy objectives—full employment or price level stability—that will emerge if the contractive or expansionary forces arising from the balance of payments should lead to external equilibrium.

There may, of course, be a combination of both disequilibria: some deflationary unemployment and some balance of payments deficit or some balance of payments surplus and a bit too much inflation.

The changes in the exchange rate which are required to correct a given dilemma situation are likely to be underestimated by governments and even by economists for one or more of the following reasons:

• Corrective changes in exchange rates have mostly been considered as measures of last resort. The International Monetary Fund rule that the disequilibrium must be a fundamental one has probably more often than not delayed the appropriate action. In these circumstances, the exchange rate has to change much in a short time, first to catch up with the changes that would have been necessary in order to correct or prevent the (small) disequilibriums during the time when they accumulated. In the second place, it is necessary that the spot rate is permitted to move—or is moved —beyond the equilibrium point; otherwise there would be too few speculators who are prepared to act as countervailing forces vis-à-vis the natural tendencies of sluggishness, which favor extrapolating expectations.[7]

• In judging the combined size of the disequilibrium in the dilemma case, attention is focused on the balance of payments, quite in accordance with the prevalent view that the exchange rate is an instrument of balance of payments policy. The domestic policy objective is then likely to be left out of consideration.

• In the case of an upward revaluation that is to remove a balance of payments surplus and to alleviate inflationary pressures, one easily forgets to take into account that domestic producers may be able to raise prices in their export markets where they probably have some influence on the price level which affects import prices. Of course, the same price pressures would have developed—although more slowly—if the balance of payments surplus had been removed without revaluation by means of an internal adjustment inflation.

The change in the exchange rate per unit of time that is necessary can be reduced by widening the band and by not intervening within the band. The rate can then quickly adjust in response to an external disturbance and can prevent the emergence of a disequilibrium for some time. Some investors may have to revise their plans and decisions, but such revisions are to avoid a disappointment later on and to prevent a misallocation of resources which is bound to arise if a necessary change is delayed by Central Bank intervention in the foreign exchange market.

The necessary change in the exchange rate can be reduced by adopting complementary measures of demand management. This implies that the objective is to restore or to maintain balance of payments equilibrium and that there is scope for complementary measures. If a devaluation is to become fully effective with regard to the trade balance, it has to be accompanied by measures to reduce domestic absorption. Under a pegged rate, these measures will be delayed because they appear painful and although they will be painful only if they have to be drastic because of a long delay. Nominal wages that have increased too much during this period may become the cause of minimum wage unemployment, if corrective measures of demand management are taken later on. If they are not taken at all for fear of unemployment, the devaluation will have to be much stronger and quicker to permit prices in the export and import substitution sector to rise faster than nominal wages (minus productivity increases), so that domestic absorption is being reduced via the wage lag.

In the case of an external disturbance that leads to a balance of payments surplus, the possibility of delaying action may have even stronger consequences, as the case of West Germany shows. Under a regime of flexible rates, revaluation would probably have started in 1966 and would have forced and enabled the Central Bank to ease rather than tighten monetary conditions. "There is no reason to assume that something like the recession of 1966–67 would have occurred."[8] Apart from the recession there would not have been an export-induced boom, combined with the longest wage lag after the war, and an excess demand at fairly stable prices that all contributed to making the West German economy even more export biased. How else but with a strong profit squeeze can such a bias be corrected? This is part of the explanation why the 1971 float was so furiously fought by business.

The degree of exchange rate flexibility that is desirable because of different attitudes toward inflation (different trade-offs and/or different policy preferences) may be large in the usual sense of the term. In a more sophisticated sense, that is, if flexibility is measured by exchange rate deviations from a predictable trend, it may become nil, for example, in the extreme case that the differences can be taken as constant.

The type of exchange rate system relevant in this context would be the preannounced crawl, as it was suggested in 1966 by the German Expert Council with a view to reducing internal inflation by the annual percentage of the crawl below what would have been compatible (under constant rates) with the then expected inflationary trends in major partner countries (3 to 4 percent). It is the property of a preannounced crawl that it can be expected to have an immediate and full impact on domestic interest rates for loans maturing within the time span for which the crawl is announced. Moreover, this crawl can be considered neutral with regard to employment as well as to the balance of payments since wage increases and domestic production costs can be expected to be correspondingly lower. This would permit exporters and producers in the import-competing sector to remain as competitive as they were before and as they would have been with constant exchange rates (other things being equal).

That the arrangement would be neutral with regard to capital movements is evident from the fact that international interest rate differentials would accommodate to the annual rate of the crawl. By the same token the domestic growth rate would not be affected. If the domestic economy is a kind of price leader, it cannot be excluded that the crawl arrangement increases inflationary pressures in dependent partner countries. The latter would, of course, be free to join the crawl, which would amount to creating an optimum currency area of the Grubel-Salin type. The German Expert Council explicitly envisaged this.[9]

A preannounced crawl with a narrow band is a pedagogical rather than a practical device. It can easily be turned around to show that if wage, price, and monetary-fiscal policies were predictable, the unpredictable element in a fully flexible rate system would be very small. What functions then would speculators have to perform? They would have to live on information about structural changes and their impact on trade and capital flows and on rumors about changes in monetary-fiscal policy. Structural changes are with us anyhow and everywhere and should, of course, be anticipated not only in the foreign exchange market. As regards monetary policy, it must be consistent with the objectives of public policy and with the situation as it develops. Under flexible exchange rates, monetary policy will be more powerful; it can work more smoothly and can be less erratic. If it is sufficiently consistent, it will be anticipated after some time by stabilizing speculators. There is no need for official intervention. A semantic question: Is this very much or very little exchange rate flexibility?

To mitigate the impact of cyclical fluctuations abroad on the domestic economy requires genuine room for exchange rate fluctuations. This case can best be explained by starting with the assumption that the domestic money supply is subject to a rule which would ensure price level stability in isolation. The stock of money would increase by the rate of growth of potential output corrected for trends in the demand for money resulting from rising incomes per head, changes in concentration ratios, and similar structural factors that have all been discussed in the old debate on neutral money. It should also be assumed that the government sector behaves cyclically neutral, a line of conduct that is difficult to define but an interesting subject of research in West Germany.[10] Under these assumptions an open economy can be considered to be cyclically stable in isolation. This amounts to saying that all cyclical disturbances will come from abroad and that the exchange rate is used as a shock absorber. When foreign demand accelerates in a cyclical upswing, the exchange rate appreciates and becomes a brake on the volume of exports and places importers into a better position vis-à-vis their foreign competitors on the tighter world markets. For domestic importers and exporters total demand is more stable than it would be under fixed exchange rates, but the steady expansion of the money supply does, of course, not guarantee complete cyclical stability in the face of foreign demand that is likely to induce fluctuations in the income velocity of money. The width of the band required for this kind of immunizing exchange rate flexibility would probably not exceed 6 percent for countries like Germany.[11]

If the objective is complete immunization or even an exportation of cyclical fluctuations originating in the domestic economy, including the government sector, then more exchange rate flexibility is necessary. This model needs a countercyclical rather than a neutral expansion of the money supply. Whether monetary policy can be used as an effective countercyclical instrument is beyond the scope of this chapter. What matters here is another problem. It is not unreasonable to assume that other countries pursue similar objectives. If the internal and the external situation were alike, the exchange rate would remain constant (in the absence of trend divergences), which means that there is a de facto harmonization of policies. If, on the other hand, the domestic and the foreign economy are in a seesaw position, opposite monetary policies would be required; they would reinforce the fluctuations in the exchange rate. Unless the monetary policies are destabilizing by themselves, the entrepreneurs and the employees in both countries would enjoy a more secure position.

Both cases of immunizing exchange rate flexibility assume nonintervention in foreign exchange markets. They imply policies which are predictable either with regard to the target variable (money supply) or with regard to their countercyclical effectiveness, so that speculation can be expected to be stabilizing.[12]

Intervention may fulfill a useful function if it is used as a measure to reinforce domestic policies. If, for example, a strategy for reducing inflation is to be embarked upon, it may be advisable to combine restrictive monetary policies with interventions in foreign exchange markets to bring about a more rapid upward revaluation at the expense of accumulated foreign exchange reserves, even if the balance of payments is in equilibrium. This combination lays the emphasis on the foreign trade sector[13] and uses more intensive competition from abroad as an instrument for controlling the price and wage level and for breaking up tacit agreements about restrictive investment behavior in periods of declining profits.[14] Interventions in foreign exchange markets may thus help to achieve stabilization without stagnation. The intensification of competition from abroad must, of course, remain within tolerable limits in order not to provoke a wave of pessimism in the business community.

Intervention in the downward direction may be part of a strategy to raise the level of employment, to attract foreign capital, to reduce outmigration by creating new and better jobs, and to increase the rate of growth of GDP above what it otherwise would be. The intermediate target is to reduce real wages in comparison to productivity and to raise the real rate of return on investment, first of all in the foreign trade sector and— eventually—in the other sectors as well. For this purpose the competitive position of the export and the import competing sector must be artificially improved by lowering the real rate of exchange.[15] The undervaluation of the currency must be maintained for a sufficiently long period, if outmigration of labor and capital is to be effectively checked and even to be reversed. A necessary condition for success is the existence of substantial money illusion, notably among workers and trade union leaders. Since money illusion is becoming scarce nowadays, wage and price controls may be needed as a substitute if the strategy of a growth-accelerating downward drift of a floating exchange rate is to be successful. The degree of exchange rate flexibility required for such a strategy is fairly large, depending upon the existing money illusion and the effectiveness of measures used to check the devaluation-induced inflation.

The opposite is the strategy of a growth-curbing upward flexibility. The final purpose here is to reduce the yield on domestic investment, to promote capital exports and to create fewer jobs that attract labor from less developed partner countries. For growth-minded economists this objective may appear absurd as long as it is not realized that immigration creates social problems and therefore external costs, and that an inflow of capital into a highly developed country may not only be at the expense of economic growth elsewhere but also a source of overcongestion and environmental problems. From a cosmopolitan point of view, the objective appears quite fair, and looking at it from the point of view of European integration it may be crucial indeed. Perhaps it is a necessary condition for the growth-accelerating strategies in other countries to become successful at all.

The growth-limiting upward drift of the exchange rate requires the use of foreign exchange reserves rather than of money illusion. It is, therefore, feasible only for countries that have accumulated foreign exchange reserves in a period of undervaluation, that is, in a period in which growth of GDP has been accelerated at the expense of other countries. The balance of payments mechanism under fixed exchange rates would, of course, enforce a growth-limiting process of inflation in such a country, if

• the exchange rates were irrevocably fixed, so that trade unions would pursue a balance of payments–oriented wage policy,

• national authorities would be unable to control the inflow of foreign funds, so that a national stabilization policy would immediately appear self-defeating, and

• the direct international price equalization mechanism would work without friction.

The desirable degree of upward flexibility is, of course, greater in the case of a growth-curbing strategy than in the case of intensifying competition from abroad discussed above. In the latter case the deterioration in the competitive position of domestic producers must be small enough to let entrepreneurs hope that they will be able to neutralize the unfavorable impact on profits by means of investments and innovations. The growth-curbing strategy, on the other hand, implies an upward drift of the exchange rate that is believed to lead to a sustained deterioration of the competitive position.

A final point refers to the desirable degree of exchange rate flexibility in the case that a new European money (call it Europa) is to be launched in competition with national currencies. The Federal Trust proposal[16] suffers from not taking account of Gresham's Law which must be invalidated by exchange rate flexibility. Moreover, the use of Europa needs subsidization and/or legal privileges. In contrast to the authors of this proposal the present writer—in sympathy with von Weizsäcker and others—strongly believes that Europa should outcompete the national currencies by better fulfilling the functions of a unit of account and a store of value (including the contract currency for long-term loans) by being a more stable currency, perhaps tied to some wholesale or consumer price index. Apart from this, the desirable degree of exchange rate flexibility in this case is unlimited. Particularly in the phase when Europa is generally believed to become the dominant currency, there is likely to be a flight out of national currencies in anticipation of further falls in their exchange rate. Supporting national currencies in this phase by intervention on foreign exchange markets would only prolong the process and would thus be undesirable if European monetary integration through Europa is seriously considered to be a desirable goal for this decade.

**Evaluation and Concluding Remarks**

Table 15.1 surveys exchange rate and demand policies for fifteen alternative combinations of policy objectives and constraints. It is sufficiently descriptive to be self-explanatory. Let me here merely summarize the cases

**Table 15.1**
Exchange rate policies for alternative combinations of policy objectives and constraints

| Policies | I *Prevent deficit* in balance of payments arising from domestic *expansion* relative to abroad | II *Prevent surplus* in balance of payments arising from domestic *contraction* relative to abroad | III *Correct deficit* (and replenish reserves) having arisen from domestic *expansion* relative to abroad | IV *Correct surplus* (and reduce reserves) having arisen from domestic *contraction* relative to abroad | V *Mitigate* the impact of foreign recession on the domestic economy |
|---|---|---|---|---|---|
| Objectives and constraints | No return to more unemployment | No return to more inflation | No return to more unemployment | No return to more inflation | Maintenance of balance of payments equilibrium |
| Exchange rate | Downward float | Upward float | Devaluation or downward float, steeper than in case I | Revaluation or upward float, steeper than in case II | Downward float |
| Demand management | Less restrictive than with a fixed rate | Less expansionary than with a fixed rate | More restrictive than before, temporarily more restrictive than in case I, less restrictive than with the old fixed rate | More expansionary than before, temporarily more expansionary than in case II, less expansionary than with the old fixed rate | Steady expansion of money supply |
| Incomes policy | Wage and price increases should not absorb competitive advantage gained through downward float, so that the trade balance remains unchanged while income increases relative to abroad | Wage and price increases should contribute to bringing about a deterioration of the competitive position so that trade balance remains unchanged while income contracts relative to abroad | Wage and price increases should absorb competitive advantage gained through devaluation or downward float, so that the trade balance can be improved without more unemployment | Wage and price increases should contribute to bringing about a deterioration of the competitive position, so that the trade balance worsens without more inflation | Analogous to case I |

**Table 15.1** (continued)

| | VI<br>*Neutralize*<br>the impact of foreign recession on the domestic economy | VII<br>*Mitigate*<br>the impact of a foreign boom on the domestic economy | VIII<br>*Neutralize*<br>the impact of a foreign boom on the domestic economy | IX<br>*Correct*<br>underutilization of resources due to domestic recession | X<br>*Correct*<br>excess demand due to a domestic boom |
|---|---|---|---|---|---|
| Objectives and constraints | As in case V | As in case V | As in case V | No balance of payments deficit | No balance of payments surplus |
| **Policies** | | | | | |
| Exchange rate | Downward float steeper than in case V | Upward float | Upward float steeper than in case VII | Devaluation or enforced downward float | Revaluation or enforced upward float |
| Demand management | Accelerated expansion of money supply | As in case V | Decelerated expansion or even contraction of money supply | Expansionary, as in case IV | Decelerated expansion or contraction of money supply |
| Incomes policy | Analogous to Case I | Analogous to case II | Analogous to Case II | Wage and price increases should not absorb competitive advantage gained through devaluation or downward float, so that mprovement in competitive position can contribute to further increased resource use | Wage and price increases could be strong enough to bring about a temporary deterioration of competitive conditions which would worsen the trade balance and would be compatible with induced capital inflows |

**Table 15.1** (continued)

| Objectives and constraints / Policies | XI *Mitigate* the effects of internal cyclical tendencies on the domestic economy | XII *Prevent* the effects of internal cyclical tendencies on the domestic economy | XIII *Reduce* domestic below foreign price trends | XIV *Accelerate* growth of GDP | XV *Decelerate* growth of GDP |
|---|---|---|---|---|---|
| | Balance of payments equilibrium | As in case XI | No balance of payments surplus | No balance of payments deficit | No balance of payments surplus |
| Exchange rate | Free float that induces countercyclical reactions in the trade balance | Free float with stronger fluctuations and stronger counter-cyclical trade balance reactions | Free float with announced monetary strategy (a) preannounced crawl (b) | Devaluation, enforced downward float | Revaluation or enforced upward float |
| Demand management | Steady expansion of money supply | Countercyclical monetary policy | Steady expansion of money supply (a) balance of payments oriented (b) | Expansionary monetary policy | Restrictive monetary policy |
| Incomes policy | More price and wage flexibility—shorter lags | As in case XI | Adjust wage and price increases to the announced monetary strategy (a) adjust wage increase and interest rate to preannounced crawl (b) | Wages and prices should not absorb competitive advantage gained through devaluation or enforced downward float, so that resource use and attractiveness to capital and entrepreneurial activity is increased | The slowdown of wage and price increases should not fully offset revaluation or enforced upward float, so that the competitive position deteriorates and the attractiveness to capital, labor, and entrepreneurial ability is reduced. |

with a view to drawing some conclusions for the desirable degree of exchange rate flexibility.

If the objective is

• to prevent a balance of payments deficit or surplus from arising out of
domestic or external causes—cases I, II—

• to mitigate the impact of a foreign recession or boom on the domestic
economy—cases V, VII—or

• to mitigate the effects of internal cyclical tendencies on the domestic
economy—case XI—

then there is need for a downward and upward flexibility of the exchange
rate. Such flexibility is limited provided that domestic demand management
(monetary policy) is attuned to exchange rate flexibility by being

• steady—as in cases V, VII, and XI—

• or more steady (less restrictive or expansionary) than the objective would
require with a fixed rate—cases I and II.

Much larger changes in exchange rates per unit of time will result or are
necessary,

• in all cases mentioned if monetary policy is not attuned to exchange rate
flexibility and is, therefore, too unsteady,

• if the exchange rate has been pegged for some time, so that a surplus or
a deficit in the balance of payments must be corrected—cases III and IV,

• if demand management has failed to prevent a domestic recession or
boom—cases IX and X—so that corrective rather than preventive policies
have to be adopted,

• if the objective is to neutralize (rather than mitigate) the impact of a
foreign recession or boom on the domestic economy—cases VI and VIII—

• if the domestic economy is unstable in isolation (perhaps as a result of
unsteady fiscal policies) and if exchange rate flexibility and countercyclical
monetary policies are adopted to stabilize the domestic economy, which
implies stronger countercyclical reaction of the trade balance than under a
regime of fixed rates—case XII.

While the greater exchange rate flexibility (larger changes per unit of
time) would be desirable from a national point of view in all cases mentioned in the previous paragraph, they would not necessarily be desirable

from the point of view of the world economy. It would rather be desirable to have rules

• that force countries to an early upward or downward float, so that the surpluses and the deficits in the balance of payments which must be corrected are smaller than under the present system,

• that force countries to pursue a less unsteady monetary policy,

• that force countries to harmonize these policies,

• that prevent countries from pursuing a destabilizing fiscal policy.

It is debatable whether—as in case XII—a combination of countercyclical monetary policy and exchange rate flexibility, which would cause countercyclical reactions in the trade balance, should be ruled out, except in specific cases, where

• the country is small so that the "export of the domestic cycle" is only an insignificant disturbance for the rest of the world,

• the country, although not so small, has a structure of exports and imports that is fairly diversified,

• a large country happens to be in a cyclical seesaw position in relation to another large country, with which it is closely integrated (West Germany and France in the middle of the sixties).

On a similar footing as these exceptions in case XII should be clearly the case of a country that needs countercyclical policy and exchange rate flexibility to neutralize its domestic economy against disturbances arising in a dominant partner country (Canada in relation to the United States)—cases VI and VIII.

A free upward float with a clearly announced monetary strategy to reduce domestic below foreign price trends (case XIII) meets with no objections from a cosmopolitan point of view. Countries should rather be encouraged to start such a policy and to join the starting country, thus creating blocs of greater price level stability. The same would hold true for the preannounced crawl, as long as the currency area developing out of it does not become dominant. If too many countries join, the emphasis must shift from the fixed crawl to a common expansion of the money supply as a unifying factor, that is, from an external to an internal target variable.

This then leaves us with cases XIV and XV—the use of exchange rate flexibility to produce an undervaluation or overvaluation for the purpose of speeding up and slowing down economic growth via a profit rise or profit squeeze that is not too short-lived to induce an inflow or outflow of long-term capital (direct investment). There is probably no objection on cosmopolitan grounds against developing countries' moving from an over-valuation to an undervaluation of their currencies. On the contrary. Such a change will cure several diseases at the same time:

• it will permit LDCs to remove exchange controls—in itself a major obstacle to the free flow of capital into the Third World;

• it will make the price of imported capital goods high enough to let investors think twice about labor-saving techniques and give incentives for the use and development of capital-saving, labor-using (intermediate) technology;

• both the inflow of capital (at unsubsidized interest rates) and the incentives to choose more labor-intensive techniques will help to solve the unemployment problem;

• in the same way the tendencies toward a dual economy and an unequit-able income distribution would be weakened, although the primary effect would appear to be a worsening of the barter terms of trade of labor in relation to capital;

• while their commodity terms of trade are bound to worsen, the less-developed countries (LDCs) would become more attractive sellers for foreign importers, who might find it worthwhile in a buyers' market to supply their know-how and market information to the LDCs and sup-port their efforts to change from import substitution to export diversifi-cation, including efforts to increase the supply of exportables through direct investment.

Perhaps, more LDCs will learn by experience that the right answer to a deterioration of the terms of trade is not a defensive action (strengthening of their monopoly power), but a future-oriented change in the export mix, that is, a change in favor of products with a high-income elasticity of demand. Concern with static notions of the terms of trade may—in a growing world economy—be misplaced emphasis that leads to misguided policies.

In principle, developed countries should not be allowed to have their currencies undervalued vis-à-vis the Third World. On the contrary. They would probably benefit from a (symmetrical) overvaluation—case XV— for the following reasons:

• imports would become cheaper;

• import competition from LDCs would relieve inflationary wage pressures;

• it would also force structurally weak industries either to speed up technological progress or—if this is impossible or undesirable in the long run—to release resources for the benefit of the LDCs (capital outflow) or for the development of service-intensive and research-intensive growth sectors;

• it would slow down immigration;

• it might help against the danger of congestion.

Overvaluation—case XV—although intended to decelerate the growth of GDP, might in fact help to accelerate the rise in the standard of living of the working class and contribute to impoving the quality of life, just at a time when there is a high-income elasticity of demand for it.

The only problem left is whether developed countries which stretch out into the periphery of Europe and which suffer from unemployment in their peripheric regions should be allowed to adopt an exchange rate policy to accelerate the growth of GDP. An alternative would be that countries in the center of the European industrial system adopt very clearly an exchange rate policy to decelerate growth. One or the other strategy is a substitute for a coordinated wage policy that lets wages in the central areas rise faster than at the periphery—or for a deliberate and well-designed regional policy to subsidize wages (rather than investment) in the peripheric areas. Without such a wage policy or regional policy the enlarged common market may be very far from an optimum currency area and may not even be a feasible one.

Why there should be any limitation to exchange rate flexibility in the form of a "band" defined by an upper and a lower supporting point is a question to which economics does not provide an answer that appears satisfactory. At least it would have to outweigh the objection that fluctuations within a band might be quite erratic, as the edges will attract the rate under the pressure of one-way speculation.

George N. Halm a proponent of the band, calls the support points "guideposts, clear signals for the monetary authority to support the adjustment process through domestic monetary policies," and he thinks of a hand of 10 percent (5 on either side).[17] This to my mind raises the following questions:

If support policy is compatible with domestic objectives, why wait until the exchange rate has reached the support point?

If support policy is in conflict with domestic objectives, why should it receive priority at a preannounced support point?

It is true that intervention automatically entails some support policy, but is it not equally true that Central Banks can overrule the effects on the domestic money supply—in the expansionary direction by using up foreign exchange reserves and in the contractionary direction by accumulating reserves for a very long period until speculation is induced to anticipate a parity change?

Will the exchange rate, when it is being supported, not be a wrong rate in the sense that it distorts competitive positions and misguides the allocation of investment among countries and between domestic and foreign trade sectors?

An escape from these questions is offered by combining the band with a crawl or sliding parity. Changes in reserves would be the natural guidance for parity changes. And parity change should become mandatory, a point which is particularly relevant for countries requiring upward flexibility, but having an influential export lobby. An operational formula that ties parity changes directly to changes in reserves could perhaps be constructed although it would not easily find acceptance. If already small changes in reserves would call forth parity changes that would bring reserves back to their old level, the arrangement might come close to unlimited exchange rate flexibility. Some friction, however, would still remain—because of the changes in reserves—and hence some delays in the adjustment process that would temporarily lead either the exchange rate or the interest rate to change more than under full exchange rate flexibility.

If the argument for support points rests on the need to counter fluctuations due to destabilizing speculation, it misses the point. Counterspeculation may be necessary if central banks and governments do not adopt, as they ought to under flexible rates, a less erratic policy. But the proper institution to carry out this task would be a separate stabilization fund which must try to maximize profits from speculation (but without intentionally inflicting losses on nondestabilizing speculators).

If the economic arguments for support points are weak and if it is necessary to devise crawl arrangements for minimizing actual intervention, the case for the band must rest on political rather than economic arguments, that is, on assumptions that take public prejudices and habits of thinking formed under fixed exchange rates as given for the time being, until the learning process has proceeded far enough. This is certainly the more realistic approach for the short and the medium run.

What is important is that the public and the world economy need not pay too high a price for such concessions to realism. The exchange rate has to be able to adjust quickly enough so that there is no distortion of competitive conditions among domestic and foreign producers and among producers in the domestic sector and the export and import competing sector. Otherwise the allocation of capital among countries, the rate of growth of GDP, and the international division of labor will be influenced in a nonrational way.

A well-known economist once accused me of advocating the fragmentation of the world economy. I do not mind, but the point is that artificially institutionalized integration that creates rigidities is likely to lead to excess agglomeration and polarization, unless this can be compensated by measures requiring a high degree of political solidarity. It is true that there are important economies of scale, but there may also be diseconomies of institutional integration which may be felt in terms of social tensions and which may eventually lead to a breakdown or to separation, unless the larger system has sufficient internal flexibility and sensitive signals for adjustment processes that are speedy and smooth rather than delayed and abrupt.

## Notes

This chapter was originally presented at the Conference of the Royal Economic Society at Ditchley Park, January 1973. I am grateful to H. Müller-Groeling, H. M. Stahl, W. Tyler, and R. Vaubel for helpful suggestions but retain full responsibility for remaining errors and omissions.

1. Cf. Robert A. Mundell, "A Theory of Optimum Currency Areas," *The American Economic Review*, Vol. 51, Menasha, Wisc., 1961, 657sqq.

2. Ronald I. McKinnon, "Optimum Currency Areas," *American Economic Review*, 53, 1963, 717sqq.

3. Peter B. Kenen, "The Theory of Optimum Currency Areas: An Eclectic View," in *Monetary Problems of the International Economy*, ed. by Robert A. Mundell and Alexander K. Swoboda, Chicago and London, 1969, 41sqq.

4. Cf. Herbert G. Grubel, "The Theory of Optimum Currency Areas," *Canadian Journal of Economics*, 3, Toronto, 1970, 318sqq. Pascal Salin, *Optimum Currency Areas—An Opening Statement*, manuscript, March 1970.

5. *Integration Through Monetary Union?* ed. by Herbert Giersch, Symposium 1970, Institut für Weltwirtschaft Kiel, Tübingen, 1971.

6. Herbert Giersch, "Marktintegration, Wechselkurs und Standortstruktur," in *Fundamentale Fragen künftiger Währungspolitik*, Frankfurter Gespräch der List Gesellschaft, 5.–6. 3. 1965, Veröffentlichungen der List Gesellschaft, Reihe D: Gutachten und Konferenzen, Bd. 46, Basel u. Tübingen, 1965, 47sqq.

7. Exchange rate adjustments under the traditional system are correctly considered disruptive for international trade and payments; the exchange rate is kept too long

in disequilibrium and has to move (to be moved) into the opposite disequilibrium position in a fairly short time. No wonder that the technostructure feels embarrassed; it imputes the uncertainty to the cure rather than the underlying disease, particularly in cases of an upward adjustment. The point has wider implications: whenever prices are prevented from adjusting themselves to changing conditions, distortions in the structure of production develop. If, then, the price mechanism is suddenly allowed to play its role, there will necessarily be tendencies for cobweb-type fluctuations, which most people are afraid of, as the discussion before the return to flexible prices in West Germany in 1948 has made abundantly clear.

8. Herbert Giersch and Wolfgang Kasper, "A Floating German Mark: An Essay in Speculative Economics," in: *Approaches to Greater Flexibility of Exchange Rates, The Bürgenstock Papers*, arranged by C. Fred Bergsten, George N. Halm, Fritz Machlup, Robert V. Roosa, ed. by George N. Halm, Princeton, N.J., 1970. 353 (quoted as *The Bürgenstoch Papers*).

9. Sachverständigenrat zur Begutachtung der gesamtwirtschaftlichen Entwicklung, *Expansion und Stabilität, Jahresgutachten 1966/67* (quoted as Sachverständigenrat, *Jahresgutachten 1966/67*), Stuttgart u. Mainz, 1966, para. 274.

10. Sachverständigenrat, *Jahresgutachten 1964/65*, sqq. *Fiscal Policy and Demand Management*, ed. by Herbert Giersch, Symposium 1972, Institut für Weltwirtschaft Kiel, forthcoming.

11. Giersch and Kasper, "Floating German Mark."

12. Speculation should be clearly distinguished from arbitrage, which is often called and denounced as speculation, notably by monetary authorities who rely on discretionary policies and discretion in attempts at pursuing inconsistent policies, e.g. defending unrealistic parities and disequilibriums, and which sometimes are in favor of more exchange rate flexibility as a deterrent against what they call speculators. It is exactly those misuses of exchange rate flexibility that have contributed to discrediting a system of greater exchange rate flexibility. Nonintervention in foreign exchange markets is a safeguard against such misuse; it forces monetary authorities to concentrate on monetary policy proper and prevents them from attempts to correct the market signals rather than their own policies.

13. H.-M. Stahl, P. Trapp, "Konzept einer stabilitätsorientierten Wechselkurspolitik", in: *Beiträge und Stellungnahmen zu Problemen der Währungspolitik*, Hrsg. von Hubertus Müller-Groeling, Kieler Diskussionsbeiträge, 10, Juni 1971, pp. 19sqq. *Die Lage der Weltwirtschaft und der westdeutschen Wirtschaft im Frühjahr 1971*, Beurteilung der Wirtschaftslage durch Mitglieder der Arbeitsgemeinschaft deutscher wirtschaftswissenschaftlicher Forschungsinstitute e.V., Bonn, Essen, 29. April 1971 [Common Report of the German Economic Research Institutes], repr. in: ibid., 9sq.

14. H. Giersch. "Some Neglected Aspects of Inflation in the World Economy." *Public Finance/Finance Publiques* 28 (1973): 105–123.

15. Throughout the chapter the exchange rate is defined as the amount of foreign exchange received for one unit of domestic currency. This permits the use of

words like devaluation, downward float, and lowering of the exchange rate as synonyms as far as the direction of the change is concerned.

16. Federal Trust for Education and Research, *European Monetary Integration*, A Federal Trust Report, London, 1972.

17. George N. Halm, "Toward Limited Flexibility of Exchange Rates," in *The Bürgenstock Papers*, 11.

# 16

## Some Neglected Aspects of Inflation in the World Economy

Inflation has accelerated in most industrialized countries since the end of the Korean War boom, as table 16.1 indicates.

### Diagnosis

Price inflation is said to be the consequence of "too much money chasing too few goods." Since there exists no money that is not supplied or tolerated by central banks, we can say with greater precision: Inflation results when *monetary authorities fail to resist the pressures to create too much money*, that is, more money than would be needed for chasing the goods and services that firms and individuals are prepared to supply at prices consistent with a constant consumer price level.

This definition has several *implications*:

First, there is an *optimum rate of increase in the quantity of money*. It is equal to the rate of increase in the quantity of goods and services which firms and individuals are prepared to supply at prices consistent with a constant consumer price level, plus the increase in the quantity of money which the public wants to hold for reasons other than chasing goods and services. The optimum rate of increase in the money stock, calculated this way, may not be much higher than 5 or 6 percent for most industrialized countries except Japan and a few other countries with rapid growth.[1] It is difficult to find a country whose money stock has not grown excessively by this standard in recent years.

Second, monetary authorities *fail to resist* pressures to create too much money for several reasons:

Reprinted with permission from *Public Finance/Finances Publiques* 28 (1973): 105–124. Copyright 1973 by Foundation Journal Public Finance.

**Table 16.1**
Inflation rates in selected countries

|  | 1952–55[a] | 1956–60[a] | 1961–65[a] | 1966–69[a] | 1970–73[a,b] |
|---|---|---|---|---|---|
| United States | 0.8 | 2.0 | 1.3 | 3.8 | 4.7 |
| Canada | 0.6 | 1.9 | 1.6 | 4.0 | 4.7 |
| Japan | 4.2 | 1.5 | 6.0 | 5.0 | 7.3 |
| Great Britain | 4.7 | 2.7 | 3.5 | 4.2 | 7.9 |
| EEC[c] | 1.5[d] | 3.2[d] | 3.5[d] | 3.2[d] | 5.9[e] |
| Germany | 0.5 | 1.8 | 2.8 | 2.4 | 5.4 |
| Netherlands | 1.5 | 2.8 | 3.6 | 5.1 | 7.0 |
| Belgium | 0.4 | 1.8 | 2.5 | 3.4 | 5.2 |
| France | 2.9 | 5.9 | 3.8 | 4.1 | 6.0 |
| Italy | 2.1 | 1.9 | 4.9 | 2.4 | 6.6 |

Sources: OECD *General Statistics 1964* and OECD *Main Economic Indicators*.
Note: Consumer price index.
a. Average annual rates (arithmetic mean of annual rates).
b. Including estimates for 1973 IV.
c. Excluding the United Kingdom, Ireland, and Denmark.
d. Weighted with GNP in the last year of the respective period.
e. Weighted with GNP in 1971.

• In an open economy with fixed exchange rates, central banks are required to buy unlimited amounts of foreign currency against national currency. With flexible rates, they are sometimes under pressure to intervene in the market to keep the price of foreign exchange high for the benefit of domestic producers. Such interventions lead to an undesirable increase in the money supply.

• There is political pressure on central banks to keep interest rates low, both to help small business and to ease the interest burden of the public debt.

• Governments that are committed to ensure a level of employment which is higher than would otherwise prevail exert pressure on central banks to be permissive in boom periods and to expand the money supply at the first indication of a downswing.

• Business and the banking community often believe that it is the government's and the central bank's responsibility to avert bankruptcies and solvency crises. Governments, instead of stepping in directly, often urge central banks to assume responsibility by pursuing a more expansionary policy.

Third, the above definition also covers the possibility of *seller's inflation*: The prices at which sellers are prepared to supply the quantities consistent with full employment are higher than the prices consistent with price level stability; alternatively, the quantities supplied under conditions of price level stability are below the quantities consistent with full employment and optimum capacity utilization. We do not have perfect competition in goods and factor markets without search costs and transaction costs, and we must, therefore, accept in the medium run some excess capacity and also some "natural unemployment" due to elements of monopoly, friction, and search activity. Moreover, there is the unemployment which well-meaning but unenlightened governments create by fixing and raising minimum wages.

This underutilization of resources tends to disappear in boom periods, when monopoly prices lag behind effective demand and when wages lag behind demand, productivity, and profits, thus temporarily creating a set of relations between nominal demand, on the one hand, and prices and wages, on the other hand, that resemble or approximate those prevailing under perfect competition. In other words: As far as volumes are concerned, time lags are a temporary substitute for perfect competition.[2]

The wage lag may even lead to conditions of a sellers' market for labor, where employers deliberately develop search activities and a kind of active labor market policy (retraining, payment of relocation costs, providing housing for workers, etc.) of their own. The wage lag thus reduces frictional unemployment. In countries with an open labor market it may even happen that the number of vacancies becomes a multiple of the number of registered unemployed persons.[3]

The counterpart in commodity markets is a price lag and an excess demand for products, measured in terms of unusually long delivery periods. Excess demand in this sense, resulting from an upward inflexibility of prices, is accepted by entrepreneurs as a purchase of security at the expense of potential profits; it enables firms to make productivity gains by reducing the range of products in favor of those which can be produced in larger quantities at lower costs. This is tantamount to an improvement in the division of labor among regions and countries as well as firms and can again be counted as a temporary partial approximation to a world of quasi-perfect competition.[4]

The blissful situation of excess demand with prices, wages, and interest rates lagging behind is unstable due to the existence of excess profits. It is bound to reverse itself into an inflationary recession as soon as wages catch up, and prices are pushed up to (and above) their equilibrium level under the pressure of increasing unit labor costs. Whatever attempts are made to defend profit margins—sometimes described as markup inflation—they only succeed for a brief period. Experience shows that the wage-price spiral, even if it becomes a price-wage spiral, is not yet permitted to become a runaway inflation.[5] To stop a cost-push inflation (which is in effect a "lagged demand-pull inflation") always means a profit squeeze and hence a decline in investment, in employment, and in capacity utilization. The unemployment and excess capacity which one would usually expect from imperfect markets and insufficient competition and which are conspicuously absent during the boom at last show up in the slump when sellers' markets turn into buyers' markets and when insufficient demand makes sellers' competition quite intense, presumably as intense as it might have been all the time in the absence of monopoly elements.

Over the whole cycle we probably have just about the unemployment and the excess capacity that conform to the prevailing divergence from perfect markets and perfect competition. I should, however, not exclude the possibility that the cycle of excess demand and inflationary recession still has a (small) positive effect on the average level of resource utilization. The condition for this is that workers and entrepreneurs have enough money illusion and that the money illusion exploited during the late upswing and boom is being quickly restored afterward when inflation slows down in the late slump and the early upswing. Such a cycle of exploiting and restoring money illusion can go on as long as the public is made to believe that inflation is not persistent or that, if inflation has become persistent, it will not, or not yet, become an accelerating inflation.

This statement follows from the well-known hypothesis that it is not inflation as such but unexpected inflation that raises the level of employment and capacity utilization. Money illusion is thus an imperfection which compensates for monopoly elements and other market imperfections. Unfortunately on this score, we may now be quite close to the end of money illusion in most countries in the Western world. Money illusion may have had a long life in previous centuries and decades; but in this age of communication and inexpensive information, it is bound to disappear much more quickly. Hence, we shall find it more and more difficult to raise the trend rate of employment and capacity utilization above the natural level by having resort to unexpected inflation. Keynesian remedies to monopolistic lapses from full employment may henceforth require not merely inflation but an accelerating inflation. This compels us to look for other "means to prosperity."

One alternative to unexpected inflation is incomes policy, a set of measures to prevent prices and wages from rising as much as they would otherwise do. To be quite explicit, I assign incomes policy the role of raising the trend level of employment, although most people, including politicians with a short time horizon, consider incomes policy as a means toward price level stability.

My argument is this: To achieve price level stability, incomes policy is neither a necessary nor a sufficient condition in the longer run. If we adopt the appropriate monetary policy, we shall, after some time, have price level stability, however at a lower level of resource utilization; if we use incomes policy without the appropriate monetary policy, we shall merely substitute repressed inflation for open inflation.[6] Hence, incomes policy is useful only in combination with an appropriate monetary policy. In this case, it serves the important function of preventing the level of resource utilization from falling as much as it would do otherwise.[7]

Following Gottfried Haberler (1971) we may distinguish between two types of incomes policy. Let me call the type that acts directly on prices and wages "conventional incomes policy," and the other type, which concentrates on competition as an indirect control mechanism, "radical incomes policy."

*Conventional incomes policy,* in the form of moral suasion, gentlemen's agreements, and price and wage controls, tries to stabilize the quasi-competitive prices and wages that prevail in boom periods and is thus a substitute for inertia, time lags, and money illusion; however, it may paralyze the market and it is likely to strengthen monopoly power through its appeal to the social responsibility of trade unions and business organizations as quasi-governmental institutions. It is directed at the symptoms and may reinforce the causes of the dilemma.

*Radical incomes policy,* on the other hand, strikes at the roots: monopoly power, insufficient competition, and market imperfections. There is a wide spectrum of measures which fall into this category. They range from the dissolution of monopoly and the control of monopoly power[8] to the adjustment of exchange rates in favor of foreign producers[9] and the subsidization of innovation, of patent licensing in nonmonopolistic forms, and of adjustments to structural change. A radical incomes policy means that business and labor feel competition to be (about) as severe as in periods of recession, but with a higher capacity utilization and a lower level of unemployment than a recession usually entails. More severe competition has the consequence that a higher GNP, and a higher level of employment, are associated with a given level of profits. Alternatively, more severe competition leads to a situation in which a given GNP, and employment level, are associated with lower profits.[10]

Effective demand can and will be maintained because more severe competition compels firms to invest more at every given rate of profit for the sake of their survival. Firms have to maintain investments in spite of lower profits and greater reliance on outside finance. The competition that brings this about we call Z-competition, in contrast to competition which results from a mere fall in demand (D-competition). What is being squeezed out of profit by more Z-competition is the monopoly element rather than the cyclical demand element—contrary to the usual profit squeeze in cyclical downswings when the monopoly element (Z-competition) remains untouched and the cyclical demand element disappears (D-competition increases). What is meant, can perhaps be best illustrated by the upward floating of the deutsche mark in 1971. It invited Z-competition from abroad, produced a profit squeeze at low unemployment, and became thus a substitute for a recession (increase in D-competition) that would have been due after the long upswing and boom following the 1966–67 recession (which was of the high unemployment type).[11]

A Z-competition effect similar to revaluation emanates from the removal of barriers to imports. In the fifties and the early sixties, European countries quite often took steps toward increased market integration as a means to fight excess demand and inflation at home. Whether the Common Market of the Nine will deliberately use this opportunity as courageously as some member countries did in the past, for example, West Germany under the leadership of Ludwig Erhard, remains to be seen—but I doubt it.[12] Particularly the mercantilists among the nine will find it difficult to understand that free imports from abroad should be in their own interest, apart from being in the interest of the world at large. Advanced countries can easily obtain more Z-competition from imports if they turn their attention to the potential supply from less developed countries. They can go as far as

• to remove all barriers to imports from low-wage countries, even if the imports are considered to be disruptive, and

• to encourage—through capital aid and through especially designed tax incentives to capital exports—an export-oriented industrialization in the less developed countries (LDCs).

Instead, we observe the growth of nontariff barriers everywhere, and this with the blessing and encouragement of governments, including the U.S. Congress and the Nixon administration and, unfortunately, not excluding even the government of West Germany.

At the same time, we observe that governments, which impede the free import of labor in the form of labor-intensive products, do not hesitate to allow free immigration of workers from low wage countries at least in continental Europe. This looks like an inconsistency, but becomes plausible under the following conditions:

First, workers who are allowed or invited to come into the country are not really considered to be competitors to domestic workers, at least in the beginning. Since they are handicapped by language difficulties, they may be channeled into complementary jobs on the lower strata, where they help to increase the value of the marginal product of domestic workers, who can move up more quickly.

Second, foreign workers are welcome because they are complementary to domestic capital equipment, quite in contrast to labor-intensive imports which can be close substitutes for the products of domestic firms. That the business community is keen on hiring foreign workers, although hiring costs are substantial and foreign workers are to be paid the same wages as domestic workers, is an indication that wages are below what would be the equilibrium level in the absence of labor immigration. The inflow of foreign workers helps to defend traditional profit margins and puts a brake on the rise of labor costs and prices.

Third, in contrast to American unions, unions in some European countries are perhaps much less interested in maximizing real wages and may be more interested in maximizing membership for its own sake or for political reasons beyond the labor market.

Seen as a whole, the coexistence of barriers to labor-intensive imports and free immigration of labor in Europe looks like a well-designed mercantilistic policy. Of course, mercantilism is not withering away with the nation-state, since it corresponds so well to the preoccupations of producers and sellers—in contrast to consumers—and of politicians who think in terms of economic growth and power rather than in terms of economic and social welfare.

Immigration is probably often an inferior alternative to imports of labor-intensive products from low-wage countries, inferior from both a national and a world economic point of view. It can cause environmental costs in the immigrant areas and may become a brain and activity drain in developing countries. Certainly, it has great disadvantages in comparison with a well-designed program that would concentrate on measures to promote the reverse flow of resources: the transfer of capital, technology, know-how, and skill to the low-wage countries with a view to importing from them more labor-intensive manufactures and sun-intensive tourist services. That this reverse flow of resources is not brought about by market forces to what I consider the desirable extent may be largely due to the mercantilistic prejudices and practices already mentioned, to exchange controls, which restrict the flow of capital, and to risks of an essentially political nature. These obstacles and imperfections should be removed or compensated for the benefit of world economic development as well as in the interest of a radical incomes policy in advanced countries.[13] From a national point of view there is probably no either-or alternative between immigration and capital exports; it may even be necessary to have both: more competition in labor markets and more competition in commodity markets through capital exports. Should there now be an excess immigration of foreign workers into advanced countries, it would presumably quickly diminish to optimum proportions, once governments took adequate measures to encourage the flow of capital and technology to countries with an abundant labor supply.

Inflation is sometimes related to the struggle for income distribution. This diagnosis deserves careful consideration in any program for price level stability, since it cannot be denied that—at least in some advanced countries—the income distribution has been changing in favor of wages, at the expense of income from property and entrepreneurial activity. Was this change the result of trade union pressures (relative increase in—or better utilization of—union monopoly power) or was it the natural consequence of labor's becoming scarcer relative to capital in the process of capital accumulation? As there is (yet) little evidence for the first of these two hypotheses,[14] it may be dropped in favor of a more careful examination of the possibility that labor scarcity in advanced countries has become a factor contributing to world inflation. As an indication and illustration, take West Germany after the building of the Berlin Wall, when an important source of labor supply suddenly dried up. Wage costs increased considerably, and attempts at shifting higher costs onto prices succeeded (in spite of the temporary increase in competition which the revaluation of the deutsche mark in March 1961 had brought about). If these attempts had failed completely and if the price level had been kept stable by pursuing a restrictive monetary policy, the level of capacity utilization and employment would have fallen for some time. Thus it can be said that unexpected inflation helped to mitigate the consequences of an unexpected decline in profits. The point may perhaps, be generalized in form of the presumption that unexpected changes that the market mechanism is unable to digest in the short run and that, therefore, would lead to a temporary drop in economic activity can equally lead to a wave of inflation, if the money supply is elastic. Even more generally, unexpected changes are comparable to an increase in friction in the working of the price mechanism; they worsen the trade-off that exists, in the short run, between (less) unemployment and (more) inflation. The policy conclusion following from this seems to be twofold: First, feed the price mechanism with reliable information on structural changes that are likely to take place in the foreseeable future, so that firms and other decision-making units can, if necessary, prepare themselves for quick adjustment. Second, remove all obstacles to quick adjustment and promote the specific adjustment processes required.

The adjustment that an increase in the shortage of labor requires can be on the following lines: (1) an (accelerated) inflow of foreign workers; (2) an (increased) export of capital; (3) a substitution of capital for labor by introducing labor-saving devices in individual industries; (4) a change in the structure of production that reduces the share of labor-intensive industries in favor of imports and raises the share of labor-saving (capital-intensive) industries in favor of exports.

The first two forms of adjustment have already been dealt with. It may be useful to repeat that it was immigration rather than capital exports that proved relevant in the historical case, to the detriment, however, of a regionally balanced growth in individual advanced countries as well as in Europe at large.[15]

The third type of adjustment was successfully attempted in a number of industries. In a period when labor becomes short and increasingly expensive relative to capital, it pays to introduce labor-saving automatic devices, even if they cause high investment and user costs. The saving of wage costs per unit of output may be almost completely matched by additional capital costs, at least at the beginning when the capital goods incorporating the (induced) labor-saving innovations are not yet produced on a large scale. The inflationary cost pressures ease only gradually when capital-saving innovations make the labor-saving innovations markedly cheaper. The other disadvantage of this type of adjustment is that it raises the capital intensity of production in the world at large. In contrast to induced immigration and induced capital exports, it does nothing to reduce structural unemployment in third countries; instead it contributes to maintaining, and perhaps even widens, the gap between the rich and the poor countries.

The fourth mode of adjustment to labor scarcity in advanced countries has an unemployment-reducing effect in the rest of the world. In this respect it can be considered a type of harmonious adjustment, like capital exports. It is harmonious also in a second sense. Unlike labor-saving innovations and immigration, it does not generally raise the marginal efficiency of investment and hence the scope for capital growth (and pollution) in the advanced countries. It merely favors investment in capital-intensive export industries in a relative sense, namely, to the extent that additional imports need to be paid for by additional exports. On the other hand, it negatively affects investment in the production of labor-intensive import substitutes. This will tend to reduce the real rate of interest and should, therefore, help to promote capital exports.

Both the export of capital and the import of labor-intensive products would have been stronger had the shift in income distribution from profits to labor not been reduced or delayed by an accelerated inflow of foreign labor and by inflationary pressures that were not anticipated by trade unions (wage lag). Had the market mechanism been allowed to play its role in the foreign exchange market and had the central bank been under the obligation to defend price level stability, the outcome would have been somewhat different. The central bank would have fought wage pressures by tightening the money supply. This would have led to an upward revaluation in the foreign exchange market and hence to increased competition from abroad, mainly in labor-intensive lines of production. Perhaps some lines of production might have directly moved to low-wage countries, thus reducing the need for importing foreign labor or making it unnecessary to introduce labor-saving devices. Flexible exchange rates would thus have probably shifted the emphasis to the harmonious forms of adjustment and away from the alternative forms that are likely to have contributed to widening the gap between the advanced and the developing countries—in Europe as well as in the rest of the world. What is relevant for inflation is this: Flexible rates, combined with the appropriate monetary policy, would immediately invite increased competition from abroad with heavy emphasis on labor-intensive import substitutes. To peg the rate when it would and should move upward proves thus to be an inflationary as well as a mercantilistic device.

For this and similar reasons, there is little doubt that the extension of the price mechanism into the field of foreign exchange transactions must form an important point in any radical program for price level stability. The objection that flexible exchange rates are not always optimum exchange rates does not invalidate the case, since it follows from a nirvana approach. Objections based on the experience of 1971 carry little weight, since they refer to cases where flexible rates were prevented from playing their proper role, be it by central bank interventions in the interest of domestic producers, be it by declarations that the float is merely temporary and will quickly end with a return to the old parity or the fixing of new intervention points by some urgently needed international conference.

Flexible exchange rates are more often optimal for the international division of labor and for the flow of capital from affluent to developing countries than politically fixed or pegged exchange rates can possibly be.

With really flexible rates, there is no scope for a mercantilistic national growth policy by means of an undervaluation that gives domestic producers a competitive advantage in domestic and foreign markets. The "overindustrialization" of West Germany and the "underindustrialization" of France, both in a relative sense, would not have coexisted and caused so much political concern, had France not had an overvalued and Germany an undervalued currency for most of the time. A similar effect was presumably produced by the overvaluation of sterling, while with flexible rates there would have been no need for balance-of-payments restrictions on capital exports.

With really flexible rates between developed countries, on the one hand, and the developing countries, on the other, there would have been in the former more competition from low-wage producers, and there would have been in the latter more incentive for export diversification in contrast to the inflationary import-substitution strategies that were adopted far too often. Less undervaluation of the currencies of the advanced countries vis-à-vis the group of developing countries would also have been the best means of promoting the flow of direct investment from the former to the latter; and if the latter had not had overvalued currencies, foreign investment would have been more attracted by the export sector than by the import-substitution sector.

It appears difficult to understand how political forces should have worked for an exchange rate policy that involves undervaluation in the advanced countries and overvaluation in the developing countries. More specifically, what forces (ideologies, prejudices, or group interests) work in favor of currency overvaluation in developing countries? Possible answers are (1) the combination of fixed exchange rates and strong inflationary pressures, arising from ambitious development goals and permissive monetary fiscal policies, (2) an elasticity pessimism with regard to foreign demand and domestic supply for exports, combined with the belief that overvaluation brings substantial welfare gains in the form of better terms of trade, (3) the belief that exchange controls can he used as an effective means of controlling the whole economy and that an economy controlled in this way will develop faster and will show both a more equal income distribution and a greater independence from the more advanced countries, and (4) the sheer interest of powerful groups that derive specific benefits from handling and influencing bureaucratic exchange controls.

There is no doubt that at least some of the arguments and prejudices working in favor of overvaluation, exchange control, and import substitution have their roots in what has been experienced and taught during and after the Great Depression of the interwar period, when the world economy disintegrated. The market mechanism, however, can normally do better than what it is allowed to do in periods of worldwide monetary contraction. The postwar period shows abundant examples to support this point. If world economic disintegration was the answer to worldwide contraction, worldwide integration and reintegration appears to be the appropriate answer to world inflation.

Integration in this context relates to functional or market integration, not to institutional integration (which is almost the opposite in spirit and effect). Politicians, businessmen, and other noneconomists seem to consider integration to be an essentially institutional phenomenon that produces— by means of negotiations—inter- or supranational government, equality and equal competitive conditions, fixed exchange rates and harmonized policies, multinational corporations and (why not?) equally international unions (as countervailing power)—everything bigger and better. I shall argue in the following that institutional integration—viewed as a process —is likely to have phases in which monetary policy is becoming more permissive, while upward pressures on costs and prices increase.

Harmonization of monetary policies (in the European Economic Community and elsewhere) is thought to be institutionally enforced by narrowing the margins for exchange rate flexibility. This is like forming a price cartel in the hope that it will somehow be supplemented by an agreement to limit production and supply or by even higher forms of cartelization, including merger.[16] However, while the price cartel is likely to break down unless its members agree on limiting production, an exchange rate cartel of central banks, although it could be supported by a common quantity-of-money rule, can also be safeguarded by solidarity, mutual help, and a common determination to defend it. The reason for this is that central banks are not bound to concentrate on maximizing real profits. They are, therefore, free to adopt emotional ideologies that help defend their usually too permissive policies in the name of some superior social or international responsibility. Moreover, the production of money is nearly costless; so there is no limit to help those poor brethren that run out of foreign exchange because of their permissiveness. Fixed exchange rates that must somehow be supported by solidarity agreements make the most permissive central bank the leader in the money supply process. And no governor of a central bank will be effectively criticized for participating in this inflationary game, if and when he can resort not only to the goal of full employment but also to the goal of international solidarity.

An international harmonization of wage policies which is required if a system of permanently fixed exchange rates is to function smoothly without periodic crises is likely to add to inflationary pressures for one or more of the following reasons:

If an individual worker threatens to go on strike unless he receives a substantial pay increase, he is facing a considerable employment risk. The company union of a small firm is equally aware that the competitive system is likely to hit back with employment sanctions, if excessive wage claims were supported by a correspondingly long strike action. But when the firm and the union are big enough, their collective bargaining ceases to be a strictly private affair, because if they priced themselves out of the market, they would create a local, regional, or national unemployment problem that immediately calls forth government action, say in the form of direct subsidies. But what is granted to group A will quickly be demanded by group B and will rapidly be generalized, particularly in a system that is as transparent and as much based on equity and equality principles as modern society. Direct subsidies that are quickly generalized are not very different from a monetary-fiscal policy that is subject to a de facto full employment guarantee and that must, therefore, ensure that higher costs can be shifted onto higher prices. Such an inflationary monetary-fiscal policy is the almost inevitable consequence of a wage movement on a broad front. Now, we have already in the existing national economies such broad movements, partly due to imitation and partly due to ex ante coordination. However, there is still strong resistance from export-intensive firms and industries. They cannot be helped by a permissive monetary policy under fixed exchange rates, and their resistance must be even greater if they know from experience that the government, in the interest of stability, may from time to time make anti-inflationary monetary policy more effective by letting the exchange rate float (upward). However, the relevant export sector that is bound to resist inflationary wage pressures, necessarily becomes smaller in a monetary union with permanently fixed exchange rates among member countries and with an internationally coordinated wage policy to support them. The reason is simply that several countries, taken together, export a smaller share of their (common) GNP to the rest of the world than each country in isolation. Or, in other words, an enlarged area is faced with a smaller outside world and hence with less competition from abroad. This loss in terms of cost-controlling competition must somehow be compensated by a more restrictive monetary-fiscal policy if the formation and enlargement of common markets is to be prevented from having a leverage effect on world inflation.

This supports the argument in favor of the monopoly solution to the problem of monetary integration (one central bank) or, alternatively, it supports the view that smaller monetary systems, connected through flexible exchange rates, are more stable and need a less powerful monetary authority, since they can rely much more on the controlling forces of competition from abroad. Common markets, based on institutional integration, thus make not only for bigger business but also for bigger unions and bigger governments and central banks. If bigger governments and central banks cannot be created quickly enough as a countervailing power we shall have more inflation—unless we cut the responsibility of the central banks by reducing collective, and increasing individual, responsibility for full employment and full capacity utilization.

There are two supplementary reasons why exchange rate unions tend to be more inflationary than the participating countries would otherwise be— that is without permanently fixed exchange rates among each other.

One reason follows from the fact that in a larger system there are greater productivity differentials between central and peripheric regions. This would not matter if a larger system also permitted correspondingly larger wage differences between advanced and backward regions. However, if a system is conceived to be or to become a political unit, it will be under strong pressures to artificially reduce the existing interregional wage differentials, according to the plausible principle of "equal pay for equal work." Such pressures will become strong in the trade union movement, and they will be supported by employers' associations in the high-productivity areas. Artificially high wages in low-productivity regions mean that firms in high-productivity areas are exposed to less price competition. It becomes easier to form and to stabilize cartels. A monetary policy that tries to compensate for this reduced competition in the interest of price level stability will tend to accelerate the locational adjustments by endangering jobs in the high-cost regions at the periphery. It will drive both capital and labor from the periphery to the already congested areas in the center, which offer a higher productivity, but with private costs often lower than social costs. An inflationary monetary policy will slow down this process —by exploiting money illusion—and it will, therefore, be chosen at least as a short-run remedy. The correct long-run answer would, of course, be wage subsidies for low-productivity areas, but unless such subsidies are tied to severe conditions they may merely increase the scope for wage pressures. If the interregional wage distortion leads to more permissive monetary policy, the inflation resulting from it may become an accelerating one, since inflation clouds rather than removes the basic wage distortion. One mechanism would be that unions in high-productivity areas perceive a large wage drift as a result of the monetary policy that is required to maintain employment in the high-cost, low-productivity areas. This wage drift would force them to pursue a more aggressive wage policy since they must avoid losing members or having wildcat strikes on a company level.

The second reason why exchange rate unions tend to be more inflationary than individual countries is that they reduce the opportunities for an incomes policy of the conventional type. In a small, individual country it appears much easier to bring together the persons and institutions concerned and to convince them that inflation of wages and prices does not pay. Moreover, if the exchange rate is flexible, monetary authorities can —by pursuing a sufficiently restrictive policy—make sure that prices of traded goods and of tradables cannot be increased without heavy sanctions in terms of reduced sales. A wage restraint will thus by no means lead to higher profits and export surpluses; instead, the fruits of stabilization efforts are internalized, a necessary condition for bringing about a concerted stabilization effort that is designed to achieve price level stability without a fall in employment. Conventional incomes policy may be partly or wholly successful if a country is suffiently small, so that mutual control is as effective as in a small cartel or in a narrow oligopoly. Since a small country is very open to foreign competition, the conventional incomes policy cannot do much harm to the competitive system of control. Actually, a small country is in the enviable position of automatically having a radical incomes policy—through its openness to foreign competition on a broad front and through the strong influence of the exchange rate that is governed by monetary policy—and by having a fair chance for a conventional incomes policy to safeguard full employment. In a large common market with permanently fixed exchange rates among its members, all this is the other way round.

If we look at the world in this way we are led to the presumption that one of the fundamental causes of inflation in our time is related to the collectivization of the employment risk. Under conditions of competition, the employment risk is private, and everybody knows that he is in danger of pricing himself out of the market. The risk is also felt in the narrow oligopoly which is subject to competition from abroad. It is only in a closed economy—or in an open economy isolated by downward flexibility of the exchange rate—that the employment risk can be collectivized, whereby the downward flexibility of the exchange rate is a necessary condition for an inflationary monetary policy, not limited by the balance of payments constraint, and for a sufficient protection against competition from abroad. Therefore, it is not surprising that the full employment philosophy, which implies a collectivization of the employment risk, has been developed in the context of a closed economy, that it was most frequently applied in the quasi-closed economy of the United States, and that the United Kingdom, in order to maintain the full employment objective as a collective responsibility, has taken resort to downward flexibility of exchange rates. Promoters of exchange rate flexibility, therefore, consist of two different groups—one group wants flexibility as a means toward stability; the other group favors flexibility as a means of safeguarding the collectivization of the employment risk and does not care very much about inflation. In summary, it does appear that the reprivatization of the employment risk is a necessary condition for a return to stability. But this requires a rethinking of many problems and a rewriting of quite a few textbooks in economics—and perhaps several decades of teaching those who will form the establishment.

**Policy Conclusions**

The preceding diagnosis, it is hoped, has brought to light a number of points that are worth including in any program to halt inflation. They may be reformulated in terms of the following policy proposals:

First, make monetary policy free from any other obligation so that it can be concentrated on the single goal of supplying just as much money as is needed for the public to absorb the goods and services at prices consistent with a constant consumer price level. Only a single and clear-cut goal permits a clear judgment as to whether the monetary authority effectively does what it has to do as a government agency under parliamentary control. Whether the target for monetary policy shall be price-level stability directly, or the intermediate rule of expanding the money supply by a percentage corresponding to the growth of potential output, is a question of secondary importance. Both the price-level rule and the quantity-of-money rule can be introduced smoothly and gradually; for example, in a transitional period of, say, five years, price level increases might he tolerated, provided they were distinctly smaller in each successive year and would not exceed 1 percent in the last year. Similarly, the quantity-of-money rule might first be applied within a band of tolerance that would narrow down year by year to one percentage point above and below, say, 5 percent in the fifth year.

Second, make it definitely clear to businessmen and to workers and unions that the government and the central bank have no other full employment commitment than that implied by the money supply rule. Once the central bank has complied with its commitment, it is the responsibility of wage and price setters to be careful not to price themselves out of the market and to compete for total demand by fixing wages and prices as low as is necessary to achieve what they consider to be optimum employment and optimum capacity utilization. Wage and price guidelines may be of use in an intermediate period, but as an instrument of teaching what is wise in the interest of individual employment rather than as an instrument of preaching what is right and what is wrong for a fictitious entity, called economy. The learning process might be accelerated in a transitional period, if the government expressively limited the payment of adjustment subsidies to such firms and groups that stayed within the guidelines. In this period the government would still bear part of the employment risk, provided that firms and groups of workers behaved such as to minimize the risk.[17]

Third, encourage competition by making individual markets and the economy as a whole as open as possible to newcomers and to imports from low-wage countries. The type of competition that matters is not so much the number of sellers in an unspecifiable "relevant" market, but the easy intrusion of products that are less expensive, more durable, better designed, or more advanced. Business should be advised that the rule of the game is for each firm to protect itself against actual and potential competition by offering more and by asking for less. The only aid to be expected from government may be a premium on quick adjustment to competition from low-wage countries and to changes in the structure of world demand.[18] To protect governments from the pressure to grant protection, the business community must be made to understand that the international competitive game never takes place under conditions of equality. If domestic producers are at a net disadvantage compared with foreign producers, this is in most cases a reliable indication for the beneficial effects that would result from shifting investment, production, and know-how to foreign locations and from importing the goods instead of producing them at home. Balance-of-payments problems need to be of no concern to business firms, since there is always an exchange rate to ensure equilibrium.

Fourth, in the interest of more competition in the advanced countries and a more balanced growth of the world economy, there should be reconsideration of the (real) rates of exchange between the group of advanced countries and the group of developing countries. This should become a major topic for negotiations within the new Group of Twenty.

Fifth, improve the market mechanism! This is possible

• by supplying consumers with inexpensive information on the prices and qualities offered and producers with inexpensive information on what competitive pressures they will have to face in the process of international market integration and economic growth;

• by removing artificial barriers to transactions, including taxes, and possibly also

• by subsidizing real transaction costs if they severely inhibit arbitrage processes;

• by promoting the building up of forward markets in commodity transactions as well as foreign exchange;

• by feeding the information system of the market with unambiguous information about the future course of government policy and by avoiding unnecessary shifts in strategies, and

• by liberating governments and public authorities from tasks that can more effectively be carried out by private organizations under competitive conditions.

There may be numerous objections against each of these five complex policy conclusions. Some people will say that nothing can really be changed in this direction. If this is so, we shall have to learn to be happy with the world economy as it is and with the world inflation as it will develop after the end of money illusion has finally come.

**Notes**

1. A constant consumer price level need not be the optimum in the long run. A falling price level has several advantages. If money income per capita remains constant there is no need for adjusting income tax schedules and legally fixed nominal amounts, such as fines, taxes, subsidies, etc. Moreover, "it follows from welfare maximizing principles ... that the optimal monetary policy entails deflation of prices at a rate equal to the rate of return on non-monetary assets," so that it provides "an implicit rate of return on money sufficient to encourage optimal holdings of it, that is, to reduce the marginal private cost of money-holding to equality with its (approximately zero) marginal social cost" (Johnson 1968). On the other hand, a constant consumer price level has the advantage that the representative consumer can make a more rational choice since an absolute rise or fall in a price can be interpreted as a relative change in the same direction and magnitude.

The argument is less convincing when there are rapid changes in the commodity composition of the consumer's basket and when technological progress leads to quick changes in the quality structure. Finally, the consumer's basket may become more or less representative of what the consumer wants. How much increase in the price level is compensated by the fact that—in some countries at least—private goods have become free public goods and have become available to more people? Does the price level rise when indirect taxes make private goods more expensive but are used as a means to finance the supply or free public goods? Such questions, although important, fade into the background in view of the high rates of inflation prevailing nowadays in the real world.

2. However, this situation is characterized by excessive profits.

3. This was quite common in West Germany in upswing and boom periods. A number of points have to be considered when explaining this. First, the number of vacancies may be inflated, since a vacancy can be registered without costs and in several places. Second, selective imports of foreign labor contribute to reducing frictional unemployment in the immigrant country, but the unemployment which immigrant workers leave behind—and perhaps create—at home is left out of account. Third, the migrating workers move from low-wage areas to already congested high-wage areas where their marginal social product may be smaller than their marginal private product. Fourth, migration into West Germany might have been smaller and capital exports out of West Germany greater if the deutsche mark had not been undervalued for most of the time, according to many observers. Undervaluation makes the locations within the currency area artificially attractive for investments and hence for complementary labor. Insofar, it can be considered as a means toward increasing the rate of growth of gross domestic product, partly (at least) at the expense of growth in low wage areas.

4. The word *partial* is inserted to indicate that, in conditions of excess demand or high demand, there is, of course, less competitive pressure toward lowering costs.

5. Although some governments and central banks would like to care little about inflation, they are forced to do so in an integrated world. Under fixed exchange rates they run into balance of payments difficulties, and under flexible rates they might quickly learn how demoralizing it is to be warned by an exchange rate that shows an accelerating decline under the pressure of elastic inflationary expectations. On the other hand, there are countries where people are really worried about inflation. Here the government is pressured by public opinion to make bold attempts at restricting foreign and domestic demand sometimes at the end of the boom.

6. I should not deny that this substitution may temporarily create, or help to restore, money illusion. But if we are close to the end of money illusion in modern society, the trick will not do for long; soon it will also be considered morally questionable and become a burden on the government's credibility.

7. This is the reason why the German Council of Experts (Sachverständigenrat zur Begutachtung der gesamtwirtschaftlichen Entwicklung) in its 1965 report *Stabili-*

*sierung ohne Stagnation* suggested incomes policy as part of a program for stabilization without stabilization crisis.

8. Much could already be gained by legally preventing merger. Had the removal of barriers to trade within the Common Market that was so much greeted by economists as a process leading to more competition not been followed by a wave of European mergers, mostly of already large firms, the prospects for competition would look much brighter. Where monopoly power cannot be shaken (by inviting competition from abroad, by promoting innovation and patent licensing, or by subsidizing adjustment to structural change) public ownership or regulation appears as a means of last resort, if dissolution into several independent units is judged to cost too much (in terms of social rather than private costs per unit of output) even in the longer run. These points have been sufficiently discussed in the literature. What is new and what deserves more attention in the future is the problem of multinational corporations if the latter do not generate enough workable competition among their subsidiaries and if they prove to be strong barriers to entry. The difficulties become even larger if multinational corporations lead to the emergence of multinational unions as "countervailing power" in the labor market and as the other half of the "double monopoly" relevant in this context.

9. To use revaluations as a means of stabilization policy has, of course, the drawback that it reduces the pressure of competition in other countries. Foreign governments that are equally interested in more competition from abroad could, therefore, raise the beggar-my-neighbor complaint. But when in May 1971 West Germany let the deutsche mark find a higher level in the market, nobody outside Germany was angry about the "clean floating." The only complaints came from German producers, supported by nervous politicians and journalists, who confused the profits of large corporate firms like VW with the welfare of the population. It is true that those countries which refused to float in 1971, or which preferred "polluted floating," had higher rates of inflation in subsequent periods, but this was their free choice. On monetary grounds, it appears that a beggar-my-neighbor complaint cannot be justified if and when a country deliberately revalues to reduce its foreign exchange reserves by not more than it had previously accumulated in a process of imported inflation. The reimport of stability that was formerly exported by the force of imported inflation can hardly be considered an unfriendly act.

10. This relationship between the rate of profit, the level of GNP, and employment, and the severity of competition (being the reverse of the degree of monopoly) is illustrated in the following figure.

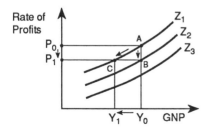

Each curve $Z_1$, $Z_2$, ..., depicts the possible combinations of profit rates and GNP associated with a given degree of competition. Curve $Z_2$ represents a higher degree of competition than $Z_1$ and is, therefore, combined with lower rates of profit at given levels of GNP. If inflation is fought by monetary policy alone, the economy moves along $Z_1$ in the downward direction (from $A$ to $C$), because profits fall when rising costs can no longer be shifted onto higher prices, and investments decline when profits fall with given Z-competition. However, if Z-competition can be increased sufficiently (point $B$ on $Z_2$), profits are reduced without a subsequent fall in investment, since more Z-competition means more investment and a higher GNP at given levels of profit. However, it is only a special case if the (downward) shift from $Z_1$ to $Z_2$ exactly compensates for the upward slope of the curve in the relevant range.

11. Unfortunately, the government became quite nervous when the business community complained that life had become too difficult under free exchange rates. The real problem, however, was not exchange rate flexibility but the increased Z-competition. These stabilization efforts touched, for the first time, the export business, which had learned in 1966–67 how advantageous a recession can be if it alleviates cost pressures at home without reducing the possibility of selling at rising prices abroad, This contrast to 1966–67 was reflected in the public debate, since the big firms of the exporting sector used to have a much louder voice than the many small firms of the domestic sector that went bankrupt in 1966–67. The 1971 downswing, which was merely a profit squeeze at high employment, consequently got the stigma of a big crisis, whereas the high unemployment recession four years earlier had been belittled in influential quarters as an inevitable, long-overdue structural change. From this one may gather how much resistance a radical incomes policy would meet in business circles which are accustomed to reducing investment when profits go down, but cannot afford to do so when it is more Z-competition rather than less demand (more D-competition) that brings profits down.

12. One reason is that the European Economic Community hardly offers any chances for economists of the neoliberal type to play an influential role. Another reason is that a larger area is bound to be more protectionist because it is more diversified in its production structure and has less to gain from (more) foreign trade.

13. If it appears paradoxical that real resources should be transferred to other countries in the interest of higher employment and more price level stability at home, the reader must be reminded that the intermediate target is more sellers' competition, that is, an improvement in that odd system of social control, which compels participants to serve ends which they do not and need not accept as their objectives.

14. This may become different as soon as unions succeed in coordinating their wages policy on an international level, a point, that will be referred to later.

15. Immigration tends to favor the large cities and agglomeration areas that require additional mobile workers for further growth. In the absence of immigration, in-

dustry would have been forced to invest more in peripheric areas with an immobile rural population.

16. The Smithsonian agreement of December 1971 can be considered a price cartel not backed by a quantity cartel. Such price cartels can survive only if participants agree on a division of the market on geographic lines (*Gebietskartell*), and that is what happened when more restrictions were placed on the free movement of capital by Switzerland and Germany in June 1972.

17. I personally see no serious objection against the government's establishing an insurance agency that would cover structural risks, in terms of paying adjustment subsidies in certain cases, against the promise of following certain guidelines to be established by the agency. However, I should prefer to limit such contracts in time and to prevent renewals, so that the arrangement does not become a permanent device for shifting the risk from private firms to public authorities. In any case, if the government is to overtake some part of entrepreneurial and private risk, it should be paid for by the beneficiaries within the framework of a clear contract.

18. Quick adjustment is a necessary condition of survival for firms that face a low-income elasticity of demand. The only genuine help governments can give is to pay a premium for the transfer of resources to alternative uses. The appropriate device would be a subsidy based on the volume of resources transferred (e.g., jobs), preferably at a rate declining from year to year. The rationale for this is that mobility costs are high in the short run and approach zero in the long run. Moreover, declining rates ensure that mobility subsidies are a temporary device.

## References

Haberler, Gottfried. 1971. *Incomes Policies and Inflation: An Analysis of Basic Principles*. Washington, D.C.: American Enterprise Institute for Public Policy Research.

Johnson, Harry G. 1968. "Problems of Efficiency in Monetary Management." *Journal of Political Economy* 76:971–90. Reprinted in Johnson, Harry G. ed. 1972. *Readings in British Monetary Economics*. Oxford: Clarendon Press.

# 17

Index Clauses and the
Fight against Inflation

Economic growth proceeds in business cycles extending over several years. From cycle to cycle the value of money has shrunk more and more during the last ten to fifteen years. At the end of the present cycle, there will probably be a decline in the rate of price increase, especially if stability continues to be the aim of demand management. But there is reason to expect that this decline will again be only temporary. For, unless we have some new ideas, it will be impossible to apply the brakes to inflation without causing some loss of employment. As soon as the rate of unemployment is clearly rising again, the need for another "leap forward" will be felt too keenly for policy makers to resist. The business cycle that will then begin will bring a renewed acceleration of inflation, and so on. This, at any rate, is what things look like if the past trend of inflation is projected into the future.

Past experiences leave their imprint on expectations. If the rates of price increase abate in the near future, many people will undoubtedly feel reassured and will no longer be thinking of the overall trend. But it is equally certain that the accelerated pace of inflation in the subsequent boom will be a source of disappointment, giving rise to an even more intense pessimism. Reflecting this state of mind, interest rates, real estate prices, and wage increases will contain higher inflation components. This adjustment will probably take place much more swiftly in the future than it did in the past. People have learned how to live with inflation; they have become used to it. To the extent that the experience of inflation gives rise to expectations of future inflation which are then built into the prices, wages, and interest rates agreed upon for the future, it becomes itself an element of cost

Reprinted with permission from Herbert Giersch, Milton Friedman, William Fellner, Edward M. Bernstein, and Alexandre Kafka, *Essays on Inflation and Indexation*. Washington, D.C.: American Enterprise Institute for Public Policy Research, 1974, 1–24. Copyright 1974 by The American Enterprise Institute for Public Policy Research, Washington, D.C.

inflation, and thereby a driving force in the inflationary process. Those who have hedged against inflation by acquiring real assets or by incurring huge debts will soon cease to be enemies of inflation. And those who anticipate the full extent of a prospective inflation, who are able to conclude collective wage agreements for relatively short terms, or who know that wildcat strikes will not be persecuted will no longer consider the fight against inflation to be a matter of particular importance. Moreover, when the population has grown accustomed to inflation, restoration of monetary stability becomes more difficult, more time-consuming and, possibly, more painful. At least this holds so long as our economic policy lacks new inspiration.

The classical prescription for curing the economy of the habit-forming drug of inflation is clear: The only way to achieve a gradual stabilization of the value of money without causing any substantive decline in employment is to eliminate, everywhere and simultaneously, the expectation of inflation by lowering, step by step and in a manner avoiding frictions, the rate of growth in the money supply and in wage increases—which in due course would also permit a reduction in interest rates. In 1965, such a program was advocated by the German Council of Economic Experts as "concerted action" with a view to avoiding a stabilization crisis (such as we actually did get afterward). But such a program would presumably be rejected today as it was then—all the more so since, in the meantime, the task has become more difficult and the sociopolitical climate has grown colder. At the same time, just as in the earlier instance, a decrease in employment would be considered too high a price to pay for monetary stability. What path can lead us out of this blind alley?

A program attacking the problem of prices directly, that is, by a price freeze, would presumably be popular because it would seem to hold out the prospect of a radical cure. To be sure, in the Federal Republic as in other countries, there are also economists who *would* advocate it. There exists, after all, a doctrine—one that commands and deserves attention—which makes direct intervention in product and factor prices appear to be a viable solution. With respect to the question of what determines the price level in an economy that is either virtually closed or has a floating currency, two schools of thought stand in opposition to each other. The "monetarists," reasoning along the lines of the old currency theory, read the famous quantity equation of exchange[1] from left to right, implying that (assuming the velocity of circulation as given) the quantity of money determines the price level of commodities and services traded (the national product). The other group, which may be considered Keynesian, reasons the other way. With Joan Robinson—and approximately in accord with the banking theory—this group holds that the volume of transactions and the price level are determined exogenously, thus representing data to which the volume of money and its velocity of circulation adjust themselves.[2] Now, if it is believed that the price level is a political phenomenon,[3] the idea of subjecting it to control by political agencies is not farfetched. John Kenneth Galbraith and all those economists who applauded Nixon on August 15, 1971, have drawn this inference—it being obvious by then that incomes policy as a milder form of controlling the price level had not worked well.

By contrast, the monetarists have no sympathy for price freezes. They stress the importance of controlling the quantity of money. The inflation which is in store for us is, according to them, programmed in advance by the development of the money supply.

On the average, a change in the rate of monetary growth produce a change in the rate of growth of nominal income about six or nine months later.... On the average, the effect on prices comes about six to nine months after the effect on income and output, so the total delay between a change in monetary growth and a change in the rate of inflation averages something like 12–18 months.[4]

It is true that one cannot determine in advance the precise rate of monetary expansion which monetary policy must aim at in order to achieve stability in the value of money. But it can be said that the rate lies in the neighborhood of the rate at which the productive potential of the economy as a whole is growing. In the process of stabilization it is impossible to make sure that physical quantities will not respond in a manner entailing some reduction in employment. But these effects can be mitigated by a policy under which the process of bringing the rate of monetary expansion down to the level of the "stability rate" moves only gradually.

To avoid major repercussions in physical quantities, it is also necessary that people keep their price and income demands flexible. These demands should be based not on inflation rates of the past, but rather on those lower future inflation rates which monetary policy will tolerate. This is exactly what will be achieved by concluding agreements containing cost-of-living escalator clauses.

Escalator clauses of one form or other have, in fact, been advocated by monetarists (for example, Milton Friedman) and by their precursors (for example, Irving Fisher), as well as by Edgeworth, Marshall, the earlier Keynes (1927), Musgrave, Machlup, Palander, Slichter, Tobin, and, in the German-speaking countries, by Jöhr, Pfleiderer, Stucken, and Timm.[5]

On the other hand, there is the widespread opinion that index clauses accelerate the inflationary process. Those who start from the assumption that the level of wages and prices is determined historically and politically must be inclined to hold this view. But the view also depends on the further assumption that a monetary inflation potential exists:

• either because—as is typical at the beginning of an inflation—an unanticipated monetary expansion has taken place, creating an excess supply of money; or

• because the central bank, for reasons of external economic policy, is not in a position to limit the volume of money effectively (for example, when, under free convertibility and fixed exchange rates, the currency of the country is undervalued), which means that the supply of money is very elastic.

In these cases, the price increase is not limited by anything that happens on the money side, but only by frictions and lagged responses ("inertia"), or by moral suasion vis-à-vis various social groups and institutions—those engaged in collective wage bargaining, suppliers of goods or services, and government officials. The price rise may also be limited by expectations which only incompletely anticipate an impending shrinkage of the value of money (the "money illusion"), with the result that inflation-caused losses arise. Under such circumstances the inflationary process would indeed be accelerated if important brakes were loosened, say, by permitting—let alone advocating—escalator clauses in collective wage agreements.

However, what we are having at present is a fully developed inflation, not an incipient one. Nor has much of the money illusion remained with us. Besides, ever since flexible exchange rates and swift adjustments of parity values have become the general practice, we have seen that the central bank is fully able to apply the monetary brakes. So let us assume that the central bank uses the means at its disposal to reduce the rate of monetary growth to a level compatible with stability.

If escalator provisions are forbidden and not in use, there is a strong tendency to build the inflation rate of the past into the new collective agreements, especially in those cases where no loss in employment has occurred as yet. For example, if a 4 percent rise in productivity is in prospect, and if the rate of inflation in the recent past was 8 percent, then wage increases to the tune of 12 percent will have to be expected. (All figures represent annual rates.) Now if the central bank succeeds, by a restrictive credit policy, in reducing the price increase from 8 percent to 5 percent, the rise in real wages will not be 4 percent but 7 percent, far exceeding what would be in line with the growth of productivity. This would entail a marked decline in employment, a typical stabilization crisis which, by all experience, would very soon lead to a resumption of the expansionist policy.

By contrast, if wage contracts with escalator clauses are permitted and are in use, the reduction in the rate of inflation will not result in unintended rises in real wages that would bring about losses in employment. This is so because in this case collective bargaining agreements provide for a rise in real wages at a specified rate, namely, the rate that conforms to the rise in productivity—let us again say 4 percent—and for a variable inflation adjustment determined ex post in conformity with the inflation that actually took place. No matter how high or low the inflation rate, real wages rise 4 percent, neither more nor less. If the rate of inflation can be brought down from 8 percent to 5 percent, nominal wages will not rise by 12 percent but only by 9 percent. If it proves feasible to reduce the inflation rate to zero, nominal wages will be only 4 percent higher, and so stabilization policy will not send up real wages by more than that rate. Hence, if wages are tied to a cost-of-living index, the risk of a decline in employment is minimized. Wages with escalator provisions are flexible wages. They, and only they, open the way to a prompt and consistent stabilization without any stabilization crisis and without wage control. If the escalator clause operates symmetrically, that is, downward as well as upward, then even an outright decrease in the price level will not result in any loss of employment.

Escalator clauses in capital transactions have similar effects. For example, with escalator provisions in loan contracts, creditor-debtor relations are "as if" the value of money were still (or again) stable.[6] In lieu of a fixed nominal interest rate of, say, 11 percent, consisting of a "real" rate (3 percent) and an inflation rate (8 percent) that has been assumed ex ante, only the "real" interest rate is settled as a fixed component. The nominal interest payments, as well as the amount representing capital repayment, vary automatically (ex post) with the actual rate of inflation. If the inflation was correctly anticipated by the contracting parties, loans with escalator provisions will neither benefit nor harm anybody. If the prospective rate of inflation has been generally underestimated, escalator clauses prevent an inflation-caused gain from accruing to the debtor; they protect in this case creditors and savers. It is true that the number of people inclined to combat inflation would thereby decrease, but so would the number of those interested in the continuation or acceleration of the inflationary process. If the inflation is being slowed down, contrary to the interests of those who incurred debts carrying high interest rates, then those debtors whose loans have escalator clauses will not be disappointed, nor will they undergo any crisis caused by an excessive debt burden. Those who have financed their investments by credit contracts under which the "real" interest rates do not go up when the actual inflation rate stays below the expected one need not be afraid of stabilization. At the time they made the investments, it was already necessary for them to figure things out "as if" the value of money were stable. For these reasons, loans with escalator provisions, besides protecting creditors and savers, provide protection from a stabilization crisis. Therefore, such loans should not only be permitted; they should also be encouraged by all means.

Furthermore, loans carrying escalator clauses help to avoid or to reduce those distortions in the structure of production and prices that originate in an inflation-caused flight from money into real assets. Under inflation, money loses its ability to function as a store of value. This makes investors, fearing further shrinkage of money value, turn to gold, real estate, houses, and condominium apartments. If the supply of these assets is elastic, real productive forces are being channeled into such "concrete gold." Loans with escalator clauses do preserve real values; they are therefore an effective device for preventing an inflation-induced building boom and an updrift of real estate prices that otherwise would be unavoidable under high and rising expectations for further inflation.

The sooner we introduce loans with escalator clauses, and the wider they spread, the less reason there will be to expect that stabilization will cause a breakdown in the construction sector, and the easier it will be, therefore, to return to monetary stability.

A number of arguments against escalator clauses have been raised in the literature and must be discussed here. For the sake of completeness we first mention a few objections that can be dealt with briefly.

1. It is objected that escalator provisions do not, in inflation, provide any protection for holders of cash. This is, of course, true, but would be an objection only if someone said that such provisions are a panacea.

2. It is argued that escalator provisions are to the disadvantage of the weaker market parties because, unlike the more powerful parties, they cannot secure acceptance of these provisions. This argument overlooks the following: The more powerful parties use their opportunities anyway, regardless of whether there are escalator clauses or not. Indeed, one might well think that if escalator provisions were forbidden, the weaker market

parties, which by all experience are the ones that have to have the strongest apprehensions regarding the risk connected with inflation, would be deprived right at the outset (by the law itself) of an important chance to hedge against the unpleasant consequences of inflation.

3. Mention is sometimes made of the possibility that the government, at some future time, might go back on its promise to insure the real value of the government securities in the hands of the public, or that it might even forbid, retroactively, the use of escalator clauses in private contracts. This apprehension is based on experiences under governments that cannot be compared with a government under which the rule of law is established, as it is in the Federal Republic.

4. The fear is sometimes voiced that the government might manipulate the price index. In the light of some isolated events abroad, this fear is perhaps not without foundation. But in the Federal Republic, with its independent statistical agencies, the situation is, after all, quite different. Besides, an alert and watchful community is nowadays so informed about matters of economic policy that the risk of manipulation can be kept within narrow limits. As a debtor in loans with escalator clauses, the government may be interested in manipulating the index downward. But this cannot possibly be justified as an act of self-defense—all the less so since the real revenue from taxes rises with the inflation (unless the tax rates themselves are pegged to an index). For the rest, should the government as a debtor owing loans with escalator clauses try to tamper with the price index, it would jeopardize its credit rating for a long time to come.

The objection that any index measures the shrinkage in money value only incompletely carries little weight: an inadequate index is always better than no index at all.

5. It has been argued that loans having escalator provisions leave debtors in the dark about the actual cost of the loan, thereby making exact calculation more difficult for them. This objection, however, is couched in terms of nominal values. Basically, the inflation itself is what makes calculation difficult. Those who wish to facilitate their calculating job by clinging to nominal values merely facilitate a job of miscalculating. Only those who calculate in real terms calculate correctly. And finally, if stabilization is being achieved, debtors should be glad that with the escalator provision they have settled for a variable inflation component.

The reminder that escalator clauses do not remove the causes of inflation and therefore cure only symptoms is in itself conclusive, but is not relevant in the framework of an anti-inflationary monetary policy. If the objection goes further and refers to real rather than monetary causes of inflation (for instance, to a shortage of supply caused by a crop failure or to an energy crisis), then we must remember that the temporary shortage means a slowing down of growth in real terms, of productivity gains and, therefore, of the increase in real incomes. One should expect monetary policy to take the slowdown into account by expanding the money supply less than would otherwise be appropriate. Thus, when food prices go up as a result of a crop failure, this should be offset by the absence of price increases that would otherwise be possible and by bringing about more price decreases. A monetary policy that does not take account of a shortage in supply becomes a contributing cause of inflation. So, even here, everything depends on monetary policy. If there are no escalator provisions and if monetary policy remains lax, there will probably be an inflationary wave; it will ebb after some time, when the nominal income claims will have lost enough of their real value. If many contracts with escalator clauses are in force, a lax monetary policy may indeed result in steeper price increases. All the heavier is the responsibility of monetary policy. This policy must make it clear that in any case, under monetary stability as well as under inflation, a temporary supply shortage entails smaller increases in real wages, lower real profits, and lower real interest rates.[7]

A few critics think that escalator clauses tend to freeze the structure of prices and incomes. If I see things in their true light, this objection has three aspects.

First, the objection seems to say that escalator clauses make the conclusion of longer-term contracts attractive. The counterargument is simple: This, precisely, is the purpose. In the absence of escalator provisions, the uncertainty that accompanies an inflation produces short-term agreements, quite contrary to the basic interests of the market participants who, after all, do need security for longer-range planning and thus do need contracts that will remain binding over longer periods. In capital transactions, contract terms are shortened because interest rates depend on the rate of inflation and are therefore unpredictable for longer periods. As for collective wage agreements, in phases when the inflationary process is slowed down, employers fear that long-term contracts will be to their disadvantage; in phases of accelerating inflation, trade unions have analogous misgivings. In the first case, what is to be feared is an inordinately heavy cost burden. In the second, there is reason to fear the outbreak of wildcat strikes following upon an unanticipated decline in consumer purchasing power. It may well be true that negotiations about contracts with escalator clauses—like those about longer-term contracts in general—will be longer and harder because more is at stake, and also because, in this case, there is no chance that divergent expectations regarding the inflation will make it easier to reach an agreement. As a compensation, there will be no disappointments and none of the wildcat strikes that arise out of frustrated hopes. All in all, we can say that escalator provisions make the conclusion of an agreement as difficult, and its term of duration as long, as would be the case if the value of money were stable.

Second, the argument seems to say that escalator provisions in collective wage agreements impart too much rigidity into relationships among wages in the various sectors and industries. Here, too, the answer is that escalator clauses merely establish conditions exactly equivalent to what would obtain if the value of money were stable, and that, consequently, they cannot in the long run produce anything that would not exist under monetary stability as well. The essence of the objection presumably lies in the question of whether we need some minimum of inflation in order to bring about changes in the structure of real wages without nominal wages having to shrink anywhere. Primarily, the problem concerns the structurally weak sectors which, unless they are given watertight shelter from foreign competition, must lay off some workers anyway. In such sectors it may in general be impossible to secure the adoption of escalator provisions, even if they are permitted; at least it will be impossible to obtain them together with real wage increases fully reflecting the progress of productivity in the economy as a whole. If, in such cases, labor nevertheless presses for such real wage increases, layoffs will inevitably be accelerated, and the labor supply available to sectors having a positive growth potential will thereby be increased.

Moreover, escalator provisions may vary from case to case. In certain borderline situations it may be that the purchasing power of only part of the wage increases is guaranteed, or that compensation for a loss in purchasing power will be granted only with considerable delay. This would correspond to a situation where the workers, even in the face of an unexpectedly sharp decline in the value of money, do not feel strong enough to resort to wildcat strikes.

Third, behind the rigidity argument there could be the question of whether escalator provisions in collective wage agreements—if they stipulate full compensation for any loss in purchasing power and thus fix the real wage for the entire duration of the contract—might not cause undesired declines in employment. This point is to be taken very seriously. The objection implies that we need inflation because it corrects downward, in the degree required to avoid employment losses, those increases in real wages which the trade unions think they have secured by their demands for nominal wages. Basically, the argument says that it is necessary for us to have, permanently, an inflation that exceeds labor's expectations for inflation. Where this is the actual situation, a return to monetary stability seems anyway out of the question because of the huge losses in employment that would then be unavoidable. However, at least two points are open to doubt.

For one thing, labor is today so experienced in matters of inflation that an employment policy based on the Keynesian prescription, presupposing "money illusion," no longer holds out any promise of lasting success. For another, we must not overlook the fact that, in their wage bargaining, employees and trade unions do take the risk of unemployment into account —even if they do not admit it because they are interested, for reasons of negotiating tactics and political strategy, in placing the responsibility for full employment squarely upon the government. The notion that the volume of employment in an enterprise, in an industry, or in a region depends on the relation of real wages to labor productivity may be unpalatable, but if it is correct, as it undoubtedly is, it will spread, at least "under the counter." Here, escalator clauses may be helpful. By making negotiations about real wages possible, they offer to the parties in collective agreements the chance of eliminating unemployment risks, especially during a process of stabilization. On the other hand, whenever one oversteps the right boundary in real wages, the unemployment risk will become apparent, and the link just mentioned will stand out clearly. Nothing could contribute more to achieving, simultaneously, monetary stability and high-level employment than such an object lesson during the period of stabilization.[8]

Some political weight attaches to the objection that the decision to permit escalator provisions in a trotting inflation will be interpreted as an act of despair and as an indication of willingness to capitulate. This objection becomes irrelevant, however, when escalator clauses are permitted and introduced in order to make sure that a monetary policy program aiming at price stability will not be endangered by a worsening of the employment situation or by crises originating in overindebtedness.

A special problem is posed by declines in employment caused by a cost-oriented pricing policy on the part of business. Again and again we see business firms raising supply prices after wage negotiations and pointing out that they can absorb only part of the wage increases agreed upon—the part that is in line with the progress in productivity. The firms emphasize that the increased costs must be reflected in higher prices in order to keep profit margins intact. At the beginning of a "wage round," not only must all firms in one particular business sector expect wage increases of a specified extent, but often many other sectors have to face the same wage increases. Hence, one can foresee quickly by what percentage the cost level in the economy as a whole will rise and by what percentage, on the average, business will therefore raise supply prices. Assuming that the government will ensure the maintenance of full employment, they can also figure out quickly how much the incomes of the broad masses will rise, and how much room for increases in market prices will thereby be created on the demand side.

All they have to do is deduct the percentage increase in quantities supplied—which reflects the increase in productivity if the physical volume of work performed is assumed as constant—from the average percentage increase in wages, and take due account of a possible change in the rate of saving. If the rate of saving remains constant, there is as much room for price increases as the cost increases indicate. This means that, as a rule, the divisions in a business firm that calculate the costs of production and the divisions that analyze market conditions can take for their points of departure the same date relating to the economy as a whole. If the policy of the central bank brakes the expansion of the money supply, thereby narrowing the scope for passing on price increases while the pricing policy of business enterprises is dominated by the divisions calculating the costs of production, there will be shrinkages in quantities produced and supplied.

In these circumstances, escalator clauses in wage agreements have a major advantage which, to my knowledge, has not yet been mentioned in the literature. They weaken the influence upon business pricing policy of the divisions concerned with calculating costs, as compared with the influence of the divisions concerned with market analysis, and they force these latter divisions to use criteria other than wage increases. The arguments of the divisions calculating supply prices lose in weight because, under a regime of escalator clauses, the cost increase cannot be determined in advance but only ex post. This is an observation which entrepreneurs stress as an objection to escalator clauses, and which economists should stress as an important argument in favor of these clauses in a stabilization program. It is true that uncertainties of the kind mentioned also affect the divisions engaged in market analysis. But these divisions have another indicator for estimating how much price increase demand will absorb: the rate of increase in the supply of money minus the rate of increase in the real national product. If the divisions engaged in market analysis rather than the divisions engaged in calculating the costs of production gained the decisive

influence on the actual pricing and if the market analysts concentrated on
the increase in the volume of money rather than on the increase in wages,
the goal of stabilization without appreciable negative responses of quantities might prove to be attainable.

In the Federal Republic, the discussion of escalator clauses turns on
whether paragraph 3 of the Currency Act of 20 June 1948 should be
applied. The main purpose of this provision, under which, in principle,
permission is required for the use of escalator clauses, was to make the
newly introduced deutsche mark the only legal contract currency. If I see
things correctly, it was—quite wrongly—considered necessary to expedite the movement away from barter transactions which had become quite
popular before the currency reform and to prevent the use of foreign
currencies. As a matter of principle, the Bundesbank has refused to permit
the use of escalator clauses in the capital and money markets, and it has
adopted a restrictive attitude with respect to such clauses in other fields
also. Exceptions are long-term rent contracts (over at least ten years) and
the sale of real estate to be paid for by an annuity over at least ten years
or by a life annuity. This leads to the grotesque situation that anybody
wishing to protect his money from the risk of inflation must first acquire
real estate. Whether permission would be required for escalator provisions
in wage contracts is a matter of controversy.

From a legal and political point of view, the prohibition of escalator
clauses represents a restriction of the freedom of contract; it is an element
of authoritarianism. So long as the rates of inflation were tolerable, the
Bundesbank's tutelage over the citizens caused little resentment. But at
present the situation is different. When contracting parties are uncertain
about the future development of monetary values, when they are in the
dark as to what they are fixing in real terms by fixing future payments in
nominal terms, why should they not be given the option to eliminate the
risk of inflation from their contractual relationship? All we have said so far
points to the conclusion that such freedom could harm third parties only if
monetary policy is not oriented toward stability. The agencies in charge
should therefore regard the establishment of freedom of contract in matters
involving money as a challenge to themselves. Our reference here is to the
Bundesbank which, by issuing a general permission, could immediately and
without difficulty make paragraph 3 of the Currency Act inoperative for all
practical purposes.

Inflation-caused distortions appear also in public fees and fines that are
expressed in absolute figures, and especially in progressive income taxes
and in the exemptions and exclusions allowed by the tax law. It is only fair

that exemptions and exclusions in systems of direct taxes should not lose their importance, thereby giving rise to an unintended tax progression effect at the wrong place. Likewise, it is only fair that the rates of wage and income taxes be automatically lowered in order to ensure that tax progressivity will not begin at ever-decreasing real incomes, thus allowing the government to profit from the inflation through the progressivity of the tax structure. Furthermore, to the extent that interest receipts merely compensate for the loss in the value of property held in money form, they should be exempt from income tax. Otherwise, there would be an unintended taxation of property. Maybe this exemption would also give an impetus to saving and capital formation. On the other hand, interest payments on borrowed capital need to be deductible as costs only to the extent that they exceed the depreciation of the debts. As for tax-allowable depreciation charges on fixed assets, if the original asset values on which the depreciation charges are based were allowed to rise along with the rise of a general price index, we should be coming closer to depreciation allowances based on replacement costs—which is the economically correct method of computing these allowances. This step, too, would help to avoid an unintended taxation of property; moreover, it would probably induce many small- and medium-size firms to switch from the incorrect calculation based on nominal values to calculation in real terms. This would prevent them from making erroneous decisions that are conditioned by, and in turn aggravate, an ongoing inflation.

A program of stabilization without stagnation and loss of employment can be combined with tax reduction quite well. Alleviations in the field of taxation relieve the pressure of costs. This is especially true of wage taxes. In an ever-growing number of countries, the increases in these taxes that will take place under a progressive tax structure are being allowed for at the time when wage demands are being advanced. Often labor unions think not only in real terms but also in terms of disposable income. The loss of tax revenue resulting from an adjustment of the tax system must be offset by raising loans, preferably by issuing purchasing-power bonds, on the capital market. If it were to be expected that the substitution of proceeds from loans for revenues from taxes would have short-run inflationary effects, it would be necessary to resort to open-market policy by issuing additional loans and inactivating the resulting budgetary surpluses within the confines of the central banking system.

My final result can be summarized as follows. Contrary to widespread prejudices—which I myself could get rid of only after prolonged thinking, and which again and again prevail "intuitively" when for some time one does not think hard about the problem but allows oneself to be impressed by conventional wisdom—I have reached the conclusion that in the present phase of the inflationary process escalator provisions would no longer have any accelerating effect on inflation. On the contrary, by forcing people to behave as they would if the value of money were again stable, they could help to avoid a stabilization crisis and thereby contribute to the actual restoration of monetary stability. In any case, however, a necessary precondition for a return to stability is a restrictive monetary policy.

**Notes**

My thanks for numerous suggestions go primarily to Hans Möller, Alfred Müller-Armack, Otto Pfleiderer, and Hans Willgerodt for the detailed comments they have offered on earlier drafts. Grateful acknowledgment for such suggestions is also due to my collaborators at the Institut für Weltwirtschaft, in particular to Adolf Ahnefeld, Hubertus Müller-Groeling, Klaus-Dieter Schmidt, and Peter Trapp. In the work on the latest version, I was greatly helped by continuous discussions with Roland Vaubel. Of course, none of the persons named is in any way responsible for such mistakes and shortcomings as may still be in the text. This chapter was originally published as Kiel Discussion Paper No. 32, Institut für Weltwirtschaft, Kiel, October 1973; I revised it for the English edition, and Eric Schiff translated it.

1. $MV = PQ$, where $M =$ volume of money, $V =$ velocity of circulation of money, $P =$ average price level, and $Q =$ quantity of output traded.

2. On this contradistinction of views, see Joan Robinson, "Quantity Theories, Old and New," *Journal of Money, Credit, and Banking* 2 (1970): 504ff.

3. Joan Robinson writes: "The main moral of the General Theory can be expressed by saying that the general price level in terms of money is not a monetary phenomenon; its movement depends mainly on money-wage bargains; that is to say, it is very largely a political phenomenon." Ibid., p. 512.

4. M. Friedman, "The Counter-Revolution in Monetary Theory," First Wincott Memorial Lecture, Occasional Paper 33 (London: Institute of Economic Affairs, 1970), p. 22ff.

5. M. Friedman, *An Economist's Protest: Columns in Political Economy* (Glen Ridge, N. J., 1972), p. 84ff.; M. Friedman and F. Machlup, in "Monetary Policy and the Management of the Public Debt: Their Role in Achieving Price Stability and High-Level Employment," U.S. Congress, Joint Committee on the Economic Report, Replies to Questions and Other Material for Use of the Subcommittee on General Credit Control and Debt Management, 82d Congress, 2d session (1952), p. 1105ff.; for the reference to S. H. Slichter, see ibid., p. 1111ff.; Irving Fisher, assisted by H. R. Cohrssen, *Stable Money: A History of the Movement* (New York, 1934), p. 112; I. Fisher, assisted by H. G. Brown, *The Purchasing Power of Money, Its*

Determination and Relation to Credit, Interest, and Crises (New York, 1911); W. S. Jevons, *Money and the Mechanism of Exchange* (London, 1875), p. 332ff.; F. Y. Edgeworth, *Papers Relating to Political Economy* (London, 1925), vol. 1, section 3; A. Marshall, *Money, Credit and Commerce* (London, 1923), p. 36ff.; Marshall, "Answer to Questions on the Subject of Currency and Prices," *Third Report of the Royal Commission Appointed to Inquire into the Depression of Trade and Industry* (London, 1886), p. 423, in Marshall, *Official Papers* (London, 1926), p. 10ff.; Marshall, "Remedies for Fluctuations of General Prices," *The Contemporary Review*, March 1887, in *Memorials of Alfred Marshall*, ed. A. C. Pigou (New York, 1956), p. 188ff.; J. M. Keynes, statement before the Committee on National Debt and Taxation (Colwyn Committee), *Minutes of Evidence* (London, 1927), vol. 1, p. 278K.; Keynes, "The Colwyn Report on National Debt and Taxation," *The Economic Journal* (London), vol. 37 (1927), p. 211ff.; Keynes, "The Prospects of Money," *The Economic Journal*, vol. 24 (1914), p. 610ff.; Keynes, "Review of Fisher's 'Purchasing Power of Money,'" *The Economic Journal*, vol. 21 (1911), p. 393ff.; G. L. Bach and R. A. Musgrave, "A Stable Purchasing Power Bond," *The American Economic Review*, vol. 31 (1941), p. 823ff.; T. Palander, *Värdebeständighet: Ett problem vid sparande, livförsäkringar och pensioner* (Stockholm, 1957); J. Tobin, "An Essay on Principles of Debt Management," in *Fiscal and Debt Management Policies*, a series of research studies prepared for the Commission on Money and Credit (Englewood Cliffs, N.J., 1963), p. 202ff.; W. A. Jöhr, "Inflationsbekämpfung und Indexierung," comments on H. Sieber, "Lösung des Inflationsproblems durch Indexierung," *Wirtschaft und Recht* (Zurich), vol. 19 (1967), p. 38ff.; O. Pfleiderer, "Berücksichtigung der Geldentwertung bei der Besteuerung von Zinserträgen," *Zeitschrift für das gesamte Kreditwesen* (Frankfurt), vol. 18 (1965), p. 886ff.; Pfleiderer, "Zur Frage der Zulassung von Wertbeständigkeitsklauseln im langfristigen Kapitalverkehr" (unpublished manuscript); R. Stucken, "Die wertbeständigen Anleihen in finanzwirtschaftlicher Betrachtung," *Schriften des Vereins für Socialpolitik* (Munich, Leipzig), 1924; Stucken, *Was stimmt nicht mit unserem Geld?* (Hamburg, 1967), p. 82ff.; H. Timm, "Der Einfluss von Geldwertsicherungsklauseln auf Geldkapitalangebot und -nachfrage und auf die schleichende Inflation," *Jahrbuch für Nationalökonomie und Statistik* (Stuttgart), vol. 180 (1967), p. 313ff.; "Geldwertsicherungsklauseln in der schleichenden Inflation," *Wirtschaftsdienst* (Hamburg), vol. 52 (1972), p. 641ff.

6. What is being agreed upon is a repayment exceeding the original loan by the percentage by which the price index—say, the cost-of-living index—has risen by the time of repayment. A further point of the agreement provides for a "real" interest rate, which means that the annual or semiannual interest payments, like the sum representing repayment, will rise in proportion to the shrinkage in money value that has taken place in the meantime.

7. If the wage agreements contain escalator clauses, the loss in real income shows, during the terms of the agreements, in those incomes that are not fixed contractually, that is, in profits. Since, for them, escalator provisions are excluded by definition, the system is not blocked, as is sometimes believed. In the new wage bargaining it will come to light whether the entrepreneurs are able partially to offset the losses of profits by making smaller concessions on real wages. This would amount to an ex post acknowledgment of the fact that, due to the crop

failure, the progress in productivity was smaller than had been assumed in the earlier agreements.

8. This reasoning is not invalidated by the consideration that in the central regions of Western Europe a steeper rise of real wages appears definitely desirable over the long pull if one wishes to curb the demand for foreign labor and to expedite the shift of job-creating investments from the central to the peripheral regions. See Giersch, "Beschäftigungspolitik ohne Geldillusion" [Employment policy without money illusion] in *Die Weltwirtschaft* (Tübingen), no. 2 (1972), p. 127ff.

# IMF Surveillance over Exchange Rates

Exchange-rate surveillance is regarded as necessary for two reasons, which are expressed in the following quotations:

1. Each IMF-member shall "avoid manipulating exchange rates or the international monetary system in order to prevent effective balance of payments adjustment or to gain an unfair competitive advantage over other members."[1]

2. "Sound economic policy calls for a greater brake on movements in exchange rates than private speculators can always be expected to provide."[2]

The first argument implies that government or central-bank intervention might be harmful in special cases, while the second one states that interventions are necessary to stabilize the market. Both together call for a controlled and coordinated intervention in foreign-exchange markets.

This view may be contrasted to an alternative policy system, which is characterized by the following three "commandments":

1. Governments and central banks should proceed toward full convertibility for short-term as well as long-term capital movements.

2. Central banks should announce and thus commit themselves to a money supply strategy for the foreseeable future.

3. Central banks should refrain from intervening in foreign-exchange markets.

The first two points of this package, which aim at the improvement of free exchange markets, may be acceptable also to proponents of surveillance,

Reprinted with permission from *The New International Monetary System*, edited by Robert A. Mundell and Jacques J. Polak. New York: Columbia University Press, 1977, 53–68. Copyright 1977 by Columbia University Press.

while the last one is generally not—except if surveillance over exchange rates is interpreted as "surveillance over nonintervention," but this does not seem to be what the proponents of surveillance have in mind.

Commandment 1, which goes beyond guideline 5 of the present IMF guidelines for the management of floating rates, is a precondition for a well-functioning foreign-exchange market.[3]

Commandment 2 pays tribute to the fact that exchange rates are closely connected to monetary policy. As the exchange rate is the relative price of two monies, it is extremely difficult to make any forecast about exchange-rate changes in the absence of reliable information about the future money supplies. A more predictable money-supply policy would therefore render exchange rates more predictable and reduce uncertainties and transaction costs in a multicurrency world.

Commandment 3 rests on the assumption that once central banks have disclosed their money-supply strategies, they cease to have better information and hence a basis for a better judgment than private market participants. It can also be taken to imply that central banks might rather irritate private stabilizing speculation, which can be expected to be even more effective under conditions of full convertibility and preannounced money-supply policies.

Several objections may be raised against this position. I first deal with two major objections against a preannounced monetary policy, and then turn to the arguments against nonintervention.

The first objection against preannounced monetary growth rates is that monetary policy can no longer be used as an instrument of discretionary demand management. This argument does not convince me, as I believe to observe forces that have largely destroyed the effectiveness of discretionary monetary policies as a tool of demand management.

1. Inflation has reduced the available stock of money illusion so that monetary policy has become less potent as a means of raising the level of employment and capacity utilization above its sustainable trend value. In the same way, inflation and the destruction of money illusion have shortened the time lag between monetary growth and its impact on the price level (more rational expectations).

2. Flexibility of exchange rates further shortens this time lag. If monetary authorities expand the money stock for employment reasons, they immediately induce a depreciation of the exchange rate, so that at least import prices will rise more quickly than under fixed exchange rates. The acceleration of monetary growth thus transforms itself earlier into price rises. The

destruction of exchange-rate illusion adds to the decline of money illusion mentioned above.

3. The price of attempts to restore money illusion by engineering a recession or foreign-exchange illusion by selling foreign exchange (including borrowed exchange) seems to be rising. This price is, of course, to be expressed in opportunity costs, that is, in the costs of alternative strategies. The best alternative strategy, at least in advanced countries, appears to be one that anticipates rational expectations and fully incorporates them as part of a new economic policy.

4. In a world of declining money illusion and foreign-exchange illusion, governments and central banks are increasingly forced to recognize and to concede quite openly that monetary policy is price-level policy and that the level of employment and capacity utilization in any one area (firm, region, or national economy) is being determined by those who conclude wage contracts binding others (collective wage bargaining with minimum-wage effects) or who fix product prices. This entails a shift of responsibility from governments to markets and from (short-term) demand management to (long-term) supply policies, including policies to maintain and strengthen competition and the flexibility of relative prices and wages.

5. The announcement of money growth targets in the United States, Germany, Switzerland, and other countries and the emphasis on steadier policies are illustrations of the fact that the required change in economic policies has already begun.

Thus I envisage a transition toward forms of economic policy in which steadiness and predictability play a greater role than discretion and policy uncertainty. This transition should help to improve the functioning of decentralized planning in domestic and international markets and should facilitate the international ex ante coordination of policies.

The second objection against a preannounced monetary policy is that unexpected shifts in the demand for money may lead to deflationary or inflationary results. A monetarist's answer to this objection would be that the demand for money (or the income velocity) is rather stable over the longer run, although it is not constant over the cycle. He would add that the time lags tend to vary and thus to be fairly unpredictable; monetary acceleration or deceleration in order to neutralize changes of demand originating from the real sector may, therefore, even turn out to be procyclical. He would thus recommend a stable monetary expansion.

In my opinion the most important aspect of monetary policy is that monetary growth rates are predictable—they need not be constant. In the present circumstances monetary growth rates still must be different from the long-term trend, because we still have to cope with the cyclical disturbances resulting from past errors of monetary policy (fast monetary acceleration followed by unanticipated monetary deceleration). If, despite preannounced money growth rates, there are still marked shifts in demand arising from the real sector, they might (hopefully) be met by fiscal policy within the constraints of the preannounced monetary targets.

Thus far the discussion has mainly concentrated on the relation between money held by domestic residents in the country of origin and domestic expenditures. But should we not take a wider view to include changes in the international demand for money, that is, shifts in currency areas? In the international competition of currencies, a good currency will be preferred to a bad currency as an asset by official as well as by private holders. Foreigners can thus "immigrate" into a country's currency area or enlarge it. If this additional demand is not accommodated, the domestic economy will experience an unintended and unanticipated deflation combined with an equally unforeseen appreciation of the exchange rate. On the other hand, the country whose currency has become less attractive will suffer from inflationary pressures combined with a devaluation of its currency. A stabilizing strategy would therefore involve an immediate reduction of the money-supply target in the latter country and an additional monetary expansion in the former country, in other words, in both cases a deviation from the preannounced rate.

The immediate correction of the target is mainly a problem of information. As to changes of demand by foreign central banks, the problem can be solved rather easily: all that is required are notifications once foreign central banks have decided to hold larger (or smaller) amounts of the currency in their reserves. The matter can then be settled between the central banks outside the exchange market. In this case, the monetary authorities can still follow the concept of preannounced targets, if the money-supply target is defined in a way that it does not include foreign official holdings.

A more difficult question relates to what can and should be done if there is little or no such instant information about demand from private foreign-exchange holders. One answer is that central hanks will have to watch what is going on in the market and accommodate after the event. This strategy has three important drawbacks:

1. Reliable indicators for a sustained shift in the international demand for money may not be readily available.

2. If monetary accommodation takes place with a time lag, it may be a source of cyclical disturbances.

3. Deviations from, or unanticipated revisions of, money-supply targets, although accommodating, may create uncertainties in foreign-exchange markets.

A second answer is to regard changes in the international demand for money as similar to changes in domestic demand for money, and stick to the preannounced rates for the sake of credibility. This solution seems to have a special appeal to large countries, where changes in the international demand for money can be expected to be fairly small in relation to its stock of money.

A third answer is to replace the money-supply target by an exchange-rate target with an endogenous money supply. The exchange-rate target has to be announced vis-à-vis another currency area (single currency or basket of currencies). In this case, the country can still choose its own rate of inflation, if the monetary expansion in the reference currency area is known.[4] If the desired rate of inflation in the dependent country is lower than in the reference currency area, the exchange-rate target would have to be formulated as a preannounced upward crawl. The advantage of this solution is that unexpected movements in the international demand for domestic money ("immigration" or "emigration") will be endogenously compensated, and negative effects on the demand for domestic goods or services can be avoided. This solution appears to be especially favorable to small countries with a small stock of money, where changes in the international demand for money have a strong influence on the domestic economy.

On the other hand, a preannounced exchange-rate target means that the country cannot rely on the exchange rate as a protection against foreign fluctuations in the demand for domestic goods, which is especially important for small countries with a large foreign-trade sector. This can be demonstrated by a brief example: Country X chooses the same rate of inflation, which is to be expected for the reference currency area and announces as its target to maintain the present exchange rate;[5] in other words, the country has decided in favor of a fixed exchange rate. Consider now two symmetrical cases of foreign disturbances:

1. Foreign demand for domestic products *falls* unexpectedly because of a foreign recession due to an insufficient monetary expansion compared with the announced rate or to changes in the real sector. In order to prevent a

devaluation of its currency, country X has to use contractive policies, that
is, to import deflation.

2. Foreign demand for domestic products *rises* unexpectedly. In order to
prevent an appreciation of its currency, country X has to increase its money
supply, that is, to import (additional) inflation.

To prevent the import of such disturbances I have advocated flexible exchange rates even for small countries, where the foreign trade sector tends
to be relatively large.[6]

The choice to be made here is between protection against foreign disturbances in the demand for domestic currency (preannounced exchange-rate
changes and endogenous monetary expansion) and protection against foreign disturbances in the demand for goods and services (preannounced
monetary expansion and endogenous exchange-rate changes). The decision
will depend on: the reliability of monetary policy in the reference currency
area; probability of strong shocks arising from the foreign real sector;
capability of the domestic government sector to compensate for cyclical
disturbances arising from abroad (fiscal policy); and the flexibility of domestic wages and prices in response to changes in foreign demand.

My personal view is that as long as there is no clear evidence for a
dominating influence of unforeseen shifts in currency areas, not only larger
but also small countries should announce money-supply targets and leave
the exchange rate to the market. The risk of unexpected changes in the
international demand for money can be reduced by choosing a rather short
announcement period. On the other hand, the period must be sufficiently
long to represent at least a reasonable short-term planing period for firms
and trade unions. Both points, aggregately seem to recommend an announcement period of about one year.[7] If, as a result of this policy, the
present heavy shifts in international portfolios will have slowed down, a
somewhat longer announcement period may be advisable, especially for
larger countries.

Having discussed the role of central banks as producers of currencies via
their monetary policy, we can now turn to the influence that official authorities can or should exert on the demand side by selling or buying foreign
currencies; this relates to commandment 3, which states that the exchange
market should be left to private market participants and that official authorities should not intervene.

The first possible objection to this commandment is that official interventions are necessary, because private speculators, if left alone, will cause
heavy and costly fluctuations of the exchange rate. There are two points in

this objection:

1. Private speculators cannot do the job of stabilization.
2. Official intervention (speculation) can do it better.

The debate about the quality of private speculation has been a long one; let me briefly summarize two ideas that I regard as especially important in this connection:

1. Sharp fluctuations in the exchange rate are generally the result of heavy changes in the underlying economic conditions. There is much reason to assume that these changes have in most cases not been caused by a highly unstable private sector but rather by government policies, for example, by unforeseen stop-and-go monetary policies or massive short-term interventions in the exchange market. Preannounced government policies will greatly reduce insecurity and improve the efficiency of stabilizing speculation.

2. Private speculators have an interest in stabilizing the exchange rate, as they gain when they buy at a low rate and sell at a high rate. There is a possibility that some speculators might try to push the rate above its equilibrium value in the hope that unexperienced speculators will take this as a signal to buy and cause an even further rise of the rate. However, this not only a very risky strategy, but also requires a strong market position, a high degree of insecurity, and considerable differences in information. Whether any private speculator has a dominating position in the exchange market must be doubted regarding the large number of banks and other companies acting in the market.

Yet, even with more comprehensive information about government policies it is not to be expected that private speculation will smooth all fluctuations in the exchange rate; the adjustment process may be too slow or there may be overshooting of equilibrium rates.[8] However, even if overshooting exists, this is not yet an argument for government or central-bank interventions. To effect stabilization, official authorities must know when the rate is overshooting.

The only convincing reason why an official authority should be a better speculator than private market participants is that it has better information. In respect to a central bank, this essentially means better information about its own monetary policy. If monetary growth rates are preannounced, the information gap disappears and with it the argument for official interventions: private and official agents having the same level of information can only differ in interpreting the data. Under these conditions it is doubtful whether official authorities will make better forecasts than private agents. As Milton Friedman has pointed out, the latter, after all, "are risking their own money."

A second source of better central-bank information may stem from consulting the International Monetary Fund (IMF), but IMF information is to be regarded as a public good and should therefore be freely disseminated; in this case, the information argument disappears.

If we look at the exchange-rate system during the last three to four years [1973—77] three points have to be stressed:

1. It is increasingly admitted that flexible exchange rates have generally worked rather well.

2. There have been marked fluctuations in some exchange rates.

3. There have been large-scale official interventions between currencies with fixed rates and those with floating rates.

The question of interest, which those in favor of official interventions will have to face, is whether central banks made a gain or a loss from their exchange-market operations. My impression is that official interventions have to a great deal delayed rather than expedited the necessary exchange-rate adjustments by leaning against the wind.

The second possible objection against commandment 3 is that international institutions should leave the choice as to which assets a central bank elects to hold in its portfolio to the bank itself and not prevent it from buying or selling foreign currency.

Exchange-rate interventions would not pose a great problem if central banks were entrusted with the task of stabilizing speculation. Under flexible exchange rates their mandate could then he defined as follows: maximize profits from exchange-rate dealings and other open-market operations under the constraint that the money supply is increased at the preannounced rate. The question as to whether it is advisable to let official agents speculate with taxpayers' money in this narrow sense is not of international concern.

A problem arises, however, as to whether a central bank has a strong position in the exchange market, for instance, because of large foreign exchange holdings. Under these circumstances, it cannot be completely excluded that the central bank in pursuing a profit-maximizing policy might attempt to gain from starting a destabilizing speculation. In this case a second constraint has to be added: any official speculator should behave like a competitor in a polypolistic market; otherwise, exchange-rate interventions would have to be ruled out completely as under commandment 3.

At this point it seems appropriate to discuss briefly whether foreign currency can be an attractive asset for a central bank. In so doing, it appears legitimate to apply the Keynesian motives for holding money to central banks.

1. Under flexible exchange rates the transaction demand and the precautionary demand for money play no role, as the central bank has extremely long-term liabilities (its own money), so that there is no need to hold liquid assets.[9]

2. The speculative motive can apply to central banks, which expect that a foreign currency will appreciate at least as much as is necessary to compensate for the foregone interest earnings.

Apart from these motives, a central bank may wish to acquire liquid foreign reserves in order to make use of external economics, for example, of the benefits from confidence which the country gains in international financial markets.

In the following we shall consider different cases of interventions that might be expected to take place, if commandment 3 does not (yet) apply. We shall first discuss interventions under short-term asset-return aspects and long-range development aspects and then consider interventions as an instrument of demand management, including "beggar-my-neighbor" policies.

A country may regard its holdings of foreign currency as being too large and wish to sell its excess reserves against other assets with a higher return. For the foreign central bank this amounts to an additional fall in the demand for its money. If the latter has fixed a monetary target net of foreign official exchange holdings, the decline in demand has to be neutralized. The easiest way of doing so is to offer the foreign central-bank assets with a higher rate of interest to replace the low-interest debt (money).

The adjustment process will work rather smoothly if notification between central banks about their foreign-exchange operations, as mentioned above, is made compulsory.

In the opposite case, a central bank may wish to increase its foreign reserves. Apart from speculative demand, the reason may be to increase international confidence into the country's economy. This argument, which is especially important for less developed countries, is closely connected to the convertibility postulate (commandment 1). Foreign investors are inclined to regard a high level of foreign-exchange reserves as an index of the country's ability to resist pressure toward restricting convertibility on balance-of-payments grounds. Countries with a low standing in international capital markets may thus be justified to increase their liquid reserves in an effort to show that they are likely to be good debtors. The investment in international liquidity may then pay off in terms of lower interest rates for foreign funds. Once the country has gained sufficient standing in international financial markets, a process that can be promoted most effectively by accepting and adhering to commandment 1, liquid reserves may be less necessary. Reserves can then be transformed into other assets urgently needed for producing goods and services.

As to exchange-rate interventions in connection with demand management policies, we may distinguish four cases:

I. Expansionary monetary policy plus acquiring foreign reserves.

II. Expansionary monetary policy plus selling foreign reserves.

III. Contractive monetary policy plus acquiring foreign reserves.

IV. Contractive monetary policy plus selling foreign reserves.

Case I, which can be described as the strategy for an "export-led upswing," corresponds to the classical "beggar-my-neighbor" policy of "exporting" unemployment. Four points have to be made here:

1. The extent to which employment rises depends on the prevailing degree of money illusion and exchange-rate illusion. An "export-led-upswing" can be expected to take place only in connection with an especially high degree of exchange-rate illusion, since the exchange rate will depreciate more, and import prices will rise faster, than in the alternative case of an expansionary monetary policy via domestic open-market operations. Thus, the more rational the expectations, the smaller will be the increase in employment.

2. Whether employment abroad actually falls will essentially depend on whether the additional demand for money can be accommodated, for the deflationary effect will come about because the foreign official demand for *money* rises unexpectedly. (Nobody would complain about "beggar-my-neighbor" policies if goods were purchased instead of currency.)

The solution to the problem of accommodation is notification. Any additional demand for money by foreign central banks could then be met by automatically expanding the money supply, so that the additional demand for foreign exchange is neutralized.

3. Moreover, one has to remind oneself that the purchase of foreign exchange is not without cost; the official authorities must either spend less on domestic goods or borrow at high rates of interest or impose a tax on the public. In our case, where the purchase is financed by monetary expansion, the cost consists of an inflation tax on money, the proceeds of which are going to the foreign central bank.[10] This means that the foreign country will even benefit from the attempted "beggar-my-neighbor" policy.

4. Finally, it can be shown that in general it would be less expensive for society to achieve the mercantilistic goal of promoting export and import-substitution industries by means of a direct subsidy rather than by an undervaluation of the currency.

Taking these points together, it appears that in a system of preannounced money-supply targets and an agreed notification on interventions, there would not be much reason to worry about "beggar-my-neighbor" policies.

The same applies for "interventions on cross purposes." The problem of internationally inconsistent policies seems to be most relevant for the duopoly case, when two countries intervene because they consider their respective currencies to be overvalued. The danger in this case is that A may be successful in appreciating B's currency until B discovers it and launches a counterattack. Exchange rates would then fluctuate in a seesaw fashion. This, however, could be prevented very easily if the intervening authorities would have to notify each other; B would learn immediately what A is doing and could react without a time lag. The efforts would neutralize each other and would, therefore, probably not be undertaken.

The second case represents a "domestic upswing" strategy. The idea behind this policy is to prevent a fast decline of the exchange rate and a corresponding rise in import prices, which would otherwise come about because of the expansionary monetary policy. It is a strategy to make use of exchange-rate illusion, so that employment effects from increasing the money supply are not too weak and not too short-lived. In this case, foreign exchange is sold in order "to buy time," which, however, cannot be purchased in unlimited amounts.

The "domestic-upswing" strategy can be described as follows: The central bank buys domestic securities against its own money (expansionary open-market policy). This will induce a fall of the interest rate and a depreciation of the domestic currency. In order to prevent the latter, the central bank has to sell foreign exchange (including borrowed reserves) against its own money. The monetary expansion due to the open-market policy must be stronger than the monetary contraction due to the exchange-market operation, so that there is a net increase in the money supply. This result is achieved if the central bank sells enough currency to cause the foreign interest rate to fall; the lower domestic interest rate is then compatible with the original exchange rate. Or to state it another way, as the exchange rate is the relative price of two monies, monetary expansion can be achieved without altering the exchange rate, if the supply of the foreign currency rises correspondingly—or if the demand for foreign currency falls, which amounts to the same.

A "domestic-upswing" policy thus implies an expansion of both the domestic and the foreign money supplies relative to demand. This means that the foreign country is faced with an inflationary pressure. But if there is notification, the foreign central bank can neutralize this effect by a contractionary monetary policy. Under these circumstances, the expansionary country cannot prevent a depreciation of its exchange rate and a "domestic upswing" policy is no longer possible. (Apart from this, a policy based on the exploitation of illusion is hardly effective, once monetary expansion is preannounced.)

Cases III and IV are symmetrical to cases I and II. A contractive policy as under case III place the main burden on the domestic sector while the export- and import-substitution industries benefit from the prevented exchange-rate appreciation. Case IV, on the other hand, implies a rather rapid and pronounced appreciation. This might help to break inflationary expectations in the export- and import-substitution industries and to alleviate cost pressures arising from the import side. However, it also depresses profits in the export- and import-substitution sector.

Again, in a system where interventions are duly notified, foreign central banks can neutralize the inflationary (case IV) or deflationary (case III) impact on their economics by accommodating the additional fall-rise in the demand for their currencies. Thus any country would be free to protect itself against monetary effects of exchange-rate interventions by foreign authorities.

In conclusion, the following remarks are presented:

1. The most promising international economic policy reforms, in my opinion, are those that help to improve the system of free markets. This essentially requires a reduction of government restrictions and regulations, which interfere with the efficient working of the market mechanism. In respect to the exchange market, this means to prevent new impediments to international transactions and to take progressive steps to abolish existing restrictions, as is implied in commandment 1 above.

2. Markets will work better when more information is provided about future economic policies. Thus governments should announce their intentions well in advance. Once overall government behavior has become more predictable, markets can be expected to show more stability. Regarding exchange markets, it is of special importance to know which monetary strategy a government or central bank will pursue. In this chapter, it is argued that generally the information problem can be solved best if the monetary authorities commit themselves to a preannounced money-supply target, as it is implied by commandment 2. Difficulties may arise from unexpected fluctuations in the private demand for money, especially shifts in currency areas, and may call for a shorter announcement period, especially for smaller countries. On these grounds, an announcement period of about one year has been regarded advisable under the present circumstances. Once fluctuations have dampened, a somewhat longer announcement period should be considered, especially for larger countries.

3. If unforeseen shifts in the foreign demand for money are regarded to be more important than unforeseen shifts in the foreign demand for goods and services, a country may decide to have an exchange-rate target with an endogenous money supply. The term money supply in commandment 3 would then have to be replaced by the term *exchange rate*.

4. Strategies with either a money-supply target or an exchange-rate target are preferable to policies where targets are kept secret, are internally inconsistent, or are inconsistent over time (target switching). Unforeseen or inconsistent policies, especially if they appear in a stop-and-go fashion, will exert damaging real effects not only on their own economy, but on other countries as well and can, therefore, be regarded as harmful also from an international standpoint. Thus the transition to foreseeable government policies should be considered a matter of international concern.

5. As to official exchange-rate intervention, one possibility is to accept commandment 3, that is, to permit no interventions. This, however, seems to be a rather long-term solution. If central banks still want to use the instrument of exchange-rate interventions, which may be even necessary in the period of transition, when past errors have to be corrected, it seems to be appropriate to replace commandment 3 by another commandment that can be briefly stated as, "No intervention without notification." As has been shown above, notification enables a country to protect itself against the monetary effects of exchange-rate intervention by foreign authorities and is thus an efficient means to prevent competitive devaluations.

The role of the IMF in this system can be conceived as follows:

1. The IMF will be an international center of information.

2. The IMF should use all of its influence to reduce restrictions that affect international transactions and to prevent governments from introducing new restrictions—an aspect that seems to be of special importance in the present situation.

3. The IMF may encourage its members to lay open their longer-term economic strategies and prevent them from making inconsistent promises, from pursuing inconsistent policies, and from losing credibility as a result of both.

4. The IMF can support the efficient working of the exchange market by encouraging the announcement of money-supply targets (or possibly exchange-rate targets); this may include surveillance over announced targets.

5. Since official exchange-rate intervention cannot realistically be prohibited (surveillance over nonintervention) on a short-term basis, the IMF may establish a system of immediate notification on interventions. Exchange-rate surveillance in the narrow sense will then consist of surveillance over notifications.

**Notes**

In preparing the chapter, I greatly benefited from constructive cooperation and many suggestions by Harmen Lehment, who, however, should not be debited with any of the remaining shortcomings.

1. Section one of the proposed new Article IV of the IMF Articles of Agreement.

2. Richard N. Cooper, "Prolegomena to the Choice of an International Monetary System," Center Paper No. 239, Economic Growth Center, Yale University, 1976, p. 96.

3. Full convertibility would especially help many developing countries to become more attractive to foreign capital.

4. This implies that at least one country must have a money-supply target.

5. This abstracts from expected changes in the real sector.

6. See Herbert Giersch, "Enterpreneurial Risk under Flexible Exchange Rates," in *Approaches to Greater Flexibility of Exchange Rates. The Bürgenstock Papers*, George N. Halm, ed. (Princeton, N.J.: Princeton University Press, 1970), p. 149.

7. This is in agreement with the present policy of the Deutsche Bundesbank.

8. It should, however, be noted, that in a would with imperfect information and thresholds in the adjustment process "overshooting" may even play a useful role, if it speeds up necessary economic changes, which would otherwise be delayed.

9. Even under fixed exchange rates, foreign reserves are not absolutely necessary, as a country can prevent a devaluation not only by selling foreign exchange, but also by selling domestic securities.

10. This implies that the foreign central bank does not increase its currency holdings but spends the money it acquired in the accommodation process.

# 19

## Monetary Policy: Does Independence Make a Difference?

### with Harmen Lehment

If countries are ranked in respect to their degree of price level stability since the collapse of the Bretton Woods system the list is topped by Switzerland and Germany—two countries with relatively independent central banks. Of course, the independence of central banks may not be the only explanation for this result. Thus, one has to take into account that public aversion against inflation is probably stronger in these two countries, partly due to Germany's experiences. We shall argue, however, that at least in the case of the Federal Republic of Germany the independence of the central bank has been an additional factor for the relatively low German inflation rates, although it should not be forgotten that the current rate of inflation in Germany is still far from representing price level stability.

This chapter is organized in two parts. The first part, "Independence: What For?" deals with the role of monetary policy in solving the assignment problem. It will be shown that the adjustable peg system of Bretton Woods prevented a rational solution to the assignment problem in the Federal Republic.

In the second part, "Independence: From Whom?" we analyze the dependence of the German central bank from domestic and foreign governments in a brief historical survey stretching back to 1875. It will be argued—inter alia—that both the hyperinflation of 1922−23 and the Great Depression starting in 1929 have been the result of monetary mismanagement by the central bank and cannot he attributed to government interference with monetary policy.

Reprinted with permission from *ORDO* 32 (1981): 3−15. Copyright 1981 by Gustav Fischer Verlag.

## Independence: What For?

As in many other countries the government of the Federal Republic of Germany is committed to simultaneously pursuing the macroeconomic goals of "price level stability," a "high level of employment," and "external economic equilibrium." The relevant laws also mention "adequate economic growth" and limit the choice of instruments to those compatible with the framework of a market economy.[1]

When the German Economic Expert Council (Sachverständigenrat) was first confronted with the magic policy triangle of price level stability, full employment, and external equilibrium, it came out (in 1964) in favor of flexible exchange rates (for external equilibrium and as a precondition for domestic price level stability) in a report that was published under the programmatic title *Stable Money—Steady Growth*. However, it must be admitted that the council failed to present a clear-cut analysis of the policy assignment problem with respect to the domestic targets of price level stability and full employment. This assignment problem stems from the theorem (first stated by Tinbergen) that the number of (suitable) instruments must (at least) be as large as the number of separate targets. The problem is boiling down to the question: who has comparative advantage for securing price level stability and who should be responsible for attaining and maintaining full employment?

In the following we shall consider three possible solutions to the assignment problem:

1. The central bank is responsible for full employment, whereas the responsibility for a stable price level rests with trade unions.

2. The central bank's policy is directed toward both targets.

3. The central bank is made responsible for achieving the target of price level stability; the target of full employment is left to the wage and pricing policy of labor and business.

The rule that labor unions are responsible for price level stability usually appears plausible to laymen who feel that costs determine prices and who do not visualize "demand-pull" inflation resulting from an overly expansionary monetary policy. But will an assignment which places responsibility for price level stability with the trade unions be efficient? Why should trade union leaders be content with low wage increases when they have reasons to anticipate that the central bank, in pursuit of the full employment goal, will accommodate whatever wage increase has been decided upon? There may be two reasons for a positive answer:

First, there may exist a combination of high public aversion against inflation and a desire of trade union leaders to gain status and to assume public responsibility. Experience shows, however, that one can hardly expect that trade unions will consider price level stability to be their principal objective. When membership is voluntary and when unions have to rely on membership contributions, they then can hardly refrain from pressing for wage increases in excess of what is compatible with cost level stability.

Second, there is the possibility that organized labor is striving for political power and concessions (like the introduction of codetermination in Germany) which induce unions to sacrifice short-term wage gains for syndicalist objectives. But such a political bargain will contribute to the target of price level stability for a limited period only, while it is likely to entail a lasting erosion of the market economy.

An assignment which places responsibility for price level stability with autonomous labor unions must, therefore, be regarded as inefficient in the medium run.

It is worthwhile to note, however, that a moderate wage policy may be a precondition for price level stability in an adjustable peg regime. Under such a system, the assignment problem cannot be solved in a simple and rational way. For a small, open economy (or for a medium-sized economy which does not supply the dominant international money) the reasoning is as follows:

The domestic price level is determined by the foreign price level and the exchange rate, if not in the short run then at least in the medium run. To prevent an imported inflation a revaluation of the exchange rate has to be enacted; but under the adjustable peg system this is only justified when a fundamental disequilibrium in the balance of payments persists, that is, after a surplus in the basic foreign balance has emerged. Such a surplus, which requires that domestic wage and price increases are sufficiently low, can be brought about only by permanently teaching labor unions and business that they are responsible for price level stability. This happened in Germany in the late sixties. Despite excess demand for labor—with guestworkers filling the gap—union leaders were criticized for pursuing an inflationary wage policy.

Thus, moral suasion and not the system of fixed exchange rates was the true source of wage discipline in those years. The exchange rate system in which the deutsche mark faced pressure to revalue against the reference currency would have permitted higher wage increases than those which actually took place.

The more quickly the exchange rate is adjusted after labor unions have been effectively educated to behave as if they had responsibility for price level stability, the more stable will this solution of the assignment problem be. When in 1964 the German Economic Expert Council came out in favor of flexible rates, it thought along those lines. This is why at the same time it submitted a formula for a cost-neutral wage policy that, incidentally, took account of changes in the terms of trade and in capital costs per unit of output. If the wage formula implies a constant domestic price level, all improvements in the terms of trade (due to exploiting a high-income elasticity of foreign demand for the export basket or to a more rapid productivity growth in the international sector) will show up in a real appreciation of the exchange rate. In this model exchange rate policy, thus, ratifies domestic wage policy; and monetary policy is not directed to maintaining the prevailing exchange rate.

If exchange rates are not adjusted quickly enough, wage discipline is bound to collapse. For unions will soon discover that the resulting excess demand for labor causes a strong wage drift and subsequent wildcat strikes. This was the case in Germany in 1969, when labor unions became gradually convinced that they could—and in the interest of external equilibrium should—switch to a balance of payments–oriented wage policy.

A solution of the assignment problem which leaves out labor unions and which attributes the twin task (1) of generating (and perhaps even guaranteeing) a high level of employment and (2) of maintaining reasonable price level stability to the central bank is bound to produce business cycles of the go-and-stop type. This can be demonstrated as follows:

Assume a starting position in—what Schumpeter called—"a neighborhood of equilibrium" and that it contains classical unemployment over and above search unemployment.[2] In this case the question comes up whether unemployment should be fought on the wage front or by monetary acceleration. The solution which is most easily adopted is monetary acceleration, and this mainly for two reasons: First, the option of letting unemployment have its impact on wage negotiations or the national wage round is considered to be too time-consuming and also has the stigma of lacking compassion. Second, it is difficult to identify classical unemployment as distinct from Keynesian unemployment, since there are always visible cases where an underutilization of the labor force coexists with an underutilization of physical capital (although the explanation can well be that complementary capital, or the jobs incorporated in complementary capital, have been made obsolete exactly by an excessive rise of real wages).

If the central bank fights classical unemployment by monetary accelera-tion there tend to be positive short-run effects on output and employment. They result from time lags in price and wage adjustments which are due to money illusion or contractual rigidities. It has to be noted that these time lags have probably become shorter in the last few years, because of two reasons [as has already been stated in chapter 18 (p. 292)]:

1. Past inflation has reduced the available stock of money illusion so that monetary policy has become less potent as a means of raising the level of employment and capacity utilization above its sustainable trend value. In the same way, inflation and the destruction of money illusion have short-ened the time lag between monetary growth and its impact on the price level (more rational expectations).

2. Flexibility of exchange rates further shortens this time lag. If monetary authorities expand the money stock for employment reasons, they immedi-ately induce a depreciation of the exchange rate, so that at least import prices will rise more quickly than under fixed exchange rates. The accelera-tion of monetary growth thus transforms itself earlier into price rises. The destruction of exchange-rate illusion adds to the decline of money illusion mentioned above.

With inflation rates rising above the tolerance level the central bank which feels responsibility not only for employment but also for price level stability has to put the feet on the monetary brake and to engage in a policy of monetary deceleration until at least a partial victory can be claimed on the inflation front. Given the time lag in the effect of monetary policy on prices and wages, unemployment will again rise. The result is a policy-determined cycle. It will start anew once the public has substituted unemployment for inflation as the number one enemy.

Unless labor reacts quickly in moderating wage claims during recessions one must expect inflation rates to rise from cycle to cycle. This is why the German Economic Expert Council in the 1967 recession advocated monetary-fiscal expansion only with the proviso that labor unions would support it by a deliberate policy of wage restraint and with the veiled reservation that the increasing potential for price rises would quickly enough be cut by upward revaluations of the exchange rate. In the absence of such supporting policies one might also find unemployment to increase from cycle to cycle. Rising inflation and rising unemployment produce a positive feedback once high and volatile inflation rates impair productivity growth (as they seem to do in some countries, including the United States) and once a slowdown in productivity growth (and even a fall in absolute labor productivity) reduces the scope for higher real wages without higher unemployment. The solution described thus means: monetary policy walks up and down the so-called Phillips curve, but by doing so it shifts the curve in a way that the supposed trade-off between unemployment and inflation turns out to be worse from cycle to cycle.[3] There is now considerable evidence that this has been the case in many countries in the seventies. If the combinations of inflation and unemployment rates are shown in a diagram, one does not observe a stable Phillips curve but instead Phillips "curls" or "loops" which in some countries (United States, United Kingdom, Canada, France) show a distinct move toward the northeast,[4] depicting a tendency for both higher inflation and higher unemployment. A solution under which the central hank is made responsible for both price level stability and full employment must, therefore, also be regarded as inefficient.[5]

This leaves us with the third assignment strategy which is medium term oriented and explicitly acknowledges that an expansionary monetary policy cannot remove classical unemployment except in the short run. Under this strategy monetary policy is conceived to be price-level policy and the level of employment and capacity utilization in any one area (firm, region, or national economy) is considered to be determined by those who conclude wage contracts binding others (collective wage bargaining with minimum-wage effects) or who fix product prices. This entails a shift of responsibility from governments to markets and from (short-term) demand management to (medium-term) supply policies, including policies to maintain and strengthen competition and the flexibility of relative prices and wages.[6]

The best way by which monetary policy may achieve its goal of medium-term price level stability would be to let the money supply grow at the same rate as potential output plus—eventually—a correction term which accounts for

• an increase in capacity utilization (if there is an initial recession),

• a so-called unavoidable rate of inflation (in the context of a gradualist strategy to fight inflation—an approach which may be appropriate for countries with low inflation rates),

• a change in the velocity of money resulting from money being a luxury good,[7] the reduction in expected inflation rates which leads to an increase in the demand for money,[8] shifts in international currency preferences.[9]

Since December 1974 the Bundesbank has regularly announced a monetary target for the following year. While this is a step toward a solution of the assignment problem as just described it has neither led to the disappearance of business cycles nor has it so far achieved the task of price level stability. One reason for this result is the fact that the Bundesbank has reserved itself some leeway for discretionary action—either by announcing a target band (as for 1979 and 1980) or by installing an option to deviate from the target. This scope for discretionary action has been the main cause of the present business cycle in Germany: The monetary expansion in 1978, which was far above the target, led to the 1979 upswing and a new surge in inflation, while the subsequent sharp restriction of monetary growth rates to levels at the lower end of the announced band contributed to the recession which started in the second quarter of 1980.

## Independence: From Whom?

If one speaks about the independence of a central bank, in most cases one means independence from the domestic government. But there may be (and has been, at least in Germany) another limit to the autonomy of a central bank, namely the dependence from foreign governments or monetary authorities (including international organizations). In the following we shall deal with both of these two aspects.

### Independence from Domestic Government

Apart from moral suasion there are mainly three ways by which the domestic government can control the course of monetary policy:

1. direct functional dependence, that is, the government is authorized to give instructions to the president or the board of the central bank;

2. indirect functional dependence through the exchange rate system: the government fixes the external value of its currency in terms of gold or another currency and thereby establishes a target to which monetary policy must be geared;

3. personal dependence which results from the right of the government to appoint and to discharge the board members of the central bank.

### 1875–1914

When the Reichsbank was founded in 1875 the board of the Reichsbank was subordinated to the prime minister (Reichskanzler). Interestingly, the close, direct, functional dependence went along with a relatively high degree of personal independence as (until 1924) the president and the other board members were appointed for lifetime. More important than the direct functional dependence of the Reichsbank was the indirect functional dependence through the gold standard, which—although working far from perfectly—governed the course of monetary policy in Germany until 1914.[10]

### 1914–1918

The gold standard was abandoned at the outbreak of World War I. The main target of monetary policy was shifted from external stability toward the financing of the war. Although inflation was suppressed, the wholesale price index more than doubled between summer 1914 and autumn 1918. The Reichsbank did not oppose the large monetary expansion; it is remarkable that the president of the Reichsbank even denied a connection between inflation and monetary expansion—in his view the increase in the money supply was only a response to the additional demand for money resulting from a rise in prices and wages, a larger territory, and a high propensity to hoard.[11]

### 1918–1922

Whereas other countries like Britain and France had experienced a similar wartime inflation as Germany, the postwar development was quite different. For while the former two countries returned to a more stability-oriented policy, the Reichsbank continued to finance government expenditures on a large scale. This led to a new surge of inflation rates. The index of wholesale prices which by the end of the war had been at 234 rose to 5,430 in March 1922.

### 1922–1923

The Allied countries suspected that the German government was consciously destroying its currency in order to demonstrate its inability to pay the war reparations.[12] They therefore urged the German parliament to establish an autonomous status of the German central bank, in order to put the board of the Reichsbank in a position to pursue a stability-oriented monetary policy against the interest of the German government.

The law establishing the autonomy of the Reichsbank was passed in May 1922. The hopes for a more stability-oriented monetary policy, however, did not materialize. The Reichsbank continued to finance government expenditures through the printing press. Independence had not made a difference. This was mainly due to the attitude of the head of the Reichsbank. The Reichsbank, whose president Havenstein had been in office since 1908, felt committed to put the request of the German government for financial support above the target of monetary stability. Moreover, there was an apparent incapability on the part of the Reichsbank to recognize the fact that monetary expansion was the main reason for the inflation.

The inflation culminated in the hyperinflation of 1923, which led to the breakdown of the financial system and forced the government to reform the monetary system. The successful issue of the Rentenmark in November combined with drastic restrictions on central bank credits to the government and a fixing of the exchange rate against the dollar led to a rapid stabilization (internally and externally) of the German currency. In its actions the government was not supported by the Reichsbank; it even was a reform against the Reichsbank. This has been one of the few cases in history where a government in its fight against inflation was more determined than the central bank.[13]

### 1924–1933

The experience of 1922–1923 had shown that the independence of a central bank was no sufficient condition for a stability-oriented monetary policy. The Allied countries therefore urged restrictions on the Reichsbank's policies. These demands found their way into the Bank Act of 1924. While this act preserved the direct functional and personal independence of the Reichsbank from government,[14] it strictly limited the volume of Reichsbank credits to government and, thus, removed the main source of the preceding hyperinflation. Even more important was the return to a de facto gold standard. From today's point of view it is interesting that some authors regarded this step as a potential source of inflation; v. Eynern[15] argued that a massive sale of gold by the United States might lead to a "gold-inflation," which through the guarantee of the Reichsmark to purchase gold at a fixed rate would also spread to Germany.

As we know today, the true problem of the return to the gold standard turned out to be not inflation but deflation. Under the system of fixed exchange rates the depression, which originated in the United States, rapidly spread to other countries including Germany. Both the German government and the Reichsbank pursued a drastic deflation policy to defend the external value of the Reichsmark. The money supply declined, the price level fell sharply—the wholesale price index which was at 137.2 in 1929 dropped to 110.9 in 1931—and unemployment rose drastically.

In summer 1931 the Reichsbank could no longer support its currency on the exchange markets. In July 1931 the full convertibility of the Reichsmark was abolished. There has been much speculation about the possible economic and political development in Germany if instead of restricting convertibility the German monetary authorities had decided on a devaluation of their currency—as the British authorities did a few months later.[16] However, it should be noted that in those years there was a widespread agreement on the priority of the external stability over the internal stability of the Reichsmark, the main reason being the traumatic experience of 1922–33 and the popular belief that a devaluation of the Reichsmark would lead to a new outbreak of inflation.[17] As the hyperinflation in 1922–23 the great depression in Germany cannot be attributed to a lack of independence of the central bank but only to monetary mismanagement.

*1933–1945*

Under the Hitler government which seized power in January 1933 the autonomy of the Reichsbank was abolished in two steps. The Bank Act of October 1933 enabled the government to appoint and to discharge the president of the Reichsbank and the other board members and, thus, removed the personal independence of the Reichsbank. Through the Bank Act of February 1937 the board of the Reichsbank was directly subordinated to the government. The government used its position to finance a large part of its expenditures through monetary expansion. In a letter of January 7, 1939, the leading members of the Reichsbank protested against the inflationary spending policy of the government.[18]

As a result, the president of the Reichsbank, Schacht, and three other members of the board were replaced. The Reichsbank was now under the complete control of the government; its predominant task was to provide the financial means for the war. Parallel to the experience of World War I, the monetary expansion ended in a huge postwar inflation, this time repressed by price controls combined with comprehensive rationing.

*1948–1973*

The currency reform of 1948 replaced the Reichsmark by the deutsche mark. The new currency was first issued by the Bank deutscher Länder which in 1957 was transformed into the Deutsche Bundesbank. In 1958 the full convertibility of the German currency—which had been abolished in 1931—was restored.

As to the independence from government the German central bank after 1948 was placed into a similar position as in the Bank Act of 1924: direct functional and personal independence[19] but an indirect functional dependence through fixed exchange rates. Like in the Weimar Republic the exchange rate system led to a severe conflict between external and internal stability. But whereas the problem of the early 1930s had been imported *deflation*, the problem now took the form of imported *inflation*.

The limits to the autonomy of the Bundesbank which resulted from the exchange-rate system became first visible in 1960 when the Bundesbank was forced to pursue an overly expansionary monetary policy, because the government refused an appreciation of the deutsche mark.[20] Only after price increases had accelerated in early 1961 the government reluctantly decided on a 5 percent revaluation of the deutsche mark. In July 1968 the German Economic Expert Council—after having repeatedly favored exchange-rate flexibility or early adjustments of parities—explicitly urged for an appreciation of the mark, a position that was supported by the Bundesbank in September 1968. The government again rejected a revaluation of the mark which was, thus, postponed until it became unavoidable in autumn 1969. During this phase "the Bundesbank's anti-inflationary monetary policy was thrown completely out of gear."[21]

Soon after the appreciation the conflict between internal and external stability arose again. In the period of January 1970 to March 1973—which included a brief interval of floating (from May to December 1971), the Smithsonian realignment, the introduction of heavy controls on German capital imports, and a 10 percent revaluation of the deutsche mark in February 1973—the Bundesbank's net foreign reserves rose by approximately 60 billion deutsche mark. In March 1973 the parity-system finally collapsed. The fetters which the fixed deutsche mark dollar rate had put on the independence of the Bundesbank were removed.

It is certainly difficult to give a precise answer to the question what would have happened if there had been no exchange-rate restrictions to the Bundesbank's monetary policy and, thus, greater independence from government. The experience of 1960–61 and 1968–69, however, suggests that at least in these two cases independence would have made a difference. For it is very likely that without the government's refusal to revalue the deutsche mark monetary policy had been less expansionary and more conducive to price level stability.

### 1973 and Afterward
The transition to a floating deutsche mark/dollar-exchange rate did not remove all external restrictions to the Bundesbank's monetary policy. The

exchange-rate of the deutsche mark remained fixed vis-à-vis the other currencies of the European "snake" (which in 1979 was replaced by the European Monetary System). However, mainly because of the dominating position of the deutsche mark these restrictions have been—at least so far—much less severe than the restrictions which had resulted from the fixed deutsche mark/dollar-rate.

The collapse of the parity system enabled the Bundesbank to concentrate on internal stability. As already noted the Bundesbank has regularly announced a money supply target since December 1974.[22] With the exception of 1979, however, the actual increase of the money supply has deviated from the target.

The main deviation took place in 1978 when the money supply rose by 11.4 percent instead of the announced 8 percent. The main reason for this deviation can hardly be seen in the external constraint through fixed exchange rates in the "snake." Although "snake"-interventions contributed to the rise in the money supply, the most important factors for the monetary expansion were the voluntary interventions to stop the decline of the dollar. The sharp increase of the money supply during this period can be regarded as the main cause for the rise of inflation rates in 1979–80 to levels of about 6 percent. The far-reaching independence which the Bundesbank has enjoyed since 1973 has, therefore, not prevented serious violations of the aim of price level stability and a loss of credibility concerning the implementation of preannounced monetary targets. It may be argued, however, that these violations would have been even stronger had monetary policy been controlled by the government. Thus, when the Bundesbank finally returned to a less expansionary monetary policy at the beginning of 1979, the competent government official in the Ministry of Finance openly opposed this step.

Looking back at the German experience since 1948 it can be concluded that the independence of monetary policy from government tends to be favorable to the objective of price level stability. The Bundesbank was in general more concerned about inflation (or was earlier aware of inflationary dangers) than the government. In this respect the party structure of the government hardly made a difference: conflicts about the course of monetary policy in which the Bundesbank favored a less expansionary course arose under the Adenauer government (as in 1960–61), under the great coalition of christian democrats and social democrats (as in 1968–69) and more recently under the government of social democrats and liberals.

Independence from Foreign Governments and Monetary Institutions

*The Experience during the Weimar Republic*
The reform of the monetary constitution in Germany after World War I
was heavily influenced by the Allied countries. The main result of this
influence was the independence of the Reichsbank from the German government which was introduced in 1922 and confirmed in the Bank Act of
1924. It is important to note that a direct functional or personal dependence of the German Reichsbank from foreign governments was not established (although there had been plans that pointed into this direction). The
foreign control over the Reichsbank's policies was limited to the surveillance over the provisions of the 1924 Bank Act which had been the subject
of an international agreement. The surveillance function of foreign governments which was institutionalized in the Bank Act of 1924 was removed by
the revision of the Bank Act in 1930. The main achievement, however,
which had been due to the foreign influence, that is, the direct functional
and personal independence of the Reichsbank, remained until it was finally
destroyed by the Hitler government.

*The Experience after World War II*
When the Federal Republic of Germany joined the International Monetary
Fund (IMF) the German Central Bank faced—apart from moral suasion—
three potential sources of dependence of the IMF. First, the IMF was entitled to combine balance-of-payments credits with specific demands in respect to the course of monetary policy. This aspect—which has been
important for some countries—did not play a role for Germany which
turned out to be a country with a very strong currency. Second, the IMF
might have opposed a revaluation of the deutsche mark. Again, this aspect
has not played a role. The resistance against the appreciation of the deutsche mark—which proved harmful for a stable monetary policy in several
periods—was not of international origin but came from the domestic government. Third, the credit facilities of the IMF (and the more recently
created facilities of the EMS) enable foreign governments or monetary
institutions to induce an expansion of the money supply in Germany. The
use of these credit facilities played a substantial role, although until now it
cannot be made responsible for an overly expansionary policy, since the
Bundesbank has the means to neutralize the resulting change in its money
supply by other measures. The main importance of these credits lies in their
effect on the international distribution of seigniorage gains. Since these
credits are given at interest rates below the market rate, the borrowing

institutions benefit whereas the Bundesbank (and in the end the German taxpayers) faces a corresponding loss in income.

## Conclusion

Independence of a central bank from government interferences is no guarantee against monetary mismanagement as evidenced, for example, by the hyperinflation of 1922–23 which occurred at a time when the German Reichsbank enjoyed a status of almost complete independence.

The postwar experience in Germany, however, suggests that the independence of the Bundesbank from government directives tended to be conducive to price level stability in the Federal Republic as the Bundesbank was generally more concerned about inflation (or earlier aware of inflationary dangers) than the government.

Nevertheless, one has to take account of the fact, that since the collapse of the parity system in 1973 and the resulting far-reaching functional independence of the Bundesbank, monetary management was still far from perfect. Apart from the consideration that the Bundesbank's choice of denominating its monetary target in terms of central bank money may be regarded as inferior compared to a target for M1, the major mistake was the fact that the Bundesbank exceeded its monetary target for 1978 by a substantial amount—a mistake which was later openly admitted by the president of the Bundesbank.[23] It should be noted, however, that the main reason for the deviation from the monetary target was not an attempt by the Bundesbank to pursue a Keynesian employment policy. The main reason rather was that the Bundesbank thought to observe an unforeseen increase in the demand for German currency indicated, inter alia, by the substantial real revaluation of the deutsche mark against the dollar. While it cannot be excluded that such a change in preferences actually took place in 1978 as a result of changes in international currency preferences, it is apparent that the Bundesbank overestimated the size of this factor. Moreover, empirical investigations for West Germany reject the thesis that real exchange-rate changes are a sufficiently reliable indicator for autonomous changes in the demand for money.[24]

This observation suggests that because of the lack of reliable indicators for changes in the demand for money deviations from monetary targets in a medium-sized country like Germany may easily be counterproductive for the objective of monetary stability and that central banks in such countries may be well advised to forgo the scope for discretionary action which so far they have reserved for themselves.

## Notes

1. See *Gesetz über die Bildung eines Sachverständigenrates zur Begutachtung der gesamt-wirtschaftlichen Entwicklung* (Aug. 14, 1963) and *Gesetz zur Förderung der Stabilität und des Wachstums der Wirtschaft* (June 8, 1967).

2. Classical unemployment can arise:

• when equilibrium wages have fallen below subsistence levels (because of capital destruction, immigration, or excessive population growth) and when minimum wages are introduced as a matter of legislation or social convention;

• when excessive real wages have been indexed or when equilibrium nominal wages have been overindexed;

• when supply shocks or labor-augmenting innovations bring about a deterioration of labor's terms of trade vis-à-vis capital or nature and when real wages are inflexible downward;

• when labor unions raise their degree of monopoly or use their monopoly power;

• when interregional or interindustrial wage differentials are reduced in collective bargaining or when labor monopoly power is used for narrowing wage differentials between skilled and unskilled workers.

3. See Milton Friedman, Nobel Lecture: Inflation and Unemployment, *Journal of Political Economy* 85 (1977), pp. 451–472.

4. See, e.g., Bank for International Settlements, Fiftieth Annual Report, Basle 1980, p. 23.

5. When the failure of the central bank's attempt to reach both targets becomes apparent, there is the danger that the government will switch to an authoritarian solution of the assignment problem by introducing controls of wages, prices, and exchange rates and other restrictions which impair the functioning of markets.

6. Responsibility of the central bank for unemployment is in this setting strictly limited to avoiding Keynesian unemployment. The central bank can discharge this part of its duties by announcing and securing a rate of growth of the money supply that would allow (not bring about) full employment. Moreover, it would be helpful if the implications of the money target for a full-employment-oriented wage policy are made sufficiently clear to the public—preferably through advice from independent institutions, such as the Economic Expert Council in Germany. Spelling out the wage policy implications has a pedagogic value. It can help labor union leaders to explain to the rank and file what is required for achieving and maintaining full employment in given circumstances. It also seems useful for enlisting public support to an employment-oriented wage policy whereever labor unions care for public opinion. Moreover, pronouncements about current and future equilibrium wages based on the employment situation in certain sectors and regions seem to be essential for a policy of rational expectations insofar as the rational expectation hypothesis implies that the agents have a sufficient knowledge of the functioning of the system of relative prices and wages as an allocative device.

As a final point it may be worth considering whether there should not be a constitutional or legal rule that allows every citizen who feels excluded from active participation in the labor market to challenge the binding nature of minimum wages established by law or by collective bargaining.

7. See Milton Friedman, The Demand for Money, Some Theoretical and Empirical Results, *Journal of Political Economy*, 67 (1959), pp. 427–455.

8. See Carlos Rodriguez, A Simple Keynesian Model of Inflation and Unemployment under Rational Expectation, *Weltwirtschaftliches Archiv* 144 (1978), pp. 1–11.

9. See Herbert Giersch, IMF Surveillance over Exchange Rates, in: *The New International Monetary System*, ed. Robert A. Mundell and Jacques J. Polak, New York 1977, pp. 53–68.

10. See Knut Borchardt, Währung und Wirtschaft, in: *Währung and Wirtschaft in Deutschland 1876–1975*, ed. Deutsche Bundesbank. Frankfurt/M. 1976, pp. 3–55.

11. See Heinz Haller, Die Rolle der Staatsfinanzen für den Inflationsprozeß, in: *Währung und Wirtschaft in Deutschland 1876–1975*, ed. Deutsche Bundesbank, Frankfurt/M. 1976, p. 130.

12. See Gert v. Eynern, Die Unabhängigkeit der Notenbank, Berlin 1957, p. 6.

13. See Otto Pfleiderer, Betrachtungen zur Stabilitätspolitik, ed. Herbert Giersch, Kieler Vorträge, 90, Tübingen 1980.

14. The president and the other members of the board were appointed by the General Council (Generalrat) in which government representatives had no seat.

15. See Gert v. Eynern, *Die Reichsbank, Probleme des deutschen Zentralnoteninstituts in geschichtlicher Darstellung*, Jena 1928, p. 114.

16. Haberler convincingly argues that the appropriate way of dealing with the Great Depression would have been a simultaneous devaluation of all currencies against gold (see Gottfried Haberler, How Important is Control over International Reserves, in: *The New International Monetary System*, ed. Robert A. Mundell and Jacques J. Polak, New York 1977, p. 116).

17. See for a more detailed discussion Heinrich Irmler, Bankenkrise und Vollbeschäftigungspolitik (1931–1936), in: *Währung und Wirtschaft in Deutschland 1876–1975*, ed. Deutsche Bundesbank, Frankfurt/M. 1976, pp. 305–307.

18. Excerpts of this letter are reprinted in Karl-Heinrich Hansmeyer und Rolf Caesar, Kriegswirtschaft und Inflation (1936–1948), in: *Währung und Wirtschaft in Deutschland 1876–1975*, ed. Deutsche Bundesbank, Frankfurt/M. 1976. pp. 382–383.

19. The direct functional independence is guaranteed in section 12 of the *Gesetz über die Deutsche Bundesbank* (June 26, 1957). The strong personal independence results from the fact that less than 50 percent of the members of the Zentralbankrat are appointed at the suggestion of the federal government (the others being suggested by the regional governments) and that the term for which they are appointed is relatively long (normally eight years).

20. The policy of the Bundesbank in this period has later been openly described as a "capitulation" (Otmar Emminger: *The D-Mark in the Conflict between Internal and External Equilibrium, 1948–1975, Essays in International Finance*, 122, Princeton (N.J.) 1977, p. 15).

21. Ibid., p. 26.

22. This target relates to the monetary base as defined by the Bundesbank (Zentralbankgeldmenge); it shows a similar behavior as M3.

23. See Otmar Emminger, Konjunktur, Geldpolitik, Geldwertstabilität: Ausführungen auf der Jahrestagung des Bundesverbandes der Deutschen Industrie, Bonn, 12. Juni 1979, in: *Deutsche Bundesbank, Auszüge aus Presseartikeln*, 1979, Nr. 40, vom 15. Juni 1979.

24. See Enno Langfeldt and Harmen Lehment, Welche Bedeutung haben "Sonderfaktoren" für die Erklärung der Geldnachfrage in der Bundesrepublik Deutschland? in: *Weltwirtschaftliches Archiv* 116, no. 4 (December 1980).

# 20 Real Exchange Rates in a Catching-up Process

## The Short and the Longer View

The public policy debate tends to be dominated by short-run considerations. This holds for Keynesian economists and for policy-makers in general. Both tend to have a time horizon not extending beyond a two- or
three-year period. In focusing on the short run, they are likely to overlook
the fundamentals below the surface. These fundamentals, I suggest, are
more relevant than is usually assumed. They relate to the real sector and
hence to markets that are slow to adjust. Adherents of the rational expectations school suffer from a similar bias. They stress the absorption and
processing of new information and thus tend to see an economy with
short-run equilibriums. This makes them pay less attention to the operation
of market forces, which are sluggish and tied to past plans and decisions,
rational or not, many of which can be corrected only gradually in the
course of time. But time lags and boomerang effects do matter. What is
treated as an exogenous "shock" in a rational expectations model is often,
in a longer perspective, the more relevant part of economic life that has to
be explained. Monetarists, it is true, have a longer time horizon when it
comes to judging the Phillips curve and the effects of alternative monetary
regimes; but their approach leads them to neglect institutional rigidities,
including labor market problems. It is here that the supply siders have a
role to play, but only if they go beyond the tax issue to encompass the
whole supply side in the spirit of classical economics.

It is the purpose of this chapter to correct some of these shortcomings
and to lengthen the time horizon in the public debate about exchange

Reprinted with permission from *Public Choice, Public Finance and Public Policy: Essays in
Honour of Alan Peacock*, edited by David Greenaway and G. K. Shaw. Oxford: Basil Blackwell, 1985, 176–192. Copyright 1985 by David Greenaway and G. K. Shaw. The original
paper was entitled "Real Exchange Rates and Economic Development."

rates, notably about the dollar–deutsche mark (DM) rate. Long-term interest rates, most of all the real rate of interest and the profitability of investment, will be brought into focus. The hypothesis emerging from this chapter is that the dollar is likely to remain strong for fundamental reasons, that is, for reasons rooted in the real sectors of the U.S. and European economies. Temporary declines for short-term reasons are not, of course, excluded. They should therefore not be viewed as disproving the central thesis: what matters in the longer run are the vitality of an economy and its place and role in world economic development.

The longer run is to be understood as comprising more than one decade and at least one turning point in what Schumpeter called a "Kondratieff cycle." This widening of the time horizon brings to mind the fact that the real exchange rate between the dollar and the deutsche mark, that is, the exchange rate adjusted for relative inflation, is now (end of July 1984) close to what it was in the 1950s, when most people thought it to be in equilibrium. To be sure, the United States and the Europe of today are not the same as they were thirty years ago. But such historical comparisons may still serve as a useful background for forming a broad judgment about the present and the future.

In a shorter perspective, that is, in comparison with the mid-1970s, the dollar appears to be grossly overvalued and U.S. interest rates look exotic. Within a Keynesian framework of thought, both can be seen as the result of a large U.S. budget deficit which the Federal Reserve is unwilling to finance (Marris 1984; Blanchard and Dornbusch 1984). Monetary and fiscal policy are seen to work against each other in the United States, and the overindebted countries have to carry the double burden of high interest rates and an expensive dollar. If only the U.S. government could be induced to reduce its deficit sharply by raising some taxes or by reversing a previous income tax cut, both the dollar and real interest rates in the world would fall and find an acceptable equilibrium level (Bergsten 1982). This is the view prevailing in the international economic policy discussion.

A dramatic picture presents itself when cyclical forces are brought to the foreground in this Keynesian framework. The strength of the U.S. upswing that developed in 1983 despite high interest rates is then seen to be the result of deficit spending (Marris 1984). Much of the investment appears to be of the induced type (described by the acceleration principle), just as are the capital imports that the United States needs in order to finance the current account deficit. These induced capital imports support the exchange rate of the dollar. Sooner or later, perhaps in 1985, the present business cycle will collapse. Then the world will experience both a sharp decline of U.S. interest rates and a downfall of the dollar below its equilibrium level, causing disruptions and new imbalances in the world economy. So this story goes. But it may well be that in the United States the fundamental conditions for investment and growth, and hence for a strong dollar, have improved relative to the fundamentals in Europe so that the dollar can remain strong irrespective of cyclical forces.

Monetarists usually take a longer view than politicians and Keynesians. Their assertion that an exchange rate is the relative price of two monies appears trivial at first glance, but their insistence on the quantity theory of money and its implications for the monies' domestic purchasing power certainly extends the time horizon. Moreover, they stress the real component in nominal interest rates and would therefore, also join my train of thought toward (changes in) real exchange rates. The bridge to the fundamentals is the concept of confidence in the long-run stability of the currency's domestic purchasing power. How a shift of confidence from one currency to another leads to currency substitution, and thus changes the real exchange rate, shall be considered below.

In a monetarist perspective budget deficits are likely to destroy confidence. As Latin American experience—and earlier European experience—amply shows, budget deficits are often the result of fiscal irresponsibility; they can induce central banks to pursue an inflationary policy designed to finance the deficits and to reduce the real value of the outstanding public debt. But this is not what has happened so far in North America and present-day Western Europe. If markets were suspicious in this respect, the dollar would be weak rather than strong.

Financial analysts watching day-to-day developments relate the strong dollar to high U.S. interest rates, which they as well as monetarists (Mascaro and Meltzer 1983) partly attribute to the volatility of Federal Reserve (Fed) policy. But doubts come to mind immediately: would a less volatile Fed policy weaken the dollar? The answer will, of course, be no on monetarist grounds. We come closer to the fundamentals when we raise the question how the U.S. economy can afford to pay the risk premium for this volatility, given the fact that its real sector is prospering and obviously has fully adjusted to current interest rate levels. The answer is to be found in a correspondingly high profitability (or marginal efficiency) of investment, which can be due either to the cut in business taxes or to technological innovation or to the downward flexibility of real wages in the U.S. labor market. In an interdependent system it is, of course, difficult to single out any one of these factors. But it is significant that they all belong to the real sector and explain why this sector has enough vitality to support a strong dollar.

## Purchasing Power Parity

Those who say that the dollar is overvalued have, of course, an implicit norm of what its exchange rate would be in "normal" circumstances, or ought to be on efficiency grounds. Sometimes they implicitly or explicitly use a reference period or entertain the idea that the dollar will settle on a level in the middle between the high value it achieved in 1984 and its trough in 1978. All this boils down to the question of what fundamentals really determine the external value of a currency in the medium run.

The appropriate starting point is the purchasing power parity (PPP) doctrine which is based on the law of one price. This law holds for tradables between any two countries if trade is not restricted and if tariffs and taxes, transport, and transactions costs are low enough to be ignored.

Deviations from this norm arise because the basket that is used to measure the purchasing power in the countries to be compared includes not only standardized commodities for which the law of one price may be taken to hold, but also goods and services that do not enter trade at all. We call them local goods or nontradables. If the relation between the prices of tradable and the prices of nontradables develops differently in the countries concerned, we will find that the exchange rate (which makes the price of tradables equal) will deviate from PPP. These are long-run deviations. We can observe them in international comparisons between more developed countries and less developed countries, and we think that they are also likely to play a role in a process of catching up or lagging behind. The major points and cases will be spelled out below.

Before doing so I propose to focus on a range of goods that are neither purely local goods (like the service of land in housing rents) nor standardized commodities to which the law of one price applies fairly well. These goods—call them "manufactures"—are sold not in perfect markets but under conditions of monopolistic competition. They include such specific items as custom-tailored capital goods, consumer goods fulfilling country-specific tastes, and new products that can earn a monopoly rent but must create their own markets first. Although these manufactures—and a great number of quite specific services—are tradables, they are not strictly subject to the law of one price. Together with tradables and nontradables, they form part of the PPP basket.

## Temporary Deviations from PPP

Changes in the price of these manufactures relative to the price of standard-ized commodities can lead to a deviation from PPP provided there is no compensating change in the relative price of nontradables. Ignoring non-tradables for the moment, we can say that changes in the price of manu-factures relative to the price of standardized commodities matter in our context if they affect the terms of trade. This is the case in the following examples.

A country removing restrictions on its foreign trade in manufactures must, at least temporarily, lower the price of its exports in order to squeeze itself as an aggressive seller into tight world markets; perhaps it also has to pay more for the import of intermediate goods. This deterioration of the terms of trade goes along with a devaluation of its currency in real terms. This benefits the export sector and the import substitution sector at the expense of the domestic sector: the latter shrinks relative to the interna-tional sector. Let me call this the case of an export drive. It applied to West Germany in the early 1950s.

The export drive is, of course, facilitated if the exchange rates are fixed to begin with and if they happen to be fixed in such a way that the country can run an export surplus and the central bank can accumulate the other country's currency. This was relevant for Europe and for much of the Western world during the period of the so-called dollar shortage. While the process of dollar accumulation gradually achieved its purpose, the down-ward deviation from PPP ought to have been corrected gradually to avoid an overshooting. But such overshooting did take place. A dollar overhang developed which again led to a rather drastic reversal of the real exchange rate at the time when the Bretton Woods system broke down. An over-shooting in the reverse direction—an excessive devaluation of the dollar as it happened in the 1970s—was perhaps necessary for shifting resources in Europe from the export sector to the domestic sector and in the United States from the domestic sector to the export sector. The United States had to become a relatively cheap country for Europeans, and Europe a rela-tively expensive country for tourists from America. "Relative" here means compared with PPP, but even more so in comparison to the period when Europe responded to the so-called dollar shortage.

Another deviation from PPP equilibrium, which is also connected with the terms of trade, takes place when a country, instead of squeezing itself into export markets, finds its export mix of manufactured products faced with a high-income elasticity of demand and uses this demand-pull for expanding its export volumes instead of raising prices. The international sector grows at the expense of the domestic sector. The terms of trade are worse than they could be. Sooner or later the country will, like West Germany at the end of the 1960s, discover that it has an oversized export sector. An adjustment process will gather momentum, either in the form of a domestic cost-push—higher wages and costs at the given exchange rate—or in the form of a currency revaluation at constant prices. This adjustment process amounts to an improvement in the country's terms of trade. All rents from superior design and quality, from reliability and punctuality, which were formerly used for promoting volumes will then be collected in the form of higher export prices. This improvement in the terms of trade goes along with an upward deviation from the previous real exchange rate, most likely also with an overshooting compared with long-run PPP.

Furthermore, changes in the terms of trade that involve a deviation from PPP, and thus have an effect on the real exchange rate, will have to be brought about to accommodate capital movements that are exogenous to the economic system. One case involves reparation payments under conditions of full employment. Their transfer in real terms requires a shift of resources from the domestic sector to the export sector and hence a real devaluation of the country's currency, so that the export sector and the import substitution sector find their terms of trade vis-à-vis the domestic sector improved.

A parallel case is that of a country that has lived on capital imports and has run into excessive debt. In order to regain confidence in its viability and to improve its standing in international capital markets, it must shift resources from the oversized domestic sector to the export (and import substitution) sector and thus improve its balance on current account. A real devaluation of the exchange rate, involving a worsening of its international terms of trade, is necessary in such a case to remedy an otherwise hopeless situation.

The last case refers to a country that insulates itself from cyclical fluctuations in international demand. In a worldwide recession, a firm can maintain its sales by undercutting its competitors' prices. A country full of such firms in its export and import-substitution sectors, supported by downward flexibility of wages, could maintain a high level of employment by exhibiting such price flexibility. Its trade balance on current account will then improve; its terms of trade become worse. In comparison with PPP and the situation before the recession, the exchange rate will be considered undervalued. A good substitute for this is a devaluation. Although some observers will call this a beggar-thy-neighbor policy, the strategy is perfectly defensible if the recession has its origin abroad. No valid objection on cosmopolitical grounds can be raised against it. Clearly, if every country behaved in the same way, without delay the real quantity of money in the world (or the price of gold under a gold standard) would go up, and the Haberler–Pigou effect would come into play. In the case of such a simultaneous action temporary deviation from PPP would, of course, be observable. The preceding argument applies symmetrically to the case of a country insulating itself from a worldwide boom (Giersch 1970).

**Sustained Deviations from PPP**

So far we have used the notion of PPP in a fairly loose fashion by concentrating on manufactures and standardized commodities and leaving local goods and their prices out of the picture. It is now time to shift the emphasis. In the long run, there is no reason to believe that the prices of manufactures will behave differently from the prices of standardized commodities. Market imperfections and processes of the kind described above fade into the background, and the relative size of the domestic and the international sectors can be taken to be in equilibrium. This means that the rewards for capital and labor are the same across sectors within the country.

But this intersectoral equalization of factor rewards does not exclude intersectoral productivity differentials. Indeed, they become important for explaining permanent deviations from PPP. They matter in intercountry comparisions if—but only if—they are different in the countries to be compared. In order to bring this into sharp focus, we consider only local goods that are not traded at all and international goods (traded goods) for which the law of one price holds. The main proposition here is that the production of tradables is subject to the productivity whip of competition (or what Samuelson 1984 calls a "Darwinian–Toynbeean challenge process"), whereas local goods are produced behind the shelter of transport costs and hence with much slack (x-inefficiency) or with an inferior technology.

There is no reason to expect greatly different productivity differentials between countries that have attained similar levels of overall productivity and development. Nevertheless, there are always exceptions. Thus, we observe that some local goods in Europe and some services that are more strictly regulated on the old continent (e.g., air freight, road haulage, postal services) are distinctly more expensive in comparison with internationally traded goods than they are in the much larger markets of the New World. If the European Community (EC) would deregulate and form a really common market, Europe would be even cheaper for U.S. visitors than it is now.

As a general rule, however, poorer countries should be cheaper in PPP terms than richer countries, just as poorer regions or cities in the same country tend to have a lower cost of living level than richer regions or cities, where the costs of local goods and services are boosted by the scarcity element in housing rents—unless these nontradables are produced with a correspondingly high productivity. The rule of rich countries being expensive countries holds to the extent (1) that local goods have significant weight in the PPP basket and (2) that in the course of the development process productivity in the international sector rises more than in the local sector. The second condition is essential. The proposition has been formulated by Balassa (1964), although somewhat differently, and can be traced back to Harrod (1933) and—with some modifications—even to Ricardo (1817).[1] As indicated, it can be supported by the presumption that competition is a productivity whip that operates more forcefully in the international sector than in the sector producing local goods.

As a corollary, countries in a catching-up process, that is, countries becoming richer relative to their trading partners, will have an exchange rate that, although still undervalued in absolute PPP terms until they have fully succeeded in catching up, is becoming less and less undervalued. Compared with the past, the catching-up country will experience an upward revaluation in PPP terms. Some observers using the past as a norm may even (wrongly) interpret it as an overvaluation. The process bringing this about includes not only competition, which raises productivity in the international sector more than that in the local sector, but also the technology transfer from the more advanced countries. This presumably also affects the international sector more strongly, or earlier. Apart from the technology transfer, the catching-up country is likely to benefit from capital imports. This, again, will affect primarily its international sector, and not so much—or only with a time lag—its domestic sector. Capital imports, of course, mean a deficit in the external balance on current account, and those who (wrongly) judge the exchange rate with the norm of a current account equilibrium will see a strong (perhaps additional) reason to say that it is overvalued.

When the German Economic Expert Council in 1964 passed its first judgment on the DM–dollar exchange rate, the dominant view of the public was that the (fixed) rate was still what it ought to be. This is why the Expert Council, considering the catching-up process and its effect on PPP,

said that the Federal Republic of Germany, which had been a cheap country
(in PPP terms) at the beginning of the catching-up process, should have
ceased to be one; the exchange rate, therefore, was to be judged as undervalued, and a revaluation (or an upward float) was to be put on the policy
agenda (Sachverständigenrat 1964). But none of us at the time thought that
the revaluation required for these reasons would he more than 5–10 percent. There is no reason to question this judgment in retrospect. As the real
exchange rate of the dollar against the DM is now (July 1984) about 5
percent higher than it was in 1964, the dollar on these (partial) grounds
appears to be overvalued by 10–15 percent. The undervaluation of the
DM in the 1950s and the 1960s took care, of course, of the original "dollar
shortage" and contributed to the accumulation of the dollar overhang mentioned above. There is therefore no additional item to be added on this
account if we make a historical comparison the basis of our judgment.

**Currency Disturbances: The Downfall and Renaissance of the Dollar**

Historical comparisons with the 1950s and 1960s are valid only to the
extent that the decline and rise of the dollar in the 1970s can be considered
an episode arising from exceptional circumstances. Without going into
detail we may just note:

1. the financial implications of President Johnson's Great Society program;

2. the inflationary financing of the Vietnam War;

3. the price control experiment of the Nixon administration;

4. the overdue breakdown the Bretton Woods system;

5. the 1973 oil shock;

6. Watergate;

7. the bad luck of the United States under the Carter administration; and

8. the rise of inflation (to almost 14 percent) and of inflationary expectations until late 1979.

This period, however, also includes events in the real sector which can
be taken to have led to a reversal of the trend. Worth mentioning are the
deregulation of the trucking and airline industries; the creation of millions
of new jobs in response to demographic changes; the emergence of new
technology centers which had hardly any parallel in the rest of the world,
perhaps not even in Japan; and the astonishing fact that real wages declined, partly under the impact of inflation, partly in response to demo-

graphic changes and increasing female participation rates. Immediately crucial for the dollar exchange rate was, of course, the monetary stance adopted in late 1979, which led to positive and high real rates of interest, which had been negative when the dollar was at its low.

A country like the United States, which previously performed a leadership role but lost ground in this respect to its competitors, will suffer a devaluation of its currency in real terms for the following reasons:

1. If technological leadership is being lost, the (transitory) monopoly rents from innovation or from superior quality will disappear: people will have to work harder to export more to pay for the same volume of imports.

2. Monetary leadership may be lost, in the sense that assets denominated in the country's currency, including cash, suffer a decline in foreign demand because foreigners (as well as domestic holders of such assets) lose confidence in the currency's long-term stability in terms of domestic purchasing power. In order to describe this case I prefer to use the metaphor that "portfolios emigrate" or that "the currency area implodes." Emigration in this sense implies immigration into another currency area, which tends to become larger (Giersch 1977). The "implosion" goes along with a devaluation of the real exchange rate in a process of currency substitution.

If a country such as the United States after 1979 resumes its leadership role in the field of technology, or as a trustworthy supplier of the Western world's international money, it will experience a sharp upward revaluation of its real exchange rate. Why then should we be so surprised about the renewed strength of the dollar?

**Growth Equilibrium**

What would real exchange rates look like in a smoothly growing world economy? A first answer is that they should not be judged by the yardstick of current account balance because there is a positive role to play for autonomous capital flows from richer to poorer countries. Wilhelm Röpke once said that people in the upper floors of the income pyramid tend to devote themselves to capital formation while the inhabitants of the lower floors take care of population growth. I prefer to use the metaphor of a Thünen cone (Giersch 1949, 1979) for portraying the world economy, or any spatial system with rich center and poor peripheries. The cone can grow in a smooth fashion, that is, with a minimum of structural change, if the marginal efficiency of capital tends to rise everywhere at the same rate and if capital flows from the rich center, where the marginal propensity to save is high, toward the periphery, where it is closer to zero. However smooth the growth process may be thought of, it must be sustained by the creation and application of new knowledge, presumably in the center, in order to prevent a fall in the profit rate under the impact of Ricardian constraints (rising rents). But such innovative growth in the center goes along with what we call "locational innovations." This means that the optimum location for producing standardized commodities is moving from the center toward the periphery.

To bring about this locational shift, the countries closer to the periphery must make themselves attractive by having their domestic resources "undervalued" via the exchange rate. Undervaluation in this specific sense means "in terms of costs for the production of standardized industrial commodities," for brevity's sake called "Heckscher–Ohlin" goods. The counterpart to this are high and rising rents and wages for local labor in the center; these push the locus of production of Heckscher–Ohlin goods out to the countries closer to the periphery. The structure of real exchange rates must reflect this structure of cost incentives. If the overvaluations and the undervaluations (in this sense) are not sufficiently pronounced, the process of locational shift (locational innovations) will be retarded. Retardation grants excessive time for process innovation to defend the old locations for Heckscher–Ohlin goods. A reversal of factor intensities is then likely to emerge, as we observe it in Thünen's stationary model in the case of wood, as a result of relatively high transport costs for this commodity. Defensive process innovations are, of course, also promoted by protectionist policies. Undervaluations and overvaluations have to be more pronounced if, in addition to transport costs, such policy-induced resistances are to be overcome.

This spread argument for real exchange rates is a close cousin of the amendment to the PPP theorem discussed above. There the reason was the high price of local commodities in rich countries (say, housing rents) which are part of the PPP basket; here, however, the reason is the price of inputs for Heckscher–Ohlin goods and an international cost differential needed to induce and support this continuous process of locational innovations. There, it was a cross-section comparison that would make sense even if the world economy were in a stationary equilibrium; here, we have overvaluation and undervaluation as part and parcel of a moving equilibrium, as the incentive system necessary for bringing about the minimum adjustment needed for a process of trickling down. We may still say that the law of one price holds for standardized commodities (apart from transport costs) at any moment in time, but then we have to consider that the value of the stock of fixed capital used in producing these goods goes down in the advanced countries under the influence of an exchange rate that people may feel to be overvalued. At the same time, the low valuation of the exchange rates of the less advanced countries raises the marginal efficiency of capital for the (potential) production of Heckscher–Ohlin goods in these countries.

This model of a smoothly growing world economy offers itself as a reference system against which important disequilibrium cases can be judged. With regard to the United States and the dollar, we can summarize so far as follows:

1. As a rich country, the United States ought to run an export surplus to support the outflow of capital to poorer countries. Yet, given the fact that there are poorer countries which have overborrowed and must regain confidence on world capital markets by servicing—and perhaps temporarily repaying—their debt, a deficit in the U.S. current account may help to prevent a debt crisis. Imagine what would happen if the United States now behaved in a similar way as it did in the interwar period, when Germany tried to pay off its reparation debt but failed because the final recipient— via the interallied war debt—did not cooperate by running a current account deficit.

2. A high valuation of the dollar may hurt numerous firms producing Heckscher–Ohlin goods and stimulate protectionist demands in the United States. Yet this is exactly the type of competitive pressure that is needed for the relocation of these industries to less advanced parts of the world economy.

### Growth Leadership

Countries leading in world economic development must be engines of economic growth. Those who advocate an expansion of demand— implying that demand is the limiting factor—focus on budget deficits. The "Reagan deficit" is thus seen as a source of growth.

However, the same observers who support Keynesian remedies for unemployment and stagnation criticize this deficit for raising the level of interest rates in the world. Some of them would like Europe and Japan to have higher public deficits instead of the United States, implying (or not?) that the level of interest rates in the world would be different in that case. (Would it really be lower if the world economy substituted second-rate borrowers for the very best public borrower it currently has?)

Nevertheless the Reagan deficit deserves criticism, first, if it has to be considered as an act of dissaving for the world economy as a whole, or, second, if it implies a waste of capital compared with a situation in which total public expenditure in the United States were the same, but the counterpart of the deficit were (additional) productive investment—say, in infrastructure instead of public consumption or rearmament. As always, the resulting judgment depends upon the reference systems chosen and the way the alternatives are evaluated.

If the Reagan deficit is seen to be the result of the cut in income taxes and business taxes, one can well argue that this cut is equivalent to a productive investment, to the extent that it helped to improve the incentive system and to raise the motivation level in society, including the propensity to work, to invest, and to innovate. It is true that our bookkeeping rules do not allow us to consider this as an investment, but in certain circumstances it may be a better form of investment than an outlay for hardware of the same magnitude. Whether this interpretation has some value, however, can be judged only in the long run, or perhaps in comparison with Europe, where taxes are higher and where motivation levels appear to be lower.

From a European perspective or a vantage point that permits a long-run view, the United States can be seen to behave as an engine for world economic growth. Its real sector seems to have adjusted to the growth conditions of our time much better than the real sector in large parts of Europe. In order to support this view, we may note or recall the following interrelated points.

1. While Europe suffers from a level of real wages that is still too high (Giersch 1978; Artus 1985) and from a rigid wage structure which does not allow sufficiently for relative scarcities (excessive wages for unskilled workers and for workers in structurally weak regions; too small wage incentives —after taxes and deductions for social security—for attaining qualifications, for accumulating human capital, and for moving to better-paid jobs elsewhere), the United States has a balkanized and hence more flexible labor market and a union system that has become much weaker after the strike of the air controllers and the severe 1982 recession. Instead of shortening the working week and reducing the retirement age, which is on the agenda in Europe, the United States has raised the retirement age and also the number of jobs that support going real wages.

2. In Europe, profits are still low compared with the interest that can be earned on financial assets (Dicke and Trapp 1984). They fail to respond to

the shortage of productive capital relative to the supply of labor—the combination of capital shortage and unemployment that emerged in the 1970s (Giersch 1978). The U.S. economy, on the other hand, has succeeded in raising profits to levels that match the high real rates of interest that exist and that are likely to prevail as long as the structural unemployment (or capital shortage unemployment) calls for giving capital formation the first priority in the growth process. This is mainly due to flexibility of the U.S. labor market.

3. In large parts of Europe, including the north of West Germany, people still believe technology to have a labor-saving bias, as one may expect it to have if real wages are excessively high; therefore, they adopt an attitude that amounts to opposing technical progress (Europessimism). In the United States the population has never been really affected by such opinion trends and seems to have almost maintained, or even recently strengthened, its optimism toward the future course of economic development and technological advance.

4. In the United States public opinion seems to have recognized that government regulations and private barriers to entry weaken the economy's capacity to adjust to future developments. In Europe large sections of society still cling to policy conceptions and political ideas that are closer to state regulation, corporationism, or the traditional guild society (Eurosclerosis). There may have been some shift to conservatism on both sides of the Atlantic, but conservatism in Europe essentially means conserving traditional structures rather than conserving the flexibility of society.

Taken together, these judgmental propositions (perhaps very subjective ones, short of further research which appears desperately needed in this field) suggest that the United States is already much better prepared for starting a new spurt in economic development—at least in comparison with Europe, perhaps less so in comparison with Japan. In this perspective, Europe is seen to be in the very early phase of an adjustment process that is likely to cover more than one of the short-term business cycles that we have become accustomed to observe. In my opinion (or my unspecified socioeconomic model), the transatlantic time lag in the real sector's adjustment to faster growth may well lie in the range of five to ten years. It could be shortened by a concerted movement toward freer trade among Western countries. Freer international trade would surely help to break up internal protection in Europe's domestic markets. In that case, the immense productivity source of international trade and of competition from abroad could be tapped. This would allow monetary policy to anticipate a somewhat faster growth of potential output. But the prospects for such a move within the next couple of years appear to be dim.

## The Short and the Longer View in Contrast

The transatlantic time lag in the adjustment to high real rates of interest and to new technologies supports an explanation for the strength of the dollar and for the superior performance of the U.S. economy which has its foundations in the real sector rather than in the monetary-fiscal policy mix. The following statements may help to bring the two alternative explanations into sharp contrast.

If the Reagan deficit is the villain or the piece, capital imports into the United States are of the induced type. They will fade away with the weakening of the present upswing, so that the dollar will decline to correct a current account deficit which corresponds with the budget deficit. If, however, it is the high marginal efficiency (profitability) of investment in the United States that is the dominant force in the scenario, the capital flows into that country are more of the autonomous type. They will then decline only slightly during the next recession, which itself will be weaker if autonomous investments in the United States remain fairly strong. To the extent that the profitability differential between the United States and Europe is decisive and does not substantially decline, the real exchange rate of the dollar will continue to have strong fundamental support.

The short-run explanation suggests that European countries ought to boost domestic demand by running higher fiscal deficits. They would weaken the induced flow of investible funds into the United States and thus contribute to bringing down the external value of the dollar. The longer-run explanation offered here suggests that Europe should imitate the United States in reducing real wages, in changing its attitude towards technical progress, and in opening up its markets, so that European markets become more flexible and more attractive to potential entrepreneurs. It is only in such a process of revitalization that Europe will regain its former competitiveness in long-term capital markets. Only then will the fundamentals induce a weakening of the exchange rate of the dollar vis-à-vis European currencies—then, however, in combination with a faster growth of potential and actual output in Europe. In this longer-run perspective there is no reason to object to potentially higher budget deficits in Europe, if they arise not from higher public spending but from tax cuts, which raise the profitability of investment and, by reducing marginal taxes for wage earners, raise the motivation level of the labor force and the whole population.

The dominance of the short-run explanation in the public discussion has drawbacks for a lasting therapy of Europe's economic problems. By making investors believe that the real value of the dollar will come down quickly, this explanation discourages U.S. foreign direct investment in Europe. It also makes European firms pessimistic about the longer-run prospects for exporting to the U.S. market. In the longer-run perspective, the high dollar will raise the profitability (marginal efficiency) of investment in Europe's export sector. This structure of exchange rates could well transmit part of the driving power for sustainable growth that the U.S. economy develops to Europe and other countries, However, Europe is unlikely to take advantage of it if the high external value of the dollar is considered to be a short episode rather than a replay of the development that Europe experienced in the 1950s and 1960s.

The view that real interest rates will come down rather quickly makes investors believe that it is not worthwhile reversing the current bias in investment and even in applied research, which favors capital-intensive and labor-saving technologies in sharp contrast to a situation that displays a shortage of productive jobs in relation to an abundant supply of labor.

The idea that Europe—and West Germany in particular—needs just a little bit of fiscal expansion supports populist pressures. This may very well weaken the efforts to reduce the waste element in public expenditures in order to free resources for productive investment in the private sector, which would be the right response to Europe's capital shortage-cum-unemployment. Moreover, the concentration on vague macroeconomic concepts like deficit spending impairs the chances for tax cuts designed to promote capital formation and the creation of new firms on the old continent.

Emphasis on short-run measures to boost demand may do less harm in the United States, where real wages were brought down in the 1970s partly under the influence of unanticipated inflation. But in inflation-experienced Europe, with fairly centralized wage bargaining in many countries, the wage problem will have to be tackled directly. Centralized unions always tend to maintain that unemployment is not their fault and must, therefore, be due to exogenous factors (like technical progress) or to a deficiency of overall demand. But although it is effective demand that matters, that is, demand in relation to supply prices, the unions yield to strong membership pressure for raising real wages when demand improves so that "job owners" fully benefit from any productivity advance, cyclical or trend based. It is true that a learning process has started in Europe, here and there; but it may be swamped by a policy debate which ignores the microeconomic foundations and depicts the U.S. policy as the source of the evil. The problem is not only the real wages paid out to the employees, but the numerous restrictive regulations and practices which raise the shadow wage for the employers, as they often make the hiring of new workers an almost irreversible decision. Irreversibility here and a belief in the reversal of the strengthening of the dollar add up to a situation that is not nearly as encouraging for Europe as the situation was under U.S. growth leadership in the 1950s and 1960s.

## Conclusions

If there is to be a brand name for distinguishing this longer-view interpretation of the present dollar–DM rate, it may be called a "flagship hypothesis." By raising the marginal efficiency of investment, the U.S. economy is speeding up its trend rate of growth relative to the laggards in the convoy. The driving power is autonomous investment rather than induced investment of the accelerator type. The capital imports into the United States, which compensate for the crowding-out effect of the Reagan deficit, are therefore more trend based than cyclical. They raise the external value of the dollar and thus weaken the competitive position of the less productive parts of U.S. manufacturing, to the benefit of locations in countries with lower labor costs. Some of the laggards have to transfer debt services; others see the marginal efficiency of investment in their export sector improved, but have difficulty in making full use of this imparted and imported driving force. This speeding up of the pacemaker and lagging of the followers is a plausible explanation for the transatlantic tensions in the field of economic policy.

At the end of a tiring series of reflections, an applied economist must try to arrive at a hard conclusion. To make it short, I would be more than mildly surprised if the real exchange rate of the dollar vis-à-vis the deutsche mark dropped by more than 10 or 15 percent on average during any period of twelve months over the next three years.[2] This rests on the (realistic) condition that the United States remains on a monetary path which does not give rise to inflationary expectations (as it did in the second half of the 1970s). Moreover, the flagship hypothesis suggests that the range for the fluctuations of the dollar might even have a somewhat higher floor. In subsequent years Europe may well succeed in lowering this floor, just as the world may succeed in bringing down the real rate of interest by accelerating capital formation and economizing on the use of capital. But such success on the exchange rate front will largely depend upon how far the old continent regains its strength in curing Eurosclerosis.

## Notes

This piece was written in the summer of 1984 and addresses itself to explaining the foreign exchange situation at a time when the world was puzzled by a strong dollar and a strong U.S. upswing. I am grateful for helpful comments on earlier drafts to many of my collaborators in the Kiel Institute of World Economics, notably R. Fürstenberg, H. Schmieding, and F. Weiss.

1. "Since gold rewards are proportional to efficiency in the output of tradable goods, highly efficient countries may find the gold cost of providing their ... services, in which proportional economies cannot be made, higher than in the less efficient countries.... The efficient countries will therefore tend to have a high cost of living" (Harrod 1933, 68). And Ricardo notes: "the prices of home commodities and those of great bulk, though of comparatively small value, are, independently of other cause, higher in those countries where manufactures flourish" (Ricardo 1817, 23). For a discussion of Ricardo's contribution to the PPP theory see Officer (1982) and Samuelson (1984).

2. When this chapter was drafted, toward the end of July 1984, the exchange rate was approximately DM 2.85 to the dollar.

## References

Artus, Jacques R. 1984. "The Disequilibrium Real Wage Hypothesis: An Empirical Evaluation." *IMF Staff Papers* 31:249–302.

Balassa, Bela. 1964. "The Purchasing Power Parity Doctrine: A Reappraisal." *Journal of Political Economy* 72:584–596.

Bergsten, C. Fred. 1982. *The International Implications of Reagonomics.* Kieler Vorträge, N.F., no. 96. Kiel: Institut für Weltwirtschaft.

Blanchard, Olivier, and Rudiger Dornbusch. 1984. "U.S. Deficits, the Dollar and Europe." *Banca Nazionale del Lavoro Quarterly Review,* no. 148:89–113.

Dicke, Hugo, and Peter Trapp. 1984. "Zinsen, Gewinne und Nettoinvestitionen: Zu den Bestimmungsfaktoren der Sachvermögensbildung westdeutscher Unternehmen." Institut für Weltwirtschaft, *Kiel Discussion Papers,* no. 99.

Giersch, Herbert. 1949. "Economic Union Between Nations and the Location of Industries." *Review of Economic Studies* 17:87–97.

Giersch, Herbert. 1970. "Entrepreneurial Risk Under Flexible Exchange Rates." In *Approaches to Greater Flexibility of Exchange Rates: The Bürgenstock Papers,* 145–149. Edited by George N. Halm. Princeton, N.J.: Princeton University Press.

Giersch, Herbert. 1977. "IMF Surveillance Over Exchange Rates." In *The New International Monetary System,* 53–68. Edited by Robert A. Mundell and Jacques J. Polak. New York: Columbia University Press.

Giersch, Herbert. 1978. Preface to *Capital Shortage and Unemployment in the World Economy.* Edited by Herbert Giersch. Tübingen: J. C. B. Mohr.

Giersch, Herbert. 1979. "Aspects of Growth, Structural Change, and Employment: A Schumpeterian View." *Weltwirtschaftliches Archiv* 115:629–652.

Harrod, Roy F. 1933. *International Economics*. London: Nisbet.

Marris, Stephen N. 1984. "The Dollar Problem." Statement on H.R. 585 before the U.S. House of Representatives Committee on Banking and Urban Affairs, Subcommittee on Domestic Monetary Policy, Washington, D.C.

Mascaro, Angelo, and Allan H. Meltzer. 1983. "Long and Short Term Interest Rates in a Risky World." *Journal of Monetary Economics* 12:485–518.

Officer, Lawrence H. 1982. *Purchasing Power Parity and Exchange Rates*. Greenwich, Conn.: JAI Press.

Ricardo, David. 1817. *On the Principles of Political Economy and Taxation*. London: Murray.

Sachverständigenrat zur Begutachtung der Gesamtwirtschaftlichen Entwicklung. 1964. *Stabiles Geld—Stetiges Wachstum. Jahresgutachten 1964/65*. Stuttgart: W. Kohlhammer-Verlag.

Samuelson, Paul. 1984. "Second Thoughts on Analytical Income Comparisons." *Economic Journal* 94:267–278.

# Index